SAFETY NETS AND BENEFIT DEPENDENCE

RESEARCH IN LABOR ECONOMICS

Series Editor: Solomon W. Polachek

IZA Co-Editor: Konstantinos Tatsiramos

RESEARCH IN LABOR ECONOMICS   VOLUME 39

SAFETY NETS AND BENEFIT DEPENDENCE

EDITED BY

STÉPHANE CARCILLO
OECD and IZA

HERWIG IMMERVOLL
OECD and IZA

STEPHEN P. JENKINS
London School of Economics & Political Science and IZA

SEBASTIAN KÖNIGS
OECD and IZA

KONSTANTINOS TATSIRAMOS
University of Nottingham and IZA

IZA

Emerald

United Kingdom − North America − Japan
India − Malaysia − China

Emerald Group Publishing Limited
Howard House, Wagon Lane, Bingley BD16 1WA, UK

First edition 2014

British Library Cataloguing in Publication Data
A catalogue record for this book is available from the British Library

ISBN: 978-1-78190-936-2
ISSN: 0147-9121 (Series)

ISOQAR certified
Management System,
awarded to Emerald
for adherence to
Environmental
standard
ISO 14001:2004.

Certificate Number 1985
ISO 14001

INVESTOR IN PEOPLE

CONTENTS

v

LIST OF CONTRIBUTORS

Lorenzo Cappellari	Università Cattolica Milano and IZA
Sarah Carpentier	University of Antwerp
Kenneth Y. Chay	Brown University
Norma B. Coe	University of Washington
Jorgen Hansen	Concordia University and IZA
Dean R. Hyslop	Victoria University of Wellington
Stephen P. Jenkins	London School of Economics and IZA
Sebastian Königs	OECD and IZA
Stephan Lindner	The Urban Institute
Xingfei Liu	IZA
Magnus Lofstrom	Public Policy Institute of California and IZA
Karel Neels	University of Antwerp
Austin Nichols	The Urban Institute
Anna Persson	The Swedish Social Insurance Agency
Karel Van den Bosch	University of Antwerp
Ulrika Vikman	Institute for Evaluation of Labor Market and Eduction Policy (IFAU)
April Yanyuan Wu	Boston College
Xuelin Zhang	Statistics Canada

EDITORIAL ADVISORY BOARD

PREFACE

Social protection systems are intended to support households in financial difficulties, a role that has been underlined during the recent "Great Recession" in many countries around the world. Over the period 2007–2011, social transfers paid in cash increased by more than 2 percentage points of GDP in a majority of OECD countries.[1] Patterns of transitions into and out of benefit receipt are key measures of the effectiveness of social protection systems. Increases in economic need should be reflected in an increase in inflows to receipt, but benefit receipt should not hinder and should ideally support a swift return to self-sufficiency. Means-tested social assistance (SA) or "welfare" and other minimum-income benefits are of particular interest as the stakes of finding a suitable policy configuration are especially high. On the one hand, those requiring support typically have little or no other resources to fall back on and may suffer acute poverty if minimum-income support is difficult to access. On the other hand, benefit levels tend to be well below commonly used poverty thresholds, and long spells of benefit receipt are therefore a social concern as well as being costly for governments.

Almost all OECD and EU countries operate comprehensive means-tested benefit programs for working-age individuals and their families. These benefits have a major role as "social protection floors," either providing last-resort income support alongside primary income-replacement benefits or acting as a principal instrument for delivering support. As anti-poverty measures, they reduce income disparities at the bottom of the income range and, as such, are important redistribution policies. Equally important, they provide safety nets for individuals experiencing low-income spells and so help smooth income levels over time. Government spending on such benefits is a significant item in the public finances of OECD and EU countries. As with other components of social spending, the aftermath of the Great Recession has created not only greater demand for social support but also increased pressures to reduce or control spending.

The nature of last-resort benefits has been changing over time, notably as a consequence of the "welfare to work" reforms introduced in countries such as the United States, the United Kingdom, Australia, New Zealand,

and Germany. These reforms may affect the extent of income support that these benefits can provide, the transitions into and out of benefit receipt, and the levels, trends, and composition of social spending. Social assistance benefit receipt is therefore at the core of social policy concerns.

This volume presents new results on the dynamics of social assistance, minimum-income and related out-of-work benefits in a range of different country contexts. It contains eight articles, seven of which were presented at the IZA/OECD/World Bank Conference on "Safety Nets and Benefit Dependence" in Paris in May 2013.[2] The articles shed light on benefit spell durations, the movements into and out of receipt of safety net benefits, the individual or family characteristics associated with these movements, the extent of state dependence or "scarring," and the interaction of various welfare programs. The results establish an evidence base for an informed policy debate in a range of OECD countries. They also provide methodological background for future work on benefit receipt patterns.

One article is methodological, evaluating alternative approaches to differentiate genuine state dependence from spurious correlations in binary outcomes using dynamic panel data models; three articles focus on the dynamics of social assistance receipt in various countries using the dynamic random effects probit version of these models; two articles deal with transitions into and out of social assistance emphasizing the role of public employment services and activation measures; and finally two deal with welfare program interactions. All articles utilize longitudinal data and several use register data linked to surveys.

We are pleased to publish as our lead article a previously unpublished "classic". The 2000 working paper by Kenneth Y. Chay and Dean R. Hyslop on "Identification and estimation of dynamic binary panel response models" was a pioneering and influential piece of research that has been much cited ever since, including by several of the articles in this volume. Chay and Hyslop examine the roles of sample initial conditions and unobserved individual effects in consistent estimation of the dynamic binary response panel data model. Many different specifications are considered. These include alternative random effects models in which the conditional distributions of both the unobserved heterogeneity and the initial conditions are specified, and fixed effects conditional logit models that make no assumptions on either distribution. In their revision of their paper for this volume, Chay and Hyslop now include models with the "Wooldridge" treatment of initial conditions (also used by other papers in the volume). The models are fitted to longitudinal data on welfare and labor force participation for female respondents to the US Survey of Income and Program

Participation (SIPP). There are several findings. First, the hypothesis that the sample initial conditions are exogenous is rejected by both samples. Misspecification of the initial conditions drastically overstates estimates of the state dependence and understates estimates of the short- and long-run effects of children on labor force participation. The fixed effects conditional logit estimates are similar to the estimates from the random effects model that is flexible with respect to both the initial conditions and the correlation between the unobserved heterogeneity and the covariates. For female labor force participation, there is evidence that fertility choices are correlated with both unobserved heterogeneity and pre-sample participation histories.

Between 1991 and 2005, the United Kingdom recorded a falling SA receipt rate, driven by a decline in the SA entry rate, while the SA exit rate changed much less. In the article "The Dynamics of Social Assistance Benefit Receipt in Britain," Lorenzo Cappellari and Stephen P. Jenkins analyze the dynamics of social assistance benefit receipt in Britain during this period using a multivariate dynamic random effects probit model applied to British Household Panel Survey data. The model is used to derive year-by-year predictions of aggregate SA entry, exit, and receipt rates. The analysis highlights the importance of the decline in the unemployment rate over the period and other changes in the socioeconomic environment including two reforms of the income maintenance system in the 1990s. It also illustrates the effects of self-selection ("creaming") on observed and unobserved characteristics.

As in the United Kingdom, Canada also saw falling SA participation rates since the mid-1990s and modestly increasing benefit receipt rates in the years following the recent Great Recession. In the article "State Dependence in Social Assistance Receipt in Canada," Jorgen Hansen, Magnus Lofstrom, Xingfei Liu, and Xuelin Zhang use longitudinal data from the Canadian Survey of Labour and Income Dynamics for the years 1993–2010 to document that there are substantial provincial differences in social assistance participation in Canada with higher participation rates in the Eastern part of the country. Using dynamic random effects probit models, the authors find that there is significant state dependence in social assistance, even after controlling for endogenous initial conditions and unobserved heterogeneity. The level of state dependence varies across provinces and might be associated with the generosity of provincial benefit systems.

Unlike the United Kingdom and Canada, Germany experienced relatively stable SA participation patterns in the 1990s, but thereafter there was a steep upward trend which peaked in 2006. As in the United Kingdom during the 1990s, Germany also implemented a major reform in the provision of social assistance receipt benefits in the mid 2000s (the "Hartz" reforms). In the article "State Dependence in Social Assistance Benefit Receipt in Germany before and after the Hartz Reforms," Sebastian Königs studies state dependence in social assistance receipt in Germany using annual survey data from the German Socio-Economic Panel for the years 1995–2011. As in the previous two articles, he estimates a series of dynamic random effects probit models controlling for endogenous initial conditions and unobserved heterogeneity. The estimates suggest substantial structural state dependence in benefit receipt, which is higher in Eastern Germany than in Western Germany. The results indicate that state dependence was similar before and after the Hartz reforms, and the article discusses possible reasons for this finding.

Participation rates vary not only over time but also within countries. In the article "How Do Exit Rates from Social Assistance Benefit in Belgium Vary with Individual and Local Agency Characteristics?," Sarah Carpentier, Karel Neels, and Karel Van den Bosch exploit the decentralization of the administration of social assistance benefits in Belgium to examine how much of the variation in spell lengths of benefit receipt is associated with differences in policies across agencies. Using administrative record data they analyze the monthly hazard of benefit exit for an inflow sample of benefit recipients across 574 welfare agencies. Controlling for differences in both the observed and unobserved characteristics of beneficiaries and local agencies, the authors find higher exit rates from social assistance receipt in bigger municipalities and in agencies which provide more generous cash-based supplementary assistance. They also find strong evidence of shorter benefit episodes in agencies where active labor market program participation rates are higher.

Activation of welfare recipients through job preparation and job search assistance programs, or through "workfare" in publicly provided jobs have been introduced in several countries in the past decades as a way to enhance job search incentives, work opportunities, and employment outcomes. In the article "The Effects of Mandatory Activation on Welfare Entry and Exit Rates," Anna Persson and Ulrika Vikman use register data on the entire population of Stockholm municipality in Sweden to examine the effect of mandatory participation in active programs on benefit receipt as well as on the transitions into and out of SA. Exploiting the sequential implementation of mandatory activation across the districts of Stockholm, the authors find a negative effect of activation on the SA entry rate for young and single individuals, and a positive effect on the SA exit for singles, suggesting a higher response among those with fewer family responsibilities.

Temporary assistance programs may create job search disincentives and may also influence application to other programs, which are designed for those with longer term needs such as disability insurance. In the article "The Impact of Temporary Assistance Programs on Disability Rolls and Re-Employment," Stephan Lindner and Austin Nichols examine whether participation in four temporary assistance programs in the United States influences application for disability insurance or Supplementary Security Income and re-employment. Instrumenting temporary assistance participation using variation in policies across states and over time, the authors find evidence suggesting that increased access to unemployment insurance benefits reduces disability insurance applications, increases the probability of return to work, and reduces the probability of claiming supplementary benefits.

In the last article "What Impact Does Old-Age Pension Receipt Have on the Use of Public Assistance Programs among the Elderly?," Norma B. Coe and April Yanyuan Wu examine the reasons behind the low take-up rate in means-tested programs in the United States among the elderly. By exploiting the interaction between old-age pension benefits and public assistance programs to instrument for the expected public assistance benefit level, they estimate the causal impact of benefit levels on the take-up of means-tested programs. The authors find that the low take-up among the elderly is not driven by changes in the composition of the eligible pool, that old-age pensions decrease the take-up of public assistance programs by decreasing the gains of participation, and that eligible individuals who begin receiving old-age pensions continue to participate in programs providing cash more often than in programs offering in-kind transfers. This different program response suggests that the elderly may have preference for cash over in-kind transfers.

As with past volumes, we aim to focus on important issues and to maintain the highest levels of scholarship. We encourage readers who have prepared manuscripts that meet these stringent standards to submit them to *Research in Labor Economics* (RLE) via the IZA website (http://rle.iza.org) for possible inclusion in future volumes.

Stéphane Carcillo
Herwig Immervoll
Stephen P. Jenkins
Sebastian Königs
Konstantinos Tatsiramos
Editors

NOTES

1. OECD Social Expenditure Database.
2. Financial support for the conference was provided by World Bank, OECD, IZA, and European Commission and is gratefully acknowledged. The usual disclaimer applies. In particular, views expressed in the articles are entirely those of the authors and they do not represent the official opinions of the OECD, the World Bank, the European Commission, or of individual member countries.

IDENTIFICATION AND ESTIMATION OF DYNAMIC BINARY RESPONSE PANEL DATA MODELS: EMPIRICAL EVIDENCE USING ALTERNATIVE APPROACHES

Kenneth Y. Chay and Dean R. Hyslop

ABSTRACT

We examine the roles of sample initial conditions and unobserved individual effects in consistent estimation of the dynamic binary response panel data model. Different specifications of the model are estimated using female welfare and labor force participation data from the Survey of Income and Program Participation. These include alternative random effects (RE) models, in which the conditional distributions of both the unobserved heterogeneity and the initial conditions are specified, and fixed effects (FE) conditional logit models that make no assumptions on either distribution. There are several findings. First, the hypothesis that the sample initial conditions are exogenous is rejected by both samples.

Safety Nets and Benefit Dependence
Research in Labor Economics, Volume 39, 1–39
Copyright © 2014 by Emerald Group Publishing Limited
All rights of reproduction in any form reserved
ISSN: 0147-9121/doi:10.1108/S0147-912120140000039001

1

Misspecification of the initial conditions results in drastically overstated estimates of the state dependence and understated estimates of the short- and long-run effects of children on labor force participation. The FE conditional logit estimates are similar to the estimates from the RE model that is flexible with respect to both the initial conditions and the correlation between the unobserved heterogeneity and the covariates. For female labor force participation, there is evidence that fertility choices are correlated with both unobserved heterogeneity and pre-sample participation histories.

Keywords: Binary response panel data; state dependence, unobserved heterogeneity, initial conditions; random effects and fixed effects models

JEL classifications: C23; C25; I39; J22

INTRODUCTION

Understanding the dynamic processes underlying discrete economic phenomena is a topic of considerable interest to a wide range of researchers. There is a striking commonality in the observed dynamics of several of these discrete processes, including welfare (Bane & Ellwood, 1983) and labor force participation (Heckman & Willis, 1977); firm import and export decisions (Roberts & Tybout, 1997); and the incidence of external debt crises in developing countries (Hajivassiliou & McFadden, 1998). Specifically, all of these phenomena exhibit substantial serial persistence over time.

There are two potential explanations for this serial dependence in discrete outcomes that have been emphasized in the literature (see Heckman, 1981a, 1981c). On one hand, persistence may be the result of structural or "true" state dependence in which current participation directly affects the preferences or opportunities of individuals and, therefore, an individual's propensity to participate in the future. On the other hand, persistence may also result from either observed or unobserved heterogeneity across individuals, in that individuals have different underlying propensities to experience an outcome in all periods.[1] Such persistence can be viewed as "spurious" state dependence, since current participation does not structurally affect the future propensity to participate.

In each of the examples mentioned above, distinguishing between these two sources of persistence is substantively important. For example, knowledge of the degree of true state dependence is crucial for the debate over the impact of welfare programs. If welfare has "narcotic" incentive effects, then changing welfare program parameters, such as benefits levels, can reduce the average length of welfare spells. If most participation is due to permanent characteristics (or transitory shocks), then changing the nature of welfare programs will have little real effect. In addition, accounting for true lag adjustment in participation is necessary for obtaining consistent estimates of the long-run impact of changing welfare benefits. Finally, since the outcomes examined are discrete, the existence of true state dependence suggests that small shocks to the process underlying the participation decision could have discontinuous, lasting effects.

This study evaluates alternative approaches to differentiating state dependence from spurious serial correlation in binary outcomes. In the ideal analysis, the researcher would have access to experimental data with a rich time series. Random assignment to a temporary state ensures that past participation would be unrelated to unobserved heterogeneity and that any observed serial dependence in participation could be attributed to state dependence. In the absence of this ideal, we consider nonexperimental econometric models that use the longitudinal structure of the data to control for the confounding effects of heterogeneity.

The most ubiquitous dynamic model for binary response panel data allows for unobserved heterogeneity and first-order state dependence:[2]

$$y_{it} = 1(X_{it}'\beta + \gamma y_{it-1} + \alpha_i + u_{it} > 0); \quad i = 1, ..., N; \quad t = 1, ..., T - 1 \qquad (1a)$$

$$P(y_{i0} = 1 | X_i, \alpha_i) = p_0(X_i, \alpha_i) \qquad (1b)$$

$$P(y_{it} = 1 | X_i, \alpha_i, y_{i0}, ..., y_{it-1}) = F(X_{it}'\beta + \gamma y_{it-1} + \alpha_i) \qquad (1c)$$

where y_{it} is the participation outcome for individual i in period t, and y_{i0} is the initial period observation; $1(\bullet)$ is an indicator function equal to one if the enclosed statement is true and zero otherwise; X_{it} is a vector of observables which affect participation, $X_i \equiv (X_{i0}, ..., X_{iT-1})$; α_i is an unobserved individual-specific effect that is time-invariant; u_{it} is an error term with distribution function $F(\bullet)$; and β and γ are the parameters of interest. The parameter γ is of particular interest since it represents structural state dependence in participation. On the other hand, α_i represents the source of spurious state dependence attributable to permanent unobserved heterogeneity across individuals (e.g., in earnings potential and/or tastes for leisure), while u_{it} captures transitory unobserved heterogeneity.

The econometric analysis of model (1) is complicated by two factors. First, if the pre-sample history of the process is unobservable, as is usually the case, and there exist both heterogeneity and state dependence, then mis-specifying the sample initial conditions will lead to inconsistent estimates of the model parameters, particularly the degree of structural state depen-dence. Since the extent of "initial conditions" bias is inversely related to the panel length, it could be a serious issue in applications that rely on panel data containing a small number of time periods. Second, while approaches to this problem for the *linear* dynamic regression model are well known, the binary response case is much less tractable (Heckman, 1981b).[3] Surprisingly, there is little evidence on the relative performance of different estimators that address the incidental parameters and initial conditions problems in this setting.

This study compares alternative approaches to estimating model (1). First, we analyze random effects (RE) models in which the distributions of both the unobserved individual effects and the initial conditions are specified. We estimate RE models using both the logit and probit assump-tions on the distributions of the errors, and with four alternative treatments of the initial conditions: treating the initial conditions as exogenous; in equilibrium; using Heckman's (1981b) flexible reduced-form approach; and Wooldridge's (2005) approach of conditioning the unobserved hetero-geneity on the initial values while leaving the distribution of the latter unspecified. Second, we examine dynamic fixed effects (FE) conditional logit models (Honoré & Kyriazidou, 2000), which make no assumptions on either the unobserved heterogeneity or the initial conditions but require further assumptions on the explanatory variables – for example, no unrest-ricted time effects.

The models are estimated using panel data on two different binary processes: welfare participation and female labor force participation. This empirical evaluation of model performance is attractive for two reasons. First, empirical evidence on performance based on real world data comple-ments the findings of Monte Carlo studies (e.g., Chintagunta, Kyriazidou, & Perktold, 1999; Honoré & Kyriazidou, 2000), which may be sensitive to the design of the simulations and have unknown relevance for specific empirical applications. Although the true data generating process is not known, we use a variety of specification tests to gauge the relative merits of the models. Second, the analysis provides new evidence on two empirical processes of considerable interest to labor economists.

There are several substantive findings. First, the hypothesis that the sam-ple initial conditions are exogenous is rejected by the data. Misspecification of the initial conditions results in drastically overstated estimates of the state dependence and understated estimates of the short- and long-run effects of children on labor force participation. The FE conditional logit estimates are similar to the estimates from the RE model that is flexible with respect to both the initial conditions and the correlation between the unobserved heterogeneity and the covariates. Heterogeneity appears to explain about 50 per cent and 70 per cent of the overall persistence in welfare and labor force participation, respectively. In addition, for female labor force partici-pation, there is evidence that fertility choices are correlated with both unob-served heterogeneity and pre-sample participation histories.

In the next section, we discuss the alternative RE and FE approaches and outline the specifications to be examined. The third section describes the data used, while the fourth section contains the empirical results. The fifth section concludes with a discussion of the results.

THE DYNAMIC BINARY RESPONSE
PANEL DATA MODEL

Consistent estimation of both FE and RE formulations of the model described by Eqs. (1a–1c) requires several additional assumptions. First, it is assumed that the first-order lag structure is correct, and that the observa-bles, X_i, are strictly exogenous conditional on α_i, y_{it-1}, and y_{i0}.[4] Second, the distribution function of the transitory errors, u_{it}, must be correctly speci-fied.[5] Also, Chamberlain (1993) shows that the parameters of a model with feedback (e.g., through state dependence) and random coefficients are often not identified, even in the linear case. As a result, we assume homogeneous effects of the variables of interest on participation probabilities.

In RE models, the distribution of the unobserved effects α_i, conditional on the observables X_i, is explicitly specified, as is the distribution of the sample initial conditions y_{i0}, conditional on α_i and X_i. FE models, on the other hand, require no assumptions on either the individual effects or the initial conditions, both of which are allowed to have arbitrary relation-ships with the explanatory variables. However, these models do assume that the transitory errors are i.i.d. over time with logistic distribution functions and that the explanatory variables meet additional stationarity criteria.

The specifications of the unobservables used in our analysis are chosen to span approaches that are both commonly used and can be systematically compared. To facilitate the comparison between the RE and FE conditional logit models, most of the specifications examined assume that u_{it} is i.i.d. logistically distributed. However, an advantage of some RE models, such as the probit model, is that one can relax the restriction that the errors are i.i.d. over time. Consequently, in the RE analysis, we assume that α_i is normally distributed in order to simplify the comparison between the probit and logit models. Finally, we consider three different possible relations between the unobserved heterogeneity and the exogenous variables: "pure" RE, which assume that α_i and X_i are independent; "correlated" RE, which allow α_i to be a linear function of X_i; and FE, which allow for arbitrary dependence. Table 1 summarizes the model specifications compared in this study and discussed in this section.[6]

Table 1.   Model Specifications.

Model	Treatment of		
	α_i	u_{it}	Initial conditions, other comments
Random Effects logit models			
1. RE-L1	$\alpha_i \sim N(0, \sigma_\alpha^2)$	$u_{it} \sim$ i.i.d. logistic	Exogenous: see Eq. (3)
2. RE-L2	$\alpha_i \sim N(0, \sigma_\alpha^2)$	$u_{it} \sim$ i.i.d. logistic	In equilibrium: see Eq. (4)
3. RE-L3	$\alpha_i \sim N(0, \sigma_\alpha^2)$	$u_{it} \sim$ i.i.d. logistic	Reduced form: see Eq. (5a)
4. RE-L4	$\alpha_i = \gamma_0 y_{i0} + \overline{X}_i' \lambda_0 + \eta_i$ $\eta_i \sim N(0, \sigma_\eta^2)$	$u_{it} \sim$ i.i.d. logistic	Wooldridge (2005): see Eq. (6)
5. CRE-L1	$\alpha_i = \sum_s X_{is}' \pi_s + \eta_i$ $\eta_i \sim N(0, \sigma_\eta^2)$	$u_{it} \sim$ i.i.d. logistic	Reduced form: see Eq. (5a)
Random Effects probit models			
6. RE-P1	$\alpha_i \sim N(0, \sigma_\alpha^2)$	$u_{it} \sim$ i.i.d. $N(0, 1 - \sigma_\alpha^2)$	Reduced form: see Eq. (5b)
7. RE-P2	$\alpha_i \sim N(0, \sigma_\alpha^2)$	$u_{it} = \rho u_{it-1} + \varepsilon_{it}$: $\varepsilon_{it} \sim$ i.i.d. $N(0, (1 - \sigma_\alpha^2)/(1 - \rho^2))$	Reduced form: see Eq. (5b)
Fixed Effects conditional logit models			
8. FE-L1	Unrestricted α_i	$u_{it} \sim$ i.i.d. logistic	Unrestricted y_{i0}, No covariates: see Eqs. (8) and (8a)
9. FE-L2	Unrestricted α_i	$u_{it} \sim$ i.i.d. logistic	Unrestricted y_{i0}, Covariates: see Eqs. (9) and (9a)

Random Effects Approaches

If the statistical relationships between the individual effects, initial conditions, and explanatory variables are correctly specified, then "random effects" estimators of model (1) will be consistent and efficient. First, we consider RE models that assume $u_{it} \sim$ i.i.d. logistic and $\alpha_i \sim$ i.i.d. $N(0, \sigma_\alpha^2)$, and independent of X_i. Let θ be the vector of parameters that fully parameterizes model (1) and $y_i = (y_{i0}, y_{i1}, ..., y_{iT-1})$, then the likelihood contribution of observation i is:

$$L(\theta | y_i, X_i) = \int P(y_{i0} | X_i, \alpha_i) \cdot \prod_{t=1}^{T-1} P(y_{it} | y_{it-1}, X_{it}, \alpha_i) \cdot \mathrm{d}F_\alpha(\alpha_i) \tag{2}$$

Most RE approaches also require the specification of the relation between the initial observation and the unobserved heterogeneity and observables, $P(y_{i0} | X_i, \alpha_i)$.[7] We examine four approaches to handling the sample initial conditions that have been previously proposed.

The simplest, and often naïve, approach assumes that the pre-sample history, or initial conditions y_{i0}, are exogenous and can be ignored (e.g., Heckman, 1978, 1981a, 1981c). This restriction is valid only if the process begins at the start of the observed sample period (i.e., the first period of observation is the true initial period), or if the disturbances that generate the process are serially independent, which is not the case in the presence of unobserved heterogeneity. Here, the conditional probability of the initial sample outcome is:

$$P(y_{i0} | X_i, \alpha_i) = P(y_0) \tag{3}$$

and the initial conditions are independent of the individual effects and can be ignored when estimating the structural model. However, if either observed or unobserved heterogeneity is a determining factor in the initial sample conditions, then this approach will overstate the amount of state dependence in the process. We refer to this as model RE-L1.

The second approach we consider for handling the initial conditions assumes that the dynamic stochastic process which generates the observed participation sequences is in equilibrium at the beginning of the sample period (e.g., Card & Sullivan, 1988). Here, the initial period steady-state probability of participation is:

$$p_{i0} \equiv P(y_{i0} = 1 | X_i, \alpha_i) = p_{i0}\, p_{i0}^R + (1 - p_{i0})p_{i0}^A = \frac{p_{i0}^A}{1 + p_{i0}^A - p_{i0}^R} \tag{4}$$

where $p_{i0}^{R} \equiv P(y_{it} = 1 | y_{it-1} = 1, X_{i0}, \alpha_i)$ and $p_{i0}^{A} \equiv P(y_{it} = 1 | y_{it-1} = 0, X_{i0}, \alpha_i)$ are, respectively, the "retention" and "accession" probabilities conditional on the initial period observables. We refer to Eq. (4) as the equilibrium initial conditions restriction (model RE-L2). In the logit case:

$$p_{i0}^{R} = \frac{\exp(X_{i0}'\beta + \gamma + \alpha_i)}{1 + \exp(X_{i0}'\beta + \gamma + \alpha_i)} \quad \text{and} \quad p_{i0}^{A} = \frac{\exp(X_{i0}'\beta + \alpha_i)}{1 + \exp(X_{i0}'\beta + \alpha_i)}$$

This stationarity restriction is unlikely to hold when the observable covariates are time-varying and important determinants of participation.

The third approach to the initial value problem that we examine uses a reduced-form approximation to the initial sample observation (Heckman, 1981b). This approach provides a flexible characterization of the sample initial conditions in terms of the observable covariates and unobserved individual effects:

$$y_{i0} = 1(X_{i0}'\beta_0 + \delta_0\alpha_i + u_{i0} > 0) \tag{5}$$

For the logit ($u_{i0} \sim$ i.i.d. logistic), the "reduced-form" initial conditions restriction is:

$$P(y_{i0} = 1 | X_i, \alpha_i) = \frac{\exp(X_{i0}'\beta_0 + \delta_0\alpha_i)}{1 + \exp(X_{i0}'\beta_0 + \delta_0\alpha_i)} \tag{5a}$$

This is model RE-L3.

The fourth RE approach we consider is based on Wooldridge (2005).[8] In contrast to the reduced-form approach that models the initial conditions of the dynamic process directly in terms of the observables and unobserved heterogeneity, Wooldridge specifies the unobserved heterogeneity conditional on the initial values and exogenous covariates, and rewrites the likelihood contribution in Eq. (2) as:

$$L(\theta | y_i, X_i) = \int \left\{ \prod_{t=1}^{T-1} P(y_{it} | y_{it-1}, X_{it}, \alpha_i) \right\} \cdot dF_\alpha(\alpha_i | Y_{i0}, X_i) \tag{2a}$$

Wooldridge suggests choosing a flexible form for the unobserved heterogeneity in terms of the initial period outcome (Y_{i0}) and the exogenous covariates (X_i). For example, we assume that α_i can be adequately modeled as a linear function of the initial outcome and the individual-specific means of the time-varying explanatory variables:

$$\alpha_i = \gamma_0 y_{i0} + \overline{X}_i' \lambda_0 + \eta_i, \quad \eta_i \sim N(0, \sigma_\eta^2) \tag{6}$$

where $\overline{X}_i'$ is the vector of individual-specific means of the time-varying variables. This is model RE-L4.

The reduced-form specification provides a point of departure for two further RE models that examine the sensitivity of the estimates to two of the above stochastic restrictions. First, we use the probit model (i.e., $u_{it} \sim$ normal) to relax the assumption that the transitory errors are independent over time. If the errors are autocorrelated, then estimates of the parameters of the dynamic model based on the i.i.d. assumption will be inconsistent. This is particularly true of the estimated state dependence.

We adopt the reduced-form approach to the initial conditions and maintain the assumption that $\alpha_i \sim$ i.i.d. $N(0, \sigma_\alpha^2)$ and independent of X_i. For a reasonably direct comparison with the logit model, we first estimate the probit model that assumes $u_{it} \sim$ i.i.d. $N(0, \sigma_u^2)$. We then relax the i.i.d. assumption and allow for stationary first-order autoregressive errors: $u_{it} = \rho u_{it-1} + v_{it}, v_{it} \sim$ i.i.d. $N(0, \sigma_v^2/(1 - \rho^2))$.[9] We refer to these as models RE-P1 and RE-P2, respectively. Both use the following specification for the initial conditions:

$$y_{i0} = 1(X_{i0}' \beta_0 + u_{i0} > 0)$$

Assuming $u_{i0} \sim N(0, 1)$ leads to:

$$P(y_{i0} = 1 | X_i, \alpha_i) = 1 - \Phi(-X_{i0}' \beta_0) \tag{5b}$$

where, for reasons of parsimony, we restrict the covariance between the reduced-form error and later period unobservables to be constant, that is, $\mathrm{cov}(u_{i0}, \alpha_i + u_{it}) = \sigma_0$, for $t = 1, \ldots, T - 1$.

In the second extension to the RE models, we relax the assumption that α_i is independent of X_i and consider a correlated random effects (CRE) specification for α_i in the logit model. Here, we assume that α_i has a linear relation with the (time-varying) explanatory variables:

$$\alpha_i = \sum_{s=0}^{T-1} X_{is}' \pi_s + \eta_i \tag{7}$$

where $\eta_i \sim$ i.i.d. $N(0, \sigma_\eta^2)$ and independent of X_i. Again, we use the reduced-form approximation to the initial conditions given by Eq. (5a), with η_i replacing α_i. The CRE model (CRE-L1) is the most unrestricted RE model in our analysis and provides a natural comparison for the FE conditional logit model.

Fixed Effects Approaches

If the relationships between the unobserved heterogeneity, initial conditions, and explanatory variables are misspecified, then RE estimators will be inconsistent. We therefore consider FE conditional logit estimators of model (1) that do not require any assumptions on the mixing distribution of the unobserved individual effects. If $u_{it} \sim$ i.i.d. logistic and independent of (X_i, α_i, y_{i0}) in all periods, then the incidental parameters α_i can be absorbed with the proper conditioning statement, thereby also circumventing the initial conditions problem. Here, α_i and y_{i0} are not specified and are allowed to have arbitrary relationships with X_i.

First, consider the model with no exogenous regressors ($\beta = 0$). If individuals are observed for at least 4 periods and $u_{it} \sim$ i.i.d. logistic, then γ can be identified without assumptions on the incidental parameters. In particular, there exist a set of sufficient statistics that absorb both α_i and y_{i0} when conditioned on (Chamberlain, 1985; Cox, 1958). The model is:

$$P(y_{i0} = 1 | \alpha_i) = p_0(\alpha_i)$$

$$P(y_{it} = 1 | \alpha_i, y_{i0}, \ldots, y_{it-1}) = \frac{\exp(\gamma y_{it-1} + \alpha_i)}{1 + \exp(\gamma y_{it-1} + \alpha_i)}$$

The set of sufficient statistics is $B \equiv \{y_{i0}, y_{iT-1}, s\}$, where $s = \sum_{t=0}^{T-1} y_{it}$ is the sufficiency class. Then we have the following conditional probability:

$$P(y_{i0}, \ldots, y_{iT-1} | B) = \frac{\exp\left(\gamma \sum_{t=1}^{T-1} y_{it} y_{it-1}\right)}{\sum_{d \in B} \exp\left(\gamma \sum_{t=1}^{T-1} d_t d_{t-1}\right)} \tag{8}$$

where the relationship between y_{i0} and α_i is left unspecified. Consistent identification of γ is based on the fact that this conditional probability is independent of α_i. If there is no first-order state dependence, then sequences in which individuals participate in adjacent periods should be no more prevalent than sequences that have less "clumping" of participation within a conditioning group B.

For $T=4$, conditioning on $B \equiv \{y_{i0} = d_0,\ y_{i3} = d_3,\ y_{i1} + y_{i2} = 1\}$, where d_0, $d_3 \in \{0,1\}$, gives:

$$P(y_{i0} = d_0, y_{i1} = 1, y_{i2} = 0, y_{i3} = d_3 | B) = \frac{\exp[\gamma(y_{i0} - y_{i3})]}{1 + \exp[\gamma(y_{i0} - y_{i3})]} \tag{8a}$$

Here, the following pairs of sequences give conditional probabilities that depend on γ; (1100 vs. 1010) and (0011 vs. 0101). The only difference between the sequences is the path taken in the two intervening periods that connect the same initial and final points. The presence of structural state dependence implies that the first sequence in each pair should occur more often in the data. Maximizing the sample log-likelihood analog of Eq. (8) provides an estimate of γ. This is model FE-L1.

This idea can be extended to derive a FE conditional logit estimator that is consistent and asymptotically normal in the presence of strictly exogenous explanatory variables (i.e., the logit form of model Eq. (1c)). In this case, conditioning on $\{y_{i0} = d_0,\ y_{i3} = d_3,\ y_{i1} + y_{i2} = 1\}$ will not eliminate the unobserved individual effects. However, Honoré and Kyriazidou (2000) show that if, in addition, $X_{i2} = X_{i3}$, then there exist conditional probabilities that are independent of α_i and identify β and γ. In particular,

$$P(y_{i0} = d_0, y_{i1} = 1, y_{i2} = 0, y_{i3} = d_3 | X_i, \alpha_i, y_{i0} = d_0, y_{i3} = d_3, y_{i1} + y_{i2} = 1, X_{i2} = X_{i3})$$
$$= \frac{\exp((X_{i1} - X_{i2})'\beta + \gamma(y_{i0} - y_{i3}))}{1 + \exp((X_{i1} - X_{i2})'\beta + \gamma(y_{i0} - y_{i3}))} \tag{9}$$

does not depend on the individual effects and allows for arbitrary dependence between α_i, y_{i0}, and X_i. Identification of γ comes from differences in the observed frequencies of sequences that are identical except for the path changes that occur in the intervening periods among individuals whose exogenous characteristics are stationary in the final 2 periods. β is identified from changes in the exogenous variables in the two middle periods for these same individuals.

Based on this insight, Honoré and Kyriazidou derive an estimator which puts greater weight on observations with X_{i2} close to X_{i3} (and asymptotically uses only observations where $X_{i2} = X_{i3}$). They propose the following estimator for the 4-period case[10]:

$$(\hat{\beta}, \hat{\gamma}) = \underset{\beta, \gamma}{\mathrm{argmax}} \sum_{i=1}^{N} 1(y_{i1} + y_{i2} = 1) K\left(\frac{X_{i2} - X_{i3}}{\sigma_N}\right) \ln\left(\frac{\exp[(X_{i1} - X_{i2})'\beta + \gamma(y_{i0} - y_{i3})]^{y_{i1}}}{1 + \exp[(X_{i1} - X_{i2})'\beta + \gamma(y_{i0} - y_{i3})]}\right)$$

(9a)

where $K(\bullet)$ is a kernel weighting function which gives greater weight to observations with smaller differences, and σ_N is a bandwidth that goes to zero as N increases. If $P(X_{i2} = X_{i3}) > 0$ (e.g., discrete covariates or controlled experiments) and $(X_{i1} - X_{i2})$ has sufficient variation conditional on $(X_{i2} = X_{i3})$, then the $K(\bullet)$ function can be replaced by a $1(X_{i2} - X_{i3} = 0)$ indicator function and the resulting estimator will have the usual $N^{-1/2}$ rate of convergence. However, if the regressors are continuous or have high dimension, then the estimator, while still consistent and asymptotically normal, will have a convergence rate slower than $N^{-1/2}$. Also, this rate will fall as the number of covariates increases.[11]

This approach (model FE-L2) uses differencing and matching to account for the confounding effects of the unobserved heterogeneity and initial conditions when estimating γ. In particular, individuals with nearly identical sequences and stationary observables in the final 2 periods provide the counterfactual for what would have occurred in the absence of state dependence. The estimator relies on the assumption that lagged participation is *conditionally* independent of unobservable determinants of current participation. When the conditioning statement holds, it will consistently identify the degree of state dependence under the maintained assumptions on u_{it}.

To the extent that $X_{i2} \neq X_{i3}$, the estimator will "over-difference" the data and understate the role of y_{i0}. This results in an estimate of γ that is biased down in finite samples.[12] Since the number of periods used in Eq. (9a) is fixed at 4, this bias will not decrease as T increases. Further, the importance of the initial conditions, and therefore the size of the attenuation bias, increases in the amount of true state dependence and as (X_{i2}, X_{i3}) become less stationary. In Monte Carlo experiments, Honoré and Kyriazidou (2000) find that the negative bias in the conditional logit estimator of γ increases both as the true γ and the bandwidth size, σ_N, increase. By contrast, the conditional logit estimator for β performs quite well, with a bias that falls rapidly as T increases and is relatively insensitive to both the true γ and the bandwidth choice. It is important to note, however, that the conditional logit estimator for both β and γ is substantially less biased than the inconsistent maximum likelihood estimator that estimates the FE.

Eq. (9) shows that the FE conditional logit estimator absorbs a lot of information in order to nonparametrically condition out the unobservables. Consequently, although this approach requires no parametric assumptions on α_i and y_{i0}, a correctly specified RE estimator may provide a substantial efficiency gain. To assess this trade-off, we use the Hausman (1978) specification test to compare the FE estimator (FE-L2) with the CRE estimator that uses the reduced-form initial conditions specification (CRE-L1). The RE estimator is consistent and efficient if the distributions of α_i and y_{i0} are correctly specified but inconsistent otherwise, while the FE estimator is consistent in either case. To the extent that the FE estimator of γ is biased down (e.g., due to nonstationary Xs), this test procedure will be imperfect.[13]

DATA AND DESCRIPTIVE ANALYSIS OF PARTICIPATION SEQUENCES

Several studies have applied the dynamic binary response model to a diverse array of topics.[14] However, there is little evidence on the relative performance of the different approaches used by these studies. Our objective is to empirically evaluate different estimators of model (1). To do this, we analyze two different labor market processes, female labor force and welfare participation, using data from the 1990 panel of the Survey of Income and Program Participation (SIPP).[15]

The SIPP panel contains 8 waves at 4-month intervals, covering a 32-month period. Although each wave collects information on the previous 4 months, we aggregate the monthly data to the 4-month level to mitigate the problem of misreported month-to-month changes.[16] For the welfare participation analysis, the sample contains all women who either received U.S. Aid to Families with Dependent Children (AFDC) payments during or before the sample period or whose average total family income during the sample period is below the family-specific average poverty level. For the analysis of married women's labor force participation (LFP), the sample contains continuously married women whose husbands are labor force participants in each wave of the panel. Further, both samples are restricted to women who are 18–65 years old and can be matched across each of the 8 waves. Table A1 contains summary information on the two samples.

Tables 2 and 3 presents the actual frequencies of the participation sequences observed in the data (column 1) and the predicted frequencies

Table 2. Actual and Predicted AFDC Participation Sequences.

Sequence	Actual	RE-L1	RE-L2	RE-L3	RE-L4	RE-P1	RE-P2	Sequence	Actual	RE-L1	RE-L2	RE-L3	RE-L4	RE-P1	RE-P2
00000000	1076	1037.4	1068.5	1067.3	1079.4	1059.6	1062.8	00011111	16	34.9	18.4	23.5	20.7	25.7	26.4
00000001	27	42.5	29.3	28.6	28.3	28.6	28.9	00111110	0	3.4	2.8	3.1	3.0	3.4	3.1
00000010	3	5.4	9.2	8.8	9.4	7.4	9.0	01111100	2	3.6	2.7	3.1	3.4	3.5	2.7
00000100	10	5.2	9.4	8.9	9.4	7.7	9.0	10001111	0	1.7	2.8	2.2	2.2	2.4	1.8
00001000	10	5.3	9.4	8.8	9.6	7.6	9.0	11000111	1	1.8	2.8	2.3	2.0	2.4	2.0
00010000	14	5.2	9.1	8.6	9.5	7.5	8.8	11100011	4	1.7	2.9	2.2	2.0	2.6	2.1
00100000	12	5.3	9.2	8.6	9.6	7.7	9.0	11110001	1	1.8	3.0	2.5	2.2	2.6	2.3
01000000	10	5.4	9.5	9.0	9.9	7.8	8.8	11111000	15	26.5	18.6	14.6	12.5	15.9	15.8
10000000	19	30.7	27.4	29.6	29.0	31.9	30.5	Misc.	7	3.1	7.5	8.2	7.9	9.2	9.0
Misc.	105	105.0	112.5	111.0	114.7	106.2	112.9		46	78.4	61.5	61.7	55.9	67.7	65.2
00000011	16	39.8	22.9	23.2	21.8	24.4	23.1	00111111	29	33.6	19.1	28.5	25.1	30.6	32.5
00000110	6	4.7	5.7	5.5	5.5	5.5	4.3	01111110	1	3.3	2.5	3.1	3.3	3.4	2.9
00001100	9	4.7	5.7	5.4	5.6	5.5	4.1	10011111	0	1.7	3.6	2.8	2.6	2.8	2.0
00011000	5	4.6	5.7	5.4	5.7	5.4	4.1	11001111	1	1.7	3.5	2.8	2.7	2.8	2.1
00110000	5	4.7	5.7	5.3	5.6	5.3	4.1	11100111	1	1.7	3.6	2.9	2.6	2.9	2.2
01100000	1	4.7	5.6	5.5	6.0	5.6	4.1	11110011	3	1.7	3.6	2.9	2.6	3.0	2.2
10000001	0	1.8	2.3	2.0	1.9	2.2	1.8	11111001	2	1.8	3.7	3.0	2.8	3.0	2.3
11000000	29.0	29.2	23.2	21.7	18.3	24.6	25.7	11111100	16	25.2	18.7	14.7	12.3	15.7	15.0
Misc.	12	2.3	6.1	6.4	6.7	6.7	8.1	Misc.	4	1.8	4.9	5.7	5.5	6.2	7.2
	83	96.5	82.9	80.4	77.1	85.2	79.4		57	72.7	63.1	66.3	59.4	70.3	68.5
00000111	27	37.7	20.0	21.5	18.9	22.4	22.1	01111111	34	33.0	19.7	37.3	38.1	39.9	38.2
00001110	3	4.1	4.1	3.9	3.8	4.3	3.7	10111111	6	1.8	4.8	4.2	4.3	3.7	4.1
00011100	6	4.3	4.0	4.0	3.9	4.4	3.6	11011111	0	1.7	4.5	4.0	4.0	3.7	4.4
00111000	5	4.2	4.1	4.2	4.1	4.3	3.7	11101111	3	1.7	4.8	4.1	4.0	3.8	4.4
01110000	1	4.2	4.1	4.3	4.4	4.4	3.5	11110111	2	1.8	4.7	4.2	4.2	3.8	4.4
10000011	1	1.8	2.3	1.9	1.7	2.1	1.6	11111011	3	1.8	4.7	4.2	4.2	3.8	4.4
								11111101	1	1.7	4.7	4.2	4.1	3.9	4.7

11000001	2	1.8	2.6	2.1	1.8	2.2	2.0	11111110	12	24.4	20.0	16.2	14.7	16.7	16.9
11100000	20	27.9	20.2	17.1	14.2	19.4	20.1		61	67.8	67.9	78.3	77.4	79.2	81.4
Misc.	12	3.4	8.4	8.8	8.6	9.7	9.6								
	77	89.5	69.9	67.9	61.4	73.3	69.8	11111111	364	303.3	343.5	337.7	351.8	324.0	328.0
00001111	28	36.0	19.2	22.3	19.2	24.0	24.3	Totals	1934	1934	1934	1934	1934	1934	1934
00011110	4	3.8	3.2	3.4	3.3	3.6	3.2								
00111100	3	3.8	3.2	3.4	3.4	3.7	3.0	Pearson	–	237.5	96.0	74.3	79.7	82.0	74.1
01111000	2	3.9	3.2	3.5	3.8	3.8	3.0	GOF stats							
10000111	2	1.7	2.5	2.0	1.8	2.2	1.7								
11000011	0	1.7	2.5	2.0	1.7	2.2	1.8								
11100001	1	1.8	2.6	2.1	2.0	2.3	2.0								
11110000	15	27.2	19.2	15.6	12.8	16.9	17.2								
Misc.	10	3.6	8.6	9.1	8.9	10.0	9.8								
	65	83.5	64.2	63.5	56.9	68.6	66.0								

Notes: A "1" in the tth position indicates participation in the tth period; a "0" indicates nonparticipation; and rows labeled "Misc." represent all sequences with at least three transitions in each sufficiency class.

Table 3. Actual and Predicted Labor Force Participation Sequences.

Sequence	Actual	RE-L1	RE-L2	RE-L3	RE-L4	RE-P1	RE-P2	Sequence	Actual	RE-L1	RE-L2	RE-L3	RE-L4	RE-P1	RE-P2
00000000	1162	881.0	1116.7	1114.0	1142.5	1076.4	1066.4	00011111	40	107.7	39.0	35.1	33.2	42.0	49.0
00000001	31	88.6	54.1	45.8	42.9	46.0	48.4	00111110	7	6.5	7.7	6.5	6.2	7.7	7.3
00000010	13	5.7	21.6	19.6	18.7	17.4	20.3	01111100	3	6.5	7.7	6.7	6.1	7.6	5.6
00000100	12	5.6	21.3	19.1	18.6	17.2	19.2	10001111	8	13.9	11.9	11.7	11.4	13.3	10.2
00001000	13	5.6	21.1	18.9	18.6	17.1	19.2	11000111	7	14.0	11.8	11.8	11.3	13.3	10.9
00010000	17	5.7	21.3	19.1	18.6	17.1	19.2	11100011	6	14.0	11.8	11.7	11.3	13.2	10.7
00100000	13	5.7	21.2	19.0	18.5	17.3	19.6	11110001	6	14.0	11.8	11.7	11.4	13.2	11.5
01000000	17	5.6	21.4	19.3	18.7	17.0	18.3	11111000	61	124.3	38.0	39.6	36.7	45.6	48.7
10000000	58	103.0	52.8	88.9	92.8	106.5	103.4	Misc.	64	12.9	41.6	43.0	41.3	50.4	46.7
Misc.	174	225.4	234.9	249.7	247.3	255.7	267.6		202	313.8	181.3	177.7	168.8	206.4	200.4
00000011	44	92.7	40.8	33.7	29.9	36.4	36.2	00111111	66	113.2	48.6	47.3	48.0	57.4	69.8
00000110	7	5.8	12.9	10.9	10.1	11.4	8.5	01111110	8	6.9	8.2	7.6	7.4	8.6	7.2
00001100	7	5.9	12.7	10.9	9.9	11.2	8.0	10011111	17	15.1	17.9	17.1	17.3	18.3	12.8
00011000	0	5.9	12.7	10.7	10.2	11.2	8.1	11001111	9	15.0	18.0	17.2	17.4	18.1	13.4
00110000	5	5.8	12.9	11.0	10.1	11.3	8.3	11100111	19	14.8	17.8	17.1	17.1	18.2	13.4
01100000	10	5.8	12.6	10.8	10.2	11.2	7.6	11110011	10	14.8	17.9	17.1	17.4	18.3	13.4
10000001	5	11.5	7.7	9.5	9.4	11.0	9.3	11111001	15	14.9	17.8	17.1	17.1	18.3	14.2
11000000	76.0	107.1	39.3	55.5	53.2	67.7	79.3	11111100	49	132.0	48.4	47.9	46.1	52.5	51.6
Misc.	36	6.6	27.0	30.3	28.9	33.5	36.7	Misc.	52	8.6	33.8	35.4	35.9	38.2	43.9
	190	247.1	178.5	183.3	171.9	204.9	202.1		245	335.5	228.3	223.9	223.7	247.8	239.6
00000111	39	97.2	35.9	29.5	26.4	33.4	36.2	01111111	73	120.1	76.3	84.2	94.6	95.9	96.5
00001110	6	5.8	9.6	7.9	7.1	8.8	7.6	10111111	30	15.9	36.0	34.2	36.6	30.2	33.7
00011100	4	6.0	9.5	8.0	7.1	8.7	7.0	11011111	38	15.9	36.0	34.5	37.2	30.2	35.2
00111000	4	6.0	9.5	7.8	7.1	8.8	7.0	11101111	19	15.9	35.5	34.0	36.8	29.8	34.2
01110000	3	6.1	9.5	7.9	7.4	8.8	6.5	11110111	25	16.0	35.7	34.0	37.0	30.1	34.5
10000011	10	12.2	7.9	8.9	8.4	10.5	8.0	11111011	32	16.2	35.8	34.1	37.0	29.9	34.1
								11111101	24	15.9	35.6	34.0	36.7	29.9	35.8

11000001	4	12.3	8.1	9.1	8.4	10.6	9.9
11100000	38	111.7	34.8	42.7	39.5	51.1	58.3
Misc.	46	11.2	37.4	40.2	37.6	47.0	43.2
Totals	154	268.6	162.2	161.9	148.9	187.6	183.7
00001111	36	101.9	35.2	29.9	27.2	34.9	39.6
00011110	8	6.3	8.2	6.9	6.3	7.9	7.1
00111100	4	6.3	8.2	6.9	6.1	7.6	6.2
01111000	5	6.3	8.0	6.8	6.2	7.8	5.9
10000011	6	13.1	9.1	9.5	9.3	11.1	8.6
11000011	9	13.1	9.1	9.4	9.1	11.0	9.0
11100001	7	13.0	9.0	9.4	8.9	10.9	9.7
11110000	55	118.2	34.1	38.4	35.4	45.6	50.3
Misc.	50	13.5	41.9	43.6	41.0	51.9	46.8
Totals	180	291.7	162.7	160.9	149.6	188.7	183.3
11111110	80	139.7	76.1	72.9	74.2	72.8	77.2
11111111	321	355.6	367.0	361.8	390.1	348.8	381.3
Totals	3035	2744.4	3031.3	3029.9	3020.1	2946.7	2938.6
Pearson	5663	5663	5663	5663	5663	5663	5663
GOF stats	—	1523.7	204.9	156.2	179.2	147.1	128.9

Notes: A "1" in the tth position indicates participation in the tth period; a "0" indicates nonparticipation; and rows labeled "Misc." represent all sequences with at least three transitions in each sufficiency class.

from the various RE models (columns 2–7).[17] Tables 2 and 3 summarize the welfare and labor force participation samples. For each sequence, a "1" in the tth position indicates participation in the tth period, while a "0" indicates nonparticipation. The sequences are grouped into the nine sufficiency classes (i.e., the total number of periods an individual participates during the sample frame). Within each sufficiency class, sequences with two transitions or less in their participation state are listed individually, while sequences with more than two transitions are grouped together in the "Miscellaneous" category (labelled "Misc.").

There are several noteworthy patterns in the actual frequencies. First, both processes exhibit substantial serial persistence over time. The overwhelming majority of women participate in either all or none of the sample periods, ruling out the possibility that the underlying process is independent over time. Second, it appears that this serial dependence cannot be explained solely by unobserved heterogeneity. In the absence of true state dependence, conditioning on the sufficiency class absorbs the individual effects in the logit model. Here, one might observe different frequencies across sufficiency classes but would expect very similar frequencies across sequences within a class (conditional on the exogenous regressors). However, it is clear that within sufficiency classes, most women experience sequences with few participation state transitions. For example, in the class in which women participate a total of 4 times (bottom of Tables 2 and 3), the sequences in which all participation occurs in either the first four or last four consecutive periods are the most prevalent, by far.

These patterns suggest that a model that includes state dependence and/ or serially correlated errors will fit the sequences better than one with only unobserved heterogeneity. We examine the ability of alternative estimators to distinguish between these sources of serial dependence and still fit the data well. Further, the similarity of the welfare and labor force participation patterns suggests that our findings may provide guidance for a wider set of contexts.

Before proceeding, we provide a simple descriptive analysis of the sequences that are used to identify state dependence in the FE conditional logit model. Recall that the Cox (1958) and Honoré and Kyriazidou (2000) approaches condition out α_i by fixing the initial and final states and the sufficiency class. Table 4 presents the relative frequencies and sample characteristics of the sequence pairs that provide information on γ in the 4-period case. Columns 1 and 2 compare the sequences (0,1,0,1) versus (0,0,1,1) and (1,1,0,0) versus (1,0,1,0), respectively. In the absence of state dependence (and covariate effects), the expected relative frequency would be 0.5.

Table 4.   Summary Statistics of Conditioning Sequences.

	Conditioning Sequence: Sufficiency Class $= 2$	
	$(0, d_1, d_2, 1)$	$(1, d_1, d_2, 0)$
Panel A: AFDC Participation		
Relative frequency $(d_1 = 1, d_2 = 0$ vs. $d_1 = 0, d_2 = 1)^{a}$	0.070	0.965
Period 2 to 3 change in:		
No. of children < 18	0.110	0.000
	(0.05)	(0.03)
Married	−0.005	0.018
	(0.01)	(0.01)
No. of observations	200	170
Panel B: Labor Force Participation		
Relative frequency $(d_1 = 1, d_2 = 0$ vs. $d_1 = 0, d_2 = 1)^{a}$	0.110	0.883
Period 2 to 3 change in:		
No. of children < 18	−0.008	0.034
	(0.01)	(0.01)
No. of observations	489	554

Note: Standard errors in parentheses.
[a]The first column contains the relative frequency of the sequence (0101) vs. (0011); the second column contains the relative frequency of the sequence (1100) vs. (1010).

For both processes, the (0,0,1,1) and (1,1,0,0) sequences occur much more often than the (0,1,0,1) and (1,0,1,0) sequences, with relative odds of roughly 0.9:0.1 in all cases. This implies the strong presence of positive first-order state dependence, with possibly greater dependence in AFDC recipiency (Panel A) than in labor force participation (Panel B).

The Honoré and Kyriazidou estimator also relies on stationarity of the covariates in the final 2 periods for identification. To address this, Table 4 also presents the period 2 to 3 changes in the time-varying variables for each sequence pair. It appears that the fertility of women with sequences that are informative about γ is nonstationary. Women who received welfare or did not participate in the labor force in the final period had an increase in the number of dependent children from the preceding period. Consequently, the conditional logit estimator of γ in Eq. (9a) may be biased down in small samples. More generally, since transitions into and out of welfare and labor force participation are associated with family structure changes, accounting for potential feedback relations may be important for consistent estimation of γ *and* β (for more details, see Chay & Hyslop, 1998).

EMPIRICAL RESULTS

Here, we present the results from estimating the various specifications of model (1) summarized in Table 1 for the welfare and labor force participation samples. First, we discuss the pure RE logit and probit results, which assume that α_i and X_i are independent and focus on the issues of initial conditions modeling and serial correlation in the errors, u_{it}. Goodness-of-fit (GOF) and Vuong (1989) testing criteria are used to compare these models. Then we discuss the CRE and FE logit results, with a focus on the robustness of assumptions on the (α_i, y_{i0}, X_i) relationship. Here, the Hausman (1978) specification test is used for model comparisons. In addition, we derive and implement a test of the stationarity restriction underlying the FE conditional logit model.

Random Effects Results

The alternative RE models are based on different restrictions on the distributions of the transitory errors (u_{it}) and initial conditions (y_{i0}). The logit models are estimated by maximum likelihood using Gaussian quadrature methods with 20 evaluation points (see Butler & Moffitt, 1982). The log-likelihoods of the probit models are functions of T-variate integrals that are computationally intractable when standard numerical methods are used. As a result, the probit models are estimated by maximum simulated likelihood (MSL) using the smooth recursive conditioning (SRC) simulator with 20 replications per observation.[18] To facilitate a comparison of the logit and probit models, the total variance of the unobservables is normalized to 1 (i.e., $\text{Var}(\alpha_i) + \text{Var}(u_{it}) = 1$).[19]

Tables 5 and 6 summarizes the RE estimation results for the welfare (Table 5) and labor force participation (Table 6) samples. Columns 1–3 of these tables provide the logit model results for the "exogenous," "equilibrium," and "reduced-form" specifications of y_{i0}, respectively. Column 4 contains the logit model results for the "Wooldridge" approach, which conditions the unobserved heterogeneity on the initial outcome and exogenous covariates. Columns 5 and 6 present the probit model results using the reduced-form specification of y_{i0} and assuming i.i.d. and AR(1) errors, u_{it}, respectively. The estimated sampling errors are based on the Huber–White formula for a robust estimator of the variance–covariance matrix.[20]

Row 1 of both Tables 5 and 6 contains the estimates of the first-order state dependence. When y_{i0} is assumed to be exogenous (column 1), the RE

Table 5. RE Results for AFDC Participation.

	Logit Models				Probit Models	
	RE-L1	RE-L2	RE-L3	RE-L4	RE-P1	RE-P2
Participation$_{t-1}$	2.832	1.462	1.287	1.453	1.430	1.621
	(0.05)	(0.09)	(0.10)	(0.10)	(0.12)	(0.13)
Var(α_i)	0	0.506	0.600	0.473	0.545	0.502
		(.04)	(0.04)	(0.04)	(0.04)	(0.05)
ρ	–	–	–	–	–	−0.164
						(0.04)
Race (black = 1)	0.056	0.125	0.150	0.081	0.145	0.131
	(0.05)	(0.05)	(0.07)	(0.06)	(0.05)	(0.05)
Years of education	−0.041	−0.054	−0.062	−0.044	−0.060	−0.058
	(0.01)	(0.01)	(0.01)	(0.01)	(0.01)	(0.01)
Family poverty level	0.110	0.079	0.152	−0.034	0.169	0.175
	(0.12)	(0.11)	(0.52)	(0.24)	(0.13)	(0.11)
Age/10	−0.138	0.181	0.002	−0.246	−0.024	−0.038
	(0.12)	(0.13)	(0.27)	(0.15)	(0.57)	(0.14)
Age^2/100	−0.007	−0.059	−0.038	0.004	−0.033	−0.030
	(0.02)	(0.02)	(0.04)	(0.02)	(0.08)	(0.02)
Married	−0.738	−1.019	−1.008	−1.134	−0.934	−0.919
	(0.06)	(0.05)	(0.11)	(0.14)	(0.06)	(0.06)
No. of children < 18	0.123	0.164	0.158	0.189	0.152	0.147
	(0.03)	(0.02)	(0.09)	(0.05)	(0.03)	(0.02)
Wooldridge heterogeneity:						
Participation$_0$	–	–	–	1.232	–	–
				(0.08)		
Family poverty level	–	–	–	0.315	–	–
				(0.31)		
Married	–	–	–	0.475	–	–
				(0.16)		
No. of children < 18	–	–	–	−0.102	–	–
				(0.07)		
Log-likelihood[a]	−2,672.41	−3,506.40	−3,480.82	−2,566.84	−3,484.47	−3,477.07
Vuong statistic	–	–	–	–	0.62	–

Notes: Quasi-MLE standard errors are in parentheses. The logit models are estimated using Gaussian quadrature with 20 evaluation points; the probit models are estimated by MSL, using the SRC simulator with 20 replications. The sample consists of $N = 1,934$ individuals, observed in each of $T = 8$ periods. In all models, the total variance of the unobservables is normalized to 1 (Var(α_i) + Var(u_{it}) = 1). The Vuong (1989) statistic compares the logit and probit models in columns 3 and 5. Asymptotically, this statistic is distributed standard normal; see text for more details. The Wooldridge specification for the unobserved heterogeneity in column 4 restricts the coefficients to be the same in each period.

[a]Log-likelihood values for the probit models are based on 500 simulation replications.

Table 6.   RE Results for Labor Force Participation.

	Logit Models				Probit Models	
	RE-L1	RE-L2	RE-L3	RE-L4	RE-P1	RE-P2
Participation$_{t-1}$	2.798	0.879	0.794	1.067	0.921	1.205
	(0.03)	(0.04)	(0.04)	(0.05)	(0.05)	(0.07)
Var(α_i)	0	0.711	0.753	0.550	0.707	0.633
		(0.01)	(0.01)	(0.02)	(0.02)	(0.03)
ρ	−	−	−	−	−	−0.201
						(0.02)
Race (black = 1)	0.075	0.185	0.157	0.074	0.137	0.133
	(0.04)	(0.06)	(0.07)	(0.06)	(0.06)	(0.06)
Years of education	0.038	0.077	0.075	0.036	0.075	0.071
	(0.004)	(0.01)	(0.01)	(0.01)	(0.01)	(0.01)
Husband's average	−0.135	−0.241	−0.242	−0.130	−0.237	−0.230
earnings	(0.02)	(0.03)	(0.03)	(0.03)	(0.03)	(0.03)
Husband's current	−0.080	−0.039	−0.039	−0.057	−0.038	−0.045
earnings	(0.03)	(0.02)	(0.02)	(0.03)	(0.02)	(0.02)
Age/10	0.869	1.357	1.416	1.035	1.418	1.369
	(0.08)	(0.10)	(0.13)	(0.12)	(0.11)	(0.11)
Age^2/100	−0.117	−0.186	−0.193	−0.136	−0.192	−0.185
	(0.01)	(0.01)	(0.02)	(0.02)	(0.01)	(0.01)
No. of children < 18	−0.067	−0.157	−0.138	−0.140	−0.134	−0.128
	(0.01)	(0.01)	(0.01)	(0.03)	(0.01)	(0.01)
Wooldridge heterogeneity:						
Participation$_0$	−	−	−	1.637	−	−
				(0.04)		
No. of children < 18	−	−	−	0.094	−	−
				(0.04)		
Log-likelihood[a]	−9,246.52	−11,865.42	−11,826.08	−8,583.71	−11,820.82	−11,794.63
Vuong statistic	−	−	−	−	−2.54	−

Notes: Quasi-MLE standard errors are in parentheses. The logit models are estimated using Gaussian quadrature with 20 evaluation points; the probit models are estimated by MSL, using the SRC simulator with 20 replications. The sample consists of $N = 1,934$ individuals, observed in each of $T = 8$ periods. In all models, the total variance of the unobservables is normalized to 1 (Var(α_i) + Var(u_{it}) = 1). The Vuong (1989) statistic compares the logit and probit models in columns 3 and 5. Asymptotically, this statistic is distributed standard normal; see text for more details. The Wooldridge specification for the unobserved heterogeneity in column 4 restricts the coefficients to be the same in each period.
[a]Log-likelihood values for the probit models are based on 500 simulation replications.

variance is set to 0 since the constrained estimate converges to the 0-boundary of the parameter space for both processes. This implies that there is no unobserved heterogeneity in participation propensities and that all serial persistence is attributable to γ and β. The resulting estimate of the state dependence in both welfare and labor force participation is substantial and of similar magnitude ($\hat{\gamma} \approx 2.8$). However, this estimate overstates the true γ if α_i is a determinant of the initial sample value, y_{i0}.[21]

When y_{i0} is assumed to be in a stationary equilibrium (column 2), the estimated state dependence in both processes falls substantially by almost one-half for AFDC participation ($\hat{\gamma} = 1.46$) and by 70 per cent for labor force participation ($\hat{\gamma} = 0.88$). Associated with these falls in state dependence are estimates of substantial unobserved heterogeneity in each process. In the case of AFDC, about one-half of the overall residual variation is due to unobserved heterogeneity ($\hat{\sigma}_\alpha^2 = 0.51$); this figure is 70 per cent in the LFP case ($\hat{\sigma}_\alpha^2 = 0.71$). In addition, the estimated coefficients on several covariates increase in magnitude, although the lower estimated state dependence implies that the long-run effects are less different from column 1.[22]

Column 3 of both Tables 5 and 6 presents the results of the model that uses a flexible reduced form to approximate y_{i0}.[23] Compared to the equilibrium estimates in column 2, the estimated state dependence falls about 10 per cent for each process, and the estimated importance of unobserved heterogeneity rises about 20 per cent for AFDC ($\hat{\sigma}_\alpha^2 = 0.60$) and 5 per cent for LFP ($\hat{\sigma}_\alpha^2 = 0.75$). Further, the estimated coefficients on the covariates are generally similar to those in column 2, particularly for the LFP case.

In column 4 of Tables 5 and 6 we present the estimates from a version of the Wooldridge (2005) approach that uses Eq. (6) to condition the unobserved heterogeneity on the initial conditions and exogenous variables. For each process, the estimated state dependence is higher, and the estimated variance of the random effect is lower, than in column 3. These results are consistent with the Monte Carlo simulation results reported in Akay (2012), which documented greater upward bias in the estimated state dependence and greater downward bias in the estimated RE variance for the Wooldridge approach when compared to the reduced-form approach (column 3) in short panels. The estimates of the parameters in Eq. (6) for the unobserved heterogeneity are shown at the bottom of the tables in column 4. They imply that the unobserved heterogeneity has a highly significant relation with the initial period outcome for both processes, and a statistically significant correlation with the individual-specific time averages of marital status for AFDC and of the number of children for LFP.

Comparing these specifications, the assumption that the initial sample conditions are exogenous is clearly rejected by the data. For both samples, the exogenous y_{i0} restriction leads to severely overstated estimates of γ and understated estimates of Var(α_i), compared to the other three approaches.

The estimates are more similar across these other three approaches. However, as the reduced-form model is less restrictive than the model assuming the initial conditions are in equilibrium, the evidence suggests some upward bias in the estimated state dependence in the equilibrium model, as is likely the case for our formulation of the Wooldridge approach.

Tables 2 and 3 provides further evidence that the exogenous y_{i0} restrictions do not hold empirically. Columns 2–5 of Tables 2 and 3 contain the predicted frequency of each participation sequence from the four RE logit models. The final row presents Pearson GOF test statistics, which are a quadratic form of the difference between the predicted and actual (column 1) frequencies.[24] For both samples, the GOF statistics imply that the exogenous initial conditions model provides a substantially worse fit to the sequence data than the other three approaches. Among the other three models, the reduced-form initial conditions model provides the best fit to the observed sequences, while the poorest fit comes from the model that assumes equilibrium initial conditions.

We use the RE probit model to examine the sensitivity of the parameter estimates to the assumption that the errors, u_{it}, are serially independent. The probit also allows us to gauge the sensitivity of the results to alternative specifications of the error distribution. To provide a comparison to the logit model, column 5 of Tables 5 and 6 presents the results from a probit that uses a reduced-form y_{i0} specification and maintains the i.i.d. assumption on u_{it}.[25] In general, the estimates from this model and the logit model in column 3 are similar. The most notable difference is that the probit gives slightly higher estimates of γ (by 11–16 per cent) and slightly lower estimates of $\mathrm{Var}(\alpha_i)$ (by 6–9 per cent) in both samples.

Column 6 of Tables 2 and 3 presents the predicted frequencies of the participation sequences from this probit model. The Pearson GOF statistics associated with the probit model are similar to those for the logit reduced-form model in column 4; suggesting a slightly worse relative fit for the probit model in the AFDC data but a slightly better relative fit in the LFP data.

The Vuong (1989) non-nested test procedure can also be used to compare the (i.i.d. error) probit and logit models. Here, the test statistic, V, is the normalized difference between the log-likelihood values of the two models:

$$V = (\log l_{\mathrm{L}}(\theta_{\mathrm{L}}) - \log l_{\mathrm{P}}(\theta_{\mathrm{P}}))/(N^{1/2} \cdot \omega)$$

where $\log l_{\mathrm{L}}(\theta_{\mathrm{L}})$ and $\log l_{\mathrm{P}}(\theta_{\mathrm{P}})$ are, respectively, the logit and probit log-likelihood values, and ω^2 is the sample variance of the difference in the log-likelihoods. If the two models are equivalent, then V has an asymptotic standard normal distribution under suitable regularity conditions. The last row of Tables 5 and 6 presents the Vuong statistics. For the AFDC sample, $V = 0.62$ implies that the logit and probit models are statistically equivalent. For the LFP sample, $V = -2.54$ implies that the probit specification fits the data slightly better, which is the same conclusion reached by comparing the GOF statistics in Tables 2 and 3. We conclude that the probit and logit models are complementary rather than competitive.

The final column of Tables 5 and 6 presents the results from the probit model that relaxes the i.i.d. error assumption. Here, u_{it} is allowed to follow a stationary first-order autoregressive AR(1) process: $u_{it} = \rho u_{it-1} + v_{it}$, $v_{it} \sim$ i.i.d., $N(0, \sigma_v^2/(1-\rho^2))$, $\alpha_i \sim$ i.i.d. $N(0, \sigma_\alpha^2)$, and $\sigma_\alpha^2 + \sigma_v^2/(1-\rho^2) = 1$ for identification. For both samples, the estimated serial correlation in u_{it} is negative and statistically significant, although relatively small in magnitude. While this result is counterintuitive, the model already absorbs the contribution of unobserved heterogeneity, initial conditions, and state dependence to positive serial correlation over time. Allowing for an AR(1) error results in an increase in the estimated state dependence and a decrease in the estimated heterogeneity variance. The change appears more significant in the LFP sample, partially due to its much larger sample size. On the other hand, the estimates of the covariate effects are virtually unchanged when the i.i.d. error assumption is relaxed.

The final column of Tables 2 and 3 gives the sequence frequencies predicted by the AR(1) probit model. For the AFDC sample, there is little difference in the fits of the AR(1) probit and the "i.i.d." logit and probit in columns 4 and 5. For the LFP sample, the AR(1) model fits the data better than the "i.i.d." models. This is not surprising given the significance of the estimated ρ and the increase in the log-likelihood in Tables 5 and 6. Since the estimated ρ is negative, we do not give it a structural interpretation and conclude that it acts as a "fitting" parameter. It is important to note that a probit model that allows for unobserved heterogeneity and an AR(1) error, but no state dependence, provides a much poorer fit to the sequences. Further, the resulting estimate of ρ implies that the latent process is close to a unit root. We conclude that the sequence frequencies in Tables 2 and 3 are consistent with a discontinuity in the latent process (e.g., due to structural state dependence) and not with serially correlated shocks that evolve continuously.

We summarize the "pure" RE results as follows. For all specifications, there is strong evidence of positive state dependence in both binary processes. All of the models that relax the assumption of exogenous initial conditions result in much smaller estimates of γ than the exogenous y_{i0} model. Thus, ignoring the endogeneity of y_{i0} leads to a clear overstatement of the state dependence and an understatement of the role of unobserved heterogeneity.[26] The estimates of γ and Var(α_i) are broadly similar across the other models, although we find that the Wooldridge approach estimates a higher level of state dependence and a lower unobserved heterogeneity variance than the reduced-form y_{i0} model. There is little difference between the comparable logit and probit specifications. Finally, the indicative GOF statistics suggest that the reduced-form model provides a (slightly) better fit to the participation sequences than the Wooldridge approach, despite the fact that the former estimates the initial outcome while the latter conditions on it.

A simple comparison of the estimates of γ suggests that heterogeneity explains about 50 per cent and 70 per cent of the overall persistence in welfare and labor force participation, respectively, and the estimated state dependence is greater in the AFDC sample.[27] The estimated (short-run) effects of children on labor force participation are much larger in the reduced-form y_{i0} model than in the exogenous model. This suggests that inappropriately accounting for the feedback of pre-sample participation histories into fertility choices can lead to severe bias. Finally, the less restrictive reduced-form model provides a better fit to the data than the equilibrium initial conditions model in both samples.[28]

Fixed Effects Results

The pure RE models assume that α_i and X_i are independent. If the time-varying variables, such as fertility, are correlated with unobserved heterogeneity in participation propensities, then the resulting estimates of their effects will be inconsistent. Here, we discuss the CRE and FE logit results, in which the independence assumption is relaxed.

Tables 7 and 8 summarizes the results of these models for the AFDC (Table 7) and LFP (Table 8) samples. For comparability across the models, we use the standard logit normalization for the variance of the errors, Var $(u_{it}) = \pi^2/3$. As a benchmark, column 1 presents the "re-normalized" estimates from the RE logit model in column 3 of Tables 5 and 6 (RE-L3). Columns 2 and 3 of these tables contain the CRE logit results. In the CRE specifications, Eq. (7) is used to model the correlation between α_i and the time-varying covariates; marital status in the AFDC sample, and number of children in both the AFDC and LFP samples. In column 2, the coefficients

Table 7.   CRE and FE Results for AFDC Participation.

	RE Logit Models			Conditional Logit Models	
	RE-L3	CRE-L1		FE-L1	FE-L2
Participation$_{t-1}$	3.693	3.656	3.696	3.554	3.372
	(0.15)	(0.15)	(0.16)	(0.16)	(0.26)
Var(η_i)	4.940	5.153	4.778	–	–
	(0.78)	(0.84)	(0.82)		
Race (black = 1)	0.430	0.410	0.411	–	–
	(0.16)	(0.17)	(0.16)		
Years of education	−0.177	−0.178	−0.178	–	–
	(0.03)	(0.03)	(0.03)		
Family poverty level	0.437	0.433	0.438	–	–
	(0.34)	(0.34)	(0.33)		
Age/10	0.007	−0.018	−0.061	–	–
	(0.23)	(0.63)	(0.44)		
Age^2/100	−0.110	−0.108	−0.101	–	–
	(0.03)	(0.09)	(0.06)		
Married	−2.892	−2.763	−2.752	–	−1.735
	(0.24)	(0.36)	(0.35)		(3.48)
No. of children < 18	0.455	0.375	0.382	–	0.530
	(0.08)	(0.11)	(0.11)		(0.18)
CRE:					
Married	–	−0.032	–	–	–
		(0.05)			
No. of children < 18	–	0.016	–	–	–
		(0.01)			
Log-likelihood	−3,480.82	−3,479.94	−3,464.37	–	–
Hausman statistic (d.o.f.)	–	–	–	–	2.09
					(3)
Stationarity test statistic (d.o.f.)	–	–	–	–	3.95
					(3)

Notes: Quasi-MLE standard errors are in parentheses, except for column 5 which has bootstrapped standard errors based on 1,000 replications. The sample consists of $N = 1,934$ individuals (AFDC participation) and $N = 5,663$ individuals (LF participation), observed in each of $T = 8$ periods. In all models, we use the standard logit normalization, that is, Var(u_{it}) = $\pi^2/3$. The RE-L3 model in column 1 is the same as that in column 3 of Tables 5 and 6, except for this re-normalization. The FE-L1 and FE-L2 models are based on Cox (1958) and Honoré and Kyriazidou (2000). The "Hausman statistic" tests the equality of the estimates in columns 3 and 5. The "stationarity" test statistic tests the stationarity of the errors, u_{it}. See text for more details.

Table 8.   CRE and FE Results for Labor Force Participation.

	RE Logit Models			Conditional Logit Models	
	RE-L3	CRE-L1		FE-L1	FE-L2
Participation$_{t-1}$	2.897	2.896	2.880	2.616	2.550
	(0.08)	(0.08)	(0.08)	(0.08)	(0.09)
Var(η_i)	10.016	10.023	10.243	–	–
	(0.71)	(0.70)	(0.75)		
Race (black = 1)	0.573	0.601	0.611	–	–
	(0.25)	(0.24)	(0.22)		
Years of education	0.273	0.272	0.280	–	–
	(0.02)	(0.03)	(0.02)		
Husband's average earnings	−0.883	−0.877	−0.912	–	–
	(0.11)	(0.11)	(0.11)		
Husband's current earnings	−0.142	−0.146	−0.146	–	–
	(0.07)	(0.07)	(0.07)		
Age/10	5.167	5.211	5.113	–	–
	(0.44)	(0.45)	(0.50)		
Age^2/100	−0.706	−0.714	−0.705	–	–
	(0.05)	(0.06)	(0.06)		
No. of children < 18	−0.505	−0.344	−0.334	–	−0.369
	(0.05)	(0.09)	(0.09)		(0.13)
CRE:					
No. of children < 18	–	−0.027	–	–	–
		(0.01)			
Log-likelihood	−11,826.08	−11,823.57	−11,803.42	–	–
Hausman statistic (d.o.f.)	–	–	–	–	51.47
					(2)
Stationarity test statistic (d.o.f.)	–	–	–	–	1.08
					(2)

Notes: Quasi-MLE standard errors are in parentheses, except for column 5 which has bootstrapped standard errors based on 1,000 replications. The sample consists of $N = 1,934$ individuals (AFDC participation) and $N = 5,663$ individuals (LF participation), observed in each of $T = 8$ periods. In all models, we use the standard logit normalization, that is, Var(u_{it}) = $\pi^2/3$. The RE-L3 model in column 1 is the same as that in column 3 of Tables 5 and 6), except for this re-normalization. The FE-L1 and FE-L2 models are based on Cox (1958) and Honoré and Kyriazidou (2000). The "Hausman statistic" tests the equality of the estimates in columns 3 and 5. The "stationarity" test statistic tests the stationarity of the errors, u_{it}. See text for more details.

on the full vector of X_i in Eq. (7) are restricted to be equal (i.e., $\pi_s = \pi$, $\forall s = 0, \ldots, T-1$). In column 3, this restriction is relaxed and the coefficients are allowed to vary.

For the AFDC sample, the "restricted" CRE estimates imply little (average) correlation between the family structure variables and heterogeneity in welfare propensities. The estimated π implies that marital status is unrelated to α_i. The estimated correlation between fertility and α_i is stronger but also statistically insignificant. The likelihood ratio (LR) statistic of 1.76 implies that the null that $\pi = 0$ cannot be rejected at conventional levels (2 degrees of freedom (d.o.f.), p-value $= 0.41$). The unrestricted CRE model in column 3 rejects the null of no correlation between α_i and the family structure variables at the 1 per cent level (LR $= 32.90$, 16 d.o.f., $p = 0.008$). However, the estimates of γ, $\text{Var}(\alpha_i)$, and the effects of marital status and fertility are very similar across columns 1–3, suggesting that the heterogeneity bias is small in the AFDC sample. While the estimated impact of children is 15 per cent lower in the CRE model than in the pure RE model, the sampling errors are noticeably larger.

For the LFP sample in Table 8, both the restricted and unrestricted CRE estimates imply that fertility choices are correlated with unobserved heterogeneity. In column 2, the restricted correlation between fertility and α_i is significant and suggests that women with lower latent probabilities of working have more children. Controlling for heterogeneity bias of this type reduces the estimated effect of children by one-third. The column 3 results imply that the column 2 specification of the relationship between α_i and X_i is too restrictive (LR $= 40.30$, 7 d.o.f., $p < 0.001$). However, as in the AFDC case, relaxing this restriction does not change the estimated impact of family structure on participation.

The CRE model in column 3 is the least restrictive RE approach in our analysis. However, if the relationships between α_i, y_{i0}, and X_i are misspecified in Eqs. (5a) and (7), then the resulting estimates of γ and β will be inconsistent. To examine the robustness of these assumptions, we estimate FE conditional logit models, in which α_i and y_{i0} are not specified and are allowed to have arbitrary relations with X_i.

Columns 4 and 5 of Tables 7 and 8 contain the conditional logit results from models without covariates (Chamberlain, 1985; Cox, 1958) and with time-varying exogenous variables (Honoré & Kyriazidou, 2000), respectively. Without covariates, the FE estimate of the state dependence is similar to the CRE estimate in column 3. The estimated γ is only 4 per cent lower in the AFDC sample and 9 per cent lower in the LFP sample. This suggests that the bias in the CRE estimator due to misspecification of the distribution of α_i and the relation between α_i and y_{i0} is relatively small. On the other hand, the sampling errors for the FE estimates are virtually unchanged, suggesting that the efficiency loss is small relative to the more parametric RE estimator.

The conditional logit model that includes the time-varying family structure variables provides a direct comparison to the CRE model with the reduced-form approximation to y_{i0}. Since marital status and number of children are discrete variables, the analysis can condition on women for whom these variables are stationary in the key periods. In Eq. (9a), this implies that the kernel weighting function, $K((X_{i2} - X_{i3})/\sigma_N)$, can be replaced by a $1(X_{i2} - X_{i3} = 0)$ indicator function. Thus, we avoid the choice of a kernel function and bandwidth. The resulting estimator has an $N^{-1/2}$ convergence rate and should exhibit less attenuation bias in the estimated state dependence.

Focusing first on the AFDC results in Panel A, adjusting for the effects of the family structure variables reduces the estimated γ. The RE specification of the individual effects and initial conditions appears to lead to a slight overstatement of the true state dependence by about 9 per cent. However, the FE estimate of γ has a much larger sampling error than the CRE estimate.[29] Further, the FE estimates of the effects of marital status and fertility are very similar to the RE estimates in column 1, especially given the sampling errors. This suggests that α_i and X_i are not correlated in the AFDC sample, a finding consistent with the CRE results.

The FE model results in a large loss in precision due to the matching and differencing that is required to nonparametrically absorb α_i and y_{i0}.[30] We use the Hausman (1978) specification test to compare the estimates in columns 3 and 5 and assess the trade-off between the FE and CRE models. In principle, this provides a test of the CRE assumptions that $\alpha_i \sim N(\sum_s X'_{is}\pi_s, \sigma_\eta^2)$ and $y_{i0} = 1(X'_{i0}\beta_0 + \delta_0\alpha_i + u_{i0} > 0)$, where $u_{i0} \sim$ i.i.d. logistic. Let $\hat{\theta}$ and $\tilde{\theta}$ denote the CRE and FE estimators, respectively. Then the Hausman test statistic is:

$$H = (\hat{\theta} - \tilde{\theta})' \hat{V}^{-1} (\hat{\theta} - \tilde{\theta})$$

where $\hat{V} = V(\hat{\theta} - \tilde{\theta}) = V(\tilde{\theta}) - V(\hat{\theta})$.[31] Under the null hypothesis ($\hat{\theta} = \tilde{\theta}$), H has an asymptotic chi-square distribution with degrees of freedom equal to the dimension of θ estimated in the FE model. For the AFDC sample, the H-statistic fails to reject the equivalence of the CRE and FE models ($H = 2.09$, 3 d.o.f., $p = 0.55$).

For the LFP sample, the conditional logit estimate of the fertility effect is close to the CRE estimate, implying that Eq. (7) provides a good approximation to the fertility–heterogeneity relation. Consistent with the CRE results, accounting for the heterogeneity bias arising from this correlation reduces the estimated impact of children by over 25 per cent. Similar to the AFDC results, the FE estimate of the state dependence is about 11–12 per cent lower than the CRE estimate in column 3. However, since there is very little loss in precision in the estimated γ, the Hausman test easily rejects the equality of the FE and CRE estimates ($H = 51.5$, 2 d.o.f.). Although this implies that the RE specifications of α_i and y_{i0} are statistically rejected, the differences in the CRE and FE estimates are small in magnitude. Also, if the FE estimate of γ is biased down due to "over-differencing," this test procedure will be biased and tend to reject a correctly specified RE model.[32]

Overall, the FE estimates are similar to the estimates from the CRE model that is flexible with respect to both y_{i0} and the correlation between α_i and X_i. As a final check of robustness, we test the stationarity assumption on u_{it} underlying the FE model. This assumption implies that the parameter vector $\theta = (\gamma, \ \beta')'$ is overidentified when $T > 4$. In particular, any 4-period subset of the data should result in the same estimate of θ as the 8-period estimator. This leads to a simple specification test of the stationarity assumption.

Let $\hat{\theta}$ be the 8-period estimator, and θ^1 and θ^2 be the 4-period estimators based on the first and last 4 periods of data, respectively.[33] Then a test statistic of the stationarity assumption is:

$$S = \begin{bmatrix} \theta^1 - \hat{\theta} \\ \theta^2 - \hat{\theta} \end{bmatrix}' \hat{V}^{-1} \begin{bmatrix} \theta^1 - \hat{\theta} \\ \theta^2 - \hat{\theta} \end{bmatrix}$$

where V is the asymptotic variance–covariance matrix of the vector of differences in the coefficient estimates.[34] Under the null that $\theta^1 = \theta^2 = \hat{\theta}$, S has an asymptotic chi-square distribution with k degrees of freedom, where $k = \dim(\theta)$. The final row of Tables 7 and 8 presents this test statistic. For both the AFDC and LFP samples, the S-statistic fails to reject the equivalence of the three estimators.[35]

CONCLUDING DISCUSSION

This paper has compared random effects and fixed effects approaches to estimating the dynamic binary response panel data model using two different empirical applications. The analysis has focused on two sets of issues.

First, we examined the impact of four alternative models of the sample initial conditions in the RE analysis. Second, we compared the results from the RE and FE models to gauge the robustness of parametric restrictions on the unobserved heterogeneity and initial conditions, and their relations to the observables.

The analysis leads to several substantive conclusions that might be extended to other contexts. In the RE analysis, the assumption of exogenous initial conditions is rejected in the welfare and labor force participation samples. Relative to the flexible reduced-form approach to handling the initial conditions, both the "equilibrium" and the Wooldridge approaches result in higher estimates of state dependence and lower estimated unobserved heterogeneity. Heterogeneity seems to explain about 50 per cent and 70 per cent of the overall persistence in welfare and labor force participation, with greater estimated state dependence in the AFDC sample. Even after accounting for heterogeneity and serially correlated shocks, we find that the sequence patterns are consistent with a discontinuity in the latent process.

The CRE and FE results suggest that fertility and marital status are unrelated to unobserved heterogeneity in propensities to receive AFDC. However, fertility choices are negatively correlated with heterogeneity in work propensities. Controlling for heterogeneity bias of this type reduces the estimated effect of children on labor force participation by 25–30 per cent. The FE conditional logit estimates are similar to the estimates of the RE model that is flexible with respect to both the initial conditions and the correlation between the unobserved heterogeneity and the covariates. The restrictions of the flexible CRE model on α_i and y_{i0} and their relations with X_i appear to be robust and lead to precise estimates. Further, the over-identifying restrictions of the FE conditional logit model are not rejected by the data, suggesting that it provides a valid and meaningful alternative.

Initial conditions matter in both samples and accounting for the endogeneity of pre-sample histories is crucial for consistent estimation of the structural state dependence and the effects of the covariates. Ignoring the contribution of heterogeneity to the initial sample observation leads to drastically overstated estimates of the state dependence. For the work decision, it appears that fertility choices are correlated with both unobserved heterogeneity and pre-sample histories. However, since the downward bias due to dynamic self-selection is much greater than the upward heterogeneity bias, conventional estimates of the fertility-work association understate the true impact of exogenous fertility shocks. This provides evidence that labor supply plans affect fertility choices over the life cycle and that empirical models should account for dynamic decision making (see Browning, 1992).

In the absence of experimental data, this study has examined nonexperimental methods that use the longitudinal structure of the data to control for omitted factors. A convincing quasi-experimental approach to this question would serve a twofold purpose. In addition to providing credible estimates of the structural state dependence in discrete processes, it could give additional guidance on the performance of nonexperimental approaches. Reliable, administrative data that contain many individuals observed over a long period at frequent intervals would also facilitate a comparison of different approaches to identifying the nonlinear dynamic model.

ACKNOWLEDGMENTS

We thank Colin Cameron, David Card, Paul Devereux, Bo Honoré, Hilary Hoynes, Guido Imbens, Aviv Nevo, James Powell, participants of the UC-Berkeley Labor Lunch and the 1998 Camp Econometrics, and three anonymous referees for helpful suggestions and insightful comments. Bo Honoré generously provided the code for one of the estimators used in this article. Finally, we are grateful to Stephen P. Jenkins for his encouragement and patience with the final draft. Copies of the computer programs used in the preparation of this article are available from the authors on request.

NOTES

1. The heterogeneity may be due to either permanent or serially correlated transitory differences.
2. The econometric literature on binary response panel data models that allow solely for unobserved heterogeneity is well established (see Chamberlain, 1980, 1984, 1992; Manski, 1987). However, the identification and estimation of nonlinear models that also include lagged dependent variables is much more complicated.
3. For the linear dynamic panel data model, see Anderson and Hsiao (1981), Holtz-Eakin, Newey, and Rosen (1988), Arellano and Bond (1991), Arellano and Bover (1995), and Blundell and Bond (1998).
4. Define $X_i^t = (X_{i0}, ..., X_{it})$, then the strict exogeneity condition is $E(u_{it}|X_i, \alpha_i, y_{it-1}) = 0$, or that $E(y_{it}|X_i, \alpha_i, y_{it-1}) = E(y_{it}|X_i^t, \alpha_i, y_{it-1})$. Arellano and Carrasco (2003) develop a random effects estimator for the dynamic binary choice model where the covariates are assumed to be predetermined instead.
5. Honoré and Kyriazidou (2000) develop an estimator of the model that is consistent if u_{it} is independent over time with a distribution function that is strictly increasing. However, they infer that this semi-parametric estimator has a convergence rate slower than $N^{-1/3}$ and a non-normal asymptotic distribution.

6. We also estimated specifications that assume the random effects have a common discrete distribution with a finite number of mass points. While this method allows for a relatively unrestricted specification of the individual effects (Heckman & Singer, 1984; Kiefer & Wolfowitz, 1956), the results were very similar to those obtained under the normality assumption (see Chay & Hyslop, 1998). In previous empirical applications (Chay, 1995; Hyslop, 1999), we also allowed the errors, u_{it}, to be serially correlated.

7. As noted by Arellano and Carrasco (2003) and Wooldridge (2005), alternatively, one could specify the conditional distribution of α_i given y_{i0}, $f(\alpha_i|y_{i0}, X_i)$, which allows for dependence between y_{i0} and α_i, while leaving the distribution of the initial values unrestricted. We investigate these random effects approaches as well.

8. Wooldridge (2005) examines dynamic probit, tobit, and Poisson regression, and also derives estimators for the partial effects averaged over the unobserved heterogeneity distribution. Arellano and Carrasco (2003) propose a similar approach to Wooldridge (2005) for the dynamic binary response model with random effects. One difference is that the Wooldridge approach is computationally simpler. Arellano and Carrasco (2003) find results for the labor force participation of married women in PSID data that are similar to those in Chay and Hyslop (1998) for the PSID.

9. In contrast to the linear and logit models, the probit model can distinguish first-order state dependence from first-order serial correlation (Heckman, 1978). In fact, state dependence can be distinguished from more unrestricted error correlation structures since the most general multivariate probit cannot generate a Markov chain. This result is attributable to the multivariate probit functional form (Chamberlain, 1985).

10. It is straightforward to extend this approach to more than 4 periods. See Honoré and Kyriazidou (2000) for details.

11. Hahn (1997) derives results suggesting that it is not possible to consistently estimate the model at an $N^{-1/2}$ rate.

12. For example, in the linear regression model, conditioning out α_i leads to attenuation bias in the estimated γ. To absorb α_i, the data is first-differenced or deviated from individual means, which effectively absorbs y_{i0} as well. As a result, fixed effects estimators attribute too much of the serial dependence to α_i and understate γ by ignoring the importance of y_{i0}. The estimator based on deviations from means has a bias that is inversely related to the panel length T and is large in short panels. The problem is more severe in the binary response model due to the model's nonlinear nature. For example, Heckman (1981b) finds that the inconsistent autoregressive probit that jointly estimates the fixed effects is substantially biased even when $T = 8$.

13. There are several other noteworthy points. First, while all of the approaches assume strict exogeneity of X_i in the mixture model, they allow for feedback arising from first-order state dependence. Second, the stationarity assumption implicit in the fixed effects conditional logit estimator is restrictive (e.g., unrestricted time effects are ruled out). Below, we derive and implement a test of this assumption. Further, the partial effects of the covariates and state dependence on the response probability are not identified in the Honoré and Kyriazidou (2000) model. Finally, to examine these assumptions further, we estimated the dynamic linear probability regression model using instrumental variables. The results from this approach are virtually identical to the results documented below (see Chay & Hyslop, 1998).

14. For example, see Card and Sullivan (1988), Moon and Stotsky (1993), Roberts and Tybout (1997), and Hajivassiliou and McFadden (1998).

15. In Chay and Hyslop (1998), we also used data from the Panel Study of Income Dynamics (PSID) to examine married women's annual labor force participation. The PSID and SIPP results are qualitatively identical.

16. See Marquis and Moore (1990) for a discussion of "seam bias" and measurement error issues in the SIPP.

17. The predicted frequencies are based on 1,000 simulations of each model.

18. See Gourieroux and Monfort (1993), Keane (1994), and Hyslop (1999) for more details on the use of the SRC simulator in Monte Carlo integration.

19. In the binary response framework with no random effect, the normalizations typically used are $\mathrm{Var}(u_{it}) = \pi^2/3$ for the logit model and $\mathrm{Var}(u_{it}) = 1$ for the probit model. In this case, the probit (β_p) and logit (β_L) coefficients may be compared using $\beta_p = (3^{1/2}/\pi)\beta_L$, although Amemiya (1981) suggests using the normalization factor 0.625 instead of 0.551 ($\approx 3^{1/2}/\pi$). However, the optimal normalization is less clear in logit and probit models that include normally distributed random effects.

20. Let H be the matrix of second derivatives of the sample log-likelihood with respect to the parameters and S be the matrix of first derivatives. The Huber–White estimator is $H^{-1}(S'S)H^{-1}$ and will be robust to heteroskedasticity.

21. We found that models with "semi-parametric" mass point heterogeneity were not identified in the exogenous y_{i0} specification, suggesting that the likelihood model is misspecified and/or does not converge to the consistent optimum in this case (see Chay & Hyslop, 1998).

22. In the linear model, the long-run effects of the X's are equal to $\beta/(1 - \gamma)$. When state dependence is not allowed for ($\gamma = 0$), the short- and long-run impacts of the covariates are identical (β).

23. The mass point heterogeneity model with reduced form y_{i0} was identified for both the AFDC and LFP samples and resulted in estimates nearly identical to those from the normal heterogeneity model (Chay & Hyslop, 1998).

24. For the model that assumes exogenous initial conditions, we condition on the first-period participation state and predict only the last seven participation outcomes.

25. Conceptually, the only difference between this model and the logit model in column 3 of Tables 5 and 6 is that u_{it} is i.i.d. normal rather than logistic. In practice, however, the reduced-form restrictions imposed on the two models are also different due to the difference in functional forms.

26. The fact that the estimated $\mathrm{Var}(\alpha_i)$ is 0 in the exogenous y_{i0} model suggests that the initial conditions are sufficient statistics for the unobserved heterogeneity.

27. It should be noted that this is not a formal decomposition of persistence and is only suggestive.

28. We also estimated a dynamic linear probability model in which instrumental variables are used to address the initial conditions and feedback problems (Chay & Hyslop, 1998). The results for γ and β from this approach are nearly identical to the results from the random effects logit and probit with the reduced form specification of y_{i0}.

29. The sampling errors of the estimates in column 5 are calculated using the bootstrap with 1,000 replications. The mean and median of the bootstrap estimates of γ and the children coefficient are identical to the sample estimates for both

samples. The median of the bootstrap estimates of the marital coefficient is identical to the sample estimate, but the mean is different, although similar to the random effects estimates (-2.63). This is true even as the number of bootstrap replications is increased (e.g., 2,000 replications).

30. Since there are few women who switch into or out of marriage, the FE estimate of the marital coefficient is particularly imprecise. That is, there is little variation in $(X_{i1} - X_{i2})$ conditional on $X_{i2} = X_{i3}$ among women with informative participation sequences.

31. $V(\hat{\theta})$ is the bootstrapped variance–covariance matrix of the Honoré and Kyriazidou fixed effects estimator. The consistency of the bootstrap estimator of the asymptotic variance of the HK estimator has not been proven. Also, as noted above, in our context, the HK estimator has an $N^{-1/2}$ convergence rate under the null since kernel weighting is not used. This allows for a standard application of the Hausman test. However, the application of the Hausman test would not be standard in situations where the HK estimator does not converge at the root-N rate. We thank a referee for pointing this out to us.

32. Consistent with this possibility, we found that the Cox FE estimate of γ increases in the number of time periods used. A preliminary Monte Carlo analysis also suggests that the FE estimate of γ has a small downward bias that decreases as T increases. While it is not within the scope of this study, this issue should be examined more in the future.

33. Choosing the first and last 4 periods should maximize the power of the test to reject the stationarity restriction relative to the degrees of freedom.

34. The estimator of the variance–covariance matrix of the coefficient differences was calculated using the 1,000 bootstrap replications of each of the three different estimators of θ.

35. In the linear probability model, the parameter estimates were unchanged when unrestricted state-time effects were included as controls (see Chay & Hyslop, 1998). This further suggests that non-stationarity in the errors is not a major source of bias in the conditional logit approaches.

REFERENCES

Akay, A. (2012). Finite-sample comparison of alternative methods for estimating dynamic panel data models. *Journal of Applied Econometrics, 27*, 1189–1204.

Amemiya, T. (1981). Qualitative response models: A survey. *Journal of Economic Literature, 19*, 483–536.

Anderson, T. W., & Hsiao, C. (1981). Estimation of dynamic models with error components. *Journal of the American Statistical Association, 76*, 598–606.

Arellano, M., & Bond, S. (1991). Some tests of specification for panel data: Monte Carlo evidence and an application to employment equations. *Review of Economic Studies, 58*, 277–297.

Arellano, M., & Bover, O. (1995). Another look at the instrumental variable estimation of error-components models. *Journal of Econometrics, 68*, 29–51.

Arellano, M., & Carrasco, R. (2003). Binary choice panel data models with predetermined variables. *Journal of Econometrics, 115*, 125–157.

Bane, M. J., & Ellwood, D. T. (1983). *The dynamics of dependence: The routes to self sufficiency, Prepared for the U.S. Department of Health and Human Services, Office of the Assistant Secretary for Planning and Evaluation.* Cambridge, MA: Urban Systems Research and Engineering, Inc.

Blundell, R., & Bond, S. (1998). Initial conditions and moment restrictions in dynamic panel data models. *Journal of Econometrics, 87*, 115–143.

Browning, M. (1992). Children and household economic behavior. *Journal of Economic Literature, 30*, 1434–1475.

Butler, J. S., & Moffitt, R. (1982). A computationally efficient quadrature procedure for the one factor multinomial probit model. *Econometrica, 50*, 761–764.

Card, D., & Sullivan, D. (1988). Measuring the effect of subsidized training programs on movements in and out of employment. *Econometrica, 56*, 497–530.

Chamberlain, G. (1980). Analysis of covariance with qualitative data. *Review of Economic Studies, 47*, 225–238.

Chamberlain, G. (1984). Panel data. In Z. Griliches & M. Intriligator (Eds.), *Handbook of econometrics* (Vol. 2, pp. 1247–1318). Amsterdam: North Holland.

Chamberlain, G. (1985). Heterogeneity, omitted variables bias, and duration dependence. In J. Heckman & B. Singer (Eds.), *Longitudinal analysis of labor market data* (pp. 3–38). Cambridge: Cambridge University Press.

Chamberlain, G. (1992). *Binary response models for panel data: Identification and information.* Mimeo, Department of Economics, Harvard University.

Chamberlain, G. (1993). *Feedback in panel data models.* Mimeo, Department of Economics, Harvard University.

Chay, K. Y. (1995). *Evaluating the impact of the 1964 Civil Rights Act on the economic status of Black men using censored longitudinal earnings data.* Mimeo, Department of Economics, Princeton University.

Chay, K. Y., & Hyslop, D. R. (1998). *Identification and estimation of dynamic binary response panel data models: Empirical evidence using alternative approaches.* Working Paper No. 5. Center for Labor Economics, UC Berkeley.

Chintagunta, P., Kyriazidou, E., & Perktold, J. (1999). *Panel data analysis of household brand choices.* Mimeo, Department of Economics, UCLA.

Cox, D. R. (1958). The regression analysis of binary sequences. *Journal of the Royal Statistical Society, Series B, 20*, 215–232.

Gourieroux, C., & Monfort, A. (1993). Simulation-based inference: A survey with special reference to panel data models. *Journal of Econometrics, 59*, 5–33.

Hahn, J. (1997). *Information bound of the dynamic panel logit model with fixed effects.* Mimeo, Department of Economics, University of Pennsylvania.

Hajivassiliou, V., & McFadden, D. (1998). The method of simulated scores with application to models of external debt crises. *Econometrica, 66*, 863–896.

Hausman, J. A. (1978). Specification tests in econometrics. *Econometrica, 46*, 1251–1271.

Heckman, J. J. (1978). Simple statistical models for discrete panel data developed and applied to test the hypothesis of true state dependence against the hypothesis of spurious state dependence. *Annales de l'INSEE, 30–31*, 227–269.

Heckman, J. J. (1981a). Statistical models for discrete panel data. In C. Manski & D. McFadden (Eds.), *Structural analysis of discrete data* (pp. 114–178). Cambridge, MA: MIT Press.

Heckman, J. J. (1981b). The incidental parameters problem and the problem of initial conditions in estimating a discrete time-discrete data stochastic process. In C. Manski & D. McFadden (Eds.), *Structural analysis of discrete data* (pp. 179–195). Cambridge, MA: MIT Press.

Heckman, J. J. (1981c). Heterogeneity and state dependence. In S. Rosen (Ed.), *Studies in labor markets*. Chicago, IL: University of Chicago Press.

Heckman, J. J., & Singer, B. (1984). A method for minimizing the impact of distributional assumptions in econometric models for duration data. *Econometrica, 52*, 271–320.

Heckman, J. J., & Willis, R. (1977). A beta-logistic model for the analysis of sequential labor force participation by married women. *Journal of Political Economy, 85*, 27–58.

Holtz-Eakin, D., Newey, W., & Rosen, H. S. (1988). Estimating vector autoregressions with panel data. *Econometrica, 56*, 1371–1395.

Honoré, B. E., & Kyriazidou, E. (2000). Panel data discrete choice models with lagged dependent variables. *Econometrica, 68*, 839–874.

Hyslop, D. R. (1999). State dependence, serial correlation and heterogeneity in intertemporal labor force participation behavior of married women. *Econometrica, 67*, 1255–1294.

Keane, M. (1994). A computationally practical simulation estimator for panel data. *Econometrica, 62*, 95–116.

Kiefer, J., & Wolfowitz, J. (1956). Consistency of the maximum likelihood estimator in the presence of infinitely many incidental parameters. *Annals of Mathematical Statistics, 27*, 887–906.

Manski, C. (1987). Semiparametric analysis of random effects linear models from binary panel data. *Econometrica, 55*, 357–362.

Marquis, K. H., & Moore, J. C. (1990). Measurement errors in the survey of income and program participation (SIPP) program reports, *1990 Annual research conference proceedings*, US Bureau of the Census, Washington, D.C.

Moon, C. G., & Stotsky, J. G. (1993). The effect of rent control on housing quality change: A longitudinal analysis. *Journal of Political Economy, 101*, 1114–1148.

Roberts, M. J., & Tybout, J. R. (1997). The decision to export in Columbia: An empirical model of entry with sunk costs. *American Economic Review, 87*, 545–564.

Vuong, Q. H. (1989). Likelihood ratio tests for model selection and non-nested hypotheses. *Econometrica, 57*, 307–333.

Wooldridge, J. M. (2005). Simple solutions to the initial conditions problem in dynamic, nonlinear panel data models with unobserved heterogeneity. *Journal of Applied Econometrics, 20*, 39–54.

APPENDIX

Table A1. Sample Characteristics.

	Welfare Sample	Labor Force Sample
Participation	0.30	0.68
	(0.01)	(0.01)
Age	34.05	39.04
	(0.26)	(0.13)
Race (black = 1)	0.31	0.07
	(0.01)	(0.003)
Years of education	11.26	13.21
	(0.06)	(0.04)
No. of children < 18	1.85	1.24
	(0.03)	(0.02)
Family poverty level	1026.43	—
	(7.61)	
Husband's earnings	—	2961.92
		(21.45)
No. of observations	1,934	5,663

Notes: Estimated standard errors are in parentheses. See text for sample selection criteria. Family poverty level and husband's earnings are measured monthly in 1990 dollars.

THE DYNAMICS OF SOCIAL ASSISTANCE BENEFIT RECEIPT IN BRITAIN

Lorenzo Cappellari and Stephen P. Jenkins

ABSTRACT

We analyse the dynamics of social assistance benefit (SA) receipt among working-age adults in Britain between 1991 and 2005. The decline in the annual SA receipt rate was driven by a decline in the SA entry rate rather than by the SA exit rate (which also declined). We examine the determinants of these trends using a multivariate dynamic random effects probit model of SA receipt probabilities applied to British Household Panel Survey data. We show how the model may be used to derive year-by-year predictions of aggregate SA entry, exit and receipt rates. The analysis highlights the importance of the decline in the unemployment rate over the period and other changes in the socio-economic environment including two reforms to the income maintenance system in the 1990s and also illustrates the effects of self-selection ('creaming') on observed and unobserved characteristics.

Keywords: Social assistance benefits; welfare benefits; panel data; dynamic self-selection; dynamic random effects probit

JEL classifications: I38; C23; C53

Safety Nets and Benefit Dependence
Research in Labor Economics, Volume 39, 41–79
Copyright © 2014 by Emerald Group Publishing Limited
All rights of reproduction in any form reserved
ISSN: 0147-9121/doi:10.1108/S0147-912120140000039000

INTRODUCTION

For at least two decades, 'welfare to work' ideas have strongly influenced social policy thinking on both sides of the Atlantic and in English-speaking OECD nations more generally. There has been substantial interest in reorienting the design of systems of cash transfers for poor working-age families away from schemes involving arguably passive receipt of benefits ('welfare') towards schemes in which individuals are more actively involved in meeting minimum income requirements, by increasing their labour market participation ('work'). In the USA, this reorientation is illustrated by the abolition of the Aid for Families with Dependent Children (AFDC) programme by the 1996 Personal Responsibility and Work Opportunity Reconciliation Act and introduction of the Temporary Assistance for Needy Families programme with time limited benefit payments. The Earned Income Tax Credit programme supporting low-income working families was expanded during the 1980s and 1990s and is a major antipoverty policy.

Britain's Labour Government, elected in 1997, was strongly influenced by the US reforms. It was responsible for substantial extensions to the provision and generosity of in-work benefits through the Working Families Tax Credit (WFTC) programme introduced in 1999 and modified and extended in 2003. Major social assistance (SA) benefit programmes for working-age families remain in place, however, though with some modifications in the mid-1990s that tightened eligibility requirements for unemployed people of working age.

This background raises questions such as how much did dependence on SA benefits decline over the last two decades in Britain? To what extent were policy reforms responsible for observed trends and what was the role played by other factors such as changes in the availability of jobs? This article describes SA benefit receipt dynamics in Britain over the period 1991−2005 and investigates the determinants of trends in aggregate rates of entry, exit and receipt using an econometric model fitted to household panel data together with counterfactual predictions based on the model estimates.

To set the scene, look at Fig. 1 which shows trends in SA benefit receipt in Britain between 1991 and 2005. (In these graphs and throughout the article we focus on working-age individuals; definitions and data are explained in more detail later.) Apart from the rise in receipt at the beginning of the 1990s when Britain went into recession, the percentage of working-age adults in receipt of SA halved, falling from a peak of around 12 per cent in 1993 to around 6 per cent in 2005. If the definition of SA is widened to

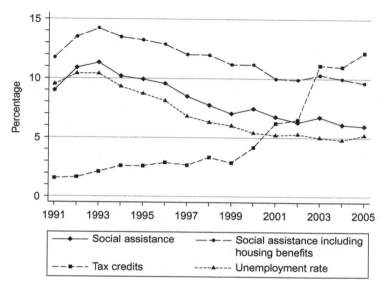

Fig. 1. Proportion of Working-Age Adults Receiving Social Assistance Benefits and Tax Credits, and the Unemployment Rate, by Year. *Notes*: Authors' calculations using data from waves 1–15 of the BHPS, except for the unemployment rate which is series YBTI from the UK Office for National Statistics, http://www.ons.gov.uk. The unemployment rate is the ILO unemployment rate for all adults (men aged 16–64, women aged 16–59), derived from the Labour Force Survey, and is a three-month average centred on the October of the year in question. The definitions of social assistance benefits, housing benefits, and tax credits are explained later.

include housing benefits (HB), the proportion in receipt each year is consistently 2–3 per cent higher, but follows a similar downward trend. Two leading explanations for these trends are the reforms to the benefit system intending to 'make work pay' and changes in the availability of jobs.

Fig. 1 shows the substantial increase over the period in receipt of in-work cash assistance ('tax credits'). The proportion of working-age adults in receipt was consistently about 2 or 3 per cent during the 1990s, until the introduction of WFTC in October 1999 after which the proportion in receipt rose dramatically to almost 7 per cent in 2002. The receipt rate then rose again significantly with the extension of eligibility in 2003. Observe that the turning points in the SA receipt rate series do not correspond closely with the turning points in the series for tax credit receipt, suggesting that in-work benefit reforms were not a major driver of the former. By contrast, note the relatively close correspondence between the trends in the unemployment rate and in the SA receipt rate. These and other explanations are examined in greater detail later in the article. We show that the story about what drove the trends is more complicated than Fig. 1 suggests.

Since changes in SA receipt rates from year to year reflect the combination of changes in annual rates of entry to or exit from receipt (which are processes with different determinants), we analyse entry and exit rates. Fig. 2 shows the trends in these SA transition rates over the period 1991–2005. The entry rate fell from above 4 per cent in 1993 to below 2 per cent in 2005. The exit rate fell from around 40 per cent to nearly 25 per cent (the greater variability in the rate at the end of the period may simply reflect small sample sizes).

We conclude that the secular decline in annual (cross-sectional) SA receipt rates was driven primarily by a decline in entry rates: the fall in the entry rate was sufficiently large that it offset the decline in the exit rate over the same period (which would increase receipt rates, other things being equal). This conclusion follows directly from the stock-flow identity that

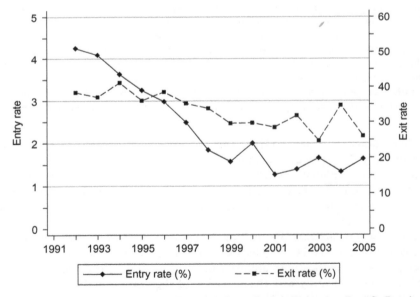

Fig. 2. Annual Rates of Entry to and Exit from Social Assistance Benefit Receipt: Working-Age Adults, by Year. *Notes*: Authors' calculations using BHPS data. The definition of Social Assistance benefit receipt is explained later.

links the proportion receiving SA in year t to entry and exit rates.[1] The importance for trends in cross-sectional receipt of changes in the entry rate rather than the exit rate echo findings reported for the USA by Grogger (2004) and Haider and Klerman (2005).

To investigate the determinants of these trends, we propose a multivariate dynamic random effects probit model of individuals' receipt probabilities and fit it to data from waves 1–15 of the British Household Panel Survey (BHPS) covering 1991–2005.[2] Dynamic random effects probit models have been used to examine benefit (and employment and unemployment) dynamics in the past, most commonly to estimate the degree of genuine state dependence. We have examined state dependence with these same data (Cappellari & Jenkins, 2008a), but in this article our focus is different.

We show how dynamic random effects probit model estimates can be used to derive year-by-year predictions of aggregate SA entry, exit and receipt rates and also, under various counterfactual scenarios, the relative importance of several potential determinants of trends in observed transition rates. As we discuss, calculation of year-by-year SA transition and receipt rates requires careful accounting for the effects of dynamic self-selection on unobservables. Our analysis highlights the decline in the unemployment rate and also other secular changes in the socio-economic environment including two reforms to the social security benefit system and also illustrates the effects of 'creaming' on observed and unobserved characteristics.

In the second section, we explain the benefit system in Britain over the period 1991–2005, referring to both SA and in-work benefits. We introduce the BHPS data used in the analysis in the third section and present the statistical model in the fourth section. Estimates and predictions are discussed in the fifth section. The sixth section provides a brief summary and conclusions.

BENEFITS AND TAX CREDITS FOR WORKING-AGE BRITONS, 1991–2005

Social Assistance benefits are income-tested 'safety net' cash benefits, sometimes called 'welfare benefits'. They are paid to bring incomes up to some minimum income level — they refer to income maintenance. By contrast, social insurance benefits refer to income replacement — payments made in response to the occurrence of particular risky events such as sickness or unemployment and for which an appropriate record of social insurance contributions exists.[3]

The System of Benefits and Tax Credits, 2005

The principal Social Assistance benefits in Britain in 2005 for people of working age are given in Table 1. Income Support (IS) and income-based Job Seekers Allowance (JSA) differ from HB and Council Tax Benefit (CTB) because receipt depends on employment status. Put differently, receipt of HB and CTB depends on income (and some other conditions) but not on employment or job search status. As Fig. 1 shows, the SA receipt rates according to both the narrower and broader definitions move in tandem over time. The populations receiving IS and JSA on the one hand, and HB and CTB on the other hand, overlap substantially, and so the choice of whether to include HB in the definition of SA benefits is of little practical importance in the current context. In the analysis presented below, we do not include HB and CTB in our definition of SA.

Alongside these benefits for non-working families, there is extensive cash support available for low-income working families, currently through the Working Tax Credit (WTC) programme. (It plays a similar role to the Earned Income Tax Credit in the USA.) The eligibility conditions relate to

Table 1.   The Principal Social Assistance Benefits in the United Kingdom for Working-Age Adults, 2005.

Benefit	Eligibility Conditions (Main)
Income Support	Income less than a specified minimum level and unavailable for full-time work (e.g. lone parent, registered sick or disabled, caring for someone who is sick or elderly).
Job Seekers Allowance (income-based)	Income less than a specified minimum level and unemployed but able to work and available to work (which has to be regularly declared).
Housing Benefit	Income less than a specified minimum level and needing financial help to pay all or part of one's housing costs.
Council Tax Benefit	Income less than a specified minimum level and needing financial help to pay all or part of one's Council Tax bill.

Notes: Income Support was introduced in 1988 (its predecessor was called Supplementary Benefit). Housing Benefit was introduced in 1983 and Council Tax Benefit in 1993. Job Seekers Allowance was introduced in 1996. See Table 2 regarding changes between 1991 and 2005.

having an income below a specified minimum level, and at least one family member in 'full-time work' defined to mean working at least 16 hours per week.

Changes in Benefits and Tax Credits, 1991–2005

Between 1991 and 2005, the system of benefits and tax credits in Britain changed substantially. The main reforms are summarized in Table 2 by year of introduction. Prior to 1996, a non-working family could be receiving IS (social assistance), Unemployment Benefit (UB, social insurance), or both. In October 1996, cash benefits for unemployed job seekers were unified under the JSA programme, with a distinction made between

Table 2. Principal Changes to the UK System of Cash Benefits and Tax Credits, 1991–2005.

Year of Introduction	Change
1996	Job Seekers Allowance (JSA) introduced in October 1996 with 'income-based' and 'contribution-based' components. JSA replaced Income Support (IS) and Unemployment Benefit (UB) for unemployed job seekers. Accompanied by more stringent job search requirements for those assessed as available for work. IS became available only to those not available for work.
1999	Working Families Tax Credit (WFTC) introduced in October 1999, and fully phased in by April 2000. This in-work benefit programme for low-income families was more generous and widened eligibility relative to its predecessor, the Family Credit (FC) programme. FC programme, introduced in 1988, replaced Family Income Supplement (FIS) which began in 1971. Administered by the income tax authorities (HM Revenue and Customs) rather than the benefits authorities (Department for Work and Pensions, and Benefits Agency).
1999	Increased support for families with children, including increases in Child Benefit (flat-rate payment per child, paid regardless of parental work status or income), and increases in the child allowances in other benefits.
1999	National Minimum Wage introduced.
2003	WFTC replaced by the Working Tax Credit (WTC) and Child Tax Credit (CTC) programmes from April 2003. WTC extended eligibility to single people and to families without children. CTC unified child allowances across benefits.

Note: See Brewer and Shephard (2004) for a concise overview of the Labour government's welfare to work policies and associated changes in the benefit system.

'income-based' JSA corresponding to the former IS and 'contribution-based' JSA corresponding to the former UB, which was a flat-rate non-means-tested social insurance benefit paid to unemployed individuals with a satisfactory national insurance contribution record. JSA also incorporated more stringent job search requirements for those assessed as available for work. Unemployed individuals with an incomplete national insurance contribution record and a sufficiently low income were also eligible to claim contribution-based JSA on a means-tested basis. Because UB payments were relatively low, most recipients' families were also eligible for IS, and it remains the case today that most JSA recipients receive income-based benefits.[4] Because of this, official statistics on JSA numbers no longer distinguish between contribution-based and income-based JSA and, also, it is difficult to identify them separately in household surveys. For this reason, we include both types of JSA in our definition of SA (see Table 2).

The other main changes were introduced by the Labour government that was elected in May 1997. The most significant reform was the replacement of the existing in-work benefits programme, Family Credit, by WFTC which was modelled more closely on the US Earned Income Tax Credit programme. Aiming to 'make work pay', WFTC had more generous payments and extended eligibility notably by lowering the number of work hours required for qualification. Take-up was substantial, as Fig. 1 illustrates. In 2003, the child allowance elements of WFTC were spun out into the Child Tax Credit programme, which aimed to unify child support payments across the income maintenance system more generally. The WFTC component supplementing earnings became WTC, and eligibility was extended to single people and to families without children. This gave another fillip to the proportion of working-age adults receiving tax credits (see Fig. 1).

Among other policy reforms introduced by the Labour government to make work pay was a national minimum wage rate per hour. And, as part of its aim to reduce child poverty, there was an increase in support for families with children through increases in Child Benefit (a universal non-income-tested benefit paid per child) and in the child allowance element of other benefits.[5]

Brewer and Shephard's (2004) summary assessment, focusing on families with dependent children, is that '[e]xamining outcomes of Labour's ultimate objectives would lead one to conclude that the make work pay policies have been a success. ... Academic studies agree that government policies were partially responsible for these changes, at least among lone parents' (p. vii).[6]

If policies making work pay are successful, we would expect them to be accompanied by corresponding reductions in SA receipt,[7] and for the turning points and inflections in SA receipt trend lines to correspond with the major changes in tax credits (1999 and 2003). Similarly, we would expect the tightening of job search requirements for unemployed people accompanying the introduction of JSA in 1996 to lead to a decline in SA receipt, other things equal. Analysis of administrative record data by Petrongolo (2009) of men aged 16–64 suggests that tighter job search requirements were successful in moving individuals off UB. Manning (2009) derives the same conclusion using Labour Force Survey data.[8]

DATA: THE BHPS

We track SA receipt among working-age adults using BHPS data from survey years 1991–2005 (waves 1–15).[9] The first wave of the BHPS was a nationally representative probability sample of the private household population, with interviews in Autumn 1991. The achieved sample consists of more than 10,000 individuals in some 5,000 households, who were re-interviewed annually. Individuals in split-off families were followed, as in other household panels such as the US Panel Study of Income Dynamics or the German Socio-Economic Panel.[10] Our analysis is restricted to 1991–2005 because the local unemployment rate series that we rely on in the econometric analysis is not available beyond 2005 (see below). In any case, the BHPS ended with wave 18 (survey year 2008).

The focus throughout is on individuals of working age. More specifically, we consider only individuals below the age of 60.[11] To avoid complications associated with education and training, we also exclude individuals aged less than 25, or individuals in families in which there are any adults of working age who are full-time students.

We define an individual to be in receipt of SA if any individual in his or her family is receiving SA benefits at the time of the BHPS interview. In Britain, assessment of benefit eligibility is based on the income of the nuclear family, the so-called benefit unit, which is a single person or a couple living together with or without dependent children. (A dependent child is aged less than 16 years, or more than 16 years but under 19 years and unmarried, in full-time non-advanced education and living with his/her parents.) It is not legal marital status that distinguishes a 'couple' from two single adults; it is living arrangements (cohabiting unions are treated like legal marriages). In the sample of SA recipients we analyse, only one-quarter are lone parents, 54 per cent live with a partner (37 per cent have a partner and children), and 21 per cent are childless single adults. We track individuals over time, not families, since families and households cannot be followed over time as a unit in any consistent manner. Families and households change their composition over time as individuals arrive (e.g. via partnership formation) or depart (e.g. via partnership dissolution). These types of change are common (Jenkins, 2000).

We define SA to include IS and either UB or JSA (of either type). This is a matter of practical necessity: it is the only definition of SA that can be measured consistently over time using the BHPS (and other British surveys). As mentioned earlier, it is difficult to reliably distinguish between receipt of contribution-based JSA and income-based JSA. Indeed, since JSA's introduction in 1996, the BHPS interview has not asked respondents receiving JSA to distinguish between the two types for precisely this reason. See Cappellari and Jenkins (2008a) for further discussion.

Our definition of SA receipt for a given year t refers to receipt at the time of the BHPS interview in survey year t (typically September or October) — this is the definition used for Fig. 1. The entry rate refers to the proportion of individuals not receiving SA at the year $t-1$ interview that are receiving SA at the year t interview and the exit rate refers to the proportion of individuals receiving SA at the year $t-1$ interview that are not receiving SA at the year t interview. Thus, the dynamics of SA receipt analysed in this article refer to transitions to and from receipt between successive annual interviews.

An alternative approach to receipt dynamics would be to take a spell-based approach, where spells are defined in terms of either consecutive 'benefit years' (meaning receipt at least once during the relevant year) or consecutive sub-annual periods such as 'months' where data are available. For the USA, the benefit year approach has been used to define spells in studies using PSID data from the pioneering analysis of AFDC benefit receipt by Bane and Ellwood (1983, 1994) onwards, while spell-based approaches based on sub-annual data have been applied in studies based on the Survey of Income and Program Participation (Chay & Hyslop, 2014; Grogger, 2004).

By focusing on transitions between annual interviews, we play to the BHPS's strengths. Wishing to minimize measurement error and respondent burden, most BHPS effort is devoted to collecting information about the various income sources received at the time of the interview and the corresponding amounts. To be sure, at each interview the survey also asks about receipt of each of a large number of cash benefits for each month between the interview month and the September of the year prior to the current survey year using the respondent's retrospective recall. There are, however, substantial complications arising in the creation of consistent monthly histories of SA receipt. Not only are there 'seam' problems to deal with (an implausible number of transitions at the seam where successive histories overlap and have to be spliced together), but there are also issues arising from the family-based measure of receipt since histories are required for all the individuals who were in each person's family month by month. See Cappellari and Jenkins (2008a) for further discussion. Addressing these issues is an important and major task and beyond the scope of this article.[12] Our approach focusing on annual SA transitions rather than spells of receipt is effectively the same as the one taken by Andrén and Andrén (2013) and Hansen and Lofstrom (2003, 2011) using Swedish administrative record data, by Hansen, Lofstrom, and Zhang (2006) and Hansen, Lofstrom, Liu, and Zhang (2014) using Canadian household panel data, and by Königs (2014) using German household panel data.

With 15 waves of BHPS data, our analysis data set contains a maximum of 15 observations per individual on SA receipt and other variables. At least two consecutive waves of data are required to estimate transition rates and any multivariate model of dynamics. We track individuals from when they are first observed as BHPS respondents until the first wave at which they drop out of the panel, either completely non-responding or with item non-response of sufficient degree that the individual's data cannot be used for estimation. If individuals rejoin the panel at some later wave, leading to gaps in benefit receipt sequences, we exclude them because taking account of intermittent participation complicates modelling substantially. Thus we focus on what is known as the 'absorbing attrition' case. The sample used for the empirical analysis is restricted to individuals of working age and not in full-time education (see earlier), and without missing data for some important explanatory variables. The basic estimation sample is an unbalanced panel of 75,988 person-wave observations for 9,036 adults. The majority of the sequences start at wave 1 (56 per cent), but there are sequences that begin at each subsequent wave as well (roughly 200−300 adults each year). See Cappellari and Jenkins (2008a) for further details concerning sample selection and demonstration that conclusions are robust to the use of a balanced rather than an unbalanced panel.

A DYNAMIC RANDOM EFFECTS PROBIT MODEL OF SA RECEIPT

Our data on outcomes consist of a sequence of ones (representing SA receipt at a particular interview) or zeros (representing non-receipt), for every adult included in the analysis sample. To analyse these data, we propose a version of the dynamic random effects probit model popularized by Heckman (1981) which also accounts for unobserved individual heterogeneity. Dynamic random effects probit models have been used to analyse SA dynamics by Andrén and Andrén (2013), Bhuller and Königs (2011), Hansen and Lofstrom (2011), Hansen et al. (2006), Hansen et al. (2014), and Königs (2014). One US application is by Chay and Hyslop (2004). The models have also been applied to other binary outcomes such as (un)employment and poverty: see inter alia Biewen (2009), Hyslop (1999), and Stewart (2007). Our model specification differs from those cited because, first, we allow the relationship between current and lagged SA receipt status to differ across individuals using an extensive set of covariate interactions.[13] Most previous studies have constrained the effects to be the same. Second, and related, we know of no previous study that has used dynamic random effects probit model estimates to predict aggregate entry and exit rates year by year in the way that we do. We elaborate on this point later.

The Statistical Model

Let p_{it}^* represent the latent propensity of SA receipt in each year of the sequence of T_i years for which an individual is observed, excluding the first year ($t = 1$), where

$$p_{it}^* = (\beta + \lambda y_{it-1})' Z_{it-1} + \gamma_i + \zeta_{it}; \quad t = 2, ..., T_i \qquad (1)$$

Each individual, $i = 1, ..., N$, is observed to receive SA ($y_{it} = 1$) in year t if $p_{it}^* > 0$, and to not receive it ($y_{it} = 0$) otherwise. Observed individual heterogeneity is measured by the vector of variables represented by Z_{it-1} (which also includes an intercept term). These variables are measured in the year at which the individual is at risk of making a transition (year $t - 1$). The interactions between the lagged dependent variable (y_{it-1}) and each element of Z_{it-1} allow characteristics to affect SA entry and exit rates differently.[14]

Unobserved heterogeneity is characterized by a fixed individual-specific component (γ_i) and a white noise error component (ζ_{it}). The errors are each assumed to have a mean of zero and be normally distributed, with the variance of ζ_{it} normalized to be one, and variance of γ_i estimated from the data. The error terms are assumed to be uncorrelated with each other, and the white noise component is assumed to be uncorrelated with each element of Z_{it}. We follow Mundlak (1978) and Chamberlain (1984), and many researchers since, in allowing for correlations between γ_i and Z_{it} by supposing that

$$\gamma_i = \xi' \overline{Z}_i + u_i \qquad (2)$$

where u_i is distributed $N(0, \sigma_u^2)$ and is assumed independent of Z_{it} and ζ_{it} for all persons and time periods. The $\overline{Z}_i$ may be defined in several ways — we follow the common practice of defining them as the longitudinal average for each individual of each time-varying characteristic within the vector Z_{it} (with the exception of intrinsically time-varying characteristics like age). Intuitively, differences in longitudinally averaged characteristics are informative about underlying individual-specific characteristics, so that the unobserved individual differences that are left (u_i) may be more plausibly supposed to be independent of observed characteristics.

There is an issue for estimation concerning the 'initial conditions' of the sequence of observations for each individual — whether y_{i1} is independent of u_i. If receipt in the initial year is correlated with the time-invariant individual-specific effect, a correlation is induced between the error term and the lagged dependent variable in Eq. (1), leading to bias in parameter estimates.

We handle initial conditions using the conditional maximum likelihood estimator proposed by Wooldridge (2005). Rather than modelling the joint distribution of the sequence of binary receipt indicators from the initial one to the final one conditioning on the set of explanatory variables, Wooldridge showed that one may model the distribution of the binary receipt indicators from $t_i = 2, \ldots, T_i$, conditioning on the set of explanatory variables and the binary receipt indicator for the initial year. Wooldridge proposed modelling the distribution of γ_i conditional on y_{i1} and either $Z_i = (Z_{i1}, Z_{i2}, \ldots, Z_{iT})$ or $\overline{Z}_i$. His model for the individual-specific component (abstracting from $\overline{Z}_i$ already incorporated using the Chamberlain–Mundlak specification) can be written as:

$$\gamma_i = a_0 + a_1 y_{i1} + u_i \qquad (3)$$

so that, subsuming the constant term a_0 into the parameter vector β, Eq. (1) becomes

$$p_{it}^* = (\beta + \lambda y_{it-1})'Z_{it-1} + \xi'\overline{Z}_i + a_1 y_{i1} + u_i + \zeta_{it}; \quad t = 2, ..., T_i \qquad (4)$$

The Wooldridge estimator has the advantages that initial conditions do not have to be modelled and estimation can be done using standard random effects probit software.[15]

The model outlined incorporates a relatively simple dynamic structure. It characterizes a first-order Markov process: transition behaviour does not depend on receipt history beyond the year before the current one. Higher order Markov models can be fitted, as Stewart (2007) demonstrates, but we find that our model characterizes aggregate trends in transition rates relatively well (see below). More flexible approaches to duration dependence can also be modelled using survival analysis methods applied to spell data. We eschew those methods because of the difficulties of deriving consistent monthly histories (see earlier) and because using the annual interview data to define spells would underestimate the prevalence of short spells. For spell length predictions from our first-order Markov model ignoring the latter issue and employing a 'steady-state' assumption, see Cappellari and Jenkins (2008a).

Prediction of Aggregate SA Receipt and Transition Rates Using Model Estimates

The dynamic random effects probit model summarizes individual probabilities of SA receipt rates in each year t, where those probabilities depend on receipt status at $t-1$. We now discuss how the model and its parameter estimates may be employed to predict aggregate SA receipt and transition rates year-by-year using the sample data.[16] We consider three sets of estimators and explain how each of them takes account of unobservable differences between individuals (u_i). We argue that the first set of estimators (labelled A) provides biased estimates of aggregate transition rates. We then introduce a second and intermediate set of estimators (labelled B) which we argue is also biased. Finally, we propose a third set of estimators (C) which is a modification of B, and which improves upon both B and A.

For estimator set A, let us first define an individual-level predicted probability of SA receipt in year $t = \tau$ as:

$$\hat{p}_{i\tau} = \Phi\left(\frac{[\hat{\beta} + \hat{\lambda}y_{i\tau-1}]'Z_{i\tau-1} + \hat{\xi}'\bar{Z}_i + \hat{a}_1 y_{i1}}{\sqrt{1 + \hat{\sigma}_u^2}}\right), \quad \tau = 1992, \dots, 2005 \qquad (5)$$

where '^' denotes a maximum likelihood estimate. This leads to a first set of estimators of the aggregate SA receipt rate ($\hat{P}_\tau^A$), entry rate ($\hat{E}_\tau^A$) and exit rate ($\hat{X}_\tau^A$), respectively: [17]

$$\hat{P}_\tau^A = \frac{1}{N}\sum_{i=1}^N \hat{p}_{i\tau} = \frac{1}{N}\left[\sum_{i=1}^N y_{i\tau-1}(1 - \hat{X}_\tau^A) + (1 - y_{i\tau-1})\hat{E}_\tau^A\right], \text{ where}$$

$$\hat{E}_\tau^A = \frac{\sum_{i=1}^N (1 - y_{i\tau-1})\hat{p}_{i\tau}}{\sum_{i=1}^N (1 - y_{i\tau-1})} \quad \text{and} \quad \hat{X}_\tau^A = 1 - \frac{\sum_{i=1}^N y_{i\tau-1}\hat{p}_{i\tau}}{\sum_{i=1}^N y_{i\tau-1}}$$

(6)

The expression for the receipt rate is the year-τ analogue of the expression for the 'population average' prediction given by Wooldridge (2005, pp. 47–48), in which unobserved differences between individuals (the u_i) are integrated out – the predictions are not conditional on the u_i – and there is no conditioning on a particular year.[18] The denominators in the expressions for the entry and exit rates are the number of non-recipients and recipients in the sample in year $\tau-1$, respectively.

Year-τ predictions based on population average estimators are biased in general. The problem is that the distribution of the u_i within each year-τ sample at risk of a transition differs from the distribution assumed for the population. The exceptional case is the first year in the sample period (year $\tau-1$ is 1991), because the wave 1 BHPS sample was a random sample of the UK private household population, and sample selection was therefore unrelated to either benefit receipt status or u_i. (The distribution of unobservables is the same among the subsamples of recipients and of non-recipients, aside from considerations related to subsample numbers.) However, in subsequent years, the samples that are at risk of making an SA transition are not randomly selected. Sample composition depends on u_i: there is dynamic self-selection and the distributions of unobservables among recipients and non-recipients will differ from each other and the population as a whole. Thus, deployment of population average estimators (based on $\hat{\sigma}_u^2$) to single years other than 1991 will lead to biased estimates of the aggregate year-τ transition and receipt rates.[19]

Consider now a second and intermediate set of estimators (B) that is based on individual-level predictions that use estimates of the u_i for each individual in the relevant year-τ sample. That is, for each τ, define

$$\hat{q}_{i\tau} = \Phi([\hat{\beta} + \hat{\lambda}y_{i\tau-1}]'Z_{i\tau-1} + \hat{\xi}'\overline{Z}_i + \hat{a}_1 y_{i1} + \hat{u}_i) \tag{7}$$

Observe the presence of the $\hat{u}_i$ in this expression: we derive estimates of u_i using Empirical Bayes methods.[20] Expressions for our second set of estimators of the aggregate SA receipt rate, entry rate and exit rate are then given by:

$$\hat{P}_\tau^B = \frac{1}{N}\sum_{i=1}^{N}\hat{q}_{i\tau} = \frac{1}{N}\left[\sum_{i=1}^{N}y_{i\tau-1}(1 - \hat{X}_\tau^B) + (1 - y_{i\tau-1})\hat{E}_\tau^B\right], \quad \text{where}$$

$$\tag{8}$$

$$\hat{E}_\tau^B = \frac{\sum_{i=1}^{N}(1 - y_{i\tau-1})\hat{q}_{i\tau}}{\sum_{i=1}^{N}(1 - y_{i\tau-1})} \quad \text{and} \quad \hat{X}_\tau^B = 1 - \frac{\sum_{i=1}^{N}y_{i\tau-1}\hat{q}_{i\tau}}{\sum_{i=1}^{N}y_{i\tau-1}}$$

These estimators are biased as well. Although the individual-level year-τ predicted probabilities for each at-risk sample are derived using each individual's $\hat{u}_i$, the estimates of the aggregate transition rates do not take full account of the effects of dynamic self-selection. We also need to adjust for how the distribution of unobservables in each at-risk sample changes over time and differs between recipients and non-recipients. Distributions are relevant since we are averaging over subsamples in Eq. (8) and the distribution of u_i within each at-risk sample differs from the distribution in the population (assumed to be normally distributed with mean 0 and variance σ_u^2).

Among those at risk of SA entry in any given year $\tau > 1$, there will be an over-representation of individuals with relatively low u_i and hence fewer entries (so SA entry rates will be under-predicted). Similarly, SA retention rates are likely to be over-predicted (SA exit rates under-predicted), this time because there is an over-representation of individuals with relatively high u_i in the at-risk sample. The magnitude of the potential problem in either case is unclear a priori, however.

So, to derive good year-by-year estimates of the aggregate receipt, entry and exit rates, one needs to also take account of dynamic self-selection. To do this, we propose a third set of estimators (C) in which we calculate individual-level predicted probabilities in the at-risk samples as for B, but then derive the estimates of aggregate SA entry rates and exit rates by weighting the individual-level predictions to adjust for the effects of the over- and under-representation that we have cited.

By analogy with the use of design weights for complex survey designs, we suggest inverse-probability-of-selection weights with the weights based on $\hat{u}_i$. For those at risk of SA exit, we propose approximating the probability of selection into receipt by $\Phi(\hat{u}_i)$ and define weight $w_i^X = 1/\Phi(\hat{u}_i)$. Individuals with relatively high $\hat{u}_i$ (more likely not to exit) are down-weighted in the exit rate calculation, as required. Similarly, we approximate the probability of selection into receipt for those at risk of SA entry by $1 - \Phi(\hat{u}_i)$ and define $w_i^E = 1/(1 - \Phi(\hat{u}_i))$ so that those with relatively low $\hat{u}_i$ are down-weighted in the entry rate calculation.[21] Our third, and preferred, set of estimators is thus:

$$\hat{P}_\tau^C = \frac{1}{N}\left[\sum_{i=1}^{N} y_{i\tau-1}\,(1-\hat{X}_\tau^C) + (1-y_{i\tau-1})\hat{E}_\tau^C\right], \quad \text{where}$$

$$\hat{E}_\tau^C = \frac{\sum_{i=1}^{N}(1-y_{i\tau-1})w_i^E q_{i\tau}}{\sum_{i=1}^{N}(1-y_{i\tau-1})} \quad \text{and} \quad \hat{X}_\tau^C = 1 - \frac{\sum_{i=1}^{N} y_{i\tau-1}\,w_i^X q_{i\tau}}{\sum_{i=1}^{N} y_{i\tau-1}} \tag{9}$$

We show in the next section that these 'individual (weighted)' estimators (C) provide good estimates of their observed sample counterparts, and better estimates than estimator sets A and B. We also report sample estimates of the distribution of $\hat{u}_i$ among SA recipients and non-recipients, year-by-year, to provide a direct look at the process of dynamic self-selection.

Observe that the impact on the SA entry rate of a factor included in Z_{it-1} depends on the coefficient in β corresponding to that factor. For example, we would expect larger unemployment rates to be associated with a larger SA entry rate and a smaller exit rate (a larger persistence rate), other things being equal. In this case, the coefficient on the unemployment rate in β (call it β_{unemp}) would be positive. As the model is non-linear, the precise effect of changing unemployment rates also depends on the values of other parameters and the other characteristics in Z_{it-1}.

The more negative (positive) an element of λ is, the higher (lower) is the exit rate, other things being equal. However, the overall impact of a covariate on the exit rate depends on the sum of the coefficients in β and λ relating to that covariate. For example, a negative association between the exit rate and the unemployment rate requires $\beta_{\text{unemp}} + \lambda_{\text{unemp}}$ to be negative. Observe that many previous studies using dynamic random effects probit models constrain the impact of covariates on entry and exit rates to be the same: the λ vector contains an intercept term and zeros otherwise. In the example just discussed, the assumption would be that $\lambda_{\text{unemp}} = 0$.

Our model accounts for trends in aggregate entry and exit rates over the sample period in two ways. One is through time-varying parameters: we allow the intercepts in β and λ to be year-specific by including year dummy variables in the vectors of covariates. Second, there are changes over time in the characteristics of the individuals at risk of SA exit or entry — not only selection on unobservables as just discussed but also changes in observable characteristics. An example of the latter is changes in the local unemployment rates that individuals face. These affect our predictions of aggregate transition and receipt probabilities because we derive them by averaging individual-specific probabilities across the individuals at risk in each year.

We assess the model's within-sample goodness of fit by comparing predicted and observed aggregate SA transition and receipt probabilities, year by year, using the three sets of estimators. We then use the model to undertake some counterfactual predictions using the 'individual (weighted)' estimators in order to summarize the relative impacts of changes such as benefit reforms and unavailability of jobs. In the first case, we compare observed aggregate SA entry, exit and receipt rates with the corresponding rates predicted by holding the year-specific intercepts in β and λ fixed at their values at the start of the period, with all other factors (parameters and characteristics in Z_{t-1}) being held fixed. (The reason for this specification is discussed in the next section.) In the second case, we compare observed rates with the rates predicted with local unemployment rates held at their levels at the start of the period. In both cases, we re-calculate $\hat{q}_{i\tau}$ under each counterfactual scenario and generate predicted transition and receipt rates year by year using Eq. (9). The larger is the difference between the counterfactual and within-sample prediction, the larger is the effect that we attribute to the factor examined.

In all our simulations, we use observed values of $y_{i\tau-1}$ to predict aggregate transition rates for year τ. That is, transition rate series are constructed by splicing together one-year-ahead predictions (consistent with the first-order Markov nature of the statistical model), rather than by constructing sequences in which $y_{i\tau-1}$ values for year τ are dynamically updated using the prediction of receipt in year $\tau-1$ made for year $\tau-1$. There are some attractions to dynamic updating but we note that our approach is the conventional one.[22] We return to this issue again later. Overall, we believe that, whereas our simulations are indicative rather than decisive, they remain valuable not least because they help one judge the economic significance of the estimated model parameters in a more helpful way than simply looking at each parameter in isolation. The characteristics included in Z are discussed next.

Explanatory Variables

Observed characteristics are summarized by sex and age, highest educational qualification and health status. Age refers to whether the individual is aged 50 or more years: we expect older workers to have less work attachment, other things being equal, and hence higher SA entry and lower SA exit rates. We distinguish four categories of educational qualification: none, low, high and missing. 'Low' refers to having passes in examinations taken at age 16 (CSE(s) and/or O-levels); 'high' refers to having passes in examinations taken at age 18 (A-level(s)) or higher qualifications such as a degree. Around one-tenth of respondents have missing data on educational qualifications: these are mostly respondents for whom only a proxy interview was gained but sufficient information was derived about other characteristics from the proxy respondent so that the individual could be included in the sample. The missing qualifications indicator is better interpreted as a control for response propensity than as a measure of educational qualifications. Health status refers to whether the respondent stated that s/he had one or more of 13 health problems.[23]

The characteristics of each respondent's family are summarized by the number of dependent children, whether the age of the youngest child is less than 5 years, and by family type (single adult, couple or lone parent). We also control whether the respondent lives in the London area (as the labour market is very different from elsewhere in the country) and housing tenure (whether the respondent lived in owner-occupied housing rather than other tenures such as social housing or renting privately). We do not suggest that tenure itself necessarily has an impact; rather it is a marker for other factors including differences in wealth and assets and local area disadvantage.

The remainder of the explanatory variables relate to the factors cited earlier in the descriptions of trends in aggregate receipt and transition rates (Figs. 1 and 2), specifically changes in the unavailability of jobs and in tax and benefit policies.

Our measure of unemployment is the unemployment rate in the individual's local area, by which we mean travel-to-work area (TTWA). A TTWA is defined with reference to commuting patterns and corresponds broadly to a city and surrounding area. More precisely, the local area unemployment rate is the ratio of the number of unemployed people to the number in the labour force in the individual's TTWA at the time of the annual interview, derived from the Joint Unemployment and Vacancies Operating System Cohort (a 5 per cent sample of all computerized claims for unemployment-related benefits selected by reference to a claimant's National Insurance Number).[24]

The impacts of benefit policy changes are accounted for by allowing the intercept terms in the SA entry and exit equations to differ by survey year. We follow this strategy rather than including measures of (say) programme generosity over time for two reasons. First, benefit rates in the UK are set nationally; there is no spatial variation across regions or states as in the USA or some European countries. Second, there have been many programme changes within the 1991–2005 period (Tables 1 and 2), and so it is difficult to identify the impact of any specific policy reform. Nonetheless, we expect that if the policy changes cited in Table 2 had had an effect on SA entry and exit rates, they would be reflected in changes in the time-varying intercepts, especially around 1996, 1999 and 2003 (see the earlier discussion).[25] At the time, we acknowledge that there may be other factors that account for the year-to-year variations that are picked up by the year fixed effects, though we cannot think of examples that are not otherwise included in the model.

Derivation of unbiased parameter estimates relies on the assumption that the explanatory variables are strictly exogenous. This assumption is relatively innocuous for factors such as local unemployment rates or changes to the benefit system. More debatable is our supposition that the impacts of a shock in an individual's SA eligibility on the individual's future housing tenure or household type are sufficiently small that they may be ignored. To account for potential endogeneity is particularly difficult and hampered, for example, by a lack of plausible instruments. For valuable discussion of the issues, see Biewen (2009).

Summary Statistics for At-Risk Groups

Changes in the aggregate SA transition rates depend in part on changes in the composition of the populations at risk. Sample characteristics and their changes over time are summarized in Table 3 in terms of sample means for the first year (1991) and last year (2005) and all years pooled (1991–2005) broken down by SA receipt status.[26]

Consider first those at risk of entry (SA non-recipients). Averaging over the period as a whole, the mean age was 41 years, half of the sample were women and just over one-half reported at least one health problem. About 13 per cent had no educational qualifications and a quarter had only low

Table 3. Explanatory Variables: Sample Means, by Survey Year and SA Receipt Status.

Variable	All Cases			SA Recipients			SA Non-recipients		
	1991	2005	All years	1991	2005	All years	1991	2005	All years
Aged 50+ years	0.14	0.22	0.20	0.10	0.25	0.16	0.14	0.22	0.20
Age (years)	39.46	41.89	40.75	36.98	41.78	39.35	39.69	41.89	40.86
Female	0.51	0.52	0.51	0.61	0.58	0.60	0.50	0.52	0.50
Health problems	0.51	0.60	0.56	0.53	0.76	0.67	0.50	0.59	0.55
Educational qualifications									
None	0.24	0.08	0.15	0.43	0.32	0.38	0.22	0.06	0.13
Low (O-levels, etc.)	0.31	0.20	0.26	0.36	0.23	0.32	0.31	0.20	0.26
High (A-levels or more)	0.39	0.59	0.48	0.18	0.36	0.27	0.40	0.60	0.50
Missing	0.07	0.13	0.10	0.03	0.10	0.03	0.07	0.13	0.10
Number of children	0.98	0.87	0.87	1.50	1.13	1.31	0.93	0.86	0.84
Age youngest child <5	0.21	0.18	0.18	0.35	0.17	0.25	0.19	0.18	0.18
Family type									
Lone parent	0.05	0.04	0.05	0.29	0.18	0.24	0.03	0.04	0.03
Couple	0.79	0.79	0.78	0.55	0.59	0.54	0.81	0.80	0.80
Single	0.17	0.17	0.18	0.16	0.23	0.21	0.17	0.17	0.17
Couple and children	0.46	0.44	0.43	0.41	0.36	0.37	0.47	0.45	0.43
House is owned	0.78	0.83	0.78	0.41	0.23	0.33	0.82	0.86	0.82
Lives in London	0.11	0.08	0.10	0.13	0.08	0.11	0.11	0.08	0.10
Local area unemployment rate (%)	8.00	2.32	5.10	8.55	2.54	6.15	7.95	2.30	5.01

Notes: Children's variables are set equal to zero if there is no child in the respondent's family. All variables are binary (0/1), except age (integer), number of children (integer) and local unemployment rate (percentage). 'All years' refers to all survey years 1991–2005. 'All cases' refers to SA recipients and non-recipients combined.

educational qualifications. The average number of dependent children was 0.84 and just under a fifth had a child aged less than 5 years. Four-fifths were part of a couple, some 17 per cent were single adults and 3 per cent were lone parents. Just over 80 per cent lived in owner-occupied accommodation, one in ten lived in the London area and the average local area unemployment rate was just over 5 per cent. These whole-period averages disguise some marked trends over time. In particular, there was a rise in the proportion reporting a health problem (up from around 50 per cent in 1991 to around 60 per cent in 2005), and even larger changes in the distribution of educational qualifications. The fraction of non-recipients with no or low educational qualifications declined from around 53 per cent in 1991 to 26 per cent in 2005. The other main variation over time was in local area unemployment rates, which declined from 8 per cent on average at the start of the 1990s to just over 2 per cent in 2005. In contrast, the means of virtually all the demographic variables (age, number and age of children, family type) changed very little.

These changes suggest that one reason for the decline in SA entry rates may be the improvement in educational qualifications (improving employability) and the decline in local area unemployment rates reflecting improved availability of jobs. The rate of decline in the average local area unemployment rate levelled off around 1997, which is consistent with the levelling off in the decline in the entry rate around that year (Fig. 2).

Consider now those at risk of SA exit. Averaging over the period as a whole, we find that compared to non-recipients, the proportion of female recipients is larger (60 per cent rather than 50 per cent), and the proportion with relatively low educational qualifications is higher (38 per cent of recipients have no educational qualifications compared to 13 per cent of non-recipients). The average number of children among SA recipients is 1.31 (compared to 0.84) and the proportion with a child aged less than 5 years is 25 per cent rather than 18 per cent. About one-quarter of recipients are lone parents but only 3 per cent of non-recipients. The proportion of SA recipients living in owned accommodation is only one-third compared with 80 per cent for non-recipients. In addition, recipients tend to live in areas with slightly higher unemployment rates than non-recipients. In sum, SA receipt is concentrated among individuals with characteristics commonly associated with labour market disadvantage.

As far as trends are concerned, there are both similarities and differences between SA recipients and non-recipients. For both groups, the prevalence of health problems rose between 1991 and 2005, but the increase is larger for recipients (from 53 to 76 per cent, compared to from 50 to 59 per cent).

Local area unemployment rates fell for both groups; so too did the proportion with no educational qualifications, but the decline in the latter was smaller for SA recipients than non-recipients. There are some distinctive demographic trends for recipients: the proportions with children and with young children in particular declined over time. There was also a decline in the number of lone parents among recipients (from 29 per cent in 1991 to 18 per cent in 2005). In principle this might be explained by a shift in low-income families with children (and lone parents in particular) from SA receipt to receipt of in-work benefits such as WFTC, but the proportions of couples with children and of lone parents was largely unchanged over the period. Another marked trend among recipients is the decline in the proportion living in owned accommodation, from 41 per cent in 1991 to 23 per cent in 2005. Put another way, the association between SA receipt and living in rented accommodation (much of which is subsidized social housing) has increased.

These patterns suggest that two trends in particular may help account for the decline in the aggregate SA exit rate over time: the rise in proportion of recipients with health problems and the large rise in the proportion living in non-owned accommodation. Both trends are consistent with a hypothesis of 'creaming' on observable characteristics: the most skilled and work-ready individuals left SA for a job, whereas the group left on SA increasingly consisted of individuals who were less well equipped for work, and for whom the probability of SA exit is relatively low. In the following section, we provide additional evidence of 'creaming' that associated with unobserved differences (dynamic self-selection).

MODEL ESTIMATES AND COUNTERFACTUAL PREDICTIONS

Model Parameter Estimates

Estimates of the dynamic random effects probit model specified in Eq. (4) are set out in Table 4. In the top half of the table, the first column of numbers refers to estimates of β and the second column to estimates of λ. In the bottom half of the table are the estimates of the effects of the longitudinally averaged variables on SA receipt propensities, the impact of being in SA receipt when initially observed, and the variance of the unobserved heterogeneity distribution.

Table 4. The Probability of SA Receipt (Dynamic Random Effect Probit Model Estimates).

Explanatory Variables (Measured at $t-1$)	β	λ
Female	−0.0895***	0.0896
	(0.034)	(0.060)
Aged 50 years or more	0.0529	0.0463
	(0.044)	(0.081)
Has health problem(s)	0.0278	−0.0143
	(0.038)	(0.057)
Educational qualifications		
Low: O-level(s), CSE, etc.	−0.2073***	−0.0534
	(0.046)	(0.071)
High: A-level(s) or higher	−0.3623***	−0.0680
	(0.045)	(0.073)
Missing data	−0.4215***	0.0318
	(0.063)	(0.150)
Number of children in family	−0.0264	0.0751***
	(0.024)	(0.027)
Age of youngest child <5 years	0.1540***	−0.1084
	(0.049)	(0.073)
Family type: lone parent	−0.0030	0.0724
	(0.095)	(0.110)
Family type: couple	−0.1214*	−0.2342***
	(0.069)	(0.079)
House tenure: owned	−0.0491	0.0145
	(0.056)	(0.059)
Lives in London (inner or outer)	0.2402	0.0472
	(0.163)	(0.091)
Unemployment rate in local area (%)	0.0323***	−0.0107
	(0.010)	(0.015)
Survey year (year t)		
1993	−0.0321	0.0049
	(0.058)	(0.118)
1994	−0.0964	−0.0659
	(0.060)	(0.121)
1995	−0.1372**	0.0462
	(0.060)	(0.122)
1996	−0.1559**	0.0013
	(0.061)	(0.124)
1997	−0.1734***	0.1401
	(0.067)	(0.135)
1998	−0.2914***	0.2572*
	(0.077)	(0.147)
1999	−0.3655***	0.3811**
	(0.082)	(0.154)

Table 4.   (*Continued*)

Explanatory Variables (Measured at $t-1$)	β	λ
2000	−0.2357***	0.2633*
	(0.080)	(0.157)
2001	−0.4262***	0.4703***
	(0.089)	(0.165)
2002	−0.3834***	0.3103*
	(0.089)	(0.167)
2003	−0.3152***	0.5179***
	(0.088)	(0.176)
2004	−0.3991***	0.2557
	(0.092)	(0.173)
2005	−0.2847***	0.4109**
	(0.090)	(0.181)
Intercept	−1.5693***	1.2370***
	(0.102)	(0.180)
Longitudinally averaged variables		
Has health problems	0.2495***	
	(0.055)	
Family type: couple	−0.1473*	
	(0.081)	
Family type: lone parent	0.6074***	
	(0.121)	
Number of children in family	0.0964***	
	(0.031)	
Age of youngest child <5 years	−0.0054	
	(0.085)	
House tenure: owned	−0.7970***	
	(0.068)	
Lives in London (inner or outer)	−0.2498	
	(0.171)	
Unemployment rate in local area (%)	0.0118	
	(0.009)	
Received SA at $t=1$	0.7658***	
	(0.051)	
σ_u^2	0.4201***	
	(0.036)	

Notes: The table provides estimates of Eq. (4) model fitted to data from waves 1−15 of the BHPS using the Wooldridge (2005) estimator. Standard errors in parentheses. *$p<0.10$; **$p<0.05$; ***$p<0.01$. Log-likelihood = −8,792.293. Number of person-year observations = 66,952. Number of persons = 9,036. Reference categories: male, aged 25−50, has no health problems, has no educational qualifications, family type is single, lives in non-owned accommodation outside the London area and the survey year is 1992. The outcome is measured in year t, and explanatory variables in year $t-1$, with the exception of the survey year indicators for which the indicator label refers to year t.

Table 4 gives that SA entry probabilities are lower for women, individuals living with a partner and without a child aged less than 5 years. There is a gradient in entry rates with educational qualifications – highest for those with no qualifications, and entry rates are lower the higher the qualifications attained (and lower still for those with missing qualifications data). There is no statistically significant association between entry rates and age, the presence of health problems, number of children, home ownership and residential location.

The greater the local area unemployment rate, the larger is the SA entry rate – which is consistent with the aggregate trend data as shown in Figs. 1 and 2.

The pattern of estimates of the survey year intercepts also corresponds with the trends in aggregate data. (The year labels given in Table 4 refer to year t for transitions between year $t-1$ and year t.) Between the mid-1990s and the mid-2000s, the coefficients become increasingly negative implying a lower SA entry rate, other things being equal. These appear to be large changes: the estimated intercept doubled in magnitude between 1995 and 2005, from -0.14 to -0.28. But are there variations in intercepts corresponding to years of major benefit reform (survey years 1997, 2000 and 2004 according to the labelling convention used in Table 4)?

The estimates suggest that the introduction of JSA, accompanied by tightening of eligibility conditions, was associated with a decline in SA entry rates. For those at risk of entry in 1996 (year $t = 1997$), the estimated coefficient is -0.17, but it is -0.29 for those at risk of entry in 1997 (year $t = 1998$) and -0.37 for those at risk of entry in 1998 (year $t = 1999$). There is also some evidence consistent with a WFTC introduction effect as the coefficient for those at risk of entry in 1999 (year $t = 2000$) is -0.24, but -0.43 for those at risk of entry a year later. In contrast, there is no similar change in the coefficients for years round the change from WFTC to WTC. We therefore find a smoking gun for some effects on SA entry rates of benefit policy reforms. We refrain from drawing stronger conclusions for the reasons described earlier.

What about the determinants of exit rates? Observe, first of all, that relatively few of the coefficients on interactions between characteristics and lagged SA receipt status are statistically significant, which suggests that the determinants of exit rates are similar to the determinants of entry rates (see earlier). However, there are exceptions: the number of children in the family, whether the respondent has a partner, and a number of the year indicators. Having more children is associated with a smaller exit rate, whereas being a member of a couple is associated with larger exit rate.

Otherwise, we find, for example and as expected, that having better educational qualifications is associated with a higher exit rate and a larger unemployment rate is associated with a lower exit rate.

There appears to be little evidence of benefit policy reform effects on SA exit rates. For the relevant survey years, observe that the sum of corresponding β and λ intercepts is close to zero: the estimates are of approximately the same magnitude and of the opposite sign. Hence the change between successive years is also negligible.

The estimates of the parameters associated with time-averaged characteristics and unobserved heterogeneity are at the bottom of Table 4. The table gives that individuals with a disposition to health problems or many children are more likely to receive SA. Family type and housing tenure also matter. Individuals who are more likely to be lone parents are more likely to receive SA, whereas individuals with a partner are less likely to. Homeowners are less likely to receive SA than renters. Experiencing persistently high local area unemployment rates does not appear to be associated with a high probability of SA receipt, other things being equal. (Thus it is the year-to-year variations in unemployment that drive changes in SA receipt, by changing exit and entry propensities.) There is statistically significant unobserved heterogeneity in addition to the heterogeneity captured by the longitudinally averaged variables: the estimate of σ_u^2 is 0.42. Finally, observe that initial conditions matter. Individuals who are receiving SA when initially observed are much more likely than non-recipients to be receiving SA in some subsequent year.

We make two further observations about the estimates before proceeding to the simulations. First, the estimates of λ are indicative not only of genuine state dependence in SA benefit receipt per se but also of heterogeneity in its degree across population subgroups. (See Cappellari & Jenkins, 2008a, for estimates and discussion.) Second, although there is a relatively large number of statistically insignificant parameter estimates in the λ column, we use the full model for the simulations because the inclusion of redundant predictors does not affect the accuracy of our predictions. It may affect their precision but that is less of an issue for our simulations.

Predictions and Counterfactual Simulations

We now show that the fitted model tracks the aggregate trends in aggregate SA transition and receipt rates and then assess the main drivers of the trends using counterfactual predictions.

Fig. 3 compares observed and within-sample predictions of SA entry, exit and receipt rates year by year.[27] Panel (a) compares entry rates; panel (b) compares exit rates and panel (c) compares receipt rates.[28] Predicted rates are based on the population average, individual (unweighted), individual (weighted) sets of estimators discussed earlier, A, B and C respectively.

The population average within-sample predictions lead to overestimates of observed SA transition rates and underestimates of receipt rates, with the exception of 1991 when the estimates match their observed counterparts for the reason explained earlier. Individual (unweighted) predictions underestimate SA entry rates. They track exit rates well (the expected underestimation turns out to be small), but receipt rates are underestimated. By contrast, the individual (weighted) estimates track both transition rates and the receipt rate very well, except at the very beginning of the period (1991 and 1992 for entry rates and the receipt rate). As discussed earlier, the differences in predictions between estimator sets are indicative of the role played by dynamic self-selection.

Direct evidence about dynamic self-selection is provided by the year-by-year estimates of the distribution of $\hat{u}_i$. Means and variances are given in Table 5 separately for individuals at risk of SA entry and SA exit. For the former group, the mean of $\hat{u}_i$ is slightly negative in each year (around -0.04) confirming that this group contains an over-representation of individuals who are less prone to SA receipt. (The mean is little different from the assumed population value, zero, because those at risk of SA entry form the vast majority in any given year.) By contrast, the mean of $\hat{u}_i$ is distinctly positive in each year (except the first) confirming that this group contains an over-representation of individuals who are relatively prone to SA receipt and, moreover, the mean increases as the period progresses, almost doubling between 1993 and 2005 (from 0.32 to 0.63). This is consistent with a 'creaming on unobservables' hypothesis – that it is more employable individuals who exit SA first and the chances of SA exit among those who remain in receipt (relatively less employable) are correspondingly lower.

Given the good within-sample fit with the individual (weighted) estimators, we proceed to counterfactual predictions based on them. The first exercise concerns the impact of the decline in unemployment rates after the early-1990s recession. To assess this, we consider what would have happened to SA entry and exit rates were unemployment to have remained at its 1993 peak and everything else were to stay the same, as discussed earlier. More precisely, individual-specific local area unemployment rates in each year are set equal to their 1993 values. The second counterfactual exercise investigates factors associated with the passage of time, including benefit

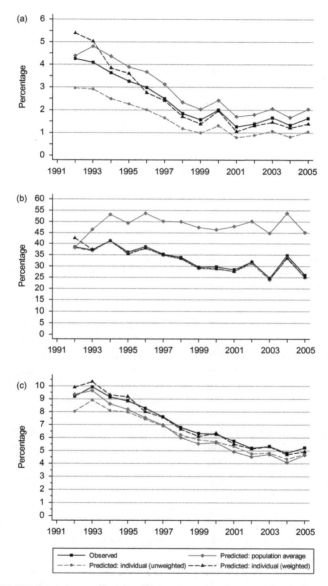

Fig. 3. Within-Sample Predictions of SA Transition and Receipt Rates, by Year and Prediction Method. (a) Entry Rates; (b) Exit Rates; (c) Receipt Rates. *Note:* Authors' calculations from BHPS data using the parameter estimates given in Table 3 and the estimators defined in Eqs. (6)–(9) and discussed in the text.

Table 5. The Distribution of $\hat{u}_i$.

Year	Individuals at Risk of SA Entry		Individuals at Risk of SA Exit	
	Mean	Variance	Mean	Variance
1992	−0.007	0.090	−0.025	0.184
1993	−0.037	0.083	0.316	0.234
1994	−0.046	0.077	0.418	0.237
1995	−0.043	0.080	0.444	0.260
1996	−0.049	0.073	0.522	0.259
1997	−0.045	0.077	0.505	0.252
1998	−0.042	0.075	0.533	0.267
1999	−0.040	0.075	0.571	0.263
2000	−0.035	0.076	0.543	0.258
2001	−0.039	0.070	0.623	0.241
2002	−0.034	0.072	0.590	0.244
2003	−0.035	0.066	0.658	0.247
2004	−0.033	0.066	0.638	0.199
2005	−0.028	0.063	0.630	0.222

Note: $\hat{u}_i$ is derived using Empirical Bayes methods (see text). Our model-based estimate of σ_u^2 is 0.4201, with the mean of u_i assumed to equal zero.

policy reform effects. We compare the within-sample prediction series with aggregate rates predicted by fixing the survey year intercepts at their estimated values for 1993, with all other factors remaining unchanged.

The two sets of counterfactual predictions and corresponding observed entry, exit and receipt rates are shown in Fig. 4, panels (a), (b) and (c), respectively. The figure suggests that the fall in unemployment rates over the period had a large impact on SA entry rates. If unemployment rates had remained at their peak level, the entry rate would have been almost 1 percentage point higher by 2005, which is large relative to the entry rate in 2005 (just over 1 per cent). Most of impact of falling unemployment rates occurred before 2000, as suggested by the aggregate unemployment rate trends reported in Fig. 1. Effects associated with passage of time itself are slightly larger still: the dashed line lies on or above the solid black line in panel (a). By 1998, the gap between the counterfactual and within-sample series had increased to around 1.1 percentage points and fluctuated around that size until 2005.

Turning now to SA exit rates, we see that if unemployment rates had remained at their early-1990s high, the exit rate would have been lower but, again, with the gap increasing fastest before 2000 and less thereafter. However, the magnitude of the predicted effect on exit rates is small

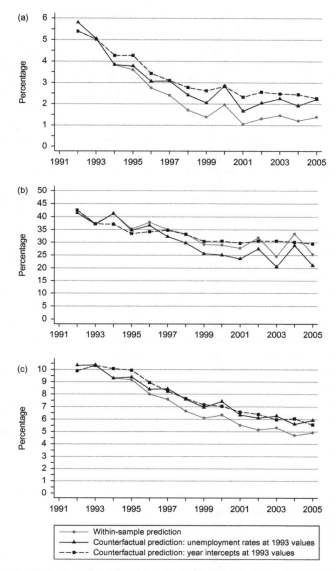

Fig. 4. Counterfactual Predictions of SA Transition and Receipt Rates, by Year. (a) Entry Rates; (b) Exit Rates; (c) Receipt Rates. *Note:* Authors' calculations from BHPS data using the parameter estimates given in Table 3. All predictions are derived using the individual (weighted) estimators shown in Eq. (9) and discussed in the text.

compared with the impact on entry rates. The difference between the series in panel (b) is just over 4 percentage points during the 2000s, which is a small gap compared to the predicted within-sample aggregate exit rate which is around 30 per cent over that same period. In addition, panel (b) provides no evidence for passage-of-time effects on SA exit rates, confirming the impressions derived from discussion of the regression table estimates. The counterfactual and within-sample series overlap substantially.

Panels (a) and (b) suggest that unemployment had impacts on both SA entry and exit rates whereas any passage-of-time time effects (including those associated with benefit reforms) were only on entry rates but slightly larger than unemployment effects in this case. When we look at the predictions for receipt rates, which reflect the combination of exit and entry rates, we see that the net effect of the two counterfactual changes is much the same from 1997 onwards, about 1 percentage point (and note that the within-sample predicted receipt rate was around 5 per cent in 2005). Thus, the sum of the two effects is around two percentage points, and we note the fall in the receipt rate over the period is about 5 percentage points.

What accounts for the remainder of the fall? Part of the explanation is changes in the distributions of observed characteristics (as discussed earlier). For example, in the fourth section we drew attention to a marked upgrading in educational qualifications among the working-age population and a halving between 1991 and 2005 in the proportion of owner-occupier SA recipients from around 40 per cent to around 20 per cent. We have investigated the impact of these two factors using counterfactual predictions as well, fixing at 1991 levels first the distribution of educational qualifications and then, second, the proportion of individuals who were owner-occupiers. In the first exercise, the impacts were small compared to the effects of falling unemployment rates or of year-specific effects discussed above. In the second exercise, there was no perceptible impact at all. For brevity's sake, we do not show the predictions here. (They are reported in the working paper versions of this article.) The point remains, nonetheless, the prediction 'gap' may be accounted for by a number of other changes, none of which individually is as large as the ones that we have focused on. Another explanation for the prediction 'gap' may be the nature of our counterfactual predictions. For example, we may have underestimated the impact of unemployment because we used observed values of y_{it-1} in the calculations rather than dynamically updated values (see the earlier discussion). With higher unemployment rates, more individuals would have been in SA receipt, and this would have knock-on implications for prediction of SA receipt status at the next wave.

SUMMARY AND CONCLUSIONS

We have analysed the dynamics of SA receipt among working-age adults in Britain between 1991 and 2005, arguing that the near-halving in the aggregate annual receipt rate over this period was driven by a decline in the annual entry rate rather than changes in the annual exit rate (which actually declined). To examine the determinants of trends in aggregate SA transition rates, we have developed a dynamic random effects probit model of SA receipt probabilities, and fitted it to BHPS data. We have discussed how one may use the model estimates to predict transition and receipt rates on a year-by-year basis and drawn attention to the issue of dynamic self-selection on unobservable characteristics. We have used the estimates to provide some counterfactual predictions of trends in SA transition rates.

Overall, our analysis of transition and receipt rate trends over the period 1991–2005 suggests two 'smoking guns'. First, there was the increasing availability of jobs, summarized by the fall in unemployment rates between 1993 and the mid-2000s. Given the substantial increase in unemployment associated with the recession that began in 2007/8, it is unsurprising that the number of individuals in receipt of SA has also increased sharply as well (Department for Work and Pensions, 2013). Second, there were a number of other changes between 1991 and 2005 in the socio-economic environment including various reforms to the benefit system. Our results are broadly consistent with the suggestion that two changes had an effect on SA entry rates: the introduction of JSA in 1996 (by making it harder to claim), and the introduction of WFTC in 1999 (making work pay and hence SA less attractive).

More generally, we have shown how year-by-year predictions of transition rates can be derived from dynamic random effects probit models. At the same time, we have highlighted a number of potential issues that need to be addressed when doing so. There is, for instance, the issue of dynamic self-selection. And we have had to grapple with the fact that year fixed effects are a crude way to consider the potential impact of benefit reforms. Researchers who apply our prediction methods in another context may not face this sort of constraint.

NOTES

1. The proportion receiving SA in year t, P_t, is given by $P_t = (1-X_t)P_{t-1} + E_t(1-P_{t-1})$, where X_t is the exit rate and E_t is the entry rate at t.

2. Suitable data for later years are unavailable: see below.

3. There are also benefits for individuals who are ill or injured that are not discussed here: Statutory Sick Pay for employees, Employment and Support Allowance (replacing Incapacity Benefit since October 2008) for those unable to work because of illness or disability and with a suitable national insurance contributions record, Industrial Injuries Disablement Benefit for those ill or disabled because of an accident or event that happened at work or in connection with work. Berthoud (2011) argues from analysis of General Household Survey data that changes in disabled peoples' employment rates or benefit payments have not coincided with major changes in the social security system's rules and procedures.

4. The most recent administrative statistics refer to February 2005. At that time, there were 687,400 JSA recipients in total, of whom 80.4 per cent were eligible to receive income-based JSA and 19.6 per cent were eligible to receive contribution-based JSA. (The latter group includes some claimants also in receipt of income-based JSA.) See Table JSA 3.1 at http://webarchive.nationalarchives.gov.uk/20130128102031/http://statistics.dwp.gov.uk/asd/asd1/jsa/index.php?page=jsa_quarterly_feb05

5. There were also a number of active labour market programmes for specific groups, the New Deals for unemployed young people and for lone parents, providing individualized help to improve job readiness and job search. Because of their targeted focus, and since they do not directly affect incomes, they are less relevant in the current context.

6. For an overview of the impact of WFTC on labour supply and other outcomes, see the *Economic Journal* Features issue on 'In-work benefit reform in a cross-national perspective' (Brewer, Francesconi, Gregg, & Grogger, 2009). Earlier research focusing on labour supply effects includes Blundell (2001), Blundell and Hoynes (2004), Brewer, Duncan, Shephard, and Suarez (2006), Francesconi and van der Klaauw (2007) and Gregg, Harkness, and Smith (2009).

7. This is because working would lead to greater income from earnings (and possibly also tax credits) that would lead to ineligibility for SA.

8. The reform did not lead to an unambiguous increase in the job-finding rate because some recipients moved instead to other benefits such as incapacity benefits (Manning, 2009; Petrongolo, 2009).

9. We use respondents to the original ('Essex') sample only. Respondents from the extension samples for Scotland, Wales and Northern Ireland incorporated in the BHPS at the end of the 1990s are not used. Taking account of the differential sample inclusion probabilities would be a large task, beyond the scope of this project, and the number of observations in the original 1991 sample is relatively large in any case (see below).

10. For full documentation of the BHPS, see http://www.iser.essex.ac.uk/survey/bhps

11. The state retirement pension age in Britain was 60 for women and 65 for men over the period that we discuss.

12. See Bhuller and Königs (2011) for a study of social assistance dynamics in Norway, comparing estimates derived from monthly and benefit year data.

13. Ribar's (2005) endogenous switching model of AFDC transitions shares this feature but he models unobserved heterogeneity differently. On endogenous switching models of transitions with unobserved transitions, see also Cappellari and Jenkins (2004, 2008b).

14. Genuine state dependence in SA receipt can also be examined using this model. If there were no covariate interactions with lagged receipt status (in which case λ is a scalar), the degree of state dependence is an increasing function of λ and common to all individuals. Our specification with covariate interactions allows for heterogeneity in the degree of state dependence. For state dependence estimates based on the same data set as this article, see Cappellari and Jenkins (2008a).

15. In our earlier work (Cappellari & Jenkins, 2008a), we showed that the Wooldridge estimator provided almost identical parameter estimates to the estimators of Heckman (1981) and Orme (2001) that also account for the initial conditions issue, for both balanced and unbalanced panels. We attribute this robustness to the long length of our panel. For other comparisons of the different estimators, see Akay (2012), Arulampalam and Stewart (2009) and Rabe-Hesketh and Skrondal (2013). We focused on estimates based on the Heckman estimator in our earlier work. Compared to the model specification employed by Cappellari and Jenkins (2008a), the main differences in the current article are that observed characteristics are now measured at $t-1$ rather than t, and a more extensive set of variables is included in the interaction between Z_{it-1} and past receipt.

16. Our predictions are of a different nature from those derived from random effects probit models by for instance Chay and Hyslop (2014), Hyslop (1999) and Stewart (2007). Aggregate transition rates are not predicted by these authors. Instead they predict the prevalence of different types of individual-level binary response sequences and compare them with prevalence of the observed types.

17. The second expression in the equation for $\hat{P}_\tau^A$ is the model-based analogue of the expression given in note 1.

18. Population average predictions in which the averaging is over all years and all individuals are also used to calculate the degree of genuine state dependence in benefit receipt (defined as the average partial effect of past benefit receipt on current receipt). For an example, see Königs (2014).

19. The problem is analogous to that which arises if hazard regression models incorporating unobserved heterogeneity are fitted to left-truncated duration data. Fitting of the standard likelihood function (which ignores the left truncation) to left-truncated data leads to biased estimates. See for example van den Berg and Drepper (2011). On dynamic selection in a different context, see also Eberwein, Ham, and LaLonde (1997, especially section 3.1).

20. Our model was fitted using the meprobit command in Stata 13 (StataCorp, 2013) and the Empirical Bayes predictions derived using the meprobit

post-estimation prediction commands. The Empirical Bayes estimate of u_i is the expected value of u_i conditional on the observed covariates and binary response and the fitted parameter estimates. See Skrondal and Rabe-Hesketh (2009) for details.

21. Other weighting schemes might be used. The merits of ours are its inverse-probability-of-selection interpretation, the relationship to the model's assumption of the normality of u_i in the population and, decisively, the fact that they work (see below). We do not impose the restriction that weights sum to one: scaling plays a role as well as the differential weighting of different individuals.

22. For example, Chay and Hyslop (2014), Hyslop (1999) and Stewart (2007) appear not to use dynamic updating when employing dynamic random effects probit model estimates to predict the prevalence of different types of outcome sequence, and nor does Hyslop (1999) when undertaking counterfactual simulations of response probabilities for a single representative individual. Dynamic updating is not mentioned by any of the articles cited.

23. The problems refer to: (1) Problems or disability connected with arms, legs, hands, feet, back or neck (including arthritis and rheumatism); (2) difficulty in seeing (other than needing glasses to read normal size print); (3) difficulty in hearing; (4) skin conditions/allergies; (5) chest/breathing problems, asthma, bronchitis; (6) heart/blood pressure or blood circulation problems; (7) stomach/liver/kidneys; (8) diabetes; (9) anxiety, depression or bad nerves; (10) alcohol or drug related problems; (11) epilepsy; (12) migraine or frequent headaches; (13) other health problems.

24. See Cappellari and Jenkins (2008a) for more details. It is not possible to construct a consistent series that not only covers the period 1991–2005 but also extends beyond 2005.

25. We also considered a quasi-differences-in-differences approach in which we also included interactions between the survey year indicators in Z_{it-1} and the presence of children: the reasoning is that the Labour government's reforms were directed primarily at families with children. As it happened, very few coefficients on interaction variables were statistically significant, and the temporal pattern of the estimates did not correspond with expectations regarding the timing of policy changes.

26. For a more detailed year-by-year breakdown, see Cappellari and Jenkins (2008a: Table 3).

27. These assessments of the goodness of fit of our predictions of aggregate rates differ from those used by authors predicting the prevalence of different types of binary outcome sequences (see note 22). Some authors fitting dynamic random effects probit models have also assessed goodness of fit in terms of the 'proportion of correct predictions': see Biewen (2009: equation 26) for a definition. Biewen (2009: Table V) reports a share of correct predictions of 94 per cent for his six-wave panel. By comparison, the individual-level predicted probabilities underlying estimator set B imply a share of correct predictions of 95 per cent for our 15-wave panel.

28. The series for the observed rates differ slightly from those shown in Figs. 1 and 2 because they are based on the estimation sample. This is smaller than the samples for Figs. 1 and 2 because of missing values on elements of Z_{it-1}.

ACKNOWLEDGEMENTS

This major revision of IZA discussion paper 4457 and ISER working paper 2009-29 was prepared with financial assistance from the ESRC Research Centre on Micro-Social Change (grant number RES-062-23-1455). For helpful comments and suggestions at various stages, we thank the editors, anonymous referees, Thomas Andrén, Martin Biewen, Ken Couch, Jörgen Hansen, Herwig Immervoll, Sebastian Königs, Alfonso Miranda, Chris Orme, Lucinda Platt, Mark Stewart, and audiences at the Universities of Melbourne, Munich, Nuremburg, and Queensland, Motu Research (Wellington), NIESR (London), SPRC (Sydney), the Welsh Economics Colloquium, the Wisconsin Summer Research Workshop, the annual congresses of the Italian Association of Labour Economists and European Society for Population Economics, the Joint OECD/University of Maryland International Conference on 'Measuring Poverty, Income Inequality, and Social Exclusion: Lessons from Europe', and the IZA/ OECD/World Bank Conference on 'Safety Nets and Benefit Dependence'.

REFERENCES

Akay, A. (2012). Finite-sample comparison of alternative methods for estimating dynamic panel data models. *Journal of Applied Econometrics, 27*(7), 1189–1204.

Andrén, T., & Andrén, D. (2013). Never give up? The persistence of welfare participation in Sweden. *IZA Journal of European Labor Studies, 2*, 1.

Arulampalam, W., & Stewart, M. B. (2009). Simplified implementation of the Heckman estimator of the dynamic probit model and a comparison with alternative estimators. *Oxford Bulletin of Economics and Statistics, 71*(5), 659–681.

Bane, M. J., & Ellwood, D. T. (1983). *The dynamics of dependence: The routes to self-sufficiency*. Report to US Department of Health and Human Services, Urban Systems Research and Engineering, Cambridge, MA.

Bane, M. J., & Ellwood, D. T. (1994). *Welfare realities: From rhetoric to reform*. Cambridge, MA: Harvard University Press.

Berthoud, R. (2011). *Trends in the employment of disabled people*. ISER Working Paper No. 2011-03. Colchester: Institute for Social and Economic Research, University of Essex. Retrieved from http://www.iser.essex.ac.uk/publications/working-papers/iser/2011-03.pdf

Bhuller, M., & Königs, S. (2011). *The dynamics of social assistance receipt in Norway*. Unpublished manuscript, University of Oxford.

Biewen, M. (2009). Measuring state dependence in individual poverty histories when there is feedback to employment status and household composition. *Journal of Applied Econometrics, 24*(7), 1095–1116.

Blundell, R. (2001). Welfare reform for low income workers. *Oxford Economic Papers*, *53*(2), 189−214.

Blundell, R., & Hoynes, H. (2004). Has in-work benefit reform helped the labour market? In R. Blundell, D. Card, & R. B. Freeman (Eds.), *Seeking a premier economy: The economic effects of British economic reforms* (pp. 1980−2000). Chicago, IL: University of Chicago Press.

Brewer, M., Duncan, A., Shephard, A., & Suarez, M. J. (2006). Did working families' tax credit work? The impact of in-work support on labour supply in Britain. *Labour Economics*, *13*(6), 699−720.

Brewer, M., Francesconi, M., Gregg, P., & Grogger, J. (2009). In-work benefit reform in a cross-national perspective − Introduction. *Economic Journal*, *119*(535), F1−F14.

Brewer, M. and Shephard, A. (2004). Has labour made work pay? York: York Publishing Services for the Joseph Rowntree Foundation. Retrieved from http://www.jrf.org.uk/bookshop/eBooks/1859352626.pdf

Cappellari, L., & Jenkins, S. P. (2004). Modelling low income transitions. *Journal of Applied Econometrics*, *19*(5), 593−610.

Cappellari, L., & Jenkins, S. P. (2008a). *The dynamics of social assistance receipt: Measurement and modelling issues, with an application to Britain*. Social, Employment and Migration Working Paper No. 67. OECD, Paris. Retrieved from http://www.oecd.org/dataoecd/30/42/41414013.pdf

Cappellari, L., & Jenkins, S. P. (2008b). Estimating low pay transition probabilities accounting for endogenous selection mechanisms. *Journal of the Royal Statistical Society, Series C (Applied Statistics)*, *57*(2), 165−186.

Chamberlain, G. (1984). Panel data. In Z. Griliches & M. Intrilligator (Eds.), *Handbook of econometrics*. Amsterdam: North-Holland.

Chay, K. Y., & Hyslop, D. R. (2014). Identification and estimation of dynamic binary response panel data models: Empirical evidence using alternative approaches. In S. Carcillo, H. Immervoll, S. P. Jenkins, S. Königs, & K. Tatsiramos (Eds.), *Safety nets and benefit dependence* (Vol. 39). Research in Labor Economics. Bingley, UK: Emerald Group Publishing Limited.

Department for Work and Pensions. (2013). Quarterly statistical summary, March. Retrieved from http://research.dwp.gov.uk/asd/asd1/stats_summary/stats_summary_mar13.pdf

Eberwein, C., Ham, J. C., & LaLonde, R. J. (1997). The impact of being offered and receiving classroom training on the employment histories of disadvantaged women: Evidence from experimental data. *Review of Economic Studies*, *64*(4), 655−682.

Francesconi, M., & van der Klaauw, W. (2007). The socioeconomic consequences of in-work benefit reform for British lone mothers. *Journal of Human Resources*, *42*(1), 1−31.

Gregg, P., Harkness, S., & Smith, S. (2009). Welfare reform and lone parents in the UK. *Economic Journal*, *119*(535), F38−F65.

Grogger, J. (2004). Welfare transitions in the 1990s: The economy, welfare policy, and the EITC. *Journal of Policy Analysis and Management*, *32*(4), 671−695.

Haider, S., & Klerman, J. A. (2005). Dynamic properties of the welfare caseload. *Labour Economics*, *12*(5), 629−648.

Hansen, J., & Lofstrom, M. (2003). Immigrant assimilation and welfare participation: Do immigrants assimilate into or out of welfare? *Journal of Human Resources*, *38*(1), 74−98.

Hansen, J., & Lofstrom, M. (2011). Immigrant-native differences in welfare participation: The role of entry and exit rates. *Industrial Relations, 50*(3), 412–442.

Hansen, J., Lofstrom, M., Liu, X., & Zhang, X. (2014). State dependence in social assistance receipt in Canada. In S. Carcillo, H. Immervoll, S. P. Jenkins, S. Königs, & K. Tatsiramos (Eds.), *Safety nets and benefit dependence* (Vol. 39). Research in Labor Economics. Bingley, UK: Emerald Group Publishing Limited.

Hansen, J., Lofstrom, M., & Zhang, X. (2006). *State dependence in Canadian welfare participation*. IZA Discussion Paper No. 2266. Institute for the Study of Labour (IZA), Bonn. Retrieved from http://ftp.iza.org/dp2266.pdf

Heckman, J. J. (1981). The incidental parameters problem and the problem of initial conditions in estimating a discrete time-discrete data stochastic process. In C. F. Manski & D. McFadden (Eds.), *Structural analysis of discrete data with econometric applications*. Cambridge, MA: MIT Press.

Hyslop, D. (1999). State dependence, serial correlation and heterogeneity in intertemporal labor force participation of married women. *Econometrica, 67*(6), 1255–1294.

Jenkins, S. P. (2000). Modelling household income dynamics. *Journal of Population Economics, 13*(4), 529–567.

Königs, S. (2014). State dependence in socialassistance benefit receipt in Germany before and after the Hartz reforms. In S. Carcillo, H. Immervoll, S. P. Jenkins, S. Königs, & K. Tatsiramos (Eds.), *Safety nets and benefit dependence* (Vol. 39). Research in Labor Economics. Bingley, UK: Emerald Group Publishing Limited.

Manning, A. (2009). You can't always get what you want: The impact of the UK Jobseeker's Allowance. *Labour Economics, 16*(3), 239–250.

Mundlak, Y. (1978). On the pooling of time series and cross section data. *Econometrica, 46*(1), 69–85.

Orme, C. D. (2001). *Two-step inference in dynamic non-linear panel data models*. Unpublished manuscript, University of Manchester. Retrieved from http://personalpages.manchester.ac.uk/staff/chris.orme/documents/Research%20Papers/initcondlast.pdf

Petrongolo, B. (2009). What are the long-term effects of UI? Evidence from the UK JSA reform. *Journal of Public Economics, 93*(11–12), 1234–1253.

Rabe-Hesketh, S., & Skrondal, A. (2013). Avoiding biased versions of Wooldridge's simple solution to the initial conditions problem. *Economics Letters, 120*(2), 346–349.

Ribar, D. C. (2005). Transitions from welfare and the employment prospects of low-skill workers. *Southern Economic Journal, 71*(3), 514–533.

Skrondal, A., & Rabe-Hesketh, S. (2009). Prediction in multilevel generalised linear models. *Journal of the Royal Statistical Society (Series A), 172*(3), 659–687.

StataCorp. (2013). *Stata Release 13. Statistical software*. College Station, TX: StataCorp LP.

Stewart, M. B. (2007). The interrelated dynamics of unemployment and low pay. *Journal of Applied Econometrics, 22*(3), 511–531.

van den Berg, G. J., & Drepper, B. (2011). *Inference for shared-frailty survival models with left-truncated data*, IZA Discussion Paper No. 6031. Institute for the Study of Labour (IZA), Bonn. Retrieved from http://ftp.iza.org/dp6031.pdf

Wooldridge, J. M. (2005). Simple solutions to the initial conditions problem in dynamic, nonlinear panel data models with unobserved heterogeneity. *Journal of Applied Econometrics, 20*(1), 39–54.

STATE DEPENDENCE IN SOCIAL ASSISTANCE RECEIPT IN CANADA

Jorgen Hansen, Magnus Lofstrom, Xingfei Liu and Xuelin Zhang

ABSTRACT

This article analyzes transitions into and out of social assistance (SA) in Canada. We estimate dynamic probit models, controlling for endogenous initial conditions and unobserved heterogeneity, using longitudinal data extracted from the Survey of Labour and Income Dynamics (SLID) for the years 1993–2010. The data indicate that there are substantial provincial differences in SA participation with higher participation rates in the eastern part of the country. However, since the mid-1990s, participation rates have fallen substantially in all provinces with only a modest increase at the end of the observation period. Results from the probit models suggest that there is a significant time dependency in social assistance, even after controlling for endogenous initial conditions and unobserved heterogeneity. The extent of this state dependence varies across provinces.

Keywords: Social assistance; state dependence; unobserved heterogeneity; endogenous initial conditions; transitions; Canada

JEL classifications: I30; I38; J18

Safety Nets and Benefit Dependence
Research in Labor Economics, Volume 39, 81–105
ISSN: 0147-9121/doi:10.1108/S0147-912120140000039002

INTRODUCTION

Since the mid-1990s, many countries have experienced large declines in the number of social assistance (SA) or welfare recipients.[1] For example, between 1995 and 2005, the welfare participation rate dropped by around 30 percent in Canada and 50 percent in the United Kingdom and the United States (see Cappellari & Jenkins, 2013; Scholz, Moffitt, & Cowan, 2009). These declines coincided with significant improvements in the labor markets. Further, in the United States, a number of important welfare policy changes occurred during this period, such as the introduction of work requirements for welfare recipients and time limits on aid, increased minimum wages, and expansion of the Earned Income Tax Credit program (see Blank, 2002; Moffitt, 1999).

In order to understand changes in observed utilization of welfare programs, it is necessary to understand the underlying dynamic processes. A large body of literature has documented the existence of substantial state dependence in welfare utilization over time (Andrén & Andrén, 2013; Blank, 1989; Cappellari & Jenkins, 2013; Chay & Hyslop, 2014; Engberg, Gottschalk, & Wolf, 1990; Finnie & Pavlic, 2013; Hansen & Lofstrom, 2009, 2011; Hansen, Lofstrom, & Zhang, 2006; Königs, 2013; Riphahn & Wunder, 2013).[2] In this article, we examine factors that underlie welfare reliance and follow the literature and define persistence simply as the probability that a current welfare recipient remains on benefits another year while state dependence refers to the difference between the persistence probability and the probability of entry into benefits.

One reason for state dependence in welfare participation is that previous participation directly affects current participation. Possible explanations for this include human capital depreciation (in which case the stock of human capital depreciates during the period an individual is not active in the workforce) or signaling (potential employers believe that a person who has been unemployed or on welfare is not as productive as an identical applicant who has not experienced these events). In either of these cases, employment opportunities are reduced as a result of welfare participation and policies, such as changing the benefit levels or introducing labor market training, may be relatively effective in reducing welfare caseloads.

The relationship between past and current participation in a welfare program may also be due to time-invariant individual factors, such as time-invariant preferences (with respect to leisure and/or so-called stigma effects associated with participation in the transfer program). If these factors contribute to the observed, or raw, state dependence, labor market policies may be less effective. Hence, modeling the dynamics of welfare participation requires a careful treatment of how unobservable factors affect individual choices.[3]

The main objective of this article is to analyze provincial transitions into and out of welfare and to examine to what extent the raw state dependence is structural.[4] Among other things, this will enable us to infer to what extent provincial differences in SA participation are due to differences in entry rates and to what extent they are due to differences in exit rates.

To accomplish this, we estimate dynamic probit models, controlling for both endogenous initial conditions and unobserved heterogeneity, using longitudinal data extracted from the Survey of Labour and Income Dynamics (SLID) for the years 1993–2010. SLID is a rotating panel where each panel, consisting of about 15,000 households, follows the same respondents for up to six years. Every third year, a new panel is introduced.

The empirical results suggest that there is a significant state dependence in welfare in all Canadian provinces, even after controlling for endogenous initial conditions and unobserved heterogeneity. However, there is substantial variation in this structural state dependence across provinces with the lowest value observed for British Columbia (0.22) and the highest for Quebec (0.47).

These findings are consistent with the results reported in Finnie and Pavlic (2013), who use the Canadian Longitudinal Administrative Dataset (LAD). They report a similar geographical dispersion although the magnitudes of the estimated state dependence rates are lower than in this article. Our results are also consistent with those from comparable studies for other countries. For example, Hansen and Lofstrom (2009, 2011) find evidence of structural state dependence in welfare use in Sweden. Moreover, the extent of structural state dependence is greater for refugee immigrants than for natives and non-refugee immigrants. Similar results, also for Sweden, are reported in Andrén and Andrén (2013). Other studies who have reported a significant degree of structural state dependence in welfare include Chay, Hoynes, and Hyslop (1999), for the United States, and Cappellari and Jenkins (2013), for the United Kingdom.

The article is organized in the following way. In the second section, we provide background information about the SA program in Canada and show how participation varies across provinces and time. The third section describes the data and variables while we present the model and empirical specification in the fourth section. We discuss the results in the fifth section 5 and conclude in the sixth section.

SA IN CANADA

SA in Canada is the income program of last resort and it is the principal source of income for families who lack earned income and access to insurance programs for unemployment, disability, and old age. SA is a provincial responsibility, although the federal government assumes a portion of the program costs. Provinces set their own benefit levels and these have varied substantially across family types, provinces, and time periods.[5]

The SA benefits are substantially less generous than those of the Employment Insurance (EI) program, the major Canadian income replacement program for nonworking adults. For example, the average monthly SA amount for single, unattached individuals across all provinces over the period 1993–2009 was $492 (expressed in $2002). The corresponding amount for lone parents with one child over the same period equals $1,123.[6] Regular EI benefits, on the other hand, are not dependent on family type and equal about 55 percent of insurable earnings up to a maximum (in 2013 this maximum is around $3,200 per month, again expressed in $2002).[7]

Some of the provincial and time variation in SA benefits can be attributed to policy changes. Specifically, until March 1996, welfare was paid under the terms of the Canada Assistance Plan (CAP), an arrangement that allowed the cost to be shared by the federal government and the provinces and territories.

In April 1996, the Canada Health and Social Transfer (CHST) replaced CAP which implied that the federal government moved away from a shared-cost program to a lump-sum transfer of funds intended to cover not only SA but also health and education. In addition to the change in the method of transferring funds, there were substantial reductions in the dollar value of the transfers.[8] With the introduction of the Canada Child Tax Benefit (CCTB) in July 1998, the federal government assumed a greater share of the cost of welfare for families with children.[9] Further, in 2006, the federal government introduced the Universal Child Care Benefit (UCCB), and in 2007, the new Child Tax Credit program was announced.

Compared to its U.S. counterpart, Temporary Assistance for Needy Families (TANF), the Canadian SA program serves a more diverse population of recipients since unattached, childless men and women (as well as childless couples) may also qualify for benefits. Nonetheless, SA participation rates in Canada are substantially higher among single mothers (28.5 percent over the period 1993–2010 using our sample in SLID) than among unattached, childless women (15.4 percent over the same period).

In Table 1, we present SA participation rates in Canada by year and province. The entries in the table are obtained using a sample of households

Table 1. Participation in SA in Canada 1993–2010, by Year and Province.

Year	All Provinces	Province									
		Nfld	PEI	NS	NB	QC	ONT	MAN	SAS	ALB	BC
1993	0.115	0.177	0.08	0.133	0.148	0.136	0.108	0.076	0.106	0.08	0.108
1994	0.12	0.173	0.104	0.138	0.155	0.135	0.118	0.085	0.102	0.083	0.113
1995	0.121	0.179	0.114	0.137	0.156	0.133	0.117	0.082	0.115	0.083	0.112
1996	0.114	0.185	0.093	0.12	0.136	0.136	0.109	0.081	0.106	0.083	0.087
1997	0.113	0.183	0.095	0.117	0.14	0.133	0.112	0.074	0.117	0.076	0.084
1998	0.115	0.182	0.094	0.12	0.144	0.132	0.116	0.072	0.113	0.074	0.095
1999	0.097	0.192	0.087	0.084	0.102	0.125	0.086	0.052	0.1	0.072	0.079
2000	0.094	0.19	0.096	0.085	0.096	0.12	0.083	0.05	0.098	0.071	0.075
2001	0.093	0.193	0.093	0.087	0.095	0.116	0.085	0.047	0.09	0.072	0.077
2002	0.084	0.163	0.088	0.068	0.098	0.1	0.079	0.043	0.082	0.068	0.073
2003	0.084	0.158	0.087	0.074	0.09	0.103	0.08	0.04	0.086	0.062	0.067
2004	0.085	0.168	0.085	0.072	0.091	0.102	0.082	0.037	0.094	0.06	0.065
2005	0.083	0.131	0.068	0.061	0.092	0.094	0.09	0.054	0.092	0.058	0.061
2006	0.081	0.132	0.06	0.061	0.087	0.088	0.094	0.057	0.085	0.057	0.054
2007	0.083	0.143	0.058	0.058	0.089	0.089	0.096	0.058	0.095	0.055	0.052
2008	0.084	0.152	0.059	0.062	0.087	0.08	0.103	0.065	0.067	0.066	0.057
2009	0.085	0.153	0.078	0.065	0.084	0.078	0.105	0.07	0.072	0.067	0.059
2010	0.086	0.152	0.074	0.068	0.088	0.08	0.107	0.063	0.071	0.069	0.06
All years	0.096	0.163	0.085	0.085	0.103	0.106	0.102	0.062	0.096	0.07	0.075

Notes: Data from the SLID, 1993–2010. Based on a sample of men and women. Students and retirees are excluded. The numbers are weighted using longitudinal weights provided by Statistics Canada. Provinces are ordered by location from East to West. Nfld, Newfoundland and Labrador; PEI, Prince Edward Island; NS, Nova Scotia; NB, New Brunswick; QC, Quebec; ONT, Ontario; MAN, Manitoba; SAS, Saskatchewan; ALB, Alberta; BC, British Columbia.

in SLID where the response person is between 18 and 65. Furthermore, retirees and students are excluded from the sample. As shown, there have been substantial reductions in the participation rates since the mid-1990s. When aggregating all provinces, the entries in the table show that welfare participation peaked at 12.1 percent in 1995. Between 1995 and 2006, participation dropped by 4 percentage points to 8.1 percent, a reduction of 33 percent. Since 2006, participation rates have increased somewhat, an increase that coincides with the economic recession.

The table also illustrates large provincial variations in welfare use in Canada, with an average rate over the 1993–2010 period as high as 16 percent in Newfoundland and Labrador and as low as 6 percent in Manitoba. Despite the large provincial variations in SA participation rates, the change in participation over time is similar in all provinces with an increase or peak in the mid-1990s followed by a substantial reduction between 2000 and 2006. Cappellari and Jenkins (2013) report a similar pattern for the United Kingdom.

DATA

The data used in this article is extracted from Statistics Canada's SLID. SLID is a rotating, longitudinal household survey designed to capture the dynamics of the labor market activities and the well-being of individuals and their families living in Canada. Households and individuals are followed for up to six years during which information on their labor market experience, income, and family circumstances are collected. Every third year, a new panel is introduced.

The target population for SLID are persons residing in Canada, excluding residents living on the reserves or in any of the three territories, full-time members of the armed forces, and institutionalized persons. The first panel of SLID started in 1993 and the initial sample was drawn from the Labour Force Survey. Approximately 15,000 households, comprising of roughly 31,000 individuals aged 16 and over, were interviewed once or twice per year. The second panel started in 1996, the third in 1999, and so on. We use data from six panels and we have up to six years of data for households belonging to the first five panels and up to three years of data for the last panel. The number of households and individuals involved in the later panels were similar to those in the first panel.

Welfare participation is determined by household composition, income, and geographic location (which determine eligibility and welfare amounts) and household members' individual backgrounds, characteristics, and preferences. Hence it is not entirely clear whether the appropriate unit of observation is the household or person(s). Given the practical challenges of incorporating household complexity, we opt for letting the survey response person (defined by Statistics Canada) represent the household.[10] One could then interpret the person as the unit of observation but given that we define welfare participation based on any household member receiving SA, we prefer to view the household as the unit of observation.

In any given year, we retained households whose response person was between 18 and 65 years old, not retired, and not enrolled in full- or part-time schooling.[11] This means, for example, that a household whose representative was a student in the initial year of the panel but not during subsequent years is excluded from our sample the first year, but included the remaining years.

A household is defined as a welfare participating household, in any given year, if any person belonging to the household received any SA at any time during that year. Thus, the dependent variable in our analysis is equal to one if the household received SA in a particular year and equal to zero otherwise. There are some concerns about the underreporting of SA in SLID (see Kapsalis, 2001). In particular, substantial "seaming" appears to be a problem in the reporting of welfare spells. According to Kapsalis (2001), a disproportional large fraction of spells start in January and end in December. Furthermore, there are indications that households systematically underreport the SA amounts they receive.

However, none of these concerns are likely to affect the results in our study for the following reasons. First, the income information for most respondents (between 80 and 90 percent) is obtained from tax files where there is no underreporting or "seaming." Secondly, for the respondents whose income information was obtained during the interview, the issue with "seaming" may not be a major concern given that we are aggregating the time dimension from months to years.

To control for local labor market conditions, we include information on regional unemployment rates. These annual unemployment rates for each economic region are obtained from Statistics Canada.[12] In addition to regional unemployment rates, we also include controls for age, marital status, education, urban residency, number of children, as well as indicators for gender and disability status.

In Table 2, we present transition probability matrices separately for each province. The table reveals several interesting relationships and patterns. First, we examine the issue of persistence in the raw data. There are

Table 2. Transition Matrices, 1993–2010, by Province.

State at time t	State at time t + 1 Newfoundland and Labrador		State at time t	State at time t + 1 Prince Edward Island		State at time t	State at time t + 1 Nova Scotia		State at time t	State at time t + 1 New Brunswick	
	Welfare	No welfare		Welfare	No welfare		Welfare	No welfare		Welfare	No welfare
Welfare	0.856	0.144	Welfare	0.713	0.287	Welfare	0.836	0.164	Welfare	0.834	0.166
No welfare	0.022	0.978	No welfare	0.034	0.966	No welfare	0.015	0.985	No welfare	0.025	0.975

State at time t	State at time t + 1 Quebec		State at time t	State at time t + 1 Ontario		State at time t	State at time t + 1 Manitoba		State at time t	State at time t + 1 Saskatchewan	
	Welfare	No welfare		Welfare	No welfare		Welfare	No welfare		Welfare	No welfare
Welfare	0.856	0.144	Welfare	0.833	0.167	Welfare	0.829	0.171	Welfare	0.796	0.204
No welfare	0.017	0.983	No welfare	0.018	0.982	No welfare	0.010	0.990	No welfare	0.029	0.971

State at time t	State at time t + 1 Alberta		State at time t	State at time t + 1 British Columbia		State at time t	State at time t + 1 All provinces	
	Welfare	No welfare		Welfare	No welfare		Welfare	No welfare
Welfare	0.769	0.231	Welfare	0.767	0.233	Welfare	0.821	0.179
No welfare	0.016	0.984	No welfare	0.016	0.984	No welfare	0.019	0.981

Notes: Data from the SLID, 1993–2010. Based on a sample of men and women. Students and retirees are excluded. The figures are weighted using longitudinal weights provided by Statistics Canada. Provinces are ordered by location from East to West.

relatively large differences in the probability of leaving welfare in any given year across provinces. The highest exit rates are found in Prince Edward Island (0.287), Alberta (0.231), and British Columbia (0.233), while the lowest are found in Quebec and Newfoundland and Labrador (both equal 0.144). Table 2 also indicates that there is considerable variation in the entry rates across provinces with the highest reported for Prince Edward Island (0.034) and the lowest for Manitoba (0.010).

The entry and exit rates reported in Table 2 provide the anatomy of provincial welfare participation rates. For example, for the 1993–2010 period, SA participation rates in Quebec are substantially higher than in Alberta (0.106 and 0.070, respectively). The entries in Table 2 provide that the probability of remaining on welfare in the next period is higher in Quebec than in Alberta (85.6 percent for Quebec compared to 76.9 percent for Alberta). At the same time, the probability of entering welfare is about the same in both provinces (0.017 in Quebec and 0.016 in Alberta). This suggests that SA is more of a temporary income support for households in Alberta than in Quebec, where households, once they have started to receive assistance, appear to have some difficulties leaving welfare, at least relative to welfare participants in Alberta.

In Hansen et al. (2006), we provide a similar table of entry and exit rates for the years 1993–2000, a period with higher participation rates compared to the 2001–2010 period. A comparison of these transition rates with the ones in Table 2 provides an illustration of how SA utilization has changed over time. In particular, the persistence rates for all provinces are higher in this article than in Hansen et al. (2006). This suggests that it was more difficult to leave SA in the 2000–2010 period than in the 1990s. However, the entry rates are lower in this article and this explains the reduction in participation rates over the whole 1993–2010 period. Thus, while entry into SA became less likely in the new millennium, those who were on welfare found it more difficult to leave.

Given the differences in transition probabilities across provinces, we would also expect the distribution of the number of years receiving welfare to differ. Table 3 gives the number of years households have received SA for balanced panels, panels consisting of households who were observed for the entire six-year period. The entries in the table suggest that approximately 30 percent of households in New Brunswick and in Newfoundland and Labrador received SA at least once. However, in New Brunswick, around 50 percent of these households received it at most two years while the corresponding number for Newfoundland and Labrador is 32 percent. For the other provinces, 78–85 percent of households did not utilize SA at all during the period 1993–2010.

Table 3. Number of Years Receiving SA, 1993−2010, by Province.

Years Receiving SA	0	1	2	3	4	5	6
Newfoundland and Labrador	0.684	0.057	0.043	0.047	0.032	0.026	0.112
Prince Edward Island	0.817	0.066	0.040	0.019	0.007	0.018	0.034
Nova Scotia	0.803	0.047	0.033	0.017	0.020	0.013	0.063
New Brunswick	0.706	0.108	0.043	0.026	0.026	0.026	0.065
Quebec	0.781	0.040	0.022	0.020	0.020	0.023	0.093
Ontario	0.786	0.072	0.039	0.021	0.022	0.016	0.045
Manitoba	0.845	0.052	0.038	0.006	0.011	0.019	0.029
Saskatchewan	0.835	0.050	0.024	0.008	0.011	0.012	0.059
Alberta	0.832	0.046	0.027	0.026	0.018	0.016	0.034
British Columbia	0.806	0.06	0.015	0.023	0.036	0.015	0.046
All provinces	0.790	0.059	0.032	0.021	0.021	0.018	0.059

Notes: Data from the SLID, 1993−2010. Students and retirees are excluded. The figures are weighted using longitudinal weights provided by Statistics Canada. Provinces are ordered by location from East to West.

The entries in Table 3 further illustrate the difference in the composition of welfare users in Quebec and in Alberta. For instance, 27 percent of the households that received SA during this period received it for only one year in Alberta. The corresponding number for Quebec is only 18 percent. Moreover, in Quebec as many as 42 percent of all welfare participants received welfare for the whole period. In Alberta, this figure is only 20 percent.

As mentioned above, the objective of this article is to study the determinants of the transitions into and out of welfare in Canada. However, before we analyze the observed disparity in the behavior of households across provinces, we want to compare observable characteristics of households who remain in welfare (or those who remain in the "no welfare" state) with those who leave welfare (or those who enter welfare).

Table 4 gives the mean characteristics by previous year's state. In general, it appears that any movements out of welfare are associated with being married, better educated, not disabled, and male. Households who leave welfare also seem to live in areas with relatively low unemployment rates. Regarding transitions into welfare, they are associated with being single, less educated, and residing in areas with higher unemployment rates. Interestingly, the entries also suggest that older individuals are less likely to move out of previous year's state, regardless of what that state was in the previous period.

The descriptive statistics indicate that there are substantial provincial differences in welfare participation rates. Participation rates are higher in Newfoundland and Labrador than elsewhere in Canada. Furthermore, there

Table 4. Mean Characteristics by Previous Year's Welfare State, 1993—2010.

State at t	Welfare		No Welfare		Whole
State at $t+1$	Welfare	No Welfare	Welfare	No Welfare	Sample
Married	0.39	0.55	0.55	0.72	0.65
Age	43.2	39.4	40.8	42.8	41.6
Urban area	0.82	0.80	0.77	0.79	0.80
Number of children	0.91	1.15	1.10	1.04	0.97
Years of education	11.3	12.1	12.2	13.7	13.6
Regional unemployment rate (%)	8.41	8.11	8.10	7.59	7.68
Disabled	0.54	0.25	0.33	0.16	0.19
Male	0.43	0.45	0.48	0.51	0.50
Province					
Newfoundland and Labrador	0.034	0.027	0.022	0.017	0.018
Prince Edward Island	0.003	0.006	0.009	0.005	0.005
Nova Scotia	0.029	0.027	0.027	0.031	0.03
New Brunswick	0.027	0.026	0.037	0.026	0.026
Quebec	0.292	0.234	0.237	0.247	0.246
Ontario	0.397	0.381	0.386	0.372	0.376
Manitoba	0.024	0.023	0.021	0.037	0.036
Saskatchewan	0.026	0.032	0.051	0.03	0.031
Alberta	0.071	0.102	0.095	0.107	0.105
British Columbia	0.097	0.142	0.116	0.128	0.128
Number of individuals	5,034	1,193	1,182	65,566	72,976

Notes: Data from the SLID, 1993—2010. Based on a sample of men and women. Students and retirees are excluded. The figures are weighted using longitudinal weights provided by Statistics Canada. Provinces are ordered by location from East to West.

have been substantial changes in welfare use over time and these changes are similar for all provinces. The data also show provincial differences in entry and exit rates. The exit rates from SA are lowest in Newfoundland and Labrador and in Quebec, while the entry rate is lowest in Manitoba.

MODEL AND EMPIRICAL SPECIFICATION

To analyze transitions into and out of SA, we estimate dynamic probit models with random effects separately for each province.[13] As is common in the literature, we assume that the dynamic structure can be approximated by a first-order Markov model. The use of longitudinal data allows us to control for unobserved heterogeneity and to distinguish between structural and spurious state dependence.

The model can be described as follows. Assume that households (indexed by h, $h = 1, 2, ..., n$), residing in province j ($j = 1, 2, ..., 10$), choose between receiving and not receiving SA benefits in any time period t ($t = 1, 2, ..., T_i$). Let the latent variable $y_{h,j,t}^*$, which represents the value for household h residing in province j from receiving SA benefits at time t, be specified as:

$$y_{h,j,t}^* = \beta_{1,j} + X_{h,j,t}\beta_{2,j} + y_{h,j,t-1}\beta_{3,j} + \varepsilon_{h,j,t}$$

$$y_{h,j,t} = 1(\beta_{1,j} + X_{h,j,t}\beta_{2,j} + y_{h,j,t-1}\beta_{3,j} + \varepsilon_{h,j,t} > 0)$$

where $X_{h,j,t}$ is a vector of observable characteristics, including marital status, age, urban residency, number of children, educational attainment, disability status, and local labor market conditions. $1(\cdot)$ is an indicator function equal to one if the enclosed statement is true and zero otherwise, and $Y_{h,j,t-1}$ is a dummy variable indicating whether the household received SA in the previous time period. We follow Heckman (1981) and Cameron and Heckman (2001), and assume that $\varepsilon_{h,j,t}$ is characterized by the following factor structure:

$$\varepsilon_{h,j,t} = \mu\eta_{h,j} + \nu_{h,j,t}$$

where $\eta_{h,j}$ represents an unobserved household specific, time-invariant effect and μ is a factor loading parameter. The second term, $\nu_{h,j,t}$, represents a white-noise error term and is assumed to be serially uncorrelated, independent of $X_{h,j,t}$ and $y_{h,j,t-1}$, and to follow a standard Normal distribution.[14] We further assume that $\eta_{h,j}$ is independent of $\nu_{h,j,t}$ and $X_{h,j,t}$.pvr

The vector $\beta_{2,j}$ and the scalars $\beta_{1,j}, \beta_{3,j}$, and μ are parameters to be estimated. Given the distribution assumption of $\nu_{h,j,t}$, the probability that household h received SA at time t ($t > 1$), conditional on $X_{h,j,t}$, $y_{h,j,t-1}$, and $\eta_{h,j}$, can be written as:

$$Pr(y_{h,j,t} = 1 | X_{h,j,t}, y_{h,j,t-1}, \eta_{h,j}) = \Phi(\beta_{1,j} + X_{h,j,t}\beta_{2,j} + y_{h,j,t-1}\beta_{3,j} + \mu\eta_{h,j})$$

Because the state in which a family is initially observed is endogenous, we adopt a procedure similar to that suggested by Heckman (1981). For the initial period the household is observed ($t = 1$), we estimate a static probit model including $X_{h,j,1}$ as control variables. This procedure approximates the initial conditions for the model, and Heckman (1981) reports that this approximation, in a binary choice model, performs well with only a small asymptotic bias.[15] Specifically, let the value of the latent variable $y^*_{h,j,t}$ in the initial time period ($t = 1$) be specified as:

$$y^*_{h,j,1} = \theta_{1,j} + X_{h,j,1}\theta_{2,j} + \varepsilon_{h,j,1}$$

where

$$\varepsilon_{h,j,1} = \alpha\eta_{h,j} + \nu_{h,j,1}$$

and where $\theta_{l,j}$, $l = 1, 2$ and α are parameters to be estimated. As before, we assume that $\nu_{h,j,1}$ follows a standard Normal distribution.

The probability that household h received SA in the initial time period, conditional on $X_{h,j,1}$ and $\eta_{h,j}$, can therefore be written as:

$$Pr(y_{h,j,1} = 1|X_{h,j,1}, \eta_{h,j}) = \Phi(\theta_{1,j} + X_{h,j,t}\theta_{2,j} + \alpha\eta_{h,j})$$

The presence of the unobserved household specific effects, $\eta_{h,j}$, in the latent variable equations allows for a particular correlation between the stochastic terms $\varepsilon_{h,j,t}$ and $\varepsilon_{h,j,1}$ and relaxes the assumption that the initial conditions are exogenous. However, the parameters μ and α are not non-parametrically identified without further normalizations. We follow Cameron and Heckman (2001) and normalize the first two moments of $\eta_{h,j}$, $E(\eta_{h,j}) = 0$ and $Var(\eta_{h,j}) = 1$. Given these normalizations, the model can be estimated with maximum likelihood techniques.[16] The likelihood contribution for household h, given observed characteristics and unobserved heterogeneity, can be written as:

$$L_h(\eta_{h,j}) = \prod_{t=1}^{T} Pr(y_{h,j,t} = 1|\eta_{h,j})$$

However, as $\eta_{h,j}$ is not observed, we need to integrate out this term from the above likelihood to obtain the unconditional likelihood function. To do this, we follow Heckman and Singer (1984) and Cameron and Heckman (2001), and assume that the probability distribution of $\eta_{h,j}$ can be approximated by a discrete distribution with a finite number (I) of support points. In this case, integration is replaced by a summation over the number of supports for the distribution of $\eta_{h,j}$.pvr Associated with each support point is a probability, π_i, where $\sum_{i=1}^{I} \pi_i = 1$ and $\pi_i \geq 0$. To be specific, we assume that there are I types of households and that each household is endowed with a particular realization of $\eta_{h,j}$, $\eta_{h,j,i}$. Thus, the unconditional contribution to the log-likelihood function for household h is given by:

$$\log L_i = \log \sum_{i=1}^{I} \pi_i L_i(\eta_{h,j,i})$$

We found that a model with $I = 2$ fitted the data quite well. This low dimensionality has been found in many studies of mixture models (e.g., Cameron & Heckman, 2001; Eberwein, Ham, & Lalonde, 1997; Ham & Lalonde, 1996). Finally, since SLID is not a representative random sample, the likelihood function is weighted with longitudinal weights provided by Statistics Canada.

EMPIRICAL RESULTS

In this section, we report results from maximizing the likelihood function above. Because of the nonlinear nature of the model, the magnitudes of the estimated coefficients provide little information about the size of the effects of the observable characteristics. Therefore, instead of discussing the coefficient estimates, which are reported in Table A1, we focus our presentation on the transition probabilities and the state dependence. The predicted transition probabilities are the average of all households' probabilities and are calculated using the estimates reported in Table A1.

In Table 5, we present the predicted transition matrices separately for each province as well as for Canada.[17] The entries in the table refer to a specification that controls for unobserved heterogeneity and endogenous initial conditions. The entries show large provincial variations in persistence and entry rates. For instance, persistence in welfare is highest in Newfoundland and Labrador (0.552) and in Quebec (0.509) and lowest in British Columbia (0.247) and in Manitoba (0.258). Moreover, the entry rate into SA is lowest in Manitoba (0.021) and highest in Newfoundland and Labrador (0.119).

The transition probabilities reported in Tables 2 and 5 can be used to calculate the state dependence in SA for each province. We follow the literature and distinguish between raw and genuine state dependence. The former is defined as the observed difference between the state dependence and entry probabilities (reported in Table 2), while the latter is the corresponding

Table 5. Estimated Transition Matrices, 1993–2010, with Controls for Initial Conditions and Unobserved Heterogeneity.

State at time t	Newfoundland and Labrador (State at time t+1)		Prince Edward Island (State at Time t+1)		Nova Scotia (State at Time t+1)		New Brunswick (State at Time t+1)	
	Welfare	No welfare	Welfare	No welfare	Welfare	No welfare	Welfare	No welfare
Welfare	0.5519	0.4481	0.2957	0.7043	0.3892	0.6108	0.3708	0.6292
No welfare	0.1188	0.8812	0.0494	0.9506	0.0469	0.9531	0.0582	0.9418

State at time t	Quebec (State at time t+1)		Ontario (State at time t+1)		Manitoba (State at Time t+1)		Saskatchewan (State at Time t+1)	
	Welfare	No welfare	Welfare	No welfare	Welfare	No welfare	Welfare	No welfare
Welfare	0.5092	0.4908	0.3329	0.6671	0.2579	0.7421	0.2806	0.7194
No welfare	0.0352	0.9648	0.0249	0.9751	0.0214	0.9786	0.0514	0.9486

State at time t	Alberta (State at time t+1)		British Columbia (State at time t+1)		All provinces (State at time t+1)	
	Welfare	No welfare	Welfare	No welfare	Welfare	No welfare
Welfare	0.3118	0.6882	0.2466	0.7534	0.3854	0.6146
No welfare	0.0265	0.9735	0.0263	0.9737	0.0318	0.9682

Notes: Data from the SLID, 1993–2010. Entries are calculated based on estimated parameters presented in Table A1. Provinces are ordered by location from East to West.

difference obtained using a model specification that controls for both observed and unobserved heterogeneity (reported in Table 5).[18]

In Table 6, we report both types of state dependence for each province and also for Canada. The entries in the first column suggest that there is a high degree of raw state dependence in all provinces. The entries range from 0.679 for Prince Edward Island to 0.839 for Quebec. In the second column, we present the corresponding genuine state dependence for each province. As expected, there is a significant reduction compared to the entries in the first column indicating that a large fraction of the raw state dependence is due to individual characteristics (both observed and unobserved). This is especially true for Western Canadian provinces for whom most of the state dependence is due to individual heterogeneity. For Newfoundland and Labrador and Quebec however, the opposite is true.

A reduction in the estimated state dependence when controlling for unobserved heterogeneity is a common finding in the literature. For example, a series of papers on welfare dependence in Sweden, Hansen, and Lofstrom (2006, 2009, 2011) report a significant reduction in the estimated state dependence.[19] Our results are also consistent with findings from comparable studies for other countries (see Chay et al., 1999, for the United States; Andrén & Andrén, 2013, for Sweden; Cappellari & Jenkins, 2013, for the United Kingdom; and Finnie & Pavlic, 2013, for Canada).

Table 6. Genuine versus Spurious State Dependence in SA, 1993−2010, by Province.

	State Dependence			
	Raw	Genuine	Spurious	Proportion Genuine
Newfoundland and Labrador	0.834	0.433	0.401	0.519
Prince Edward Island	0.679	0.246	0.433	0.363
Nova Scotia	0.821	0.342	0.479	0.417
New Brunswick	0.809	0.313	0.496	0.386
Quebec	0.839	0.474	0.365	0.565
Ontario	0.815	0.308	0.507	0.378
Manitoba	0.820	0.237	0.583	0.289
Saskatchewan	0.767	0.229	0.538	0.299
Alberta	0.753	0.285	0.468	0.379
British Columbia	0.751	0.220	0.531	0.293
All provinces	0.802	0.354	0.448	0.441

Notes: Data from the SLID, 1993−2010. Entries are calculated based on entries in Tables 2 and 5. Provinces are ordered by location from East to West.

As mentioned in the third section, the raw persistence rates for all provinces are higher in this article than in Hansen et al. (2006). However, the predicted persistence rates from a consistent model controlling for initial conditions and unobserved heterogeneity (as well as the structural state dependence rates) are lower in this article than in Hansen et al. (2006). This suggests that heterogeneity explains more of the state dependence in SA during the period 2001–2010 compared to the 1990s. We believe this is an interesting observation that should be further explored in future work.

We also believe the finding that the source of SA dependency differs across provinces is interesting. As mentioned in the introduction, there are at least two possible reasons for structural state dependence in SA. First, the stock of human capital may depreciate during the period an individual receives welfare. Alternatively, potential employers believe that a person who has been on welfare is not as productive as an identical applicant who has not received welfare (signaling). In either of these cases, employment opportunities are reduced as a result of welfare participation.

While it is unlikely that human capital depreciation varies across provinces, there may be provincial variations in the signaling effect of receiving SA. For instance, in provinces with relatively high participation rates, the negative signal attached to receiving SA may be smaller than in provinces with low participation rates. Thus, it is possible that some of the provincial differences in genuine state dependence are due to differences in signals.

Provincial differences in genuine state dependence may also arise because of differences in the impact of unobserved heterogeneity on welfare dependence. For example, there may be differences in how individuals perceive the welfare experience and the extent to which utility from a given consumption bundle is lowered because the income generated to purchase that bundle is received from welfare instead of employment.

An alternative explanation for the observed provincial variations in genuine state dependence is differences in SA generosity. For instance, it is possible that high replacement rates generate addictions to SA and previous participation will therefore have a direct impact on current participation. In Table 7, we provide a description of SA generosity across provinces between 1993 and 2009. The entries show total welfare income as percentage of the provincial after-tax low-income cutoffs for a household consisting of a single parent with one child.[20] In parenthesis, we provide generosity rankings for each year where (1) indicates the most generous province and (10) the least generous. For the whole period 1993–2009, the most generous

Table 7. Welfare Incomes as a Percentage of the After-Tax Low-Income Cutoffs, 1993–2009, by Year and Province.

Year	Province									
	Nfld	PEI	NS	NB	QC	ONT	MAN	SAS	ALB	BC
1993	92 (2)	91 (3)	85 (4)	72 (8)	77 (7)	100 (1)	68 (10)	85 (4)	69 (9)	80 (6)
1994	91 (2)	90 (3)	86 (4)	74 (8)	78 (7)	100 (1)	68 (9)	85 (5)	64 (10)	81 (6)
1995	90 (2)	86 (3)	85 (4)	77 (7)	76 (8)	94 (1)	66 (9)	83 (5)	63 (10)	80 (6)
1996	90 (1)	82 (3)	83 (2)	76 (7)	74 (8)	78 (6)	65 (9)	82 (3)	62 (10)	79 (5)
1997	92 (1)	79 (4)	82 (2)	77 (5)	72 (8)	77 (5)	64 (9)	81 (3)	61 (10)	77 (5)
1998	94 (1)	87 (2)	82 (3)	79 (4)	71 (8)	77 (5)	63 (9)	75 (7)	62 (10)	76 (6)
1999	95 (1)	86 (2)	82 (3)	80 (4)	71 (8)	75 (6)	63 (9)	77 (5)	63 (9)	75 (6)
2000	95 (1)	88 (2)	80 (3)	80 (3)	69 (8)	74 (6)	62 (10)	77 (5)	62 (9)	74 (6)
2001	95 (1)	78 (3)	76 (5)	80 (2)	69 (8)	72 (7)	62 (9)	77 (4)	61 (10)	73 (6)
2002	94 (1)	79 (2)	75 (5)	79 (2)	70 (7)	71 (6)	64 (9)	76 (4)	59 (10)	70 (7)
2003	93 (1)	78 (2)	74 (4)	78 (2)	70 (6)	69 (7)	65 (9)	74 (4)	59 (10)	68 (8)
2004	92 (1)	79 (2)	73 (4)	77 (3)	70 (6)	69 (7)	64 (9)	73 (4)	59 (10)	67 (8)
2005	91 (1)	78 (2)	73 (5)	77 (3)	73 (5)	69 (7)	63 (9)	75 (4)	59 (10)	67 (8)
2006	99 (1)	84 (2)	78 (5)	82 (4)	77 (6)	73 (7)	67 (9)	87 (2)	66 (10)	70 (8)
2007	102 (1)	86 (2)	80 (5)	84 (3)	78 (6)	75 (7)	67 (9)	83 (4)	63 (10)	74 (8)
2008	101 (1)	86 (3)	79 (5)	84 (4)	77 (6)	75 (7)	66 (9)	87 (2)	63 (10)	75 (7)
2009	102 (1)	88 (3)	79 (5)	85 (4)	78 (6)	77 (7)	66 (10)	95 (2)	70 (9)	75 (8)
Genuine state dependence	0.433	0.246	0.342	0.313	0.474	0.308	0.237	0.229	0.285	0.220

Notes: Data from the National Council of Welfare. Nfld, Newfoundland and Labrador; PEI, Prince Edward Island; NS, Nova Scotia; NB, New Brunswick; QC, Quebec; ONT, Ontario; MAN, Manitoba; SAS, Saskatchewan; ALB, Alberta; BC, British Columbia. The entries are for single parents with one child. Generosity rankings appear in parenthesis. Provinces are ordered by location from East to West.

province is Newfoundland and Labrador, followed by Prince Edward Island. The least generous provinces are Alberta and Manitoba.

The welfare generosity rankings are positively related to the degree of structural state dependence suggesting that such dependence may be more likely to appear in provinces with relatively high benefit levels.[21] If this is the case, a change in the welfare benefit structure is more likely to change participation in generous provinces than in less generous ones. Although the analysis in this article does not allow us to address this issue further, it is an important topic with clear policy relevance and we intend to analyze this issue further in future work.

SUMMARY

This article analyzes transitions into and out of SA in Canada. We use data from the SLID for the years 1993−2010 to investigate if there are differences in transition probabilities across provinces. The data indicate that there are substantial differences in welfare participation rates across provinces. The rates are highest in Newfoundland and Labrador and lowest in Manitoba.

Furthermore, there have been substantial changes in SA use over time. Although the pattern is similar for all provinces, some have been more successful in reducing SA use than others. For instance, between 1994 and 2006, participation rates were reduced by as much as 56 percent in Nova Scotia, while in Ontario, the reduction was only around 20 percent.

The data also indicate that the transition rates are quite different across provinces. The exit rates are lowest in Newfoundland and Labrador and in Quebec, while the entry rates are lowest in Manitoba. The differences in entry and exit rates illustrate the anatomy of provincial SA participation rates. For example, we show that the participation rate is higher in Quebec than in Alberta because the probability of remaining in SA in the next period is much higher in Quebec than in Alberta, while the entry rate is similar in both provinces.

Central to the policy debate is the issue of welfare state dependence. If current welfare participation directly impacts future participation, changes in SA program parameters, including but not limited to benefit levels, can at least partially reduce participation rates. However, the success of a welfare reform is more questionable if instead the raw state dependence is due to permanent observed and unobserved heterogeneity across individuals.

To separate between the reasons for SA state dependence, we estimate dynamic probit models, including a model that controls for both endogenous initial condition and unobserved heterogeneity. This model allows us, under certain assumptions, to investigate differences in the source of SA state dependence across provinces.

The empirical results suggest that a large fraction of the observed state dependence can be attributed to unobserved heterogeneity in western Canada (Manitoba, Saskatchewan, and British Columbia), while the state dependence is more genuine or structural in Newfoundland and Labrador and Quebec. As discussed above, there are many possible reasons for these provincial differences, including differences in the signaling value of welfare receipt, preferences, and benefit generosity, and we believe that it is important to address these issues further in future work.

NOTES

1. We will use the terms SA and welfare interchangeably in this article.

2. Recent work has also shown the importance of entry rates in explaining changes in welfare use, see for instance Cappellari and Jenkins (2013) and Finnie and Pavlic (2013).

3. Following Heckman (1981), we define state dependence to be structural, or genuine, if past welfare use directly affects current probability of participation. If the state dependence is instead due to time-invariant and unobservable differences across individuals, we label it spurious.

4. There are 10 provinces and three territories in Canada. The analysis in this article is limited to the provinces since residents in any of the territories are excluded from the data.

5. Provinces also have the right to set their own benefit reduction rates.

6. Data on benefit amounts were obtained from the National Council of Welfare and are expressed in $2,002 using the Consumer Price Index. In addition to variation in benefit levels across family types, there were substantial provincial differences for given family types. For example, for single, unattached individuals, the minimum monthly benefit over this period was $289 while the maximum was $614. For a lone parent with one child, the corresponding amounts were $1,003 and $1,255, respectively.

7. Unlike the SA benefits, the EI benefits are only available for a limited time, normally up to a year. Moreover, there are a number of qualifying criteria for the EI program (searching for a job, weeks worked before becoming unemployed, etc.) that do not apply to the SA program.

8. Incidentally, the United States also switched from a shared-cost system to a lump-sum transfer program around this time. However, this change was accompanied by legislative changes which altered the fundamental character of U.S. welfare programs. See Blank (2002) for details on the U.S. welfare reform.

9. The CCTB was accompanied by the National Child Benefit Supplement.

10. The response person does not change during the panel meaning that a household is always represented by the same person.

11. A retiree is defined as a person who received payment from the Canadian (or Quebec) Pension Plan or an employer sponsored plan.

12. There are currently 76 economic regions in Canada.

13. We also estimate a dynamic probit model on aggregated data that include all provinces. For the province-specific models, the estimated entry and persistence rates are within-province predictions.

14. Note however that the permanent factor, $\eta_{h,j}$, allows for a particular form of serial correlation in ε.

15. An alternative approach, suggested by Wooldridge (2005) is to condition on the explanatory variables and the dependent variable for the initial year. The main advantage of this approach is that initial conditions do not have to be modeled. Simulation results in Akay (2012) show that both the Wooldridge estimator and the one adopted in this article perform well in relatively long panels (longer than 10 periods) while the latter performs better in short panels (like the ones used in this article).

16. See Cameron and Heckman (2001) for identification results of a similar model.

17. The results for Canada are based on aggregated data and a model specification that includes provincial effects.

18. The state dependence measures obtained using the model specification that controls for both observed and unobserved heterogeneity can be interpreted as average partial effects.

19. Hansen and Lofstrom (2006) explore the robustness of their finding toward choice of empirical methodology and find that the estimated state dependence is similar regardless of model specification. They consider three alternative specifications: the one used in this article, the Wooldridge approach, and the fixed effects logit model.

20. The data entries come from the National Council of Welfare and are only available until 2009. We use information for a single parent with one child since this is the household type with the highest SA participation rates. Moreover, we use welfare income as a percentage of the after-tax low-income cutoffs (poverty lines) for each province. The reason for using this measure, and not the benefit amounts, is that it accounts, at least to a certain degree, for provincial and time variations in the cost of living. It should also be noted that there are many aspects to welfare generosity apart from monthly benefit amounts, such as asset exemption levels, time limits, and earnings exemptions, that this exercise ignores.

21. The positive relationship remains if we consider benefit amounts instead of generosity rankings.

ACKNOWLEDGMENTS

Financial support from SSHRC is gratefully acknowledged. We are also grateful for comments from the editors, two anonymous referees and participants at the IZA/OECD/World Bank Conference on Safety Nets and Benefit Dependence in Paris.

REFERENCES

Akay, A. (2012). Finite-sample comparison of alternative methods for estimating dynamic panel data models. *Journal of Applied Econometrics, 27*(7), 1189–1204.

Andrén, T., & Andrén, D. (2013). Never give up? The persistence of welfare participation in Sweden. *IZA Journal of European Labor Studies, 2*, 1.

Blank, R. M. (1989). Analyzing the length of welfare spells. *Journal of Public Economics, 39*(3), 245–273.

Blank, R. M. (2002). Evaluating welfare reform in the United States. *Journal of Economic Literature,* 1105–1166.

Cameron, S., & Heckman, J. J. (2001). The dynamics of educational attainment for Black, Hispanic, and White males. *Journal of Political Economy, 109*(3), 455–499.

Cappellari, L., & Jenkins, S. P. (2013). *The dynamics of social assistance benefit receipt in Britain,* Unpublished paper, Universita Cattolica, Milano and London School of Economics.

Chay K. Y., Hoynes, H., & Hyslop, D. (1999). A non-experimental analysis of true state dependence in monthly welfare participation sequences, American Statistical Association. *Proceedings of the Business and Economic Statistics Section* (pp. 9–17).

Chay, K. Y., & Hyslop, D. R. (2014). Identification and estimation of dynamic binary response panel data models: Empirical evidence using alternative approaches. In S. Carcillo, H. Immervoll, S. P. Jenkins, S. Königs, & K. Tatsiramos (Eds.), *Safety nets and benefit dependence* (Vol. 39). Research in Labor Economics. Bingley, UK: Emerald Group Publishing Limited.

Eberwein, C., Ham, J., & Lalonde, R. (1997). The impact of being offered and receiving classroom training on the employment histories of disadvantaged women: Evidence from experimental data. *Review of Economic Studies, 64*(4), 655–682.

Engberg, J., Gottschalk, P., & Wolf, D. A. (1990). A random-effects logit model of work-welfare transitions. *Journal of Econometrics, 43*(1), 63–75.

Finnie, R., & Pavlic, D. (2013). *The dynamics of SA receipt in Canada.* Unpublished paper, University of Ottawa.

Ham, J., & Lalonde, R. (1996). The effect of sample selection and initial conditions in duration models: Evidence from experimental data on training. *Econometrica, 64*(1), 175–205.

Hansen, J., & Lofstrom, M. (2009). The dynamics of immigrant welfare and labor market behavior. *Journal of Population Economics, 22*(4), 941–970.

Hansen, J., & Lofstrom, M. (2011). Immigrant–native differences in welfare participation: The role of entry and exit rates. *Industrial Relations, 50*(3), 412–442.

Hansen, J., & Lofstrom, M. (2006). *Immigrant-native differences in welfare participation: The role of entry and exit rates,* IZA Discussion Paper No. 2261. Institute for the Study of Labour (IZA), Bonn.

Hansen, J., Lofstrom, M., & Zhang, X. (2006). *State dependence in Canadian welfare participation,* IZA Discussion Paper No. 2266. Institute for the Study of Labour (IZA), Bonn.

Heckman, J. J. (1981). The incidental parameters problem and the problem of initial conditions in estimating a discrete time – discrete data stochastic process. In C. F. Manski & D. McFadden (Eds.), *Structural analysis of discrete data with econometric applications* (pp. 179–195). Cambridge, MA: MIT Press.

Heckman, J. J., & Singer, B. (1984). A method for minimizing the impact of distributional assumptions in econometric models for duration data. *Econometrica, 52*(2), 271–320.

Kapsalis, C. (2001). *An assessment of EI and SA reporting in SLID*, Analytical Research Paper No. 166, Statistics Canada.

Königs, S. (2013). *The dynamics of social assistance receipt in Germany*, OECD Social, Employment and Migration Working Paper No. 136.

Moffitt, R. (1999). The effect of pre-PRWORA waivers on AFDC caseloads and female earnings, income, and labor force behavior. In S. Danziger (Ed.), *Economic conditions and welfare reform*. Chicago, IL: Upjohn Institute Press.

Riphahn, R. T., & Wunder, C. (2013). *State dependence in welfare receipt: Transitions before and after a reform*, CESifo Working Paper No. 4485, Munich: Center for Economic Studies (CES) and the Ifo Institute.

Scholz, J. K., Moffitt, R., & Cowan, B. (2009). Trends in income support. In M. Cancian & S. Danziger (Eds.), *Changing poverty, changing policies* (pp. 203−241). New York, NY: Russell Sage Foundation.

Wooldridge, J. M. (2005). Simple solutions to the initial conditions problem in dynamic, nonlinear panel data models with unobserved heterogeneity. *Journal of Applied Econometrics, 20*(1), 39−54.

APPENDIX

Table A1. Dynamic Models of Welfare Participation with Controls for Endogenous Initial Conditions or Unobserved Heterogeneity.

	Newfoundland and Labrador	Prince Edward Island	Nova Scotia	New Brunswick	Quebec
Individual characteristics:					
Married	−0.757**	−0.841**	−0.646**	−0.784**	−0.505**
	(0.085)	(0.144)	(0.081)	(0.096)	(0.044)
Age	−0.009**	−0.003	−0.005	−0.001	−0.003
	(0.004)	(0.005)	(0.004)	(0.004)	(0.002)
Urban	0.016	0.067	0.322**	−0.062	−0.015
	(0.065)	(0.097)	(0.071)	(0.062)	(0.046)
Number of children	0.197**	0.220**	0.123**	0.121**	0.087**
	(0.030)	(0.059)	(0.033)	(0.032)	(0.018)
Years of education	−0.155**	−0.097**	−0.133**	−0.122**	−0.079**
	(0.013)	(0.021)	(0.014)	(0.016)	(0.006)
Disabled	0.400**	0.610**	0.594**	0.477**	0.464**
	(0.073)	(0.123)	(0.073)	(0.070)	(0.046)
Male	−0.064	−0.065	−0.112	−0.161**	−0.071**
	(0.063)	(0.103)	(0.070)	(0.063)	(0.038)
State dependence:					
Received welfare	2.182**	1.826**	2.259**	2.054**	2.732**
previous year	(0.079)	(0.164)	(0.093)	(0.111)	(0.050)
Local labor market variable:					
Local unemployment	0.020**	0.036	0.024**	0.040**	0.048**
rate	(0.007)	(0.024)	(0.008)	(0.009)	(0.006)
Unobserved heterogeneity:					
Factor loading (μ)	0.713**	0.882**	0.477**	0.754**	0.803**
	(0.096)	(0.374)	(0.083)	(0.098)	(0.239)
Factor loading (α)	0.403**	0.369*	0.284**	0.354**	0.059**
	(0.043)	(0.191)	(0.057)	(0.095)	(0.022)
Probability type I	0.119	0.217	0.079	0.119	0.018
Number of individuals	3,680	2,089	4,838	4,741	14,319
Number of observations	21,207	11,804	27,508	26,905	82,444
Average log-likelihood	−7.165	−5.393	−7.439	−7.398	−2.707

Table A1. (*Continued*)

	Ontario	Manitoba	Saskatchewan	Alberta	British Columbia	All Provinces
Individual characteristics:						
Married	−0.609**	−0.691**	−0.736**	−0.538**	−0.411**	−0.575**
	(0.044)	(0.096)	(0.103)	(0.079)	(0.109)	(0.024)
Age	0.001	0.004	−0.003	0.010	−0.005	−0.001
	(0.002)	(0.004)	(0.004)	(0.003)	(0.004)	(0.001)
Urban	0.104**	0.001	0.241**	−0.008	0.134	0.046**
	(0.043)	(0.089)	(0.097)	(0.086)	(0.092)	(0.023)
Number of	0.116**	0.150**	0.169**	0.018	0.072**	0.087**
children	(0.016)	(0.028)	(0.033)	(0.029)	(0.030)	(0.008)
Years of	−0.063**	−0.092**	−0.132**	−0.076**	−0.066**	−0.077**
education	(0.006)	(0.013)	(0.016)	(0.013)	(0.014)	(0.004)
Disabled	0.557**	0.495**	0.428**	0.472**	0.583**	0.500**
	(0.038)	(0.084)	(0.088)	(0.071)	(0.078)	(0.021)
Male	−0.015	−0.059	−0.144	−0.095	−0.099	−0.074**
	(0.034)	(0.073)	(0.084)	(0.066)	(0.099)	(0.018)
State dependence:						
Received welfare	2.380**	2.189**	1.909**	2.334**	2.212**	2.436**
previous year	(0.053)	(0.117)	(0.104)	(0.099)	(0.188)	(0.031)
Local labor market variable:						
Local	0.065**	0.047**	0.047	0.062**	0.066**	0.045**
unemployment rate	(0.009)	(0.024)	(0.032)	(0.018)	(0.017)	(0.004)
Unobserved heterogeneity:						
Factor loading (μ)	0.717**	0.948**	0.646**	0.460**	1.145**	0.675**
	(0.071)	(0.153)	(0.076)	(0.069)	(0.351)	(0.038)
Factor loading (α)	0.262**	0.295**	0.494**	0.319**	0.747*	0.267**
	(0.032)	(0.072)	(0.044)	(0.038)	(0.434)	(0.023)
Probability type I	0.103	0.127	0.106	0.053	0.452	0.111
Number of individuals	20,387	5,151	5,039	6,604	6,128	72,976
Number of observations	121,665	30,186	29,872	37,511	35,420	424,522
Average log-likelihood	−8.2148	−7.5606	−7.5343	−7.8747	−7.2978	−7.6185

Note: Standard errors are shown in parentheses.
Significance at the 5 percent level is indicated by ** while significance at the 10 percent level is indicated by *.

STATE DEPENDENCE IN SOCIAL ASSISTANCE BENEFIT RECEIPT IN GERMANY BEFORE AND AFTER THE HARTZ REFORMS

Sebastian Königs

ABSTRACT

I study state dependence in social assistance receipt in Germany using annual survey data from the German Socio-Economic Panel for the years 1995–2011. There is considerable observed state dependence, with an average persistence rate in benefits of 68 per cent comparing to an average entry rate of just above 3 per cent. To identify a possible structural component, I estimate a series of dynamic random-effects probit models that control for observed and unobserved heterogeneity and endogeneity of initial conditions. I find evidence of substantial structural state dependence in benefit receipt. Estimates suggest that benefit receipt one year ago is associated with an increase in the likelihood of benefit receipt today by a factor of 3.4. This corresponds to an average partial effect of 13 percentage points. Average predicted entry and persistence rates and the absolute level of structural state dependence are higher in Eastern

Safety Nets and Benefit Dependence
Research in Labor Economics, Volume 39, 107–150
Copyright © 2014 by Emerald Group Publishing Limited
ISSN: 0147-9121/doi:10.1108/S0147-912120140000039003

Germany than in Western Germany. I find only little evidence for time variation in state dependence around the years of the Hartz reforms.

Keywords: Social assistance; welfare benefits; state dependence; Germany; Hartz reforms

JEL classifications: I38; J60; J64; C23

INTRODUCTION

A standard observation in data on social assistance benefit receipt is that current recipients are much more likely than non-recipients to receive benefits also in the next period. For instance, as described below, the average year-to-year persistence rate on benefits for recipients in Germany was 68 per cent over the years 1995–2011 compared to a year-to-year entry rate for non-recipients of only 3 per cent.

Two explanations for this 'state dependence' have been proposed (Heckman, 1981a, 1981b). First, there is heterogeneity in personal and socio-economic characteristics. If these characteristics affect the likelihood of benefit receipt, individuals with less 'favourable' characteristics – for instance low educational attainment or bad health – will self-select into benefits. The resulting differences in individual characteristics between recipients and non-recipients will induce differences between benefit entry and persistence rates. Any state dependence induced by heterogeneity across individuals will disappear once all relevant characteristics are controlled for, which is why it is referred to as 'spurious'. Second, the gap between persistence and entry rates might hint at potential pervasive effects of benefit receipt itself. Individuals on benefits might feel less confident, motivated or incentivized to leave benefits *as a result of benefit receipt*, or they may become accustomed to receiving transfer payments as a 'way of life' (Bane & Ellwood, 1994). Potential employers might interpret benefit receipt as a negative signal about a recipient's unobserved labour productivity when screening job applicants, which would reduce her employment prospects and thus the likelihood of becoming self-sufficient. In these cases, current benefit receipt has a *causal* effect on the probability of future receipt by raising hurdles to self-sufficiency. This effect is referred to as 'structural' or 'genuine' state dependence.

The two potential drivers of state dependence have very different implications for policy making. If benefit receipt *as such* increases the probability of future benefit receipt, policies that prevent entry or facilitate early exits from social assistance can induce a lasting reduction in receipt rates. If, by contrast, high benefit persistence is due to recipients' characteristics, policies that encourage exits from benefits are likely to have little impact unless the factors causing benefit receipt are addressed directly.

This article presents an empirical analysis of state dependence in social assistance receipt in Germany for the years 1995–2011 based on annual survey data from the German Socio-Economic Panel (SOEP). The period studied is of particular interest because it covers the far-reaching 'Hartz reforms' implemented from 2003 to 2005 that fundamentally changed the system of social assistance benefit provision in Germany. While the type of model estimated is not suited for assessing potential causal reform effects, the analysis presents evidence on both the level of state dependence as well as on potential variations in state dependence over the observation period. Sample selection criteria and the estimation technique used are similar to those in earlier analyses for other countries such that results can be compared across studies. A methodological contribution of the article lies in that it contrasts the results obtained to those reported in two recent studies for Germany by Riphahn and Wunder (2013) and Wunder and Riphahn (2014), who – for a narrower sample and based on a different modelling approach – obtain very different results.

The decomposition of observed 'raw' state dependence into its structural and spurious components has been the focus of much recent work on social assistance dynamics. Yet, the number of studies that look for structural state dependence in social assistance receipt remains small to date and the existing work is limited to a few countries.[1] Chay, Hoynes, and Hyslop (1999) and Chay and Hyslop (2014) provide evidence for state dependence in the receipt of Aid to Families with Dependent Children (AFDC) in the United States. Gong (2004) studies benefit transitions of low-income women who receive Income Support or Family Allowance in Australia and finds state dependence in both programmes. Hansen and Lofstrom (2008, 2011) and Andrén and Andrén (2013) study the native–immigrant gap in benefit receipt in Sweden. They find higher structural state dependence for migrants but emphasize the importance of unobserved heterogeneity for explaining differences in receipt rates between natives and migrants. In a study for Britain, Cappellari and Jenkins (2008) estimate stronger structural state dependence for lone parents and for recipients with one non-interrupted spell compared to individuals with a spell of work between interview dates. Hansen, Lofstrom, Liu, and Zhang (2014) report strong variations in state dependence across provinces in Canada and suggest that the level of state dependence might be positively related to benefit generosity.

I am aware of only two studies of state dependence in social assistance benefit receipt in Germany.[2] Wunder and Riphahn (2014) compare the benefit dynamics of natives and immigrants in Western Germany for the post-Hartz years 2005–2009. Based on SOEP data, they estimate a dynamic multinomial logit model with three competing states distinguishing between social assistance receipt, employment and 'inactivity' (which is defined as including unemployment). They find that persistence in social assistance benefit receipt can mostly be accounted for by observable characteristics, with only limited evidence for structural state dependence. In a recent follow-up paper, Riphahn and Wunder (2013) extend this analysis to cover the years immediately before the Hartz reform. Using the same model, they find evidence for a decline in persistence in welfare and inactivity and for a rise in frequency of transitions from welfare to work but also from work to welfare.

In this article, I follow the approach used in much of the earlier work on social assistance dynamics by estimating a series of dynamic random-effects probit models that control for individuals' observable characteristics and persistent unobserved heterogeneity. I find that even though individual heterogeneity explains most of the gap between observed benefit persistence and entry rates, there is evidence of substantial structural state dependence in social assistance. On average, benefit receipt at the last interview raises the likelihood of benefit receipt at the current interview by a factor of 3.4. This corresponds to an average partial effect (APE) of past benefit receipt on the probability of receipt in the current period of 13 percentage points. By contrast, I do not find evidence of a change in state dependence around the time of the Hartz reforms. While state dependence was lower for the years 1996–2004 than in 2005–2011, this effect seems to be primarily driven by lower state dependence in the late 1990s and a temporary spike in 2010 for Eastern Germany.

A sensitivity check shows that the estimated level of state dependence is affected by sample selection and, more importantly, by the method used for defining the benefit variable. In an attempt to reconcile my results with those presented by Riphahn and Wunder in their two recent papers, I show that using an individual-level rather than the more standard household-level definition of the social assistance variable leads to a substantial drop in the estimated level of state dependence. Moreover, findings are sensitive to the source of information used, that is, whether data on benefit receipt are taken from personal or household questionnaires. Once these issues and differences in sample selection are accounted for, the results presented in this article are consistent with Riphahn and Wunder's findings of only very weak state dependence in Germany.

The remainder of this article is structured as follows: The next section gives an overview of the institutional background in Germany during the observation period and defines the benefit variable. The third and the fourth section describe the SOEP data used in the analysis and present trends in benefit receipt and transition rates, respectively. The fifth section introduces the econometric model used for the analysis along with two extensions suited to study time variation in state dependence. The sixth section presents the empirical results about the level and potential time variation in state dependence. The seventh section concludes the article.

INSTITUTIONAL BACKGROUND AND DEFINITION OF THE BENEFIT VARIABLE

During the 1995–2011 observation period, the German social assistance system underwent far-reaching reforms. The so-called Hartz reforms, implemented by the left-of-centre coalition of Social Democrats and Greens from 2003 to 2005, resulted, among other things, in a structural change of the groups entitled to different last-resort minimum-income benefits.[3] This section describes some key features of the benefit system in the years before and after the reforms and defines the social assistance variable used in the analysis.

Institutional Background

Until 2005, the German income-support system for working-age individuals had a three-tier structure. As the top layer, Unemployment Insurance (UI) benefits (*Arbeitslosengeld*) aimed at replacing an individual's income after job loss for a limited amount of time, with eligibility being conditional on a previous work and contribution record.[4] Individuals whose entitlements to UI had expired could claim Unemployment Assistance (UA) benefits (*Arbeitslosenhilfe*). UA was earnings-related but means-tested on family-income and less generous than UI.[5] Unlike UI, UA benefits could in principle be received for an indefinite period of time under the condition that the claimant was looking for and available for work.

Finally, Social Assistance (SA, *Sozialhilfe*) served as a benefit of last resort below this primary social safety net.[6] SA was understood as a temporary emergency benefit, and eligibility required from individuals to have exhausted all alternative sources of income in the form of earnings from work, UI or UA benefit payments and financial support from direct family members. While SA had initially been primarily targeted at individuals with special needs and limited employability, a gradual tightening of eligibility criteria for UI and UA over time meant that a growing number of individuals were shifted into SA. Due to the lower benefit amounts of UA compared to UI, recipients of UA benefits moreover often qualified for SA payments as a top-up.

The fourth package of the Hartz reforms, which entered into force in January 2005, abolished this three-tier system with the aim of strengthening labour market services and intensifying the activation of unemployed job seekers. The contribution-based UI was replaced by the new Unemployment Benefit I (UBI, *Arbeitslosengeld I*), with an initially unchanged maximum benefit duration and replacement rate.[7] The more relevant change in the context of this study was the merger of UA and SA for employable job seekers into the new means-tested Unemployment Benefit II (UBII, *Arbeitslosengeld II*). The computation of UBII benefit levels follows a similar logic as for the former last-resort SA. Compared to the old UA scheme, the new UBII is typically less generous and it no longer depends on the level of previous earnings. SA continues to exist as a separate programme but is now restricted to individuals incapable for work due to sickness, disability or care duties. The Hartz reforms thus introduced a clearer distinction between the minimum-income support for employable and non-employable individuals.

Both before and after the reform, an income-tested Housing Benefit (HB, *Wohngeld*) is targeted at low-income households more broadly. Until 2005, this benefit could be claimed by individuals in work and by recipients of UI or UA benefits, while SA recipients were not entitled. Since 2005, recipients of UBII and SA receive support for eligible housing expenses as part of their benefit entitlements, while HB continues to be available for other low-income groups.

Definition of the Benefit Variable

In light of the institutional changes just described, it is not obvious what the best choice is for defining a social assistance benefit variable that allows for a consistent analysis of receipt dynamics over the entire observation period. Existing studies of social assistance dynamics in Germany focus only on relatively short time periods either before (Riphahn, 2004; Voges & Rohwer, 1992) or after the Hartz reforms (Schels, 2013; Wunder & Riphahn, 2014) and look at receipt of either SA or UBII only. Riphahn and Wunder (2013), who compare pre- and post-reform benefit dynamics for able-bodied individuals, study receipt of UA and SA before 2005 and of UBII thereafter. In this article, I choose a slightly different approach by defining a broader benefit variable that takes into account receipt of all means-tested benefits (for an overview, see Table 1).

The classification of pre- and post-reform SA and of UBII as social assistance programmes is probably uncontroversial. A categorization of UA by contrast is more difficult: As a contribution-based and earnings-related benefit, it does not correspond to the standard definition of a social assistance programme. The reason why it is included in this analysis nonetheless is that treating UA as a social assistance programme is sensible in terms of the implied benefit dynamics. The typical recipient of UA in December 2004 would go on to receive UBII in January 2005. It is not evident why such a transition should bring about a change in the individual's social assistance benefit receipt status for the purpose of this analysis. As the direct precursor to UBII, UA moreover shared a number of key features of the other social assistance programmes. Unlike UI benefits, UA

Table 1. Principal Eligibility Conditions of Social Assistance Benefit Programmes for Working-Age Individuals in Germany.

Before the Hartz Reforms	After the Hartz Reforms
Social Assistance (*Sozialhilfe*)	Social Assistance (*Sozialhilfe*)
• Lacking or insufficient social insurance contribution history and income and assets below a specified minimum level	• Lacking or expired claims to contributory UBI and income and assets below a specified minimum level
• Possibly available for (part-time) work	• Incapable of working
Unemployment Assistance (*Arbeitslosenhilfe*)	Unemployment Benefits II (*Arbeitslosengeld II*)
• History of work and social insurance contributions but expired (or lacking) entitlements to UI benefits	• Lacking or expired claims to contributory UBI and income and assets below a specified minimum level
	• Available for at least part-time work
Housing Benefits (*Wohngeld*)	Housing Benefits (*Wohngeld*)
• Income below a specified minimum level and not a recipient of SA (but possibly of UI or UA Benefits)	• Income below a specified minimum level and not a recipient of SA or UBII (but possibly of UBI)

was means-tested and could be claimed for an infinite period of time. Also, it was not paid for by social-security contributions but was tax-funded. Both of these features make it resemble social assistance benefit schemes like SA or UBII.[8] Finally, I also take into account receipt of HB as a means-tested benefit targeted at low-income benefits more broadly. HB receipt rates are however relatively low and excluding HB from the analysis does not affect its main conclusions (see Königs, 2013).

Like most comparable previous studies, I use the individual as the unit of analysis. While eligibility for social assistance benefits is determined at the level of a possibly larger 'need unit', frequent changes in household composition imply that it is not obvious how the benefit dynamics of a household could be studied over time. Since for the means test, the financial status not only of the claimant alone but of other household members matters, I categorize an individual as a benefit recipient if benefit payments are recorded for any individual in the household.[9] I measure benefit receipt using reports of receipt in both the individual and household questionnaires of the SOEP. I count receipt as occurring if there is a report in either source or both sources.[10] To account for the importance of household composition, I include partner and household characteristics as explanatory variables in the econometric estimations. The household as defined in the survey will however not always coincide with the benefit unit used by the social assistance office to assess eligibility for income-support payments.

The time interval of analysis is one year during which benefit receipt is measured only once at the moment of the interview. While respondents in the SOEP are requested to provide information on receipt of income-support payments on a monthly basis, corresponding information on personal and household characteristics is lacking that would be required to estimate the model at the monthly level. Earlier research moreover indicates that the quality of monthly data on benefit receipt derived from annual surveys is often poor. In particular, the so-called seam bias is observed in months where survey periods adjoin or overlap as respondents have apparent difficulties to answer questions that relate to early parts of the survey year (Pavetti, 1993; Blank & Ruggles, 1994). The approach of modelling benefit transitions from one interview date to the next therefore appears to be the safer option, and it has been previously used for the same reason by Cappellari and Jenkins (2008) and Cappellari and Jenkins (2014) in their analysis of social assistance receipt dynamics in Britain.[11]

DATA USED

The data for the analysis come from the German Socio-Economic Panel (SOEP), a representative longitudinal survey of private households in Germany. The panel was started in West Germany in 1984 and expanded to the territory of the former German Democratic Republic in 1990. The last wave currently available is for 2011. Over time, the sample size increased from an initial 6,000 households to around 12,300 households and 22,000 individuals in 2011.

In a sampled household, all individuals aged above 16 years are interviewed personally and one of the household members additionally completes a separate household questionnaire. All members of a sampled household are followed over time even if they leave the original household. Individuals who move into a sampled household become part of the panel and remain in the sample even in case of a split-up of that household. Household interviews are conducted annually, with the majority of interviews taking place early in the year.[12] The SOEP oversamples 'guest workers' and other immigrants, German residents of the former German Democratic Republic, and high-income individuals. For a detailed description of the dataset, see Haisken-DeNew and Frick (2005).

I construct my data set by merging the first eight samples of the SOEP (officially denoted samples A-H).[13] To separately study the benefit dynamics in Western and Eastern Germany, I split this full sample into two subsamples based on the region of residence of the sample members as explained below.

From the eight SOEP samples, I use the last 17 waves for the years 1995−2011 prior to which no question on the receipt of income-support benefits at the time of the interview was asked. I restrict the sample to working-age individuals (25−59 years) who are not dependent children and without missing information on benefit receipt and a few other important variables. I further drop observations for individuals with a partner who is not of working-age (i.e. below 25 or above 59 years), observations for individuals in a household with a working-age member in full-time education, and all observations after a gap in an individual's interview sequence.[14] Excluding the initial observation in each individual's interview sequence for which no lag is available, the resulting estimation sample consists of 17,733 individuals and 100,434 person-year observations.

I match the sample with annual data on unemployment rates in the individuals' state of residence from the German Federal Statistical Office

(Statistisches Bundesamt, 2013). These data are used to control for differences in regional labour market conditions in the econometric analysis.[15]

TRENDS IN BENEFIT RECEIPT

Germany has seen a slight rise in rates of social assistance benefit receipt
over the 17 years of the observation period. As illustrated in the left panel
of Fig. 1, the frequency of benefit receipt among working-age individuals is
initially relatively stable at around 7−8 per cent. After 2001, rates of benefit
receipt start rising strongly to peak at 12.7 per cent in 2006. The beginning
of this increase coincides with the start of a period of economic stagnation
in Germany in the early 2000s. After 2006, the year after the Hartz reforms,
the frequency of benefit receipt declines through the years of the Great
Recession and drops to below 10 per cent in 2011.

A breakdown of social assistance into the different programmes shows
that trends for the different programmes differ. Rates of HB and SA
receipt are relatively stable until 2005, but then drop visibly with the implementation of the Hartz reforms. By contrast, rates of UA receipt show an
upward trend in the first decade of the panel, which continues for the newly
introduced UBII in 2005 and 2006. The drop in SA receipt rates and the
simultaneous jump in receipt rates from UA to UBII indicate that a large

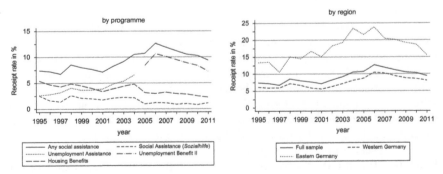

Fig. 1. Rates of Benefit Receipt. *Notes*: Rates of benefit receipt were calculated
using cross-sectional individual sampling weights. The frequency of benefit receipt is
the share of working-age individuals who live in a benefit-receiving household at the
time of the interview. The final package of the Hartz reforms entered into force in
January 2005. *Source*: SOEP (2011).

share of SA recipients were moved into UBII through the Hartz reforms. Similarly, HB receipt rates fall as recipients who are transferred from UA to UBII lose eligibility to HB. The decline in receipt rates after 2006 is primarily due to a reduced number of UBII recipients.

Patterns of benefit receipt still differ considerably between Eastern and Western Germany. As illustrated in the right panel of Fig. 1, receipt rates in Eastern Germany are substantially higher, averaging 17.6 per cent compared to 7.6 per cent for Western Germany. This difference is broadly comparable to the disparity in unemployment rates in the two parts of the country.[16] Benefit receipt rates in Eastern Germany show a weak upward trend even in the initial years of the panel and already peak in 2004. Receipt rates for Western Germany closely follow those for Germany overall, which reflects the fact that about 80 per cent of observations in the full sample are for Western Germany.

Benefit transition rates plotted in Fig. 2 show that the rise in the benefit receipt rates observed after 2001 seems to have been primarily due to a permanent drop in exit rates from benefit receipt. The share of individuals who report leaving benefits from one interview to the next falls from around

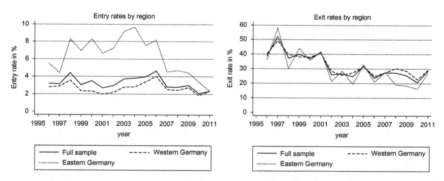

Fig. 2. Benefit Transition Rates. *Notes*: Entry rates into benefit receipt are defined as the number of individuals in receipt of social assistance benefits at time t but not at time $t-1$ divided by the total number of individuals not in social assistance at time $t-1$. Similarly, exit rates from benefit receipt are defined as the number of individuals in receipt at time $t-1$ but no longer in receipt at time t divided by the total number of individuals in receipt at time $t-1$. Individuals observed for only one of the two waves have not been used in the calculations. Benefit transition rates were calculated using cross-sectional individual sampling weights for period t. The final package of the Hartz reforms entered into force in January 2005.
Source: SOEP (2011).

or above 40 per cent until 2001 to below 30 per cent thereafter (right panel). This is remarkable, since earlier comparable work for Canada (Finnie & Irvine, 2008) and Britain (Cappellari & Jenkins, 2008; Cappellari & Jenkins, 2014) shows that declining rates of benefit receipt in these countries were primarily driven by falling entry rates while exit rates remained stable or declined as well. The rise in receipt rates in Eastern Germany during the late 1990s and, more importantly, the decline in receipt rates after 2006 appear to be due to changes in entry rates (left panel).

The breakdown of benefit transition rates by region again shows very different patterns in the two parts of the country. Exit rates are nearly identical with slightly stronger fluctuations for Eastern Germany due to the much smaller sample size. Entry rates into benefit receipt by contrast are up to four times higher in Eastern Germany than in Western Germany. They also show much more variation in Eastern Germany, rising from around 5 per cent to 8 per cent in 1998 and dropping again by the same amount from 2006 to 2007. The gap in social assistance receipt rates between Eastern and Western Germany shown in Fig. 1 is thus due to much higher entry rates in Eastern Germany.

An important implication of these benefit transition rates is that there is indeed substantial observed (or 'raw') state dependence in benefit receipt as highlighted in the Introduction. Average exit rates of around 32 per cent over the observation period imply that 68 per cent of benefit recipients in a given year will continue to receive benefits in the following year. Entry rates into benefits by contrast average only around 3 per cent over the same period. Observed state dependence is thus around 65 per cent. At least some of this effect is of course likely to be driven by differences in individual and household characteristics between social assistance recipients and non-recipients. Königs (2013) shows for instance that benefit recipients in Germany are on average substantially more likely than non-recipients to have less than 10 years of education or poor self-assessed health. Also, a larger share of benefit recipients are migrants, and the proportion of single parent households is about three times as high among benefit recipients than for non-recipients.

Based on the descriptive evidence alone it is not obvious whether there might have been a structural change in benefit receipt dynamics around the time of the Hartz reforms. Receipt rates stopped rising in 2006, the year after the Hartz reforms, to decline thereafter. This trend was driven by a strong drop in entry rates from 2006 to 2007 especially in Eastern Germany. The decline in entry rates however mirrors a comparable earlier increase in the late 1990s, and exit rates remained mostly stable during the reform years.

The econometric model presented in the following section attempts to determine whether there is evidence for 'structural' state dependence in Germany, and if so, whether the level of state dependence differs for the periods before and after the 2005 Hartz reforms.

ECONOMETRIC APPROACH

The econometric analysis is based on a dynamic random-effects probit model, the standard model in recent empirical work on state dependence in social assistance benefit receipt. This section introduces the model and proposes two simple extensions that permit studying time variations in state dependence.

Let y_{it} be a binary outcome variable such that for $y_{it} = 1$ individual i is in receipt of social assistance in period t. A latent variable specification for this outcome can be written as:

$$
\begin{aligned}
y_{it} &= \mathbf{1}\{y_{it}^* > 0\} \\
&= \mathbf{1}\{x'_{i(t-1)}\beta + \lambda y_{i(t-1)} + \mu_t + u_{it} > 0\} \quad \text{for} \quad i = 1, ..., N; \quad t = 1, ..., T_i
\end{aligned}
\tag{1}
$$

where y_{it}^* depends linearly on a vector of observable characteristics $x_{i(t-1)}$, the observed receipt status in the previous period $y_{i(t-1)}$, a period-specific effect μ_t and an error term u_{it}.[17] The latent variable y_{it}^* can be interpreted as the potential utility from receiving social assistance, with the individual choosing benefit receipt for $y_{it}^* > 0$.

The error term can be decomposed as $u_{it} = \alpha_i + \varepsilon_{it}$, where α_i is an individual-specific random intercept and ε_{it} is a transitory shock. The two error components are assumed to be mean zero and uncorrelated with each other. The persistent component α_i is by construction correlated with the lagged dependent variable $y_{i(t-1)}$ but initially assumed to be uncorrelated with the regressors $x_{i(t-1)}$, an assumption that is relaxed below. It is further assumed that the transitory shock ε_{it} is standard normal and serially uncorrelated, that the benefit receipt dynamics are correctly represented by a first-order Markov process and that the covariates $x_{i(t-1)}$ are strictly exogenous.[18]

Under these conditions, the probability of benefit receipt is given as:

$$
P(y_{it}|y_{i0}, ..., y_{iT_i}, x_i, \mu_t, \alpha_i) = \Phi(x'_{i(t-1)}\beta + \lambda y_{i(t-1)} + \mu_t + \alpha_i)
\tag{2}
$$

where x_i is the vector of an individual's characteristics in all time periods and $\Phi(\cdot)$ is the standard normal cumulative distribution function.

Following Heckman (1981a), the coefficient of the lagged dependent variable λ in such a model is interpreted as measuring 'structural' state dependence. 'Spurious' state dependence induced by permanent unobserved heterogeneity is captured by the persistent individual-specific error term α_i that might be interpreted as representing differences in unobserved labour market ability or an individual's preference for benefit receipt.

A difficulty for estimation of this model is that the specification suffers from an initial conditions bias. As for linear dynamic panel data models with unobserved heterogeneity, the individual-specific error component α_i induces a correlation between the error term and the lagged dependent variable that leads to inconsistent estimates. Integrating out the individual-specific effect α_i requires specifying its relationship with the outcome in the initial period y_{i0} that typically cannot be treated as exogenous.

The simplest approach for addressing the initial conditions problem has been proposed by Wooldridge (2005).[19] He suggests specifying a density for the individual-specific effect conditional on the outcome in the initial period and the covariates, which permits integrating out α_i. More specifically, Wooldridge sets $\alpha_i = \gamma_0 + \gamma_1 y_{i0} + x_i' \gamma_2 + a_i$, with $a_i | y_{i0}, x_i \sim \mathcal{N}(0, \sigma_a^2)$. The vector x_i contains here the values of time-varying covariates for all periods not yet already included in $x_{i(t-1)}$ and allows for a correlation of α_i with the covariates as proposed by Chamberlain (1982, 1984). Under this assumption, the joint density of $y_{i1}, ..., y_{iT_i} | y_{i0}, x_i$ unconditional on α_i simply corresponds to the likelihood of the standard random-effects probit model with the additional explanatory variables y_{i0} and x_i added in each period t and can be used for maximum likelihood estimation. In empirical practice, the vector of lags and leads of all time-varying covariates x_i is typically replaced by an individual's longitudinal averages of these covariates $\bar{x}_i$ à la Mundlak (1978). This is also what I do in this article to reduce the number of regressors and thus computation time.[20] Consistency of this model relies on the assumption that unobserved heterogeneity is uncorrelated with the regressors once between-individual differences in observable characteristics are accounted for.

Due to the non-linearity of the model, the size of the coefficient estimates is little informative about the magnitude of the implied effects on the outcome variable. To evaluate the degree of state dependence, I therefore calculate the average partial effect (APE) of benefit receipt at the previous interview on benefit receipt at the current interview. Under the assumptions just discussed, I consistently estimate an individual's expected probability of social assistance benefit receipt in period t as:

$$\frac{1}{N}\sum_{i=1}^{N}\left(\Phi(x'_{i(t-1)}\hat{\beta} + \hat{\lambda}y_{i(t-1)} + \hat{\mu}_t + \hat{\gamma}_1 y_{i0} + \bar{x}'_i\hat{\gamma}_2)(1-\hat{\rho})^{\frac{1}{2}}\right) \tag{3}$$

where $\hat{\rho} = \hat{\sigma}_a^2/(1 + \hat{\sigma}_a^2)$ is the estimated share of the variance of the composite error term that can be attributed to persistent unobserved heterogeneity (Wooldridge, 2005).

Following Stewart (2007), the APE of past benefit receipt is then defined as the difference in average predicted probabilities of social assistance receipt across individuals and time conditional on benefit receipt and non-receipt in the previous period:

$$\text{APE} = \frac{1}{NT_i}\sum_{t=1}^{T_i}\sum_{i=1}^{N}[\hat{P}(y_{it}=1|y_{i(t-1)}=1, x_{i(t-1)}, \mu_t, y_{i0}, \bar{x}_i)$$
$$- \hat{P}(y_{it}=1|y_{i(t-1)}=0, x_{i(t-1)}, \mu_t, y_{i0}, \bar{x}_i)] \tag{4}$$

The APE measures structural state dependence in absolute terms by comparing average predicted entry and persistence probabilities across all individuals over time.

Alternatively, one can express the degree of state dependence in relative terms by calculating the predicted probability ratio (PPR), i.e., the ratio of average predicted probabilities with and without benefit receipt in the previous period:

$$\text{PPR} = \frac{(1/NT_i)\sum_{t=1}^{T_i}\sum_{i=1}^{N}\hat{P}(y_{it}=1|y_{i(t-1)}=1, x_{i(t-1)}, \mu_t, y_{i0}, \bar{x}_i)}{(1/NT_i)\sum_{t=1}^{T_i}\sum_{i=1}^{N}\hat{P}(y_{it}=1|y_{i(t-1)}=0, x_{i(t-1)}, \mu_t, y_{i0}, \bar{x}_i)} \tag{5}$$

To study time variation in the level of state dependence, I estimate two different extensions of the standard model. First, I directly compare the level of state dependence before and after the Hartz reforms by rewriting the model as:

$$y_{it} = \mathbf{1}\{x'_{i(t-1)}(\beta^0 + \beta^1 H_t) + (\lambda^0 + \lambda^1 H_t)y_{i(t-1)} + (\gamma_1^0 + \gamma_1^1 H_t)y_{i0} + \bar{x}_i(\gamma_2^0 + \gamma_2^1 H_t) + a_i > 0\} \quad \text{for } i=1,...,N; \ t=1,...,T_i \tag{6}$$

where H_t is a dummy variable for the post-Hartz period that takes the value one in the years 2005–2011 and is zero otherwise.

This specification allows for differences in the processes driving benefit receipt before and after the Hartz reforms by letting the coefficients of the lagged dependence variable $y_{i(t-1)}$, of the covariates $x_{i(t-1)}$ and of the Wooldridge controls y_{i0} and $\bar{x}_i$ differ between those two periods. Unlike in the standard specification, the model now no longer includes a set of year dummies μ_t. The time trend is instead captured by an interaction of the post-Hartz dummy with the intercept term included in $x_{i(t-1)}$. Unobserved heterogeneity is assumed not to vary over time.

Second, I analyze the timing of any variations in state dependence by allowing the effect of the lagged dependent variable on the likelihood of benefit receipt to vary on a year-by-year basis. I again extend the standard specification, this time including interactions between the lagged dependent variable and calendar-year dummies. The model can be written as:

$$y_{it} = 1\left\{ x'_{i(t-1)}\beta + \lambda y_{i(t-1)} + \sum_{\tau=1997}^{2011} (\mu^\tau + \lambda^\tau y_{i(t-1)}) + \gamma_1 y_{i0} + \bar{x}'_i \gamma_2 + a_i > 0 \right\} \tag{7}$$

for $i = 1, ..., N; \quad t = 1, ..., T_i$

where μ^τ and λ^τ are the coefficients of a set of calendar-year dummy variables and of their interactions with the lagged dependent variable, respectively. The effects of all other variables are assumed to be constant over time.[21] This specification is more flexible than the one given in Eq. (6) by allowing for richer variation in the effect of lagged benefit receipt. It is more restrictive by contrast in imposing that the coefficients of other covariates do not change over time.

To quantify variations in the degree of state dependence, I predict entry and persistence rates for each individual in the sample *in each of the periods distinguished in the model* (i.e. also in those in which the individual is not observed). This is done by 'switching on' the dummy for the respective period and its interaction term (and 'switching off' period dummies and interaction terms of all other periods) for all individuals. I then use the model estimates to predict period-specific entry and persistence rates across all individuals as usual. Time variation in state dependence is given as the difference in APEs between two periods, i.e. as the 'difference in differences' between the average predicted persistence and entry rates across all individuals in two periods.[22]

The results presented in the next section were obtained using Stata's xtprobit command, which employs adaptive quadrature with 12 quadrature points for evaluation of the integrals. As a robustness check, all specifications have been re-estimated using Stata's `gllamm` command that allows for robust standard errors and the use of sampling weights (Rabe-Hesketh, Skrondal, & Pickles, 2004, 2005), but for which computation time is substantially higher. I find that the use of sampling weights leads to larger standard errors but does otherwise not strongly affect the estimation results. I therefore use weights only for the calculation of APEs and PPRs but not in the estimation process. Results from weighted estimation as well as from robustness checks for balanced panels are provided by Königs (2013).

ESTIMATION RESULTS

This section presents estimation results for the full sample and separately for Western and Eastern Germany. Covariates used in the estimation consist of personal characteristics (sex, age, years of education, health status and migrant status), household characteristics (household type, a dummy for the presence of a child aged six years or younger in the household and household size) and partner characteristics (age, years of education, health status and migrant status).[23] In the specification for the full sample, I control for region of residence using a dummy variable for Eastern Germany. I moreover include a variable measuring the annual state-level unemployment rate in all specifications to capture regional and time differences in the economic environment.

To address the endogeneity of initial conditions, I include in all specifications as 'Wooldridge controls' the receipt status in the initial period y_{i0} as well as time averages of the different family-type variables, the dummy for individuals living in a household with a child aged under six years, household size, the respondent's and her partner's health status and the regional unemployment rate.

The division of the sample into Western and Eastern Germany is based on residence in the initial period in which an individual is observed. This is meant to help avoid possible endogeneities that might arise as sample members move from one part of the country to another although such moves are infrequent.[24]

The Evidence for State Dependence

Results from the standard version of the dynamic random-effects probit model described in the previous section indicate that there is considerable state dependence in social assistance benefit receipt in Germany. Column 1 of Table 2, which gives coefficient estimates, shows that the coefficient of the lagged dependent variable is positive and strongly significant for the full sample. Table 3 presents the corresponding average predicted transition rates: I calculate an average predicted entry rate of 5.4 per cent and an average predicted persistence rate of 18.4 per cent. The resulting APE is 13.0 percentage points.

The result implies that even after controlling for observed and persistent unobserved characteristics, an individual in the sample is on average 13 percentage points more likely to report benefit receipt at the current interview if she already received benefit payments at the last interview. This corresponds to an increase in the probability of benefit receipt by a factor of 3.4 as indicated by the PPR. While an APE of 13 percentage points is substantial, the value is considerably lower than the difference between observed persistence and entry rates of about 65 percentage points as shown in Fig. 2. Most of the 'raw' state dependence is thus due to observed and unobserved heterogeneity across individuals.

Results for Western and Eastern Germany (Columns 2 and 3 of Tables 2 and 3) show strong disparities in average predicted transition rates but relatively similar levels of state dependence in absolute terms. Coefficient estimates for the lagged dependent variable are significantly positive again in both subsamples. Average predicted entry and persistence rates for Western Germany are very close to, but lower than, those for the full sample. For Eastern Germany, both predicted entry and persistence rates are substantially higher as one would expect given the much higher regional unemployment rates. State dependence in Western and Eastern Germany is comparable when measured in absolute terms at 13.5 percentage points in Western Germany and 15.2 percentage points in Eastern Germany. In relative terms, the effect of past benefit receipt is however much stronger for Western Germany where receipt rates are much lower: The PPR implies that benefit receipt at the time of the last interview raises the likelihood of benefit receipt at the current interview by a factor of 4.2 for Western Germany compared to 2.2 in Eastern Germany.

A methodological point worth mentioning is that predicted transition rates for Western and Eastern Germany are *within-sample* predictions in the sense that they have been calculated for the respective subsamples used for estimation rather than over all individuals in Eastern and Western Germany combined. A disadvantage of this approach is arguably that results are less comparable, as − due to the non-linearity of the model − they depend on the distributions of observable characteristics in the

Table 2.   Baseline Specifications − Coefficient Estimates.

	Full Sample	Western Germany	Eastern Germany
y_{t-1}	1.160*** (0.029)	1.259*** (0.036)	0.977*** (0.048)
Individual characteristics			
Female	−0.004 (0.029)	−0.010 (0.033)	0.023 (0.057)
Age	−0.078*** (0.013)	−0.077*** (0.015)	−0.080*** (0.025)
Age^2	0.088*** (0.015)	0.087*** (0.017)	0.089*** (0.029)
Years of education	−0.293*** (0.042)	−0.252*** (0.045)	−0.725*** (0.127)
Years of education^2	0.007*** (0.002)	0.006*** (0.002)	0.021*** (0.005)
Good health	−0.060** (0.028)	−0.070** (0.034)	−0.027 (0.051)
Poor health	0.080** (0.035)	0.097** (0.041)	0.020 (0.066)
Migrant	0.268*** (0.045)	0.261*** (0.046)	0.263 (0.186)
Household characteristics			
Single, with children	0.029 (0.064)	0.100 (0.082)	−0.043 (0.104)
Couple, no children	0.061 (0.073)	0.095 (0.089)	0.022 (0.132)
Couple, with children	−0.076 (0.075)	−0.061 (0.092)	−0.047 (0.131)
Child ≤ 6 years	0.096** (0.039)	0.166*** (0.045)	−0.083 (0.076)
Household size	0.062*** (0.022)	0.047* (0.026)	0.108** (0.043)
Partner characteristics			
Age	−0.018*** (0.004)	−0.016*** (0.005)	−0.021*** (0.008)
Age^2	0.022*** (0.007)	0.020*** (0.008)	0.026* (0.013)
Years of education	0.056*** (0.012)	0.046*** (0.014)	0.086*** (0.025)
Years of education^2	−0.005*** (0.001)	−0.004*** (0.001)	−0.006*** (0.001)
Good health	0.003 (0.031)	0.002 (0.038)	0.018 (0.057)
Poor health	0.155*** (0.041)	0.175*** (0.048)	0.097 (0.076)
Migrant	0.163*** (0.048)	0.163*** (0.049)	0.504** (0.201)
Calendar-year effects			
1997	−0.116** (0.055)	0.061 (0.064)	−0.525*** (0.108)
1998	0.039 (0.058)	0.097 (0.070)	0.049 (0.114)
1999	−0.100* (0.057)	−0.016 (0.068)	−0.155 (0.115)
2000	−0.076 (0.058)	−0.100 (0.070)	0.057 (0.111)
2001	−0.083 (0.052)	−0.108* (0.062)	0.066 (0.104)
2002	−0.081 (0.053)	−0.130** (0.065)	0.114 (0.106)
2003	0.097* (0.053)	0.068 (0.063)	0.278*** (0.107)
2004	0.080 (0.055)	0.054 (0.065)	0.316*** (0.115)
2005	0.129** (0.056)	0.169*** (0.065)	0.229** (0.116)
2006	0.190*** (0.060)	0.195*** (0.075)	0.410*** (0.118)
2007	−0.018 (0.058)	0.043 (0.071)	−0.005 (0.111)
2008	0.049 (0.057)	0.015 (0.069)	0.134 (0.105)
2009	0.136** (0.060)	0.158** (0.072)	0.019 (0.111)
2010	0.155** (0.063)	0.095 (0.076)	0.208* (0.115)
2011	0.084 (0.068)	0.108 (0.080)	−0.084 (0.130)

Table 2.   *(Continued)*

	Full Sample	Western Germany	Eastern Germany
Wooldridge controls			
y_0	1.268*** (0.048)	1.222*** (0.059)	1.335*** (0.086)
Avg: good health	−0.110** (0.055)	−0.080 (0.066)	−0.192* (0.103)
Avg: poor health	0.308*** (0.071)	0.332*** (0.083)	0.217 (0.143)
Avg: single, with children	0.304*** (0.093)	0.245** (0.113)	0.392** (0.173)
Avg: couple, no children	−0.360*** (0.090)	−0.447*** (0.108)	−0.250 (0.167)
Avg: couple, with children	−0.267*** (0.098)	−0.358*** (0.116)	−0.107 (0.187)
Avg: child ≤6 years	0.267*** (0.064)	0.192*** (0.073)	0.525*** (0.133)
Avg: household size	0.059** (0.028)	0.086*** (0.032)	−0.030 (0.058)
Avg: reg. unemployment rate	0.024** (0.010)	0.042** (0.018)	0.005 (0.017)
Avg: good health (partner)	−0.096* (0.057)	−0.024 (0.068)	−0.227** (0.107)
Avg: poor health (partner)	0.209*** (0.079)	0.260*** (0.092)	0.115 (0.161)
Reg. unemployment rate	0.037*** (0.009)	0.021 (0.017)	0.007 (0.016)
Eastern Germany	0.247*** (0.056)		
Constant	0.923** (0.375)	0.549 (0.423)	5.096*** (0.998)
σ_a	0.831*** (0.025)	0.773*** (0.030)	0.959*** (0.047)
ρ	0.409*** (0.014)	0.374*** (0.018)	0.479*** (0.025)
Log-likelihood	−14,538.474	−9,671.444	−4,776.992
No. of observations	100,434	79,790	20,644
No. of individuals	17,733	14,010	3,723

$*p < 0.10, **p < 0.05, ***p < 0.01.$

Notes: Standard errors are given in parentheses. y_{t-1} and y_0 are the observed social assistance receipt status in the last period and the initial observed period, respectively. All other covariates with the exception of calendar-year dummies are lagged by one period. 'Avg:' denotes an individual's longitudinal average of a variable. Values of age^2 have been scaled through division by 100. The breakdown of the sample into Western and Eastern Germany is based on region of residence in an individual's initial observed period.
Source: SOEP (2011).

Table 3.   Baseline Specifications − Predicted Transition Rates, APE and PPR.

	Full Sample	Western Germany	Eastern Germany
Average predicted entry rate in %	5.4 (0.2)	4.2 (0.1)	12.3 (0.6)
Average predicted persistence rate in %	18.4 (0.7)	17.7 (0.9)	27.5 (1.2)
Average partial effect (in ppts)	13.0 (0.7)	13.5 (0.9)	15.2 (1.3)
Predicted probability ratio (in ppts)	3.4 (0.2)	4.2 (0.3)	2.2 (0.1)

Notes: Calculations are based on the coefficient estimates presented in Table 2. All averages have been calculated using individual cross-sectional sampling weights. Standard errors in parenthesis were obtained by bootstrapping with 100 replications. Results for Western and Eastern Germany are *within-sample* predictions.
Source: SOEP (2011).

two subsamples. The reason why I have nonetheless opted for this approach is that results by region can straightforwardly be interpreted as the decomposition of the results for the full sample. By contrast, I found that *out-of-sample* predictions can give very counter-intuitive results. In particular, predicted transition rates calculated over all individuals in the full sample were higher when based on coefficient estimates obtained for either the Western or the Eastern German subsample than when based on estimates from a specification run on the two subsamples combined.

The relations between individual-, household- and partner-level characteristics and the likelihood of benefit receipt tend to have the direction one would assume. Coefficient estimates for Western and Eastern Germany are generally similar with larger standard errors for Eastern Germany as a result of the lower sample size. I therefore limit the discussion to estimates for the full sample.

Starting with the individual-level explanatory variables, a surprising finding is that, *ceteris paribus*, the sex of the respondent does not seem to be related to the risk of benefit receipt as indicated by the insignificant coefficient on the female dummy.[25] The effect of age on the outcome variable is u-shaped with a minimum at age 44 implying that young adults and older individuals have a higher probability of benefit receipt. Education is associated negatively with social assistance receipt at a slightly diminishing rate for higher years of education as suggested by the positive coefficient on the quadratic term (the minimum is at about 21 years of education). As one would expect, poor health is associated with a higher probability of benefit receipt and healthier individuals are less likely to receive benefits. Even after controlling for personal characteristics, first- or second-generation migrants are significantly more likely to receive social assistance than natives.

The first impression from a look at the coefficients of the household-level characteristics may be that these variables are not strongly associated with benefit receipt, since for instance the coefficients of all family-type variables are statistically insignificant. This result may however primarily reflect insufficient time variation in those variables over the observation period. The time averages of these variables among the Wooldridge controls are statistically significant: Living in a couple (with or without children) is associated with a lower probability of benefit receipt and being a single parent is associated with a higher likelihood of benefit receipt (both compared to the base category singles without children). These findings however have to be interpreted with care, because the time averages were only included in the specification to capture persistent differences in unobserved factors that they might be correlated with. Both household size and the dummy variable for a child aged six years and younger in the household enter positively. This might reflect the greater generosity of the means test for larger households.

Also the partner's characteristics appear very relevant for determining an individual's social assistance receipt. The variable controlling for the partner's age displays a profile similar to that of the respondent with the size of the effect falling until age 41 and rising thereafter. There is again a negative relationship between the partner's education and the likelihood of benefit receipt, with additional education reducing the risk of benefit receipt at an increasing rate. Finally, respondents whose partner suffers from poor health and those with a migrant partner are more likely to receive benefits.

Further down in Table 2, the coefficient estimate for the state-level unemployment rate indicates that living in a region with higher unemployment is associated with a higher likelihood of benefit receipt. The positive coefficient of the dummy for residence in Eastern Germany implies that even once socio-economic characteristics and the state-level unemployment rate are controlled for, the probability of benefit receipt is higher for individuals living in the east.

The model captures time trends in benefit receipt during the observation period using year dummy variables as covariates (the reference year is 1996). The large majority of year coefficients in the model is insignificant, which suggests that the model does relatively well at explaining the time trends observed in the fourth section. I obtain significantly positive coefficient estimates for the years 2005 and 2006, which indicates *ceteris paribus* a higher probability of social assistance receipt in the years directly after implementation of the Hartz reforms. Yet, this rise in the probability of benefit receipt is transitory as the estimated coefficients for the years 2007 and 2008 are very close to zero again and statistically insignificant. The coefficient estimates for the years 2009 and 2010 are positive and significant suggesting a higher probability of benefit receipt during the economic crisis. While a negative coefficient estimate is observed for the year 1997, there does not appear to be a clear time trend or any systematic difference in the probability of benefit receipt before and after the Hartz reforms.

Time Variation in State Dependence

The results presented thus far suggest that social assistance benefit receipt in Germany is characterized by a substantial degree of state dependence. As outlined in the third section, the institutional framework for the provision of minimum-income benefits in Germany underwent a major reform during the observation period. Since one explicit aim of these reforms was to strengthen the activating elements in social assistance, an interesting question is whether based on the models I can find any evidence for changes in the degree of state dependence around the time of the Hartz reforms.

I start my analysis of time variation in state dependence by explicitly comparing the periods before and after the Hartz reforms. For this purpose, I estimate the model described in Eq. (6), which interacts the lagged dependent variable and all covariates with a dummy variable for the post-Hartz years. Table 4 presents average predicted persistence and entry rates derived from this model for the two periods. Coefficient estimates are reported in Table A1 in the Appendix but are not discussed in detail.

Estimation results show an increase in state dependence from the pre-Hartz to the post-Hartz period. Average predicted entry rates into benefits

Table 4. Pre- versus Post-Hartz Variation in State Dependence.

	1996–2004	2005–2011	Δ
Full sample			
Average predicted entry rate in %	5.2 (0.2)	6.2 (0.2)	1.0*** (0.2)
Average predicted persistence rate in %	16.6 (0.7)	20.2 (1.0)	3.6*** (0.9)
Average partial effect	11.5 (0.7)	14.0 (0.9)	2.6*** (0.9)
Predicted probability ratio	3.2 (0.2)	3.3 (0.2)	0.0 (0.2)
Western Germany			
Average predicted entry rate in %	3.9 (0.2)	4.7 (0.2)	0.8*** (0.2)
Average predicted persistence rate in %	16.3 (0.9)	18.8 (1.2)	2.5** (1.2)
Average partial effect	12.4 (0.9)	14.0 (1.2)	1.7 (1.2)
Predicted probability ratio	4.5 (0.3)	4.3 (0.3)	−0.2 (0.3)
Eastern Germany			
Average predicted entry rate in %	12.0 (0.6)	13.8 (0.8)	1.8*** (0.7)
Average predicted persistence rate in %	24.8 (1.3)	30.8 (1.9)	6.1*** (2.0)
Average partial effect	12.7 (1.4)	17.0 (1.8)	4.3** (1.9)
Predicted probability ratio	2.1 (0.1)	2.2 (0.2)	0.2 (0.2)

$*p < 0.10$, $**p < 0.05$, $***p < 0.01$.

Notes: Calculations are based on the coefficient estimates presented in Table A1 in the Appendix. Δ gives the change between columns 1 and 2. All averages have been calculated using individual cross-sectional sampling weights. Standard errors in parenthesis were obtained by bootstrapping with 100 replications. Results for Western and Eastern Germany are *within-sample* predictions.

Source: SOEP (2011).

for the full sample increase by 1 percentage point from 1996–2004 to 2005–2011, with the effect being slightly lower in Western Germany (0.8 ppts) and larger in Eastern Germany (1.8 ppts). Average predicted persistence rates rise by 3.6 percentage points (2.5 ppts in Western Germany, 6.1 ppts in Eastern Germany). The implied APE rises by 2.6 percentage points for the full sample, by (insignificant) 1.7 percentage points in Western Germany and by 4.3 percentage points in Eastern Germany. Measured in relative terms, state dependence by contrast remained stable with the change in PPRs being statistically different from zero in none of the three samples. The predicted increase in state dependence for the full sample described in Table 4 is entirely due to a change in the coefficient estimates of the covariates, in particular the intercept term. Unlike for Eastern Germany, the coefficient estimate of the lagged dependent variable does not vary over time in the specification for the full sample as illustrated by the insignificant interaction term between the lagged dependent variable and the post-Hartz dummy reported in Table A1. The increase in state dependence in the data is thus entirely captured by the non-linearity of the model. This non-linearity means that changes in the effect of observable characteristics and the intercept term indirectly affect the impact of the lagged dependent variable and thus the estimated degree of state dependence. When using a non-linear model to evaluate changes in state dependence over time by interacting the lagged dependent variable with a time dummy, it is thus not sufficient to focus alone on the significance of the interaction term if the model also includes a time trend.

To assess whether the increase in state dependence over the observation period indeed happened around the time of the Hartz reforms, I estimate the alternative specification described by Eq. (7). This model allows the coefficient of the lagged dependent variable to vary on a year-by-year basis while restricting the coefficients of all covariates to be constant over time. The latter simplification however does not appear too problematic given that in the model with the post-Hartz interactions most of the time variation in benefit dynamics was due to a change in the intercept term (see the coefficient estimates presented in Table A1 in the Appendix). Fig. 3 plots the predicted yearly average entry and persistence rates (in the panels on the left) and the year-by-year time variation in the APEs compared to the initial year 1996 (on the right). Coefficient estimates for the specification are reported in Table A2 in the Appendix.

The upper two panels show changes in predicted transition rates and state dependence for the full sample. I find that entry rates in benefit receipt are very stable over time at around 5 per cent per year with rises to 6 per cent in 2005–2006 and 2010–2011. The average predicted persistence

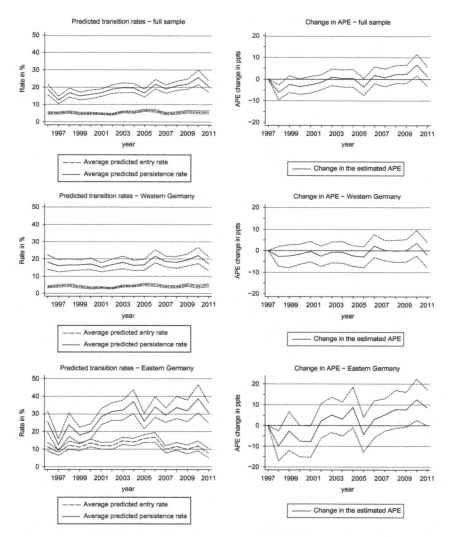

Fig. 3. Year-by-Year Variation in State Dependence. *Notes*: Calculations are based on the coefficient estimates presented in Table A2. The left panels show year-by-year averages of predicted benefit persistence and entry rates. The right panels show the change in the annual APE compared to the one in the initial year 1996. The dotted lines give the 95% confidence intervals. All averages have been calculated using individual cross-sectional sampling weights. Standard errors were obtained by bootstrapping with 100 replications. Results for Western and Eastern Germany are within-sample predictions. *Source*: SOEP (2011).

rate drops from 19 per cent in 1996 to below 13 per cent in 1997, but then starts rising to reach 20 per cent in 2003 and to peak at 26 per cent in 2010.

The top-right panel plots the variation in the APE with respect to the reference year 1996, i.e. the difference in the vertical distance between average predicted persistence and entry rates in the given year compared to that in the initial year of the observation period. As one would expect from looking at the top-left panel, the level of estimated state dependence is lowest in 1997 and then slowly starts to rise eventually peaking in 2010. The annual APE is however statistically different from the one measured in the initial year 1996 only in 1997 (when it is significantly lower) and in 2010 (when it is significantly greater). A negative blip in the change in APEs for the year 2005 is just on the border of being statistically significant.

The corresponding graphs for Western Germany − shown in the middle two panels − offer few additional insights. As observed for other specifications, average predicted persistence and entry rates are very similar to those for the full sample. The same is consequently true also for the year-to-year variations in the APEs, now however with none of the annual APEs calculated being significantly different from the one for the initial period.

Time variation in predicted transition rates appears to be stronger for Eastern Germany (bottom two panels). Results are however less easy to interpret due to the much smaller sample size and thus much wider confidence bands. Predicted benefit persistence rates are initially only slightly higher than for Western Germany however rise strongly in the early 2000s. They remain relatively stable over the second part of the observation period at around 30−35 per cent with a one-year drop in 2005. Predicted entry rates are about twice as high as for Western Germany, appear to rise through the early- and mid-2000s, but then drop substantially after the Hartz reforms from around 17 per cent in 2006 to 10 per cent in 2007.

Estimated year-by-year changes in APEs are much more pronounced in Eastern Germany. The APE appears to be around 5 percentage points lower than in the initial period in the late 1990s and around 5 percentage points higher than in the initial period from 2001. I moreover again find a strong drop in the APE for the year 2005 and a rise up to around 10 per cent for the final years of the observation period. Because of very wide confidence intervals, however, only the drops in the APE for the years 1997 and 2000 and the increase for the year 2010 are statistically significant at the 5 per cent level.

Overall, I conclude based on the model estimates that there is no evidence for a change in state dependence around the time of the Hartz reforms possibly except for a one-time drop in 2005. A specification that interacts the lagged dependent variable and all regressors with a dummy for the post-Hartz years shows that state dependence over the years 2005–2011 was 2.6 percentage points higher compared to the years 1996–2004. Allowing for year-by-year changes in state dependence however suggests that this effect is due to lower state dependence in the late 1990s and stronger state dependence during the crisis years in Eastern Germany. State dependence in Western Germany shows no significant time variation. More generally, the magnitude of estimated state dependence appears to be positively associated with benefit receipt rates being relatively low in the 1990s and increasing along with rising receipt rates from 2001 onwards. Most of these variations however do not reach statistical significance.

The Sensitivity of Results to Changes in the Methodology

The finding of positive state dependence in social assistance receipt confirms similar results from comparable earlier studies for other countries. The APE of 13 percentage points reported in Table 3 is relatively close for instance to the value of 14.4 percentage points estimated by Cappellari and Jenkins (2008) in their analysis for Britain with the same methodology. The findings just reported by contrast differ surprisingly from those presented by Wunder and Riphahn (2014) and Riphahn and Wunder (2013) in two recent papers on state dependence in social assistance receipt for Germany.

Using SOEP data for the years 2005–2009, Wunder and Riphahn (2014) estimate a dynamic multinomial logit model of transitions between receipt of 'welfare' benefits (UBII), employment and 'inactivity' (which they define as including unemployment).[26] They find evidence of structural state dependence in all three states modelled, the effect size however is much smaller than the one reported in this article. For natives, the authors calculate a predicted persistence rate in welfare of 3.1 per cent and predicted entry rates into welfare of 1.6 per cent from inactivity and of 0.5 per cent from employment. For immigrants, the predicted persistence rate is 9.0 per cent, compared to an entry rate of 3.8 per cent from inactivity and of 1.8 per cent from employment. The partial effect of past welfare receipt on welfare receipt in the current period lies thus between 1.5 and 2.6 percentage points for natives and between 5.2 and 7.2 percentage points for immigrants (Wunder & Riphahn, 2014, Table 5).[27] Since moreover exit rates to employment are higher from welfare than from inactivity for both natives and immigrants, they conclude that there is no evidence of a 'welfare trap'.

Table 5. The Impact of Sample Selection and the Definition of the Benefit Variable on Estimated state Dependence.

	Standard Sample, 2005–2009			Restricted Sample, 2005–2009		
	Entry rate in %	Persistence rate in %	APE in ppts	Entry rate in %	Persistence rate in %	APE in ppts
Benefit variable defined at the						
Household level	6.0 (0.4)	14.2 (1.4)	8.3 (1.5)	3.5 (0.5)	8.7 (1.5)	5.2 (1.7)
Individual level	4.5 (0.4)	9.0 (1.1)	4.6 (1.2)	2.7 (0.5)	5.6 (1.6)	2.9 (1.8)
No. of individuals		6,769			4,083	
No. of observations		22,289			13,249	

Notes: The standard sample is defined using the sample selection criteria outlined in the third section. The 'restricted' sample excludes individuals who live in Eastern Germany, disabled individuals and first- or second-generation migrants. The benefit variable measures receipt of UBII. For the household-level definition, I categorize an individual as a recipient if benefit payments are recorded for any member of the household; for the individual-level definition, I only use information on benefit receipt reported in the personal questionnaire. Standard errors in parentheses have been obtained from bootstrapping with 100 replications. Coefficient estimates are not reported but available from the author upon request.
Source: SOEP (2011).

One difference between my study and the one by Wunder and Riphahn is methodological. While the analysis presented in this article is based on a binary dynamic probit model, Wunder and Riphahn estimate a more complex dynamic multinomial logit model that distinguishes between inactivity and employment among non-recipients of welfare benefits. A second important difference lies in sample selection and in the way the benefit variable is defined. Wunder and Riphahn limit their attention to receipt of post-Hartz UBII and the years 2005–2009. They further restrict their analysis to Western Germany and drop individuals with a disability from the sample. Finally, Wunder and Riphahn define benefit receipt at the *individual* level using only information from the respondent's personal questionnaire. This approach is different from the one taken in this study (and in most of the related literature) of defining social assistance receipt at the *household* level.

To assess the reason for the difference in findings between the two studies, I use my simpler model described in Eq. (2) to study the UBII receipt dynamics for the years 2005–2009 only. I then vary the way of defining the benefit variable (household- versus individual-level definition) and the estimation sample (standard sample versus restricted sample of natives in Western Germany without disability).[28] The results of this exercise are presented in Table 5.

The level of estimated state dependence in benefit receipt is sensitive to both the approach used for defining the benefit variable and the sample selection criteria. For the standard sample and the household-level definition of the benefit variable, I calculate an APE of 8.3 percentage points. The disparity between this value and the much higher 13 percentage points reported for the standard specification in Table 3 reflects the lower rate of benefit receipt once SA and HB are no longer considered. Switching from the household-level to the individual-level definition of the benefit variable then reduces this APE by nearly half to 4.6 percentage points. The restriction of the sample to natives without disability in Western Germany leads to a further reduction in estimated state dependence. For the household-level definition, the estimated APE declines from 8.3 to 5.2 percentage points; for the specification that uses the individual-level benefit variable, the APE drops from 4.6 to 2.9 percentage points. This APE of 2.9 percentage points is very close to the 1.5 to 2.6 percentage points reported by Wunder and Riphahn for a similar sample and definition of the benefit variable. The APE is moreover no longer significantly different from zero even at the 10 per cent level (*t*-value of 1.62).

In a recent follow-up study, Riphahn and Wunder (2013) extend their earlier analysis to cover the pre-Hartz years 2001–2004. They again estimate a dynamic multinomial logit model with the same three competing states. For the years prior to the reforms, the state 'welfare' now consists of UA or SA receipt. Unlike in their previous study, where they used information on an individual's benefit receipt from the personal questionnaires only, Riphahn and Wunder now use only the information on benefit receipt from the household questionnaire. They then go on to model the benefit transitions of the household head (but not of the other family members). The sample is again restricted to non-disabled individuals in Western Germany. As in their previous study, they obtain a much lower degree of state dependence, with a partial effect in the post-reform years of 2.5–4.4 percentage points for natives and of 3.9–7.5 percentage points for immigrants. State dependence in welfare receipt appears to be somewhat higher during the immediate pre-reform years, but it is not obvious whether this effect is statistically significant (Riphahn & Wunder, 2013, Table 5).

Using again my simpler dynamic probit model from Eq. (2), I find that Riphahn and Wunder's focus on the benefit transitions of the household head alone has little effect on estimated state dependence in the binary case. Instead, lower levels of state dependence reported in their paper may again be due to sample selection and a subtle difference in the definition of the household-level benefit receipt variable. While Riphahn and Wunder use information on benefit receipt from the household questionnaire only, I also take into account the responses provided by each of the household members in their personal questionnaires (see endnote 10). As it turns out, for about 10 per cent of the households in which UBII receipt is reported by at least one of the household members in their personal questionnaires, no benefit receipt is recorded in the household questionnaire. I find that coding these households as non-recipient households and further restricting the sample to non-disabled natives in Western Germany induces a drop in the APE from 9.1 to 2.9 percentage points for the post-Hartz years (*not shown*). This is again much in line with the 2.5–4.4 percentage points reported by Riphahn and Wunder.

Overall, these robustness checks confirm that while the conclusions differ, the results presented in this article and in the studies by Wunder and Riphahn (2014) and Riphahn and Wunder (2013) can easily be reconciled. In particular, Riphahn and Wunder's finding of only very weak state dependence appears to be due to their focus on able-bodied individuals in Western Germany only and the choices they make when defining the social assistance benefit variable. As outlined in the third section, I believe that there are good reasons to define a social assistance benefit variable at the household level. In this case, it also seems justified to take into account all the information provided by the respondents in a household via the household questionnaire and the responses given in the personal questionnaires. Yet, there is no easy way of telling whether a benefit variable that uses information from only one of two sources really underestimates benefit receipt. If benefit receipt is misreported in some of the individual questionnaires, combining data from individual and household questionnaires might even lead to an overestimate of receipt rates and hence likely also of state dependence.

For the analysis presented in this article, this issue is arguably of lesser importance: UBII is only one of three benefit programmes considered for constructing the social assistance variable, and no information on receipt of SA or HB is provided in the personal questionnaires. Consequently, I find that using Riphahn and Wunder's approach to defining UBII receipt hardly affects the results presented above for a broader definition of the social assistance variable. More generally, the exercise presented in this section however highlights the strong sensitivity of estimation results to the way the benefit variable is defined. Researchers should therefore be very clear in stating what type of information they use for constructing the benefit variable, and potential methodological differences should be taken into account whenever results are compared across studies.

CONCLUSION

In this article, I have studied state dependence in social assistance benefit receipt in Germany using annual data from the German Socio-Economic Panel (SOEP) for the years 1995–2011. Estimating a series of dynamic random-effects probit models that control for observed and persistent unobserved heterogeneity, I found evidence of substantial structural state dependence: Benefit receipt at the last interview is on average associated with a rise in the likelihood of benefit receipt at the current interview by 13 percentage points. This corresponds to an increase by a factor of 3.4. Predicted benefit entry and persistence rates and the resulting absolute level of state dependence are higher in Eastern Germany than in Western Germany. Large disparities between observed and estimated structural state dependence however illustrate that individual characteristics are the most important determinant of benefit transitions.

An analysis of variations in state dependence over the observation period does not provide evidence of a difference in patterns before and after the Hartz reforms. A simple comparison of the periods 1996–2004 and 2005–2011 suggests that estimated state dependence was 2.6 percentage points higher in the years after the Hartz reforms than in the years before. However, looking at year-to-year changes in state dependence, I found that this effect is likely driven by a period of lower state dependence in the late 1990s and a spike in state dependence in Eastern Germany in 2010. In none of the other years, the level of state dependence was significantly different from that in the initial year 1996.

A methodological insight from this article is that the magnitude of estimated state dependence can be sensitive to the method used for constructing the benefit variable. For the means-tested UBII that was introduced by the Hartz reforms, I showed that defining the benefit variable at the individual rather than at the household level can lead to substantially lower estimated state dependence. Apparent inconsistencies between the information provided in household and personal questionnaires also affect the level of estimated state dependence. An implication of these findings is that my results can be reconciled with those reported in two recent studies by Wunder and Riphahn (2014) and Riphahn and Wunder (2013), who – based on a slightly different methodological approach – find little evidence for state dependence in UBII receipt in post-Hartz Western Germany.

The policy implications of these findings depend much on what assumptions one makes about likely sources of structural state dependence in social assistance. The results presented in this article are consistent with 'scarring' effects in social assistance that might arise if benefit receipt affects an individual's job-search behaviour or reservation wages. In this case, it is somewhat surprising that the analysis does not show a decline in the level of state dependence following the Hartz reforms. While clearly, the model estimated in this article is not suited to identify the causal effects of a policy change, one might have expected the level of state dependence to fall with the introduction of stronger job search requirements and increased incentives to take up work.

A potential explanation for the lack of measurable time variation in state dependence might be that the effect of the Hartz reforms varies by recipient group. For instance, state dependence might have declined for employable benefit recipients for whom the benefit system got less generous as they were moved from UA to UBII; no such effect might in contrast exist for those judged unable to work who received SA after the reforms. The number of recipient households in the SOEP however is too low to permit splitting the analysis by benefit programme. Separate analyses for women and men and for natives and migrants gave no evidence of time variation in state dependence for any of these groups (Königs, 2013). A point worth noting is moreover that the partial effects reported in this article are (sub)sample averages and might well differ from the effect on the 'treated' group of benefit recipients.

A different reason for why even a successful policy reform might not translate into a decline in state dependence is that it might lower both benefit entry and persistence rates, for instance as benefit generosity is reduced. Since state dependence is calculated as the difference between predicted persistence and entry rates, such a reform might not at all affect the level of state dependence. In Eastern Germany, average predicted entry rates into social assistance seem to have fallen after the Hartz reforms, while average predicted persistence rates remained relatively stable, inducing an increase in state dependence (though most of these changes were not statistically significant). A policy reform that works by keeping individuals off benefits rather than by promoting exits might thus even induce greater state dependence.

Finally, it remains unclear whether the measured state dependence in benefit receipt indeed reflects the properties of the benefit system as opposed to labour market and income dynamics more broadly. Contini and Negri (2007) for instance highlight that measured state dependence in social assistance might in reality be driven by persistence in unemployment or the detrimental effects of living in poverty. Unfortunately, little empirical evidence exists about the drivers of state dependence in social assistance, and this study is not well suited to provide any insights on this question. In the absence of (quasi-)experimental evidence, models of labour market transitions of the type used by Riphahn and Wunder that distinguish a greater number of different states may allow to shed further light on this issue.

NOTES

1. A few studies look at the related question of duration dependence in social assistance receipt using event-history models, see for instance Dahl and Lorentzen (2013) for Norway and Mood (2013) for Sweden or Schels (2013) for Germany.

2. Other studies use panel data methods to examine the determinants of social assistance receipt in Germany without looking at state dependence (Riphahn, 2004; Riphahn, Sander, & Wunder, 2013; Schels, 2013). For cross-sectional analyses of the determinants of social assistance benefit receipt in Germany, see Voges and Rohwer (1992) or Riphahn and Wunder (2012). Mühleisen and Zimmermann (1994) study state dependence in unemployment.

3. The new legislation was formally labelled 'laws for modern services on the labour market' (*Gesetze für moderne Dienstleistungen am Arbeitsmarkt*) and was subdivided into four packages, which were enacted sequentially in the years 2003 ('Hartz I & II'), 2004 ('Hartz III') and 2005 ('Hartz IV').

4. The maximum duration of benefit entitlements was 12–32 months depending on age and the previous contribution history, with the relevant thresholds changing over the observation period. Benefit levels were determined by a replacement rate of 60 per cent of previous earnings net of taxes and social-security contributions (67 per cent for individuals with children) and were independent of individual means.

5. Until the end of the year 1999, individuals could claim UA without having previously received UI under the condition that they had worked for at least 150 days over the last 12 months. From 2000, receipt of UA benefits was restricted to individuals who had exhausted their claims for UI. Replacement rates were 53 per cent (57 per cent for individuals with children).

6. Throughout this article, I distinguish between the concept 'social assistance' (noncapitalized) and the benefit programme 'Social Assistance' (SA, *Sozialhilfe*, in capital letters).

7. The maximum period of benefit entitlements remained 12–32 month depending on age until a year after the reforms. In 2006, it was lowered to 18 months but raised again to 24 months in 2008. The replacement rate remained at 60 per cent (67 per cent for individuals with children).

8. Earlier studies of immigrant–native differences in social assistance benefit receipt by Riphahn and Wunder (2012, 2013) and Riphahn, Sander, and Wunder (2013) also looked at UA, UBII and SA jointly without however accounting for receipt of HB.

9. In the estimations, I need to assume independence across individuals. Strictly speaking, this assumption is violated if in each period, a household can be represented by several observations that by construction have the same social assistance receipt status. Like earlier authors, I ignore any potential inconsistencies induced by this lack of independence. In an earlier version of this article (Königs, 2013), I however show that results differ little when the sample is split between women and men, a case in which the independence assumption is arguably more credible.

10. Questions on the receipt of minimum-income benefits by any of the members of a household are included in the household questionnaire. For UBII, an additional question is included in the personal questionnaire that is completed by each working-age member of the household. For further information on the design of the SOEP, see the following section.

11. An alternative approach frequently used is to define a 'benefit year' by setting the binary social assistance variable equal to one if any positive amount of benefit

receipt is recorded during the calendar year. This method is convenient if data come from annual administrative records where information on the amount of benefits received is available but the exact timing of payments during the year is unknown (see Andrén & Andrén, 2013; Hansen & Lofstrom, 2008, 2011; Hansen et al., 2014).

12. In the years used for the analysis just below 80 per cent of interviews have been conducted in the months January to April.

13. The samples are labelled "Residents in the Federal Republic of Germany" (sample A), "Foreigners in the Federal Republic of Germany" (B), "German Residents in the German Democratic Republic" (C), "Immigrants" (D), "Refreshment" (E), "Innovation" (F), "High Income" (G) and "Refreshment" (H).

14. The motivation for dropping households with adult full-time students is to avoid having to deal with the labour market entry of these individuals. This criterion however concerns only few observations because it is applied after having removed dependent children and individuals below the age of 25 from the sample.

15. The version of the SOEP used for the analysis does not permit for a distinction between the two German states of Saarland and Rhineland-Palatinate in each of the years of the observation period. I therefore allocate a weighted average of the unemployment rates of these two federal states to all individuals living in either of these states.

16. Over the observation period, the average of the yearly unemployment rates was 8 per cent in Western Germany compared to 16 per cent in Eastern Germany (Bundesagentur für Arbeit, 2013).

17. An alternative specification of the model uses current values of the observable characteristics x_{it}. In using lagged values $x_{i(t-1)}$, I follow Cappellari and Jenkins (2014). The difference in results between the two approaches is however modest.

18. Stewart (2006, 2007) estimates a comparable model however allowing for serial correlation in the transitory shock; Biewen (2009) permits feedback effects between the outcome variables and some of the regressors in his model of poverty dynamics in Germany.

19. The earliest and most widely used approach is due to Heckman (1981b), who suggests approximating the unknown density of $y_{i0}|x_i$, α_i, to remove the conditioning on y_{i0}. A further approach proposed by Orme (2001) is used much less frequently in practice. Comparisons of the Heckman and Wooldridge estimators by Arulampalam and Stewart (2009) and Akay (2012) suggest that neither of them is strictly superior in terms of their finite-sample properties. Cappellari and Jenkins (2008) compare all three approaches in their analysis of social assistance benefit dynamics in Britain and find that they give nearly identical results.

20. Rabe-Hesketh and Skrondal (2013) warn that especially in short panels this simplification can lead to biased estimates. They suggest that also the initial values of all time-varying explanatory variables x_{i0} should be included in the model as regressors when the simplified Wooldridge approach is used. I have tested this alternative specification and found it to give nearly identical results, which is why I only report results for the simplified Wooldridge approach.

21. The same type of specification has previously been estimated by Cappellari and Jenkins (2008) in their analysis of social assistance dynamics in Britain.

22. More specifically, in the second model extension described by Eq. (7), the difference between the predicted entry rates in year τ and the initial year 1996 is captured by the time effect μ^τ, while the difference in predicted persistence rates between the two periods is captured by $\mu^\tau + \lambda^\tau$. The magnitude of the time variation in predicted persistence and entry rates (and the difference between the two) then depends on the values of the covariates and thus varies across individuals.

23. Partner characteristics are set equal to zero if the individual is single.

24. The proportion of individuals who move from Eastern to Western Germany is indeed slightly higher among social assistance recipients than among non-recipients. However, only about 0.6 per cent of sample members who live in Eastern Germany move to Western Germany in a given year, and only about 0.1 per cent migrate in the opposite direction. Benefit-induced migration within Germany is thus unlikely to be an important issue for the analysis.

25. For a detailed breakdown of the benefit dynamics by sex, see Königs (2013).

26. For individuals who receive welfare benefits while being employed or unemployed welfare receipt is defined as the overriding state.

27. They argue that the higher welfare entry rates from inactivity rather than those from employment should be used for assessing state dependence, because transitions from employment to welfare might be influenced more by employment protection legislation than by features of the welfare system. All their predicted transition rates have been calculated for a randomly selected individual, which the authors however show to yield a result similar to the average transition rate across all individuals.

28. As in Wunder and Riphahn (2014) 'natives' are defined as sample members who are not first- or second-generation immigrants irrespective of citizenship. I do not follow Wunder and Riphahn's sample selection criteria exactly in that the upper age threshold of 59 years I use is slightly lower than theirs of 65 years.

ACKNOWLEDGEMENT

This is a shortened and revised version of a study commissioned by the OECD (contract #68627, Königs, 2013). I would like to thank Tony Atkinson, Steve Bond, Stéphane Carcillo, Patricia Gallego-Granados, Herwig Immervoll, Stephen P. Jenkins, Monika Queisser, Regina Riphahn, Kostas Tatsiramos, Christoph Wunder and two anonymous referees for helpful comments. The article has moreover benefited from the feedback I received at the joint OECD/IZA/World Bank workshop on Social Safety Nets and Benefit Dependence in Paris in May 2013. Financial support provided through the INET grant INO1200010 by the Institute for New Economic Thinking at the Oxford Martin School is gratefully acknowledged. The usual disclaimer applies. In particular, the views expressed in this article do not represent the official positions of the OECD or the governments of OECD member countries.

REFERENCES

Akay, A. (2012). Finite-sample comparison of alternative methods for estimating dynamic panel data models. *Journal of Applied Econometrics, 27*(7), 1189–1204.

Andrén, T., & Andrén, D. (2013). Never give up? The persistence of welfare participation in Sweden. *IZA Journal of European Labor Studies, 2*(1), 1–21.

Arulampalam, W., & Stewart, M. B. (2009). Simplified implementation of the Heckman estimator of the dynamic probit model and a comparison with alternative estimators. *Oxford Bulletin of Economics and Statistics, 71*(5), 659–681.

Bane, M. J., & Ellwood, D. T. (1994). Understanding welfare dynamics. In M. J. Bane & D. T. Ellwood (Eds.), *Welfare realities: From rhetoric to reform* (pp. 28–66). Cambridge, MA: Harvard University Press.

Biewen, M. (2009). Measuring state dependence in individual poverty histories when there is feedback to employment status and household composition. *Journal of Applied Econometrics, 24*(7), 1095–1116.

Blank, R. M., & Ruggles, P. (1994). Short-term recidivism among public-assistance recipients. *The American Economic Review, 84*(2), 49–53.

Bundesagentur für Arbeit. (2013). Arbeitsmarkt in Zahlen: Monats/Jahreszahlen – Arbeitslosigkeit im Zeitverlauf, März 2013. Retrieved from http://statistik.arbeitsagen tur.de/Statischer-Content/Statistik-nach-Themen/Zeitreihen/Generische-Publikationen/ Arbeitslosigkeit-Deutschland-Zeitreihe.xls

Cappellari, L., & Jenkins, S. (2008). *The dynamics of social assistance receipt: Measurement and modelling issues, with an application to Britain.* OECD Social, Employment, and Migration Working Paper No. 67. OECD, Paris.

Cappellari, L., & Jenkins, S. P. (2014). The dynamics of social assistance benefit receipt in Britain. In S. Carcillo, H. Immervoll, S. P. Jenkins, S. Königs, & K. Tatsiramos (Eds.), *Safety nets and benefit dependence* (Vol. 39, Ch. 2, pp. 41–79). Research in Labor Economics. Bingley, UK: Emerald Group Publishing Limited.

Chamberlain, G. (1982). Multivariate regression models for panel data. *Journal of Econometrics, 18*(1), 5–46.

Chamberlain, G. (1984). Panel data. In Z. Griliches & M. D. Intriligator (Eds.), *Handbook of econometrics* (pp. 1247–1318). North-Holland: Elsevier Science Publishers.

Chay, K. Y., Hoynes, H., & Hyslop, D. (1999). A non-experimental analysis of 'true' state dependence in monthly welfare participation sequences. *American Statistical Association, 1999 Proceedings of the Business and Economic Statistics Section* (pp. 9–17).

Chay, K. Y., & Hyslop, D. R. (2014). Identification and estimation of dynamic binary response panel data models: Empirical evidence using alternative approaches. In S. Carcillo, H. Immervoll, S. P. Jenkins, S. Königs, & K. Tatsiramos (Eds.), *Safety nets and benefit dependence* (Vol. 39). Research in Labor Economics. Bingley, UK: Emerald Group Publishing Limited.

Contini, D., & Negri, N. (2007). Would declining exit rates from welfare provide evidence of welfare dependence in homogeneous environments? *European Sociological Review, 23*(1), 21–33.

Dahl, E., & Lorentzen, T. (2013). Explaining exit to work among social assistance recipients in Norway: Heterogeneity or dependency? *European Sociological Review, 19*(5), 519–536.

Finnie, R., & Irvine, I. (2008). *The welfare Enigma: Explaining the dramatic decline in Canadians' use of social assistance, 1993–2005*. C.D. Howe Institute Commentary, 267. Toronto, ON: C.D. Howe Institute.

Gong, X. (2004). *Transition patterns for the welfare reliance of low income mothers in Australia*. IZA Discussion Papers, 1047. Institute for the Study of Labor, Bonn.

Haisken-DeNew, J. P., & Frick, J. R., (Eds.). (2005). DTC – Desktop Companion to the German Socio-Economic Panel (SOEP). DIW Berlin.

Hansen, J., & Lofstrom, M. (2008). The dynamics of immigrant welfare and labor market behavior. *Journal of Population Economics, 22*(4), 941–970.

Hansen, J., & Lofstrom, M. (2011). Immigrant–native differences in welfare participation: The role of entry and exit rates. *Industrial Relations: A Journal of Economy and Society, 50*(3), 412–442.

Hansen, J., Lofstrom, M., Liu, X., & Zhang, X. (2014). State dependence in social assistance receipt in Canada. In S. Carcillo, H. Immervoll, S. P. Jenkins, S. Königs, & K. Tatsiramos (Eds.), *Safety nets and benefit dependence* (Vol. 39, Ch. 3, pp. 79–103). Research in Labor Economics. Bingley, UK: Emerald Group Publishing Limited.

Heckman, J. J. (1981a). Heterogeneity and state dependence. In S. Rosen (Ed.), *Studies in labor markets* (pp. 91–140). Chicago, IL: University of Chicago Press.

Heckman, J. J. (1981b). The incidental parameters problem and the problem of initial conditions in estimating a discrete time-discrete data stochastic process. In C. F. Manski & D. McFadden (Eds.), *Structural analysis of discrete data with econometric applications* (pp. 179–195). Cambridge, MA: The MIT Press.

Königs, S. (2013). *The dynamics of social assistance benefit receipt in Germany: State dependence before and after the Hartz reforms*. OECD Social, Employment, and Migration Working Paper No. 136. OECD, Paris.

Mood, C. (2013). Social assistance dynamics in Sweden: Duration dependence and heterogeneity. *Social Science Research, 42*(1), 120–139.

Mundlak, Y. (1978). On the pooling of time series and cross section data. *Econometrica, 46*(1), 69–85.

Mühleisen, M., & Zimmermann, K. F. (1994). A panel analysis of job changes and unemployment. *European Economic Review, 38*, 793–801.

Orme, C. D. (2001). *Two-step inference in dynamic non-linear panel data models*. Working Paper. University of Manchester. Available at http://personalpages.manchester.ac.uk/staff/chris.orme/documents/Research%20Papers/initcondlast.pdf

Pavetti, L. A. (1993). *The dynamics of welfare and work: Exploring the process by which women work their way off welfare*. Ph.D. thesis, Harvard University.

Rabe-Hesketh, S., & Skrondal, A. (2013). Avoiding biased versions of Wooldridge's simple solution to the initial conditions problem. *Economics Letters, 120*(2), 346–349.

Rabe-Hesketh, S., Skrondal, A., & Pickles, A. (2004). *GLLAMM manual. UC Berkeley Division of Biostatistics*. Working Paper Series No. 160. University of California, Berkeley.

Rabe-Hesketh, S., Skrondal, A., & Pickles, A. (2005). Maximum likelihood estimation of limited and discrete dependent variable models with nested random effects. *Journal of Econometrics, 128*(2), 301–323.

Riphahn, R. T. (2004). Immigrant participation in social assistance programs: Evidence from German guestworkers. *Applied Economics Quarterly, 50*(4), 329–362.

Riphahn, R. T., Sander, M., & Wunder, C. (2013). The welfare use of immigrants and natives in Germany: The case of Turkish immigrants. *International Journal of Manpower, 34*(1), 70–82.

Riphahn, R. T., & Wunder, C. (2012). Patterns of welfare dependence before and after a reform: Evidence from first generation immigrants and natives in Germany. *Review of Income and Wealth, 59*(3), 437–459.

Riphahn, R. T., & Wunder, C. (2013). *State dependence in welfare receipt: Transitions before and after a reform.* CESifo Working Paper No. 4485. Center for Economic Studies — Ifo Institute, Munich.

Schels, B. (2013). Persistence or transition: Young adults and social benefits in Germany. *Journal of Youth Studies, 16*(7), 1–20.

Statistisches Bundesamt. (2013). Arbeitslose, Arbeitslosenquoten, Gemeldete Arbeitsstellen: Bundesländer, Jahre. Retrieved from https://www-genesis.destatis.de/genesis/online

Stewart, M. B. (2006). Maximum simulated likelihood estimation of random-effects dynamic probit models with autocorrelated errors. *Stata Journal, 6*(2), 256.

Stewart, M. B. (2007). The interrelated dynamics of unemployment and low-wage employment. *Journal of Applied Econometrics, 22*, 511–531.

Voges, W., & Rohwer, G. (1992). Receiving social assistance in Germany: Risk and duration. *Journal of European Social Policy, 2*(3), 175–191.

Wooldridge, J. M. (2005). Simple solutions to the initial conditions problem in dynamic, nonlinear panel data models with unobserved heterogeneity. *Journal of Applied Econometrics, 20*(1), 39–54.

Wunder, C., & Riphahn, R. T. (2014). The dynamics of welfare entry and exit amongst natives and immigrants. *Oxford Economic Papers, 66*(2), 580–604.

APPENDIX

Table A1. Specifications with Post-Hartz Interactions.

	Full Sample	Western Germany	Eastern Germany
y_{t-1}	1.105*** (0.036)	1.231*** (0.045)	0.863*** (0.061)
$H_t \times y_{t-1}$	0.070 (0.049)	0.005 (0.060)	0.191** (0.083)
Individual characteristics			
Female	−0.004 (0.034)	−0.020 (0.040)	0.041 (0.065)
Age	−0.067*** (0.016)	−0.074*** (0.019)	−0.035 (0.031)
Age^2	0.078*** (0.019)	0.085*** (0.022)	0.044 (0.037)
Years of education	−0.236*** (0.048)	−0.192*** (0.053)	−0.613*** (0.144)
Years of education^2	0.005*** (0.002)	0.004* (0.002)	0.018*** (0.005)
Good health	−0.038 (0.038)	0.003 (0.045)	−0.122* (0.068)
Poor health	0.112** (0.047)	0.140** (0.056)	0.058 (0.086)
Migrant	0.278*** (0.055)	0.264*** (0.057)	0.471** (0.222)
Household characteristics			
Single, with children	0.042 (0.095)	0.139 (0.122)	−0.025 (0.153)
Couple, no children	0.187* (0.102)	0.302** (0.123)	0.016 (0.186)
Couple, with children	0.001 (0.106)	0.021 (0.130)	0.059 (0.190)
Child ≤6 years	0.035 (0.052)	0.127** (0.061)	−0.180* (0.098)
Household size	0.057* (0.030)	0.069** (0.035)	0.013 (0.059)
Partner characteristics			
Age	−0.019*** (0.005)	−0.018*** (0.006)	−0.024** (0.011)
Age^2	0.026*** (0.009)	0.026*** (0.010)	0.032* (0.017)
Years of education	0.057*** (0.015)	0.040** (0.018)	0.111*** (0.033)
Years of education^2	−0.004*** (0.001)	−0.004*** (0.001)	−0.007*** (0.002)
Good health	0.013 (0.041)	0.030 (0.050)	−0.036 (0.074)
Poor health	0.208*** (0.053)	0.235*** (0.064)	0.158* (0.095)
Migrant	0.186*** (0.058)	0.198*** (0.060)	0.602** (0.239)
Wooldridge controls			
y_0	1.310*** (0.056)	1.261*** (0.069)	1.374*** (0.098)
Avg: good health	−0.153** (0.066)	−0.171** (0.081)	−0.113 (0.120)
Avg: poor health	0.269*** (0.084)	0.291*** (0.099)	0.174 (0.160)
Avg: single, with children	0.421*** (0.125)	0.315** (0.155)	0.465** (0.223)
Avg: couple, no children	−0.481*** (0.117)	−0.680*** (0.144)	−0.280 (0.212)
Avg: couple, with children	−0.235* (0.130)	−0.389** (0.157)	−0.088 (0.243)
Avg: child ≤6 years	0.352*** (0.080)	0.188** (0.094)	0.872*** (0.161)
Avg: household size	0.065* (0.035)	0.069* (0.040)	0.053 (0.073)
Avg: reg. unemployment rate	0.017 (0.012)	0.014 (0.018)	−0.015 (0.021)
Avg: good health (partner)	−0.144** (0.070)	−0.050 (0.085)	−0.246** (0.125)
Avg: poor health (partner)	0.145 (0.093)	0.211* (0.110)	0.050 (0.179)

Table A1. (*Continued*)

	Full Sample	Western Germany	Eastern Germany
Individual characteristics (post-Hartz)			
Female	−0.003 (0.045)	0.016 (0.054)	−0.020 (0.082)
Age	−0.025 (0.024)	−0.023 (0.029)	−0.026 (0.047)
Age^2	0.023 (0.029)	0.022 (0.034)	0.027 (0.055)
Years of education	−0.202*** (0.071)	−0.221*** (0.078)	−0.310 (0.198)
Years of education^2	0.006** (0.003)	0.008** (0.003)	0.009 (0.007)
Good health	−0.060 (0.058)	−0.180** (0.070)	0.196* (0.107)
Poor health	−0.071 (0.073)	−0.087 (0.086)	−0.059 (0.142)
Migrant	−0.022 (0.070)	0.002 (0.072)	−0.493 (0.301)
Household characteristics (post-Hartz)			
Single, with children	−0.047 (0.143)	−0.095 (0.183)	−0.027 (0.236)
Couple, no children	−0.263 (0.161)	−0.445** (0.197)	0.136 (0.287)
Couple, with children	−0.219 (0.163)	−0.208 (0.202)	−0.267 (0.285)
Child ≤6 years	0.075 (0.089)	0.051 (0.103)	0.114 (0.180)
Household size	0.042 (0.049)	−0.047 (0.059)	0.260*** (0.093)
Partner characteristics (post-Hartz)			
Age	0.000 (0.007)	0.003 (0.009)	−0.005 (0.015)
Age^2	0.000 (0.012)	−0.008 (0.014)	0.017 (0.024)
Years of education	−0.004 (0.022)	0.017 (0.025)	−0.064 (0.044)
Years of education^2	−0.001 (0.001)	−0.002 (0.001)	0.002 (0.002)
Good health	−0.039 (0.066)	−0.089 (0.079)	0.079 (0.120)
Poor health	−0.136 (0.086)	−0.142 (0.101)	−0.155 (0.163)
Migrant	−0.064 (0.078)	−0.101 (0.082)	−0.220 (0.331)
Wooldridge controls (post-Hartz)			
y_0	−0.078 (0.055)	−0.083 (0.069)	−0.089 (0.095)
Avg: good health	0.127 (0.098)	0.224* (0.120)	−0.066 (0.174)
Avg: poor health	0.095 (0.128)	0.099 (0.151)	0.053 (0.245)
Avg: single, with children	−0.216 (0.176)	−0.147 (0.220)	−0.010 (0.314)
Avg: couple, no children	0.242 (0.182)	0.505** (0.222)	−0.210 (0.330)
Avg: couple, with children	−0.043 (0.190)	0.079 (0.231)	−0.014 (0.349)
Avg: child ≤6 years	−0.041 (0.126)	0.081 (0.147)	−0.413 (0.257)
Avg: household size	−0.058 (0.055)	0.038 (0.064)	−0.356*** (0.110)
Avg: reg. unemployment rate	0.009 (0.017)	0.015 (0.024)	0.001 (0.028)
Avg: good health (partner)	0.187* (0.104)	0.089 (0.127)	0.326* (0.186)
Avg: poor health (partner)	0.174 (0.145)	0.103 (0.171)	0.182 (0.281)
Reg. unemployment rate	0.041*** (0.011)	0.051*** (0.017)	0.035** (0.015)
H_t × reg. unemployment rate	−0.003 (0.014)	−0.016 (0.022)	0.017 (0.019)
Eastern Germany	0.267*** (0.069)		
H_t × Eastern Germany	−0.068 (0.089)		
Constant	0.111 (0.453)	−0.045 (0.517)	2.930** (1.168)
H_t × constant	2.324*** (0.687)	2.274*** (0.797)	3.252** (1.610)

Table A1. (*Continued*)

	Full Sample	Western Germany	Eastern Germany
σ_a	0.839*** (0.026)	0.784*** (0.030)	0.953*** (0.048)
ρ	0.413*** (0.015)	0.381*** (0.018)	0.476*** (0.025)
Log-likelihood	−14,528.497	−9,664.339	−4,780.015
No. of observations	100,434	79,790	20,644
No. of individuals	17,733	14,010	3,723

*$p < 0.10$, **$p < 0.05$, ***$p < 0.01$.

Notes: Standard errors are given in parentheses. y_{t-1} and y_0 are the observed social assistance receipt status in the last period and the initial observed period, respectively, H_t is a dummy variable for the post-Hartz years 2005–2011. All other covariates are lagged by one period. Blocks of variables labelled '(post-Hartz)' have been interacted with the post-Hartz dummy. 'Avg:' denotes an individual's longitudinal average of a variable. Values of age^2 have been scaled through division by 100. The breakdown of the sample into Western and Eastern Germany is based on region of residence in an individual's initial observed period.
Source: SOEP (2011).

Table A2. Specifications with Calendar-Year Interactions.

	Full Sample	Western Germany	Eastern Germany
y_{t-1}	1.199*** (0.095)	1.359*** (0.119)	0.932*** (0.163)
Calendar-year interactions			
$y_{t-1} \times 1997$	−0.377*** (0.127)	−0.254 (0.158)	−0.522** (0.228)
$y_{t-1} \times 1998$	−0.177 (0.132)	−0.246 (0.159)	−0.181 (0.249)
$y_{t-1} \times 1999$	−0.181 (0.126)	−0.119 (0.155)	−0.425* (0.222)
$y_{t-1} \times 2000$	−0.114 (0.132)	0.050 (0.164)	−0.495** (0.230)
$y_{t-1} \times 2001$	−0.022 (0.118)	−0.107 (0.147)	0.100 (0.205)
$y_{t-1} \times 2002$	0.156 (0.124)	0.077 (0.154)	0.220 (0.212)
$y_{t-1} \times 2003$	−0.025 (0.125)	−0.103 (0.156)	0.044 (0.211)
$y_{t-1} \times 2004$	−0.001 (0.122)	−0.220 (0.152)	0.316 (0.212)
$y_{t-1} \times 2005$	−0.329*** (0.122)	−0.333** (0.153)	−0.349* (0.207)
$y_{t-1} \times 2006$	0.000 (0.124)	−0.023 (0.155)	−0.013 (0.212)
$y_{t-1} \times 2007$	0.081 (0.121)	−0.038 (0.151)	0.320 (0.212)
$y_{t-1} \times 2008$	0.133 (0.126)	−0.027 (0.156)	0.351 (0.221)
$y_{t-1} \times 2009$	0.063 (0.131)	−0.135 (0.165)	0.431* (0.224)
$y_{t-1} \times 2010$	0.321** (0.139)	0.153 (0.174)	0.542** (0.237)
$y_{t-1} \times 2011$	0.028 (0.143)	−0.254 (0.179)	0.593** (0.254)
Individual characteristics			
Female	−0.004 (0.029)	−0.010 (0.033)	0.023 (0.056)
Age	−0.079*** (0.013)	−0.078*** (0.015)	−0.076*** (0.024)
Age^2	0.088*** (0.015)	0.089*** (0.017)	0.085*** (0.029)
Years of education	−0.289*** (0.041)	−0.252*** (0.045)	−0.696*** (0.126)

Table A2. (*Continued*)

	Full Sample	Western Germany	Eastern Germany
Years of education^2	0.007*** (0.002)	0.006*** (0.002)	0.020*** (0.005)
Good health	−0.058** (0.028)	−0.069** (0.034)	−0.020 (0.051)
Poor health	0.076** (0.035)	0.095** (0.041)	0.022 (0.067)
Migrant	0.266*** (0.045)	0.263*** (0.046)	0.268 (0.184)
Household characteristics			
Single, with children	0.030 (0.064)	0.098 (0.082)	−0.046 (0.105)
Couple, no children	0.072 (0.074)	0.100 (0.090)	0.056 (0.133)
Couple, with children	−0.073 (0.075)	−0.061 (0.092)	−0.034 (0.132)
Child ≤ 6 years	0.101*** (0.039)	0.166*** (0.046)	−0.062 (0.077)
Household size	0.063*** (0.022)	0.051* (0.026)	0.102** (0.043)
Partner characteristics			
Age	−0.018*** (0.004)	−0.016*** (0.005)	−0.021*** (0.008)
Age^2	0.023*** (0.007)	0.020*** (0.008)	0.027** (0.013)
Years of education	0.056*** (0.012)	0.047*** (0.014)	0.087*** (0.024)
Years of education^2	−0.005*** (0.001)	−0.004*** (0.001)	−0.006*** (0.001)
Good health	0.005 (0.031)	0.002 (0.038)	0.019 (0.057)
Poor health	0.152*** (0.041)	0.174*** (0.048)	0.100 (0.076)
Migrant	0.164*** (0.048)	0.163*** (0.049)	0.502** (0.200)
Calendar-year effects			
1997	−0.011 (0.064)	0.120 (0.074)	−0.321** (0.129)
1998	0.079 (0.065)	0.157** (0.079)	0.074 (0.127)
1999	−0.045 (0.067)	0.016 (0.080)	−0.022 (0.130)
2000	−0.043 (0.067)	−0.122 (0.084)	0.177 (0.124)
2001	−0.072 (0.061)	−0.080 (0.072)	0.042 (0.120)
2002	−0.125** (0.063)	−0.159** (0.077)	0.051 (0.123)
2003	0.107* (0.060)	0.094 (0.072)	0.268** (0.121)
2004	0.080 (0.063)	0.109 (0.074)	0.217* (0.131)
2005	0.221*** (0.063)	0.249*** (0.073)	0.360*** (0.130)
2006	0.191*** (0.067)	0.203** (0.083)	0.417*** (0.132)
2007	−0.048 (0.069)	0.049 (0.082)	−0.142 (0.139)
2008	0.010 (0.068)	0.018 (0.082)	0.023 (0.128)
2009	0.130* (0.070)	0.196** (0.082)	−0.132 (0.137)
2010	0.070 (0.074)	0.050 (0.089)	0.045 (0.139)
2011	0.085 (0.079)	0.176* (0.090)	−0.340** (0.172)
Wooldridge controls			
y_0	1.256*** (0.048)	1.221*** (0.059)	1.307*** (0.085)
Avg: good health	−0.111** (0.055)	−0.084 (0.066)	−0.190* (0.102)
Avg: poor health	0.309*** (0.071)	0.334*** (0.083)	0.230 (0.141)
Avg: single, with children	0.299*** (0.093)	0.250** (0.114)	0.357** (0.173)
Avg: couple, no children	−0.370*** (0.089)	−0.452*** (0.108)	−0.295* (0.166)
Avg: couple, with children	−0.265*** (0.097)	−0.355*** (0.116)	−0.129 (0.186)

Table A2. (*Continued*)

	Full Sample	Western Germany	Eastern Germany
Avg: child ≤6 years	0.256*** (0.064)	0.191*** (0.074)	0.520*** (0.132)
Avg: household size	0.059** (0.028)	0.084*** (0.032)	−0.018 (0.058)
Avg: good health (partner)	−0.099* (0.057)	−0.026 (0.069)	−0.221** (0.106)
Avg: poor health (partner)	0.205*** (0.079)	0.260*** (0.092)	0.116 (0.159)
Avg: reg. unemployment rate	0.022** (0.010)	0.042** (0.018)	0.004 (0.017)
Reg. unemployment rate	0.039*** (0.010)	0.021 (0.017)	0.007 (0.016)
Eastern Germany	0.242*** (0.056)		
Constant	0.890** (0.374)	0.538 (0.425)	4.834*** (0.987)
σ_a	0.823*** (0.026)	0.778*** (0.031)	0.934*** (0.048)
ρ	0.404*** (0.015)	0.377*** (0.019)	0.466*** (0.026)
Log-likelihood	−14,507.179	−9,659.002	−4,737.816
No. of observation	100,434	79,790	20,644
No. of individuals	17,733	14,010	3,723

$*p < 0.10$, $**p < 0.05$, $***p < 0.01$.

Notes: Standard errors are given in parentheses. y_{t-1} and y_0 are the observed social assistance receipt status in the last period and the initial observed period, respectively. All other covariates are lagged by one period. 'Avg:' denotes an individual's longitudinal average of a variable. Values of age^2 have been scaled through division by 100. The breakdown of the sample into Western and Eastern Germany is based on region of residence in an individual's initial observed period.

Source: SOEP (2011).

HOW DO EXIT RATES FROM SOCIAL ASSISTANCE BENEFIT IN BELGIUM VARY WITH INDIVIDUAL AND LOCAL AGENCY CHARACTERISTICS?

Sarah Carpentier, Karel Neels and
Karel Van den Bosch

ABSTRACT

The administration of social assistance benefits is devolved to local agencies in Belgium, which raises questions about how much variation in spell lengths of benefit receipt is associated with differences across agencies. We address this issue by analysing the monthly hazard of benefit exit using administrative record data for 14,270 individuals in 574 welfare agencies. Our random-effects model allows for differences in both the observed and unobserved characteristics of beneficiaries and of local agencies. There are large differences in median benefit duration for individuals serviced by different welfare agencies: the range is from two months to more than 24 months. We find strong associations between beneficiary characteristics (sex, age, foreign nationality, citizenship

Safety Nets and Benefit Dependence
Research in Labor Economics, Volume 39, 151–187
Copyright © 2014 by Emerald Group Publishing Limited
ISSN: 0147-9121/doi:10.1108/S0147-912120140000039004

acquisition, work history and being a student) and spell length. The estimates show higher odds of exiting social assistance receipt in bigger municipalities and in agencies which provide more generous supplementary assistance, and also strong evidence of shorter episodes in agencies where active labour market programme participation rates are higher.

Keywords: Social assistance duration; local welfare agencies; municipalities; welfare; duration analysis

JEL classifications: I38; J68; R50

INTRODUCTION

Social assistance for able-bodied persons of working age in Belgium is a shared responsibility between the national state and local welfare agencies. Although there is a nationwide guaranteed minimum income, local agencies enjoy considerable discretion in how they implement the federal statutory framework on the conditions for eligibility (e.g. labour market availability) of the benefit. Local agencies can provide supplementary assistance in cash or in-kind on top of the federally defined minimum benefit level. Also, agencies have discretion in how they use active labour market programmes (ALMPs) regulated and subsidised by the federal government, and they also decide which beneficiaries they give access to these programmes. This raises the question of how much variation in spell lengths of benefit receipt is associated with differences across local agencies.

In this article, we study how the monthly hazard of exit from social assistance is associated with beneficiary and local agency characteristics in Belgium. We use a representative sample of 14,270 beneficiaries in 574 local agencies who entered social assistance in the course of 2004 and are followed for a two-year period. We use discrete-time random-effects event history analysis to examine whether the probability of benefit exit is associated with elapsed duration since the start of benefit receipt, seasonal variation in employment opportunities, benefit recipient characteristics (age, sex, nationality at birth, citizenship acquisition, recent work history and being a student), characteristics of the local welfare agencies (generosity level of supplementary assistance and participation rate in ALMPs) and municipality characteristics (local unemployment rate and municipality size).

We study exits from social assistance of any kind. An exit may result from varying types of agency policies (e.g. punitive measures versus labour market participation), changes in household income or composition (e.g. paid employment of another household member or re-partnering), becoming eligible for other social security schemes (e.g. unemployment or invalidity benefit) or moving to another place of residence (e.g. to another country).

The contribution of this study to the existing international literature on benefit dynamics lies in the combination of the following features. First, we examine administrative record data on benefit receipt rather than survey data, which allows the use of a sufficiently large sample to estimate the effects of local agency differences and which reduces measurement error. Second, the analysis of longitudinal micro data on social assistance beneficiaries is supplemented with information on local area characteristics and local agency policy from other data sources. Earlier studies have usually focused on the association of individual characteristics with benefit exit. In this article, we analyse whether agency policy and local area characteristics are associated with spell length and also whether the association with individual characteristics changes when controlling for agency characteristics. Belgium is an interesting case to look at spell lengths at the level of local welfare agencies, as social assistance is moderately to highly decentralised, with important local variations in terms of generosity and use of ALMPs. Third, to our knowledge, this article is the first study to analyse the hazard of social assistance exit using a random-effects model that includes time-varying covariates at the level of both beneficiaries and local agencies, while allowing for unobserved heterogeneity at the level of beneficiaries and agencies.

The outline of the article is as follows. In the second section we describe the Belgian social assistance scheme, with particular attention for the discretionary power of local agencies. In the third section we briefly review the literature on variation in spell length. The fourth section describes the data and introduces the model specification and covariates used. In the fifth section we use life tables to show how the conditional probability of exiting social assistance changes with elapsed duration and also to illustrate how variation in this probability is associated with agency characteristics. Next, we present the estimates of a multivariate model that shows the net effects of agency-level variables, controlling for beneficiary-level covariates. In the final section we summarise the findings, consider some limitations of the study and discuss possible implications for policy and further research.

THE BELGIAN SOCIAL ASSISTANCE SCHEME

Rights and Conditions in the Belgian Social Assistance Scheme
on the National Level

In Belgium, the non-contributory tax-financed social assistance scheme serves as the ultimate financial safety net for able-bodied persons of working age. The scheme fulfils a residual role, as it is supplementary to social insurance benefits, as well as to other categorical minimum income schemes such as the one targeted at disabled people. There are in fact two social assistance schemes, regulated by two different acts, namely the 'Right to Social Integration' and the 'Right to Social Assistance' acts. Persons with Belgian or other European nationality, as well as some categories of non-EU foreigners, are eligible for the first scheme. Other conditions include that beneficiaries are aged 18 or older and that they have insufficient economic resources. Moreover, beneficiaries must be available for work, unless they are exempt for health or other reasons (see below). People who are not eligible for the 'Right to Social Integration' can apply for benefits under the 'Right to Social Assistance'. Most of these beneficiaries are foreigners who entered Belgium less than five years earlier and, in the period of study, include asylum seekers. In principle, social assistance entitlement in both schemes is unlimited in duration, as long as the eligibility conditions are fulfilled. Persons above retirement age can apply to another social assistance scheme (i.e. the 'Income Guarantee for Older people'), which provides more generous benefits than those directed at non-retired people. At the time of study, the retirement age was 63 for women and 65 for men.

Both schemes provide a guaranteed minimum income (the 'Revenu d'Intégration Sociale' and its equivalent under the 'Right to Social Assistance'), which is defined at the federal level. It is subject to a means test, which includes the income of the partner, as well as that of children and parents living in the same household according to the de facto living arrangement. Beneficiaries are divided into three categories, depending on their household situation: single persons, persons within couples (married or cohabiting) without children and persons (single or non-single) with dependent children. Each adult in a couple without dependent children is individually entitled to a benefit, and the amounts are paid out separately. In other household situations, the benefit is paid out as a single amount to one person in the household. On 1 August 2005, the amounts were 417 euros, 626 euros and 834 euros for a person within a childless couple, a single person and a person or family with dependent children, respectively. Families with children usually also receive child benefits, which are administered by the National Administration for Child Allowances. Welfare agencies are required by law to re-assess benefit recipients' situations regularly and at least once a year. Minimum income protection in the Belgian social assistance scheme is regarded as being rather low by international standards, especially for single persons and couples with children, mainly due to the virtual absence of rent support (Cantillon, Van Mechelen, & Schulte, 2008; Saraceno, 2010).

In June 2005, 1.7 per cent of the population of working age was entitled to the guaranteed minimum income in social assistance, which by European standards is a low proportion (Carcillo & Grubb, 2006). The main reason for this is that unemployment benefits in Belgium are, at least in principle, unlimited in time (though they can be stopped under certain conditions). Hence, the long-term unemployed need not necessarily fall back on social assistance. Moreover, school leavers with a diploma can claim a flat-rate unemployment benefit (after a waiting period), without ever having had paid employment.

The rather low number of natives who have to fall back on the guaranteed minimum income in social assistance, due to the wide coverage of social insurance schemes, is one of the reasons for the high proportion of immigrants (see Table 1). Other explanations are that in the period 2002–2005 Belgium had one of the highest immigration rates per head of the population in Western Europe and also received a relatively high number of asylum seekers during the period 1999–2005.[1] Furthermore, the huge unemployment gap between Belgian-born and foreign-born persons may play a role (Corluy & Verbist, 2010; Jean, Causa, Jimenez, & Wanner, 2010). According to Corluy and Verbist (2010), non-EU-born individuals also have a higher probability to receive social assistance relative to Belgian-born individuals. This overrepresentation of foreign-born individuals is in line with the majority of the findings of European studies, though there is mixed evidence whether the higher participation rate holds controlling for (un)observed characteristics (Barrett & McCarthy, 2008; Gustafsson, 2013; Hansen & Lofstrom, 2011; Mood, 2011; Riphahn, 1998; Wunder & Riphahn, 2014; Zorlu, 2013).

During the period under study, the Belgian economy was characterised by sluggish growth and stable or slightly rising unemployment until the end of 2005, followed by an economic upturn during 2006 accompanied by a falling unemployment rate.[2]

Discretion of Local Agencies in Social Assistance

Social assistance for persons of working age is administered by local welfare agencies, called Public Social Welfare Centres. Each municipality has one and only one local agency. Local welfare agencies are autonomous organisations subject to public law. They are governed by a board elected by the local municipal council and are responsible for their own budgets. Funding comes from a variety of sources, of which the municipal subsidy and federal refunds are the most important. The federal state refunds several expenditures partially or wholly. Benefits granted under the 'Right to Social Integration' are refunded for at least 50 per cent; the federal share may increase up to 65 per cent for agencies with a high number of beneficiaries. The 'Right to Social Assistance' benefit is funded entirely by the federal government. One explicit goal of the federal subsidies is to somewhat equalise the burden of social assistance across municipalities, as larger cities bear the biggest burden. Another equalising subsidy is linked to active labour market participation efforts (see below).

In addition to the guaranteed minimum income, local welfare agencies can grant supplementary assistance in cash or in-kind. The amounts of and the conditions for supplementary assistance are completely at the discretion of the local welfare agencies resulting in very large differences between agencies (Van Mechelen & Bogaerts, 2008; see also Table 2). Agencies also have substantial discretionary power with regard to the assessment of exemption from labour market availability due to health or a limited number of other reasons (e.g. being a full-time student for persons aged up to 25, caring for a handicapped child or an intensive language course), job search monitoring, counselling, sanctioning and the allocation of individuals to active labour market and training programmes. Local discretion with regard to job seeking requirements is partly due to ambiguities in the relevant legislation (e.g. no definition of a suitable job) in combination with the absence of federal targets or profiling systems. A particular case concerns students. Full-time students aged between 18 and 25, whose parents are unable to support them and whose studies are deemed to enhance their chances in the labour market, can claim social assistance benefits. Student allowances do not cover all living expenses. They are eligible for a social assistance benefit as long as it takes a normal student to finish the (secondary or higher) education they are pursuing. Students are exempted from availability for work, but they are encouraged to do student jobs during school holidays.

Can Social Assistance Beneficiaries Choose Where to Apply?

In principle, a claimant can only apply to the welfare agency of the municipality of his or her actual and usual place of residence. This does not necessarily apply to students, who are assigned to the welfare agency of the municipality where they originally lived, and not to that of the town where they pursue their studies, and where they may also have their usual residence. However, more than three-quarters of the students receiving social assistance live in the municipality of the agency by which they are served (De Wilde et al., 2011). Another exception to the rule was made for asylum seekers. These persons (as any free citizen of Belgium) are free to settle where they want and, in practice, often choose to live in one of the bigger cities. However, in order to relieve these cities from the heavy administrative and financial burden this imposes, the responsibility for providing social assistance for asylum seekers was distributed across local agencies according to set quota, independent of their actual place of residence.

The fact that social assistance beneficiaries are free to move, in combination with the substantial variation in the generosity of supplementary assistance across local welfare agencies, opens up the possibility of 'benefit shopping', i.e. moving to a municipality where the benefit level is more generous. For a number of reasons it is unlikely that benefit shopping is an important phenomenon in Belgium. The amounts granted in supplementary assistance are specific for each individual application and, while many agencies use guidelines, these are not made public. Also, welfare agency workers enjoy considerable freedom in the application of these guidelines (Cornelis et al., 2012). This implies that even when a certain welfare agency has a reputation for being generous in supplementary benefit, social assistance beneficiaries cannot be certain that that generosity will extend to their particular case. Furthermore, moving residence can involve substantial costs. In other words, 'benefit shopping' in Belgium seems a risky strategy with uncertain benefits. Moreover, within the sample of beneficiaries used here, moves between agencies were most often towards agencies where the average level of supplementary benefit was lower or at an approximately equal level as at the agency of origin.

Active Labour Market Programmes

Subject to federal rules and an assessment by local welfare workers, beneficiaries of social assistance can enter various ALMPs. The most important of these in terms of persons reached is specifically targeted at social assistance beneficiaries. This involves employment where the wage costs are mostly completely subsidised by the local welfare agency, which is in fact also the employer. Claimants can work within the local welfare agency, or they can be seconded to other organisations. The goal is to give social assistance beneficiaries the opportunity to gain work experience or to ensure that they qualify for a social insurance income, in particular an unemployment benefit. For each beneficiary of this active labour market scheme, the federal government provides a subsidy that is equal to the guaranteed minimum income of a person living with a partner, but only for a period that is just sufficient to make the beneficiary eligible for social insurance benefits. Local welfare agencies thus have a clear financial incentive to move persons receiving a benefit under the 'Right to Social Integration' (which is generally refunded at only 50 per cent) into these ALMPs. Beneficiaries of the 'Right to Social Assistance' (for which expenditure is refunded at 100 per cent) are not excluded from these ALMPs, except for some categories of asylum seekers which are not permitted to work. In the period under study, only a small though increasing number of beneficiaries of the 'Right to Social Assistance' participated in an employment scheme.

On top of refunding the wage costs of these programmes, the federal government provides subsidies for supporting and training the participants. An additional subsidy for active labour market participation efforts is targeted at municipalities with more than 40,000 inhabitants, who have a relatively large number of beneficiaries in ALMPs. In addition to these employment programmes specifically targeted at beneficiaries of social assistance, a number of other more general ALMPs are also open to them, though these are of relatively minor importance. These involve employment that is partly subsidised and/or supported by counselling. We note that participation in ALMPs implies exit from social assistance.

LITERATURE REVIEW

The literature on social assistance dynamics identifies four kinds of variables that could influence exit rates and spell lengths. First, there are variables on the individual (or household) level. Beneficiaries can differ in their probability of exiting social assistance due to personal and household characteristics such as sex, age, household type, education or nationality. Heterogeneity in the composition of local social assistance beneficiaries populations can result in differences in the average spell length across welfare agencies.

Second, the length of the social assistance spell as such can influence individuals' probability of exiting, as a result of depreciation or stagnation of human and job-specific capital, and employers' negative perception of social assistance receipt (Andrén, 2007; Bane & Ellwood, 1994; Dahl & Lorentzen, 2003; Hansen, Lofstrom, Liu, & Zhang, 2014). This mechanism is generally referred to as negative duration dependence.

Third, the design of the social assistance scheme, such as the generosity level and the job seeking requirements, can account for variation in spell lengths. Job search theory argues that a more generous benefit is likely to raise the reservation wage and to reduce the job seeking effort, entailing a longer episode of social assistance benefit receipt (Cahuc & Zylberberg, 2004). This theoretical argument is empirically well substantiated, although the magnitude of the effect of generosity levels on episode duration is not always substantial (Atkinson & Micklewright, 1991 (for unemployment insurance); Fortin, Lacroix, & Drolet, 2004; Lemieux & Milligan, 2008 (for welfare in Canada); Moffitt, 2002 (for welfare in the USA)). Gustafsson, Müller, Negri, and Voges (2002) mention another argument with regard to the generosity of the benefit. A low benefit level may be insufficient to survive, compelling beneficiaries to seek work in the informal economy in order to attain an 'assisted equilibrium' by combining informal work and social assistance receipt. Although the guaranteed minimum benefit in social assistance is the same all over Belgium, these arguments suggest that the local variation in supplementary assistance (given in Table 2) may well translate into variation of spell lengths in social assistance.

Studies also indicate that counselling and monitoring of job seekers positively affect beneficiaries' likelihood of exiting social assistance (Boone, Frederiksson, Holmlund, & van Ours, 2001; Engström, 2009). Welfare agencies in Belgium have substantial discretionary power with regard to the assessment of exemption from labour market availability due to health or other reasons, job search monitoring, counselling, sanctioning and the allocation of individuals to active labour market and training programmes.

Available resources relative to demand may also play a role in the degree to which social assistance beneficiaries are subject to monitoring and counselling. Some welfare agencies may be overwhelmed by the number of social assistance beneficiaries relative to the number of social workers. Also, agencies in small municipalities may have less institutional capacity than those in larger communities to empower beneficiaries and to help them find a suitable job. Some studies for other policy fields suggest that this is one of the pitfalls of decentralisation (De Vries, 2000; Pollitt, 2005; Prud'homme, 1995). However, Cockx (1997) finds for Belgium in the late 1980s a lower turnover in big cities. Dahl and Lorentzen (2003) do not find a significant effect of municipality size on exit to work for the 1995 entry cohort in Norway.

A fourth set of relevant variables refers to the economic context. There is mixed evidence of the impact of conditions on the labour market on episode lengths. Hoynes (2000) reports a substantial effect of local labour market conditions and the economic cycle on the likelihood of exiting social assistance. Some studies also show that labour market characteristics can have a differential effect on individuals depending on their characteristics (Hansen, 2008; Hoynes, 2000; van der Klauw & van Ours, 2001). Other studies report no impact of local area unemployment on exit (Jenkins & Cappellari, 2014).

DATA AND METHODOLOGY

Data

We use administrative longitudinal data from the Belgian Data Warehouse Labour Market and Social Security to track individuals (not households) over time. Administrative data have the advantage, in comparison to survey data, that they provide a sufficiently large sample to study local variation in exit probabilities, while reducing measurement error. We have a one in three random sample of all beneficiaries entering social assistance in 2004 which is proportionally stratified by age, sex, province, applicable act and municipality size. All beneficiaries were aged 18−64 when entering social assistance and had not received social assistance benefits in the preceding 15 months. The sample provides 160,624 person-months of observation on 14,270 beneficiaries served by 574 welfare agencies who were followed over two years.[3] Observations are censored at the end of the two-year observation period.

Characteristics of the Beneficiaries and Local Welfare Agencies

Summary statistics about beneficiaries' characteristics are given in Table 1. Half of the persons entitled to social assistance are women and half

Table 1. Socio-Economic Characteristics of the Beneficiaries at Entry
($N = 14{,}270$).

Characteristic	Total	No Agency Change	At Least One Agency Change
Sex			
Male	49.8	49.8	49.5
Female	50.2	50.2	50.5
Age			
18–24	36.5	35.8	44.1
25–44	46.3	46.8	41.8
45 and over	17.2	17.5	14.2
Nationality at birth			
Belgian nationality	47.3	48.0	40.8
EU nationality	13.2	13.3	12.0
Non-EU nationality	38.3	37.6	45.9
Unknown nationality	1.2	1.2	1.4
Naturalisation			
No (includes Belgians at birth)	75.5	75.7	73.6
Yes	24.5	24.3	26.4
Work intensity in Belgium over the past five years			
0%	57.2	55.9	70.7
1–50%	28.0	28.4	23.9
51–75%	6.4	6.8	2.6
76–100%	8.4	9.0	2.8
Full-time student			
No student	85.4	85.7	82.7
Student	14.6	14.3	17.3
Welfare agency change over the observed period			
No agency change	91.4	100.0	0.0
At least one agency change	8.7	0.0	100.0

are men. Nearly half of the beneficiaries are aged between 25 and 44, and more than one-third are under 25. Less than 50 per cent of the sample have the Belgian nationality at birth, though one in four beneficiaries are naturalised after birth. Among beneficiaries having foreign nationality at birth, those holding non-European nationality constitute the largest group. Almost 60 per cent of the beneficiaries have not worked in Belgium in the past five years, and nearly 15 per cent are students. Nearly one in ten have switched welfare agencies at least once during the observation period.

Table 1 also provides the characteristics of those who changed agency and those who did not. Beneficiaries who changed agency are younger relative to those who did not change agency, more often hold a non-EU nationality, have less work experience in Belgium and are more often a full-time student.

Table 2 provides an overview of the characteristics of the 572 welfare agencies of the beneficiaries at entry.[4] More than 90 per cent of the municipalities (representing half of the beneficiaries) have fewer than 40,000 inhabitants. Two-thirds of the municipalities have an unemployment rate of under 10.4 per cent, and only a little more than one out of four beneficiaries live in a municipality with an unemployment rate under 10.4 per cent. In nearly 60 per cent of the local agencies (which corresponds with 52 per cent of the beneficiaries), the participation rate in ALMPs is below 10 per cent. As for the generosity of supplementary assistance, half of the

Table 2. Welfare Agency Characteristics at Entry ($N = 572$).

Characteristic	N (Beneficiaries)	% (Beneficiaries)	N (Agencies)	% (Agencies)
Municipality size				
<10,000 inhabitants	1,346	9.4	238	41.6
10,000–19,999 inhabitants	2,729	19.1	199	34.8
20,000–39,999 inhabitants	3,073	21.5	100	17.5
40,000–99,999 inhabitants	3,432	24.1	27	4.7
100,000 inhabitants and over	3,690	25.9	8	1.4
Municipal unemployment rate (quintile groups)				
<5.7%	783	5.5	114	19.9
5.7–7.4%	1,525	10.7	116	20.3
7.5–10.3%	1,767	12.4	112	19.6
10.4–13.6%	1,856	13.0	115	20.1
>13.6%	8,339	58.4	115	20.1
ALMP participation rate				
<10%	7,471	52.4	336	58.7
≥10% and <20%	6,146	43.1	191	33.4
≥20%	653	4.6	45	7.8
Generosity level (average amount per year per beneficiary)				
<€500	9,968	69.9	283	49.5
≥€500 and <€1,000	2,507	17.6	128	22.4
≥€1,000 and <€2,000	551	3.9	54	9.4
≥€2,000	188	1.3	21	3.7
Unknown	1,056	7.4	86	15.0

agencies (representing 70 per cent of the beneficiaries) on average pay less than 500 euros per year per beneficiary, whereas 22 per cent granted between 500 and 999 euros.

Definition of Exit

For beneficiaries having entered social assistance in 2004, we analyse the duration in months until their first unspecified exit. As is customary in life-table analysis and hazard models, we study duration in social assistance by estimating the (monthly) conditional probabilities of exiting for those who are still in social assistance. In calculating the episode durations, breaks of one month were not taken into account as such short interruptions are often due to administrative errors.[5]

We lack monthly data on paid labour other than the federal ALMPs to define mutually exclusive states in work and social assistance. Therefore, if beneficiaries combine participation in a federal ALMP (which usually involves full-time or four-fifths employment) with a complementary minimum income benefit, we consider their episode has ended. By contrast, we count anyone working in another type of job and still receiving complementary minimum income benefit as a social assistance beneficiary, as we cannot identify those cases accurately.

Model Specification

The administrative records provide data on social assistance spell lengths (measured in months), as well as time-varying data on the characteristics of beneficiaries and welfare agencies throughout the observation period. By the end of the observation period, spells are completed (there has been an exit from social assistance) or right-censored (a spell remains in progress). We use random-effects models, also known as multilevel models, to estimate the coefficients of a discrete-time hazard regression model, the precise specification of which is provided shortly.

The model relates the monthly probability of exiting social assistance to elapsed duration since entry to receipt (capturing duration dependence), and time-varying characteristics of beneficiaries and welfare agencies, while also controlling for unobserved heterogeneity ('frailty') at the beneficiary-level and at the agency-level. For previous examples of multilevel models applied to spell data, see Barber, Murphy, Axinn, and Maples (2000), Hedeker, Siddiqui, and Hu (2000) and Steele (2011).

We use a piece-wise linear specification for duration dependence, including as regressors binary variables identifying spell months grouped into three-month intervals (spell months $0-3$, $4-6$,..., $22-24$). We control for potential seasonal variation in employment opportunities in a given spell month by including quarter-of-the-year dummy variables.

In common with most multilevel models, we assume that the beneficiary and agency random effects are each normally distributed with zero mean with a fixed variance that is estimated from the data, and both effects are assumed to be uncorrelated with the observed regressors. Due to limitations in the software we use, MLwiN (Rasbash, Charlton, Browne, Healy, & Cameron, 2009), we assume that the random effects at the beneficiary-level and agency-level are uncorrelated.

The beneficiary-level random effect accounts for unobserved time-constant characteristics of beneficiaries that affect the hazard of leaving social assistance (Mills, 2011). Failing to control for unobserved heterogeneity would be likely to overstate negative duration dependence (Blossfeld, Golsch, & Rohwer, 2007; Jenkins, 2007; Lancaster, 1990; Wooldridge, 2002). The agency-level random effect captures time-constant between-agency variation in the hazard of exiting social assistance that is not captured by the regressors summarising observed agency characteristics.

Because 8.7 per cent of the beneficiaries change agency during the observation period, we do not have a standard multilevel model. That is, instead of every spell month for each beneficiary being consistently 'nested' within a single agency throughout the whole of each beneficiary's spell of benefit receipt, the data for each beneficiary are instead 'cross-nested'. Multilevel models that incorporate cross-nested random effects are discussed by, for example, Beretvas (2011), Fielding and Goldstein (2006), Hox (2010) and Leckie (2013). Disregarding the cross-classified structure results in a misspecified model that can lead to both negatively biased standard error estimates and inaccurate variance component estimates, while deleting the individuals with cross-classified structures reduces the generalisability of the results (Beretvas, 2011).[6]

Our model for the monthly hazard of exit from social assistance, conditional on entry in 2004, can be written as:

$$\ln\left[\frac{P(T_{ij}=t|T_{ij}\geq t)}{1-P(T_{ij}=t|T_{ij}\geq t)}\right] = \beta_0 + \sum_{k=1}^{7}\beta_k d_{ijk} + \gamma' X_{ijt} + \delta' Z_{jt} + u_i + v_j$$

where $u_i \sim N(0, \sigma_u^2)$ and $v_j \sim N(0, \sigma_v^2)$.

The expression $P(T_{ij} = t | T_{ij} \geq t)$ represents the monthly hazard, i.e. the probability for beneficiary i in agency j of leaving social assistance in month t conditional on having been in social assistance until at least month t. This is a proportional odds model (Jenkins, 2007; Singer & Willett, 2003), as the logit of the monthly hazard is related to a linear function of covariates. The model generates parameter estimates that are similar to those derived from a discrete-time proportional hazard model if the discrete hazard rate is small (Singer & Willett, 2003), as is the case in this study.

The intercept β_0 represents the log-odds of leaving social assistance in the first three spell months for a beneficiary with the mean value for each random effect (zero) while setting the observed characteristics equal to zero. The β_k represent the differences in log-odds of leaving social assistance in each spell interval k relative to the reference interval (the first three spell months), and the elements of γ and δ represent the effects of the observed beneficiary-level explanatory variables X_{ijt} (including seasonal effects) and agency-level explanatory variables Z_{jt}, respectively. The beneficiary-level random effect is u_i and the agency-level random effect is v_j, with variances σ_u^2 and σ_v^2, respectively.

The parameters of the model are identified by the assumptions made about the distributions of the random effects and, broadly speaking, their estimates have desirable properties such as consistency because of the large sample sizes involved, not only of beneficiaries but also of welfare agencies.

All model specifications were estimated using Bayesian Markov Chain Monte Carlo (MCMC) procedures as simulation studies have shown that these procedures generate less bias than likelihood-based estimation methods in case of random-effects logistic regression models (Browne & Draper, 2006). In contrast to likelihood-based procedures, which yield point estimates (and associated standard errors) of the population parameters that maximise the likelihood of the observed data, MCMC is a simulation-based estimation method which generates a chain of parameter values based on successive sampling from the posterior distributions of the model parameters (Goldstein, 2011). Estimates for the nested model derived by iterative generalised least squares (IGLS) were used as priors for the MCMC estimation of the cross-classified model (Browne, 2012). We use a burn-in of 5,000 iterations followed by a monitoring chain of 80,000 iterations, and orthogonal parameterisation to improve the efficiency of the MCMC-estimation procedure (Browne, 2012; Browne, Steele, Golalizadeh, & Green, 2009). Tables 3 and 4 report the means and standard deviations of the posterior distribution of parameter values, which have a similar interpretation to parameter estimates and standard errors obtained from maximum likelihood estimation (Goldstein, 2011; Leckie, 2013). Given that we estimate a proportional odds model, the antilog of the mean of the posterior distribution of parameter values can be interpreted as an odds-ratio (OR).

We use the Deviance Information Criterion (DIC), a Bayesian equivalent of Akaike's Information Criterion (AIC), to compare models (Spiegelhalter, Best, Carlin, & Van Der Linde, 2002). Like AIC, DIC takes into account both goodness-of-fit and model complexity. Lower values of the DIC reflect models that better fit the data.

Beneficiary-Level and Agency-Level Characteristics

The multivariate model analyses how the probability of exiting social assistance varies in terms of the following beneficiary-level covariates: (1) sex, (2) age at entry into social assistance (in years, centred at 31, quadratic effect), (3) nationality at birth, distinguishing the Belgian nationality (reference category), European nationalities,[7] non-European nationalities and beneficiaries with unknown nationality, (4) quarterly information on naturalisation status (a dummy variable contrasting foreigners who acquired Belgian nationality with Belgians and foreigners keeping foreign nationality), (5) work intensity in Belgium in the five years preceding entry into social assistance (measured in quarters and centred at value 11), (6) quarterly information on student status (a dummy variable indicating whether the beneficiary was enrolled in full-time education) and (7) change in welfare agency (a dummy variable indicating whether the beneficiary has changed welfare agency during the observation period at least once).[8]

Apart from characteristics of beneficiaries, the multivariate model analyses how the probability of exiting social assistance varies in terms of the following characteristics of welfare agencies and municipalities: (1) yearly data on municipality unemployment rate in quintile groups for 2004 (less than 5.7 per cent, 5.7–7.4 per cent, 7.5–10.3 per cent, 10.4–13.6 per cent and more than 13.6 per cent) (2) yearly data on municipality size (fewer than 10,000 inhabitants, 10,000–19,999 inhabitants, 20,000–39,999 inhabitants, 40,000–99,999 inhabitants and 100,000 inhabitants or over), (3) ALMP participation rate of social assistance beneficiaries in 2004 (less than 10 per cent, 10–19.9 per cent and 20 per cent and over) and (4) generosity level of supplementary benefit in 2004 (less than 500 euros; 500–999 euros, 1,000–1,999 euros, 2,000 euros and over and an unknown average amount per beneficiary per year). To calculate this variable, we divide the total yearly budget for cash and in-kind supplementary benefits per agency by the agency's total number of social assistance beneficiaries in the course of the year. However, a number of recipients of supplementary benefit are not entitled to social assistance. This implies that the indicator may overestimate the average supplementary benefit actually received by social assistance beneficiaries. More details on the calculation and shortcomings of the agency-level variables are provided in Appendix A. Since every municipality has one and only one local welfare agency, the municipal employment rate and the municipality size are treated as agency-level variables.

RESULTS

The results section consists of three parts. The first part uses life tables to illustrate how the conditional monthly probability of exiting social assistance changes with elapsed duration since entry to receipt (observed hazard function) and documents between-agency variation in the median duration in social assistance. Subsequently, the second part uses life tables to illustrate how the observed hazard functions of exiting social assistance are differentiated in terms of agency-level characteristics. Based on these descriptive results, the third part presents the estimates of the multivariate random-effects model that show how the odds of exiting social assistance are associated with duration since entry to receipt (Specification 1), beneficiary-level characteristics (Specification 2) and agency-level characteristics (Specifications 3 and 4).

Probability of Exiting Social Assistance by Elapsed Duration since Entry

Fig. 1 plots the discrete-time hazard function.[9] Apart from relatively high hazards in the first few months, the hazard function indicates that the conditional probability of exiting social assistance decreases over time: this may reflect both duration dependence or the increasingly selective profile of beneficiaries who are observed at longer durations. The hazard of exiting social assistance is slightly higher during the 12th month of the observation period than before or after. We assume this is due to the fact that, in practice, eligibility for benefits is re-assessed after a period of one year, and more beneficiaries leave during the last month of the year.

Of the beneficiaries in our sample, 61 per cent exit social assistance within a year, while 22 per cent where censored in social assistance at the

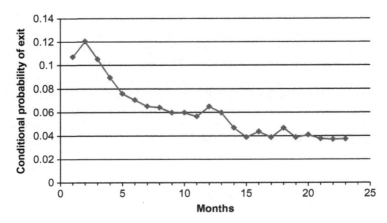

Fig. 1. Conditional Monthly Probability of Exiting Social Assistance to Elapsed Duration since Entry to Receipt.

end of the two-year observation period. The median duration of the observed spells in social assistance is 7.9 months. This median spell length is somewhat longer than estimates for the late 1980s: for beneficiaries entering between June 1987 and November 1990, Cockx (1997) reports median durations in social assistance of 4.5 and 7 months for men and women, respectively (considering changes to other agencies as exits). A median duration of approximately eight months is a medium turnover rate from an international perspective. Gustafsson et al. (2002) found that the duration of the first episode for entrants ranged from three months (in Gothenburg) to 34 months (in Lisbon).

   To explore between-agency variation, the median duration of social assistance spells was calculated for each local welfare agency having at least 20 beneficiaries in the sample. We find substantial between-agency variation. While the median duration is limited to a minimum of two months in some agencies, the median duration exceeds 24 months in five local welfare agencies. The distribution of median durations at the municipality level is skewed, however, towards shorter durations. We are unaware of previous studies on within-country local variation in duration. In Gustafsson et al. (2002) within-country variation is only based on two cities within a country: Gothenburg and Helsingborg in Sweden present similar scores (respectively three and four months), and also Milan (five months) and Turin (six months) in Italy show the same pattern. By contrast, in Spain, the findings for Barcelona (27 months) and Vitoria (12 months) diverge. In summary, the within-country variation in Belgium seems to be nearly as substantial as the between-country variation in Gustafsson et al. (2002).

Probability of Exiting Social Assistance by Welfare Agency Characteristics

To explore how the probability of leaving social assistance is associated with characteristics of local welfare agencies, we derive life-table estimates separately for groups of individuals classified according to characteristics of their benefit agency. The estimates are graphed in Fig. 2, by characteristic, and illustrate the gross effects of each agency characteristic.[10]

The differentiation of hazard in terms of municipality-level unemployment rates is pronounced during the first months: see Fig. 2(a). Welfare agencies in municipalities with low to medium unemployment rates generally have the highest exit rates, but the effect diminishes as the duration in social assistance increases. Exit hazards vary little by municipality size, but the exit probability seems to be generally lower in welfare agencies that are located in smaller municipalities: see Fig. 2(b). By contrast, hazards clearly differ by participation rate in ALMPs during the first year of the observation period: beneficiaries located in agencies with higher participation rates show higher hazards of exiting social assistance: see Fig. 2(c). After the first year, the differences between the hazard curves become less distinct which may be due to a selection effect, as beneficiaries with a more favourable profile leave social assistance already at shorter durations. Finally, we find that, during the first six months, the hazard of leaving social assistance is generally higher in local welfare agencies that provide more generous supplementary assistance: see Fig. 2(d). The hazard curve decreases rapidly after the first month for the highest generosity level: as only a small subset of beneficiaries is involved, the hazards are less stable for this group.

In summary, differences by agency type in exit hazard functions are more obvious during the first year of the observation period, with between-agency variation being largest in terms of generosity level and participation rate in ALMPs. In the next section, we will explore whether these findings hold in a multivariate model including (un)observed beneficiary-level and agency-level characteristics.

Multivariate Model Estimates of the Monthly Exit Rate from
Social Assistance

We present four specifications of the multivariate model to highlight the contribution of the inclusion of agency-level information: see Tables 3 and 4.

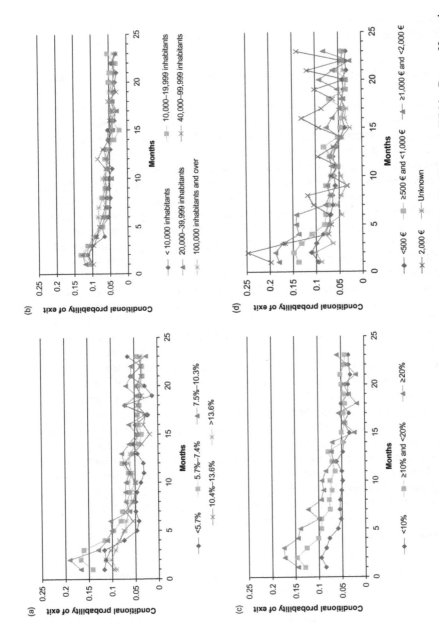

Fig. 2. (a) Observed Within-Group Hazard Function by Unemployment Rate. (b) Observed Within-Group Hazard Function by Municipality Size. (c) Observed Within-Group Hazard Function by ALMP Participation Rate. (d) Observed Within-Group Hazard Function by Generosity Level.

The first model specification only includes the elapsed duration since entry into social assistance and seasonal effects. The second specification introduces observed beneficiary characteristics as well as an individual-level random effect to account for unobserved characteristics ('frailty') affecting the odds of exiting social assistance. In the third specification, we add observed agency-level variables. The fourth and final specification in addition includes an agency-level random effect. As sensitivity tests, we fit two additional specifications, for which the estimates are presented in Appendix B. First, we estimate Specification 4 without the observed agency-level variables. This specification only includes a cross-nested agency-level random effect, as well as the beneficiary-level variables and a beneficiary-level random effect. The significant agency-level random effect illustrates that there is significant variation between welfare agencies in the odds of exiting social assistance that is not accounted for by the beneficiary-level characteristics included in the model. Second, we estimate Specification 4 for the beneficiaries in the sample that have not changed agencies.

Specification 1 only includes the duration since entry into social assistance (grouped in three-month intervals) and a variable capturing seasonal or quarterly variation in exit hazard rates: see Table 3. Apart from the variable capturing seasonal variation, this specification is the multivariate analogue of the observed hazard function pooled across all individuals shown in Fig. 1. The constant in this specification reflects the odds of exiting social assistance within three months after entry to receipt and in the first quarter of the calendar year. The parameter estimates indicate that the odds of exiting decline as the duration since entry into social assistance increases. The estimates also illustrate that the exit rate declines rather quickly during the first year in social assistance and then levels off, a pattern also seen in Fig. 1. The exit rate is subject to seasonal variation as well, with odds being significantly higher in the second and fourth quarters relative to the first quarter.

In addition to the elapsed duration since entry into social assistance and seasonal effects, Specification 2 includes beneficiary-level covariates as well as a beneficiary-level random effect to account for unobserved characteristics affecting the odds of exiting: see Table 3. This model corresponds to the standard 'frailty' model in the literature, which is commonly used when no agency-level information is available. The constant for this specification reflects the monthly odds of leaving social assistance in the period 1 January to 31 March within three months after entry into social assistance for a 31-year-old male beneficiary holding Belgian nationality, with a work intensity of 11 per cent who is not enrolled in full-time education and did not change welfare agencies during the observation period. Adding

Table 3. MCMC-Estimated Means and Standard Deviations of the
Log-Odds of the Hazard of Exiting.

	Specification 1			Specification 2		
	Mean	Std. Dev.	OR	Mean	Std. Dev.	OR
Constant	−2.21***	0.02	0.11***	−1.92***	0.04	0.15***
Duration since entry into social assistance (months 1–3 = ref. category)						
Months 4−6	−0.35***	0.03	0.70***	0.14***	0.04	1.16***
Months 7−9	−0.59***	0.03	0.55***	0.13*	0.05	1.14*
Months 10−12	−0.63***	0.04	0.53***	0.25***	0.06	1.28***
Months 13−15	−0.86***	0.04	0.42***	0.19*	0.08	1.20*
Months 16−18	−0.99***	0.05	0.37***	0.14	0.09	1.15
Months 19−21	−1.09***	0.05	0.34***	0.10	0.09	1.10
Months 22−24	−0.98***	0.05	0.38***	0.25*	0.10	1.28*
Seasonal employment opportunity (quarter 1 = ref. category)						
Quarter 2	0.11***	0.03	1.12***	0.12***	0.03	1.12***
Quarter 3	0.05	0.03	1.05	0.03	0.03	1.04
Quarter 4	0.12***	0.03	1.13***	0.15***	0.03	1.16***
Female				−0.04	0.03	0.96
Age				0.04***	0.01	1.04***
Age squared				−0.00***	0.00	1.00***
Naturalised (tv)				0.72***	0.04	2.06***
Work intensity				0.01***	0.00	1.01***
Student (tv)				−2.52***	0.07	0.08***
Agency switch				−1.40***	0.06	0.25***
Nationality at birth (Belgian = ref. category)						
EU				−0.75***	0.07	0.47***
Non-EU				−1.46***	0.06	0.23***
Unknown				−1.04***	0.19	0.36***
EU * time linear				0.00	0.01	1.00
Non-EU * time linear				0.02***	0.00	1.02***
Unknown * time linear				0.00	0.02	1.00
VARIANCE ESTIMATES FOR RANDOM EFFECTS						
Beneficiary-level				1.16***	0.10	
DEVIANCE INFORMATION CRITERION	78,378.51			71,190.20		

The reported means and standard deviations of the distributions of parameter values have a
similar interpretation as parameter estimates and standard errors obtained from maximum
likelihood estimation. Time-varying variables are denoted by 'tv'.
Significance levels: *p < 0.050, **p < 0.010, ***p < 0.001.

(un)observed beneficiary-level predictors to the model strongly affects the duration pattern of the odds of exiting. Controlling for beneficiary-level characteristics, the odds of exiting during the duration intervals after the first three months are either significantly higher or not significantly different from those during the first three months in social assistance. The negative duration dependence pattern observed in Specification 1 can thus be explained in terms of an increasingly selective composition of the risk set at longer durations.

When we control for other beneficiary characteristics, no significant difference emerges between men and women. The estimates for the quadratic specification for age indicate that the odds of exiting social assistance increase with age, but at a much lower rate at older ages. Regarding nationality, non-EU nationality at birth reduces the odds of exiting social assistance substantially compared to those of beneficiaries holding Belgian nationality. The significant interaction between non-EU nationality and the elapsed duration since entry into the social assistance scheme indicates, however, that the initial gap in the odds of exiting declines as the time spent in social assistance increases. For those holding a European nationality at birth, the odds of exiting social assistance are 53 per cent $((1 - 0.47) \times 100)$ lower than for native Belgians. Naturalised beneficiaries have odds of exiting social assistance that are 106 per cent higher than those of non-naturalised beneficiaries. The employment history is also positively associated with the odds of exiting social assistance. For full-time students the odds of exiting social assistance are 92 per cent lower than for beneficiaries who are not enrolled in education. This finding is consistent with the fact that full-time students are exempted from job searching requirements. Furthermore, changing welfare agencies during the observation period is associated with a reduction of 75 per cent in the odds of exiting social assistance.

The specifications reported in Table 4 differ from those in Table 3 in the addition of agency-level covariates in Specification 3, and, in Specification 4 additionally, an agency-level random effect. The latter specification therefore takes into account the cross-nested structure of beneficiaries in agencies. As a result, the standard deviations of the parameters for the agency-level variables are larger for Specification 4 than for Specification 3, which suggests that the standard deviations in Specification 3 are underestimated. For this reason, some associations with the odds of exiting (e.g. for unemployment rate and municipality size) appear to be statistically significant in Specification 3, whereas Specification 4 indicates that they are not. As we prefer the conservative Specification 4, and both

Table 4. MCMC-Estimated Means and Standard Deviations of the
Log-Odds of the Hazard of Exiting.

	Specification 3			Specification 4		
	Mean	Std. Dev.	OR	Mean	Std. Dev.	OR
Constant	−2.44***	0.09	0.09***	−2.41***	0.10	0.09***
Duration since entry into social assistance (months 1−3 = ref. category)						
Months 4−6	0.16***	0.04	1.18***	0.18***	0.04	1.20***
Months 7−9	0.17**	0.06	1.18**	0.18***	0.06	1.20***
Months 10−12	0.29***	0.07	1.34***	0.31***	0.07	1.36***
Months 13−15	0.23**	0.08	1.25**	0.25**	0.08	1.28**
Months 16−18	0.18*	0.09	1.19*	0.20*	0.09	1.22*
Months 19−21	0.14	0.10	1.15	0.16	0.10	1.17
Months 22−24	0.29**	0.10	1.34**	0.32**	0.10	1.38**
Seasonal employment opportunity (quarter 1 = ref. category)						
Quarter 2	0.12***	0.031	1.13***	0.12***	0.03	1.13***
Quarter 3	0.04	0.032	1.04	0.04	0.03	1.04
Quarter 4	0.15***	0.031	1.16***	0.15***	0.03	1.16***
Female	−0.04	0.03	0.96	−0.06*	0.03	0.94*
Age	0.04***	0.01	1.04***	0.04***	0.01	1.04***
Age squared	−0.00***	0.00	1.00***	−0.00***	0.00	1.00***
Naturalised (tv)	0.67***	0.04	1.95***	0.62***	0.04	1.86***
Work intensity	0.01***	0.00	1.01***	0.01***	0.00	1.01***
Student (tv)	−2.50***	0.07	0.08***	−2.49***	0.07	0.08***
Agency switch	−1.41***	0.06	0.25***	−1.40***	0.06	0.25***
Nationality at birth (Belgian = ref. category)						
EU	−0.71***	0.07	0.49***	−0.71***	0.07	0.49***
Non-EU	−1.35***	0.06	0.26***	−1.34***	0.06	0.26***
Unknown	−0.99***	0.19	0.37***	−0.94***	0.19	0.39***
EU * time linear	0.00	0.01	1.00	0.00	0.01	1.00
Non-EU * time linear	0.02***	0.00	1.02***	0.02***	0.00	1.02***
Unknown * time linear	0.00	0.02	1.00	0.00	0.02	1.00
Unemployment rate (<5.7% = ref. category, tv)						
5.7−7.4%	0.15	0.08	1.16	0.12	0.10	1.13
7.5−10.3%	0.21**	0.08	1.23**	0.17	0.10	1.19
10.4−13.6%	−0.06	0.08	0.94	−0.07	0.10	0.93
>13.6%	−0.08	0.08	0.92	−0.11	0.10	0.90
Municipality size (<10,000 inhabitants = ref. category, tv)						
10,000−19,999	0.06	0.06	1.06	0.06	0.07	1.06
20,000−39,999	0.17**	0.06	1.19**	0.22**	0.08	1.25**
40,000−99,999	0.22***	0.06	1.24***	0.18	0.10	1.20
100,000 and over	0.42***	0.07	1.53***	0.41**	0.15	1.51**

Table 4. *(Continued)*

	Specification 3			Specification 4		
	Mean	Std. Dev.	OR	Mean	Std. Dev.	OR
ALMP participation rate (<10% = ref. category)						
≥10% and <20%	0.48***	0.03	1.61***	0.43***	0.06	1.54***
≥20%	0.92***	0.07	2.50***	0.91***	0.11	2.48***
Generosity (<€500/year = ref. category)						
≥€500 and <€1,000	0.15***	0.05	1.16***	0.20*	0.08	1.22*
≥€1,000 and <€2,000	0.10	0.08	1.10	0.13	0.12	1.14
≥€2,000	0.42**	0.14	1.51**	0.47**	0.17	1.60**
Unknown	−0.14*	0.06	0.87*	−0.15	0.09	0.86
VARIANCE ESTIMATES FOR RANDOM EFFECTS						
Agency-level				0.13***	0.02	
Beneficiary-level	1.13***	0.10		1.06***	0.09	
DEVIANCE INFORMATION CRITERION	70,799.98			70,541.41		

The reported means and standard deviations of the distributions of parameter values have a similar interpretation as parameter estimates and standard errors obtained from maximum likelihood estimation. Time-varying variables are denoted by 'tv'.
Significance levels: *$p < 0.050$, **$p < 0.010$, ***$p < 0.001$.

specifications yield similar parameter estimates, we discuss the associations of the agency-level predictors with the odds of exiting social assistance on the basis of Specification 4.

The constant for Specifications 3 and 4 reflects the odds of exiting social assistance for a reference beneficiary similar to the one in Specification 2 in a municipality with fewer than 10,000 inhabitants and a very low unemployment rate, who is served by a welfare agency that has a very low generosity level and a low participation rate in ALMPs. Including the agency-level predictors in Specifications 3 and 4 does not substantially affect the parameter estimates for the elapsed duration since entry into social assistance and seasonal variation compared to Specification 2. For the beneficiary-level characteristics, parameter estimates in Specifications 3 and 4 are also largely similar to the estimates in Specification 2. However, an exception is sex in Specification 4 for which we now find that the odds of exiting for women are 6 per cent lower than for men. Also, compared to Specification 2, the estimate for naturalisation in Specifications 3 and 4 is reduced by

11 and 20 per cent, respectively. Persons who acquired Belgian nationality after birth are concentrated in cities, where exit rates are generally higher (see below).

We now turn to the agency-level variables. The estimates in Specification 4 reflect the relation between the odds of exiting and observed agency-level characteristics controlling for (un)observed individual characteristics, and other observed and unobserved agency-level characteristics. The odds of exiting social assistance do not vary significantly with the municipality-level unemployment rate. This finding differs from those in studies by Hoynes (2000) and van der Klauw and van Ours (2001), while it is in line with Cappellari and Jenkins (2014). In Fig. 2(a), we observed significant differences between agencies with various rates of unemployment, but apparently these are due to other covariates in the model.

Municipality size, however, is significantly associated with the odds of leaving social assistance: the odds of exiting are 25 per cent $((1.25 - 1) \times 100)$ and 51 per cent $((1.51 - 1) \times 100)$ higher for beneficiaries in municipalities with 20,000–39,999 inhabitants and in large cities (100,000 inhabitants and over), respectively, than those of beneficiaries in municipalities with fewer than 10,000 inhabitants. This shows that spells of social assistance receipt are generally shorter in larger cities, as illustrated in Fig. 2(b). This is in contrast with earlier findings of Cockx (1997), who reported longer durations in Belgian cities with over 100,000 inhabitants in the late 1980s. Dahl and Lorentzen (2003) concluded that municipality size does not matter in Norway.

Beneficiaries in agencies with medium to high participation rates in ALMPs have odds of exiting social assistance that are respectively 54 and 148 per cent higher than those of similar beneficiaries in agencies with low participation rates. Fig. 2(c) revealed large differences in exit rates between agencies with varying participation rates in these programmes, and these are confirmed in the multivariate analysis. Recall that participation in an ALMP implies exit from social assistance. Finally, a higher generosity level is generally associated with higher odds of exiting social assistance compared to those of agencies with low generosity levels. This finding confirms the results shown in Fig. 2(d).

To check the robustness of the findings of the cross-classified model, we re-estimated Specification 4 for beneficiaries who did not change welfare agency throughout the observation period: see Specification in Appendix B. The estimates for the subsample who did not change agencies are generally in the same order of magnitude for the beneficiary-level variables. However, omitting beneficiaries who changed agencies affects the parameter estimates for elapsed duration in social assistance: for all duration intervals the odds of exiting do not differ significantly from the first interval (one to three months in social assistance). This again suggests that the negative duration dependence pattern can be accounted for in terms of the changing profile of beneficiaries over time, similar to the results from the cross-nested model. Finally, we find that agency-level associations with the odds of exiting are slightly lower than in the cross-nested model. Excluding beneficiaries that switched agencies from the estimation sample does not necessarily remove all kinds of bias that might result from 'benefit shopping'. The remaining sample of 'stayers' might still be affected by selection bias. However, as noted in the second section, it is unlikely that many beneficiaries are motivated by higher supplementary assistance to switch agencies.

CONCLUSION

Social assistance for able-bodied persons of working age in Belgium is a shared responsibility between the federal state and local agencies. Although there is a nationwide guaranteed minimum income, local agencies enjoy considerable discretion in how they implement the federal statutory frame-work on the conditions for eligibility (e.g. labour market availability) of the benefit. Local agencies can also provide supplementary assistance on top of the federally defined minimum income level. This raises questions about how much variation in spell lengths of benefit receipt is associated with differences in local area characteristics and in local policy. Using random-effects event history analysis, we examined the hazard of exiting social assistance over a two-year observation period in a representative adminis-trative data sample of 14,270 entrants in the course of 2004 aged 18–64.

We found that the median duration varies substantially at the local level from two months to over 24 months, with an overall median duration of eight months. The magnitude of this within-country variation is nearly as large as the between-country variation found by Gustafsson et al. (2002).

We found strong associations between beneficiary characteristics (sex, age, foreign nationality, citizenship acquisition, work history and being a student) and spell length. Controlling for beneficiary characteristics, we found no evidence pointing to negative duration dependence. Beneficiaries with a more favourable profile tended to leave earlier.

The main interest of this article is the association of agency-level charac-teristics with the odds of exiting, given that agency-level information is rarely used in other studies. The local unemployment rate was not significantly associated with the odds of exiting when controlling for beneficiary-level covariates and agency characteristics, while the estimates show higher odds of exiting in bigger municipalities, and in agencies which provide more generous supplementary assistance. We also found strong evidence of shorter episodes in agencies where the participation of beneficiaries in ALMPs is higher. Including agency-level variables had a small effect on the estimates of the coefficients for a limited number of the beneficiary characteristics.

We draw attention to some methodological limitations of the present study, which may be addressed in further research. First, we note that the data applied in this study do not allow an analysis of (sustainable) labour market integration, as no distinction is made between reasons why beneficiaries exit social assistance. Moreover subsequent benefit episodes may occur (Gustafsson et al., 2002; Walker & Shaw, 1998): 26 per cent of our sample experienced more than one episode in social assistance during the 24-month observation period (disregarding breaks of one month), 21 per cent experienced two spells and 5 per cent went through three episodes. The highest number of episodes was six. Consequently, a short duration of an episode in social assistance does not necessarily reflect durable labour market integration (Gustafsson et al., 2002; Kazepov, 1999). Second, in spite of sensitivity analysis, the analysis may not fully control for possible selection bias due to 'benefit shopping'.

Despite these limitations, this study is, to the best of our knowledge, the first European study that explicitly models exit from social assistance in a decentralised scheme and uses a random-effects model that allows for differences in both the observed and unobserved characteristics of beneficiaries and of local agencies.

In Belgium, social assistance is moderately to highly decentralised, leading to important variations in welfare agency policies across municipalities, despite a national statutory framework and cost equalising mechanisms in the federal subsidies to local agencies. The findings of this study show that these variations in policy are clearly associated with differences in exit rates from social assistance. This raises a number of issues, for both researchers and policy makers. Researchers of social assistance dynamics, who have until now mainly looked at the effects of beneficiary variables and local area characteristics, should consider collecting and using indicators of local policies (including the way that national policies are locally implemented). Better policy indicators could be devised than the rather rough ones used in this study. Also, attention could be given to how these differences in policy come about. Both political preferences and variations in financial and other resources are likely to play a role. An issue that is of importance for both policy makers and researchers is that the system of partial reimbursements of social assistance benefits and subsidies for various purposes by the Belgian federal government creates incentives for local social assistance agencies to engage in particular activities and to target their efforts to particular beneficiaries. The effects and design of such incentives merit further research, which could perhaps take advantage of the literature on decentralisation and fiscal federalism. Finally, the findings could raise concerns about equity, as beneficiaries with equal characteristics are treated differently and, consequently, have different chances of exiting social assistance, depending on where they live.

NOTES

1. *Source*: Eurostat (http://epp.eurostat.ec.europa.eu/portal/page/portal/population/data/main_tables).

2. *Source*: National Bank of Belgium (http://www.nbb.be/pub/stats/stats.htm?l=en).

3. All the tables and figures included in the article are based on this sample from the Data Warehouse Labour Market and Social Security.

4. The agencies at entry cover 572 of the 574 local agencies in the sample.

5. Breaks of one month between subsequent episodes are frequent: 37 per cent of the breaks last one month. Fifteen per cent of the breaks between subsequent episodes last two months, and 10 per cent last three months. Some 37 per cent of the breaks last longer than three months.

6. We assigned individuals who were recorded as being present in more than one agency in any given month to the agency providing the highest payment amount.

7. In addition to the EU-27 countries, Switzerland, Iceland and Norway are also considered as European nations.

8. As adequate information on the actual living arrangements, which is relevant for the determination of the benefit amount, is not available in the register data, the household situation is not included in the analysis.

9. We obtained descriptive statistics on the duration in social assistance by calculating actuarial life tables (i.e. assuming that exits occur on average at the midpoint of each time interval) (Gehan, 1975).

10. In order to test whether the differences between agencies with various characteristics in Fig. 2 give rise to significant gross differences in exit for the agency-level variables, we estimated multivariate models including elapsed duration since entry to receipt and each of the agency characteristics separately (not reported). They show that differences between curves in Fig. 2 are statistically significant for each of the agency-level characteristics. The estimates for Specification 4 in Table 4 indicate

whether the agency-level covariates are significant when controlling for (un) observed beneficiary-level and agency-level characteristics.

FUNDING

This research was supported by the Agency for Innovation by Science and Technology, Flanders and by the Fund for Scientific Research [G042411N], Belgium.

ACKNOWLEDGEMENTS

The authors wish to thank the referees and editors for their detailed and constructive comments and suggestions, which were extremely helpful when revising the article. We thank also Koen Decancq, Tim Goedemé, Bea Cantillon, Michaela Pfeifer, Eva Lefevere, Chiara Saraceno, Birgitte-Pfau Effinger, Natascha Van Mechelen, Sarah Marchal, Bettina Leibetseder, Berenice Storms, Marjolijn De Wilde and Olivier Pintelon for their useful comments on earlier versions of this article. Earlier versions of this article were presented at the ISA Annual RC 19 Meeting (Oslo, 23–25 August 2012), the IZA/OECD/World Bank Conference on Safety Nets and Benefit Dependence: Evidence and Policy Implications (Paris, 21–22 May 2013) and the Young Researchers Conference 'Local Welfare Systems and Female Labour Market Participation' (Hamburg, 19–20 September 2013). The authors thank participants of those conferences for useful comments. We also extend our thanks to George Leckie for his assistance with the runmlwin module for Stata (Leckie & Charlton, 2013).

REFERENCES

Andrén, T. (2007). The persistence of welfare participation. *IZA Discussion Paper, 3100*, 1–33.
Atkinson, A., & Micklewright, J. (1991). Unemployment compensation and labor market transitions: A critical review. *Journal of Economic Literature, 29*(4), 1679–1727.
Bane, M., & Ellwood, D. (1994). *Welfare realities. From rhetoric to reform.* Cambridge, MA: Harvard University Press.
Barber, J., Murphy, S., Axinn, W., & Maples, J. (2000). Discrete-time multilevel hazard analysis. *Sociological Methodology, 30*(1), 201–235.

Barrett, A., & McCarthy, Y. (2008). Immigrants and welfare programmes: Exploring the interactions between immigrant characteristics, immigrant welfare dependence, and welfare policy. *Oxford Review of Economic Policy, 24*(3), 542–559.

Beretvas, N. (2011). Cross-classified and multiple-membership models. In J. Hox & J. K. Roberts (Eds.), *Handbook of advanced multilevel analysis* (pp. 313–334). New York, NY: Routledge.

Blossfeld, H.-P., Golsch, K., & Rohwer, G. (2007). *Event history analysis with Stata.* Mawah, NJ: Lawrence Erlbaum Associates.

Boone, J., Frederiksson, P., Holmlund, B., & van Ours, J. (2001). Optimal unemployment insurance with monitoring and sanctions. *IZA Discussion Paper, 401*, 1–30.

Browne, W. J. (2012). *MCMC estimation in MLwiN* (Vol. 2.26). Bristol: Centre for Multilevel Modelling, University of Bristol.

Browne, W. J., & Draper, D. (2006). A comparison of Bayesian and likelihood-based methods for fitting multilevel models. *Bayesian Analysis, 1*(3), 473–514.

Browne, W. J., Steele, F., Golalizadeh, M., & Green, M. J. (2009). The use of simple reparameterizations to improve the efficiency of Markov chain Monte Carlo estimation for multilevel models with applications to discrete time survival models. *Journal of the Royal Statistical Society: Series A (Statistics in Society), 172*(3), 579–598.

Cahuc, P., & Zylberberg, A. (2004). *Labor economics.* Cambridge, MA: Massachusetts Institute of Technology.

Cantillon, B., Van Mechelen, N., & Schulte, B. (2008). Minimum income policies in old and new member states. In J. Alber, T. Fahey, & C. Saraceno (Eds.), *Handbook of quality of life in the enlarged European Union* (pp. 218–234). London: Routledge.

Cappellari, L., & Jenkins, S. P. (2014). The dynamics of social assistance benefit receipt in Britain. In S. Carcillo, H. Immervoll, S. P. Jenkins, S. Königs, & K. Tatsiramos (Eds.), *Safety nets and benefit dependence* (Vol. 39, Ch. 2, pp. 41–79). Research in Labor Economics. Bingley, UK: Emerald Group Publishing Limited.

Carcillo, S., & Grubb, D. (2006). From inactivity to work: The role of active labour market policies. *OECD Social, Employment and Migration Working Paper, 36*, 1–72.

Cockx, B. (1997). Analysis of transition data by the minimum-chi-square method: An application to welfare spells in Belgium. *Review of Economics and Statistics, 79*(3), 392–405.

Corluy, V., & Verbist, G. (2010). Inkomen en diversiteit: Onderzoek naar de inkomenspositie van migranten in België. *CSB-Bericht, 5*, 1–27.

Cornelis, I., Peeters, N., Reynaert, J.-F., Thijs, P., Casman, M.-T., Nisen, L., & Storms, B. (2012). *REMI: Referentiebudgetten voor een menswaardig inkomen, een webapplicatie* (p. 181). Brussel: POD Maatschappelijke Integratie.

Dahl, E., & Lorentzen, T. (2003). Explaining exit to work among social assistance recipients in Norway: Heterogeneity or dependency? *European Sociological Review, 19*(5), 519–536.

De Vries, M. (2000). The rise and fall of decentralization: A comparative analysis of arguments and practices in European countries. *European Journal of Political Research, 38*, 193–224.

De Wilde, M., Hermans, K., Carpentier, S., De Groof, M., Cuypers, D., Torfs, D., & Cantillon, B. (2011). *Studenten en het Recht op Maatschappelijke Integratie of het Recht op Maatschappelijke Hulp* (p. 238). Brussel: POD Maatschappelijke Integratie, Armoedebestrijding, Sociale Economie en Grootstedenbeleid.

Engström, P. (2009). Vacancy referrals, job search, and the duration of unemployment: A randomized experiment. *IZA Discussion Paper, 3991*, 1–25.

Fielding, A., & Goldstein, H. (2006). Cross-classified and multiple membership structures in multilevel models: An introduction and review. University of Birmingham, Department of Education and Skills, Research Report, 791, pp. 1–66.

Fortin, B., Lacroix, G., & Drolet, S. (2004). Welfare benefits and the duration of welfare spells: Evidence from a natural experiment in Canada. *Journal of Public Economics, 88*, 1495–1520.

Gehan, E. (1975). Statistical models for survival time studies. In M. Staquet (Ed.), *Cancer therapy: Prognostic factors and criteria* (pp. 7–35). New York, NY: Raven Press.

Goldstein, H. (2011). *Multilevel statistical models* (4th ed.). Chichester: Wiley.

Gustafsson, B. (2013). Social assistance among immigrants and natives in Sweden. *International Journal of Manpower, 34*(2), 126–141.

Gustafsson, B., Müller, R., Negri, N., & Voges, W. (2002). Paths through (and out of) social assistance. In C. Saraceno (Ed.), *Social assistance dynamics in Europe. National and local poverty regimes* (pp. 173–233). Bristol: The Policy Press.

Hansen, H.-T. (2008). The dynamics of social assistance recipiency: Empirical evidence from Norway. *European Sociological Review, 24*(3), 1–17.

Hansen, J., & Lofstrom, M. (2011). Immigrant–native differences in welfare participation: The role of entry and exit rates. *Industrial Relations: A Journal of Economy and Society, 50*(3), 412–442.

Hansen, J., Lofstrom, M., Liu, X., & Zhang, X. (2014). State dependence in social assistance receipt in Canada. In S. Carcillo, H. Immervoll, S. P. Jenkins, S. Königs, & K. Tatsiramos (Eds.), *Safety nets and benefit dependence* (Vol. 39). Research in Labor Economics. Bingley, UK: Emerald Group Publishing Limited.

Hedeker, D., Siddiqui, O., & Hu, F. B. (2000). Random-effects regression analysis of correlated grouped-time survival data. *Statistical Methods in Medical Research, 9*(2), 161–179.

Hox, J. (2010). *Multilevel analysis. Techniques and applications*. New York, NY: Routledge.

Hoynes, H. (2000). Local labor markets and welfare spells: Do demand conditions matter. *The Review of Economics and Statistics, 82*(3), 351–386.

Jean, S., Causa, O., Jimenez, M., & Wanner, I. (2010). Migration and labour market outcomes in OECD countries. *OECD Journal: Economic Studies, 1*, 1–34.

Jenkins, S. (2007). *Survival analysis with Stata. Module EC968 Part II: Introduction to the analysis of spell duration data*. Essex: Institute for Social and Economic Research.

Kazepov, Y. (1999). At the edge of longitudinal analysis. Welfare institutions and social assistance dynamics. *Quality & Quantity, 33*(3), 305–322.

Lancaster, T. (1990). *The econometric analysis of transition data*. Cambridge: Cambridge University Press.

Leckie, G. (2013). Cross-classified multilevel models. Concepts. *LEMMA VLE Module, 12*, 1–60.

Leckie, G., & Charlton, C. (2013). runmlwin – A program to run the MLwiN multilevel modelling software from within Stata. *Journal of Statistical Software, 52*(11), 1–40.

Lemieux, T., & Milligan, K. (2008). Incentive effects of social assistance. A regression discontinuity approach. *Journal of Econometrics, 142*(2), 807–828.

Mills, M. (2011). *Introducing survival and event history analysis*. London: Sage.

Moffitt, R. (2002). Welfare programs and labor supply. In A. Auerbach & M. Feldstein (Eds.), *Handbook of public economics* (Vol. 4, pp. 2394–2430). Amsterdam: Elsevier.

Mood, C. (2011). Lagging behind in good times: Immigrants and the increased dependence on social assistance in Sweden. *International Journal of Social Welfare, 20*, 55–65.

Pollitt, C. (2005). Decentralization: A central concept in contemporary public management. In E. Ferlie, L. Lynn, & C. Pollitt (Eds.), *The Oxford handbook of public management* (pp. 371–397). Oxford: Oxford University Press.

Prud'homme, R. (1995). The dangers of decentralization. *The World Bank Research Observer, 10*(2), 201–220.

Rasbash, J., Charlton, C., Browne, W. J., Healy, M., & Cameron, B. (2009). *MLwiN Version 2.1*. Bristol: Centre for Multilevel Modelling, University of Bristol.

Riphahn, R. (1998). Immigrant participation in social assistance programs. *IZA Discussion Paper, 15*, 1–38.

Saraceno, C. (2010). Concepts and practices of social citizenship in Europe: The case of poverty and income support for the poor. In J. Alber & N. Gilbert (Eds.), *United in diversity? Comparing social models in Europe and America* (p. 450). Oxford: Oxford University Press.

Singer, J. D., & Willett, J. B. (2003). *Applied longitudinal data analysis. Modeling change and event occurrence*. Oxford: Oxford University Press.

Spiegelhalter, D. J., Best, N. G., Carlin, B. P., & Van Der Linde, A. (2002). Bayesian measures of model complexity and fit. *Journal of the Royal Statistical Society: Series B (Statistical Methodology), 64*(4), 583–639.

Steele, F. (2011). Multilevel discrete-time event history models with applications to the analysis of recurrent employment transitions. *Australian & New Zealand Journal of Statistics, 53*(1), 1–20.

van der Klaauw, B., & van Ours, J. (2001). From welfare to work: Does neighbourhood matter. *Journal of Public Economics, 87*, 957–985.

Van Mechelen, N., & Bogaerts, K. (2008). Aanvullende financiële steun in Vlaamse OCMW's. *CSB-Bericht, 6*, 1–21.

Walker, R., & Shaw, A. (1998). Escaping from social assistance in great Britain. In L. Leisering & R. Walker (Eds.), *The dynamics of modern society: Poverty, policy and welfare* (pp. 221–242). Bristol: The Policy Press.

Wooldridge, J. (2002). *Econometric analysis of cross section and panel data*. London: MIT Press.

Wunder, C., & Riphahn, R. (2014). The dynamics of welfare entry and exit amongst natives and immigrants. *Oxford Economic Papers, 66*(2), 580–604.

Zorlu, A. (2013). Welfare use of migrants in the Netherlands. *International Journal of Manpower, 34*(1), 83–95.

APPENDIX A: CALCULATION AND DRAWBACKS OF THE AGENCY-LEVEL VARIABLES

Table A1.   Calculation and Data Source of the Agency-Level Predictors.

Variable	Data Source	Calculation
Population size (N)	Population Register January 2004–2006	Number of inhabitants
Unemployment rate (%)	Local Employment Accounts 2004–2006	Annual mean of the share of the workforce (aged 15–64), that is job seeker and non-working
ALMP participation rate (%)	Social Integration Administration data 2004	Number of unique beneficiaries in the course of the year participating in one of the federal ALMPs in the agency, divided by the agency's number of unique beneficiaries in the course of the year
Generosity level (€) (average amount per beneficiary per year)	Dexia Survey – Welfare Agency Accounts 2004, Flemish Agency for Local and Provincial Government – Welfare Agency Accounts	Total budget for cash or in-kind supplementary assistance per agency divided by the agency's total number of social assistance beneficiaries in the course of the year

Source: Authors' compilation.

We use the municipal unemployment rate for the population aged 15–64 as a proxy for labour market tightness, as comparable data between regions on the number of job vacancies are not available. Similarly, we are not able to link unemployment rates for bigger areas to our sample of social assistance beneficiaries.

We use the participation rate in ALMPs at the agency-level as an indicator for active labour market policy. The participation rate considers all beneficiaries (not just entrants) participating in the course of the year in one of the seven federal ALMPs targeted at social assistance beneficiaries. We use this variable as we lack agency-level information on the presence and intensity of job search monitoring and counselling, punitive measures and the number of invitations to participate in a federal ALMP. Similarly, data on beneficiaries' job seeking behaviour are not available. Although beneficiaries may also move into other types of employment (e.g. interim work or a regular job), we use this measure as a proxy for the effort made by the agency to integrate beneficiaries into the labour market.

We apply the total budget for cash or in-kind supplementary benefits per agency divided by the agency's total number of social assistance beneficiaries in the course of the year. A shortcoming of this variable — the best available — is that it disregards that agencies spend a (variable) part of their budget on residents who are not entitled to the social assistance benefit. In addition, the benefit amount allocated can diverge strongly between beneficiaries within the same agency, while we apply a mean amount per beneficiary.

APPENDIX B: SENSITIVITY ANALYSIS

Table B1. MCMC-Estimated Means and Standard Deviations of the Log-Odds of the Hazard of Exiting for Specification 4 without Observed Agency-Level Variables ($N = 14{,}270$) and for the Beneficiaries without Agency Change ($N = 13{,}034$).

	No Agency-Level Variables Specification A			No Agency Switch Specification B		
	Mean	Std. Dev.	OR	Mean	Std. Dev.	OR
Constant	−2.00***	0.05	0.14***	−2.27***	0.11	0.10***
Duration since entry into social assistance (months 1–3 = ref. category)						
Months 4–6	0.17***	0.04	1.18***	0.09	0.07	1.09
Months 7–9	0.17**	0.05	1.19**	0.02	0.10	1.02
Months 10–12	0.30***	0.06	1.35***	0.09	0.13	1.10
Months 13–15	0.23**	0.08	1.26**	−0.02	0.15	0.98
Months 16–18	0.19*	0.08	1.21*	−0.13	0.17	0.88
Months 19–21	0.15	0.09	1.16	−0.19	0.18	0.83
Months 22–24	0.30**	0.10	1.35**	−0.08	0.19	0.92
Seasonal employment opportunity (quarter 1 = ref. category)						
Quarter 2	0.12***	0.03	1.13***	0.11***	0.03	1.12***
Quarter 3	0.04	0.03	1.04	0.04	0.03	1.04
Quarter 4	0.15***	0.03	1.16***	0.16***	0.03	1.17***
Female	−0.06*	0.03	0.94*	−0.07*	0.03	0.93*
Age	0.04***	0.01	1.04***	0.04***	0.01	1.04***
Age squared	−0.00***	0.00	1.00***	−0.00***	0.00	1.00***
Naturalised (tv)	0.63***	0.04	1.87***	0.62***	0.05	1.85***
Work intensity	0.01***	0.00	1.01***	0.01***	0.00	1.01***
Student (tv)	−2.49***	0.07	0.08***	−2.38***	0.11	0.09***
Agency switch	−1.40***	0.06	0.25***			
Nationality at birth (Belgian = ref. category)						
EU	−0.71***	0.07	0.49***	−0.71***	0.07	0.49***
Non-EU	−1.35***	0.06	0.26***	−1.30***	0.07	0.27***
Unknown	−0.94***	0.19	0.39***	−0.93***	0.19	0.40***
EU * time linear	0.00	0.01	1.00	0.01	0.01	1.01
Non-EU * time linear	0.02***	0.00	1.02***	0.03***	0.00	1.03***
Unknown * time linear	0.00	0.02	1.00	0.01	0.02	1.01
Unemployment rate (<5.7% = ref. category, tv)						
5.7–7.4%				0.13	0.09	1.14
7.5–10.3%				0.17	0.10	1.18
10.4–13.6%				−0.08	0.10	0.92
>13.6%				−0.125	0.10	0.88

Table B1. (*Continued*)

	No Agency-Level Variables Specification A			No Agency Switch Specification B		
	Mean	Std. Dev.	OR	Mean	Std. Dev.	OR
Municipality size (<10,000 inhabitants = ref. category, tv)						
10,000–19,999				0.07	0.07	1.07
20,000–39,999				0.20**	0.08	1.22**
40,000–99,999				0.18	0.10	1.19
100,000 inhabitants and over				0.35*	0.14	1.42*
ALMP participation rate (<10% = ref. category)						
≥ 0% and <20%				0.39***	0.06	1.48***
≥20%				0.84***	0.11	2.32***
Generosity (<€500/year = ref. category)						
≥€500 and <€1,000				0.17*	0.07	1.18*
≥€1,000 and <€2,000				0.11	0.11	1.12
≥€2,000				0.39*	0.16	1.48*
Unknown				−0.15	0.08	0.86
VARIANCE ESTIMATES FOR RANDOM EFFECTS						
Agency-level	0.24***	0.03		0.11***	0.021	
Individual-level	1.04***	0.09		0.82***	0.18	
DEVIANCE INFORMATION CRITERION	70,618.13			65,315.50		

The reported means and standard deviations of the distributions of parameter values have a similar interpretation as the parameter estimates and standard errors obtained from maximum likelihood estimation. Time-varying variables are denoted by 'tv'.
Significance levels: *$p < 0.050$, **$p < 0.010$, ***$p < 0.001$.

THE EFFECTS OF MANDATORY ACTIVATION ON WELFARE ENTRY AND EXIT RATES

Anna Persson and Ulrika Vikman

ABSTRACT

Previous literature shows that activation requirements for welfare recipients reduce welfare participation. However, the effect of mandatory activation on welfare entry and exit rates has not been fully examined. In this article, we use a rich set of register data that covers the entire population of Stockholm to study how the introduction of activation programs aimed at unemployed welfare recipients in various city districts affects the probability of individuals entering and exiting social assistance (SA). Our results show that mandatory activation has no overall average effects on SA entry or SA exit. However, we do find a significant negative effect of mandatory activation on the SA entry rate for young individuals and for unmarried individuals without children. For unmarried individuals without children, we find a positive but statistically insignificant effect on the probability to leave SA. Thus, individuals with fewer family responsibilities seem to be more responsive to the reform.

Keywords: Social assistance reform; mandatory activation program; SA entry; SA exit

JEL classifications: I38; H31

Safety Nets and Benefit Dependence
Research in Labor Economics, Volume 39, 189–217
Copyright © 2014 by Emerald Group Publishing Limited
All rights of reproduction in any form reserved
ISSN: 0147-9121/doi:10.1108/S0147-9121201400000039005

INTRODUCTION

The broad consensus in Sweden is that the welfare state has the responsibility of providing economic support to poor individuals. However, the appropriate form of poverty alleviation is a much-debated issue because receiving benefits generally conflicts with retaining work incentives (Thorén, 2008). Throughout history, the poor were often required to provide some service to society to prove themselves to be "worthy" of support. Thus, welfare recipients were commonly required to take on publicly provided, low-paying jobs or to move to workhouses to retain eligibility for benefits (Olofsson, 1996). In the last 20 years, work requirements and activation programs have again been discussed as ways of creating "the correct incentives" for both unemployed individuals and social assistance (SA) recipients in Sweden and countries such as the United States, the United Kingdom, France, and Germany (Lødemel & Trickey, 2001).[1]

The use of activation programs in Sweden has increased over the last few decades for both unemployed individuals and SA recipients (Bonoli, 2010). Many varieties of activation programs exist, and different activation programs may have very different requirements for participation. In a stricter scheme, known as "workfare," the welfare recipient is required to work in a publicly provided job to retain assistance. Less strict schemes may merely mandate participation in a job preparation or job search program. Thus, the term activation is not well defined, as it may mean very different things in different settings. In this article, we study the effects of a set of activation programs implemented in Stockholm between 1997 and 2004. In this particular setting, activation means that all unemployed applicants were required to participate in an assigned activity in order to qualify for SA benefits. The programs consisted mainly of supervised job search and language courses. In contrast to other active labor market policies, activation programs (at least in the Swedish setting) focus mostly on reducing passivity, rather than labor market training. The set-up of the programs is discussed further in section "The City Districts of Stockholm".

We study the effect of the programs on the flows into and out of SA participation in Stockholm. The identifying variation that we use has resulted from the sequential implementation of activation programs in the various city districts of Stockholm. This allows using a difference-in-difference strategy with individual fixed effects to identify the impact of the reform. Thus, we can control for changes both at the individual and district level that are not related to the activation policy. In the section "Empirical Strategy", we discuss the estimation strategy in detail. The reform has been studied previously by Dahlberg, Hanspers, and Mörk (2013), who find that mandatory activation has a positive effect on employment but no effect on the overall welfare caseload. The contribution of our article is to consider the effect on SA entry and SA exit separately. The importance of this distinction has been highlighted in a number of studies.

Besley and Coate (1992) show that the incentive effect of mandatory activation is twofold. In the short run, mandatory activation will induce individuals to refrain from applying for welfare or to exit welfare faster because of the implicit cost associated with welfare use. In the long run, people might make choices that reduce their risk of becoming welfare dependent in the future, for example, by obtaining more education, and that make welfare a less attractive alternative. Hence, mandatory activation programs affect both welfare recipients and nonrecipients through exit and entry effects, respectively. As in most theoretical work on activation requirements for welfare recipients, Besley and Coate (1992) assumes that activation does not to improve human capital but to only change individuals' incentives.[2] The importance of separating the effects on entry and exit rates has also been shown in several empirical studies, such as Grogger, Haider, and Klerman (2003) and Grogger (2004).

Our study has several methodological advantages relative to much of the previous literature. First, while welfare reforms in the US have often involved the implementation of a bundle of reforms combining work requirements, time limits, and financial incentives, such as the Earned Income Tax Credit (EITC), the reforms in Sweden that we study focused solely on activation. By using Swedish data, we can more credibly isolate the effect of activation requirements from those of other interventions. Even if other countries have recently implemented reforms that focus solely on activation requirements, for example, Denmark (Fallesen, Geerdsen, Imai, & Tranaes, 2012), we do not know of any studies that examine how SA entry and SA exit rates are affected separately by activation requirements.

Second, because we have access to data for the entire population and are not restricted to individuals in the labor force or welfare recipients, we are able to capture the full effect of activation requirements on the probability of nonrecipients entering welfare. Third, because all individuals permanently residing in Sweden are potentially eligible to receive welfare benefits, we can examine heterogeneous treatment effects across various demographic groups. Fourth, there are additional advantages to focusing on the city districts of Stockholm; namely, the districts have the same political representation and, most important, belong to the same labor market region. Thus, we can control for (unobserved) common macroeconomic shocks.

In studies on the effect of locally organized activation programs, a common concern is that the relocation of welfare-prone individuals might invalidate the exogenous variation.[3] This relocation effect has been explicitly studied by Edmark (2009) for the same reform and for most of the years that are analyzed in our study. She shows that the implementation of activation requirements did not increase the out-migration of welfare-prone individuals, and thus, we conclude that migration is unlikely to bias the results of this study.[4]

In this study, we find that mandatory activation has no average effect on the overall probability of individuals entering or exiting welfare. However, we find a negative effect of mandatory activation on SA entry rates for young individuals and unmarried individuals without children. For unmarried individuals without children, the activation requirements reduce SA entry rates by 0.2 percentage points on average (relative to the baseline average of 2.8 percent). For young individuals, the activation requirements has a rather large effect on SA entry rates into welfare, amounting to a reduction in SA entry rates by 0.9 percentage points on average (a reduction of 17.6 percent). For singe individuals, we find a positive and relatively large effect on welfare exit, which is statistically insignificant. These heterogeneous effects might occur because activation programs consist of different activities depending on the needs of the participant, and the various activities might have different effects. Our results indicate that the effects are larger for groups that can be assumed to be more mobile and to have fewer family responsibilities and are thus probably more likely to be able to accept a job offer on short notice.

The article proceeds as follows: In the section "Previous Literature", we summarize the relevant literature; then, we describe the Swedish institutions and the city districts in Stockholm in the section "Institutional Setting". In the sections "Data" and "Empirical Strategy", the data, empirical setting, and estimation strategy are presented. The section "Results" shows our results before we conclude section "Conclusions".

PREVIOUS LITERATURE

Most Scandinavian studies have found small or insignificant effects of activation on participation rates and welfare costs.[5] The previously mentioned study by Dahlberg et al. (2013) studies whether the implementation of activation requirements reduced the number of people in welfare, as well as the effect on employment (the probability of being employed in November) and economic well-being (effects on individuals' disposable income). They do not find any effect of activation requirements on the overall caseload of SA recipients or the amount of welfare benefits received. However, they find that the activation requirements reduce welfare participation among single individuals and have small positive effects on employment and disposable income.

A number of studies have investigated the effects of activation requirements on welfare recipients in the US (see, e.g., Grogger & Karoly, 2005; Hamilton, 2002). A few of these studies analyze the effects of such changes on both welfare recipients and nonrecipients. However, most previous work has consisted of experimental studies or leaver studies and therefore, by construction, has focused on exit effects and the duration of welfare participation. The results reported by these studies are mixed and vary substantially between regions and over time. For example, programs implemented in the late 1990s were substantially more successful compared to earlier programs, possibly because the later programs typically focused more on financial incentives (see, for example, Blank, 2002, for an overview). There are also some studies on the effects of welfare reform in the United Kingdom. For example, Riley and Young (2001) find that the New Deal for Young People, a welfare-to-work program for young individuals in long-term unemployment, significantly increased the employment rate in the target group.

A common finding in studies on activation requirements for unemployed individuals is that activation leads unemployed individuals to leave unemployment before activation programs start (see, for example, Black, Smith, Berger, & Noel, 2003; Geerdsen & Holm, 2007). Studies on Sweden have reported such findings for both young and old unemployed individuals (Bennmarker, Skans, & Vikman, 2013; Forslund & Skans, 2006). If this preprogram effect exists for SA recipients, we would expect to find an effect of mandatory activation on SA entry rates. However, as discussed by Moffitt (1996), the effect of activation requirements on welfare entry is ambiguous because it will depend on whether the activity is viewed as a burden or as something that might favor future employment probabilities. The program might also affect the stigma associated with welfare and thus the implicit social cost of welfare participation.

Klerman and Haider (2004) highlight the importance of examining how entry and exit rates are affected by welfare programs, together with economic conditions, because both entry and exit rates contribute to the total SA receipt. Grogger et al. (2003) reports that reduced welfare entry and increased exit rates each accounted for approximately half of the decline in US welfare caseloads during the 1990s. However, economic factors do not seem to affect SA entry and SA exit rates symmetrically. As shown by Grogger (2004), economic improvements are important in reducing entry rates, while welfare reform is more important in determining exit rates. This finding also seems to hold for Sweden. Andrén and Gustafsson (2004) study all entries into SA during two years, 1987 and 1992, and then follow the new entrants up to 1997. The labor market was very different between these two studied years, as the unemployment rate increased dramatically. In 1992, the SA entry rates were 50 percent higher than they were in 1987. Hansen and Lofstrom (2006) show that important differences exist in the flows into and out of welfare and that different SA entry rates explain the gap in welfare participation between immigrants and natives in Sweden.

Klawitter, Plotnick, and Edwards (2000) show that, for young women, US welfare entry is strongly correlated with the birth of their first child. The probability of welfare participation and the timing of entry are also associated with low education, previous poverty, and poor academic achievement. Using Survey of Income and Program Participation (SIPP) data up to 1996, Gittleman (2001) finds that state waivers before the launch of Temporary Assistance for Needy Families (TANF) increased both entry and exit rates.[6] By contrast, Acs, Phillips, and Nelson (2005) find that welfare reform significantly reduced entry rates. As an explanation for these contradictory findings, both of these studies analyze data for only a few postreform years; thus, the effects of the reforms may not be fully captured.

Moreover, there is some concern that the results should not be interpreted to indicate causal relations because, for example, the treatment of applicants or attitudes toward welfare may have changed during the reforms and because the reform serves as a proxy for other state-level changes.

Moffitt (2003) analyzes effects of nonfinancial factors, such as work requirements, on both entry and exit rates. He uses survey data for postreform years in three American cities where single mothers both on and off welfare were surveyed. The recipients were asked questions about work requirements, other requirements, and sanctions. To capture effects of the reform on entry rates, the survey includes questions to TANF applicants about various diversion programs, in which the applicant is required to work or to demonstrate job search participation prior to application. Moffitt finds that work requirements increase exit rates but have no significant effect on the entry rate of TANF applicants. The results regarding the effects of diversion programs on entry rates are mixed, possibly due to selectivity on unobservables. Because the survey focuses on TANF applicants, the study may not capture the entire effect of the policies, as some single mothers may choose to never apply to the program because of the work requirements.

Jenkins and Cappellari (2014) describe the dynamics of SA benefit receipt in Britain between 1991 and 2005 and finds that the decline in the annual SA receipt rate was driven by a decline in the SA entry rate. This can be explained by a decline in the unemployment rate over the period but also by other changes in the socioeconomic environment including two reforms in the income maintenance system in the 1990s.

INSTITUTIONAL SETTING

SA in Sweden

Sweden is divided into 290 municipalities, which are responsible for the majority of publicly provided welfare services, such as child care, education, and elder care. The local governments have also historically been responsible for relief for the poor, but labor market policies have been administered by the central government. Although SA is largely a local responsibility, national legislation establishes the main principles for benefits. The legal framework is stated in the Social Services Act, which was passed in 1982. This law ensures all Swedish citizens and foreign citizens living in Sweden financial support to maintain a "reasonable" standard of living in default of other means of support. A minimum benefit level is stated in the legal framework, but the exact level of the benefit is decided by each municipality. SA is a means-tested benefit, implying that all other financial resources (such as savings and valuable assets) must be exhausted before an individual is eligible for benefits. SA is thus a last resort when social insurance such as unemployment insurance and health insurance is not available or is insufficient. Unlike social insurance, SA is not income based. However, eligibility is universal in the sense that it is not dependent on, for example, having children, as is the case in some other countries (e.g., the United States and the United Kingdom).

During the Swedish recession and financial crisis in the 1990s, the SA caseload increased, and many municipalities faced difficulties in financing

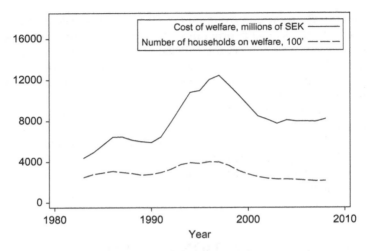

Fig. 1. Cost of Welfare (millions of SEK) and Number of Welfare Households (100s) 1983–2008. *Note*: Costs are CPI adjusted to 2000 prices. *Source:* Statistics Sweden.

the SA system. As shown in Fig. 1, both the cost of welfare benefits and the number of households receiving welfare increased until the mid-1990s, but they have decreased somewhat since then. However, the cost of benefits per household has increased substantially. In 1983, the average benefit received among those on SA was approximately 17,700 SEK (1,610 USD) per year and household (in year 2000 prices).[7] In 2008, this figure was almost 38,200 SEK (3,470 USD). Thus, individuals who were on welfare in 2008 received benefits for more months during a year and/or larger amounts of benefits than individuals in 1983.

In response to the financial difficulties and increase in the number of unemployed SA beneficiaries during the crisis in Sweden, many local governments started to develop municipal activation programs to try to move SA recipients from welfare to self-sufficiency. In 1998, the Social Services Act was changed to explicitly allow municipalities to require welfare recipients to take part in activation programs to retain their eligibility.[8] The activation programs in the Swedish municipalities consist of job search programs and education, as well as practice at job sites. In some cases, rehabilitation programs are also offered (Salonen & Ulmestig, 2004).

The City Districts of Stockholm

In Stockholm, the responsibility for many municipal services is decentralized to city districts' councils. During the time period that is relevant to this study, 18 city districts existed within the municipality. City districts are not responsible for collecting taxes and, in general, follow guidelines given by the Municipal Council. No elections take place at the city district level, and hence, the political representation is equivalent at the district and municipal levels.

In Panel A of Table 1, some characteristics of the 12 city districts used in this study for 1993 are given. The second column is the mean SA, which includes all individuals in the districts, even those who do not receive SA. As the table gives, the mean SA varies between approximately 1,070 SEK for Bromma and 6,200 SEK for Rinkeby. However, for individuals actually receiving SA, the mean SA only varies between 14,124 SEK and 20,453 SEK (see fifth column). Rinkeby is the city district that differs most from the others. The population of Rinkeby has the lowest mean disposable income and high shares of SA receivers, immigrants, and low-educated individuals, as well as the highest SA entry rates and lowest exit rates.

For approximately three-quarters of the SA recipients in Stockholm in 2005, unemployment was the primary reason for needing SA. A large portion of these individuals, 77 percent, did not meet the eligibility criteria for unemployment insurance; that is, they did not meet the work-record requirements and/or were not members of an unemployment benefit fund. However, they were registered at an employment office and were looking for and willing to accept a job (USK, 2007). These are the individuals targeted by the reforms that we study.

Using results from questionnaires and interviews conducted by Karin Edmark and Kajsa Hanspers, Dahlberg et al. (2013) reports the years in which activation requirements were implemented in the different city districts. For an activation program to be classified as mandatory, the activity must be directed to all unemployed welfare recipients, the individuals must be required to attend the activity center daily or almost daily, and welfare benefits must be strictly connected to program participation. A starting year can be determined for 12 of the 18 city districts. In the five most centrally located districts and in Skarpnäck, determining when activation programs were implemented was not possible.[9] For the central districts, the inability to determine a starting year is mainly due to the low numbers of welfare recipients in this area. In Panel B of Table 1, we also study the descriptive statistics for the districts in the nonresponse group. We find

Table 1. City District Characteristics 1993.

	(1) Share of welfare recipients	(2) Average welfare benefits[a]	(3) Average disposable income[b]	(4) Share born in non-Western countries	(5) Average benefits per recipient[c]	(6) Population	(7) Entry rate	(8) Exit rate	(9) Activation year
Panel A: City Districts Used in the Analysis									
Rinkeby	0.308	6,201	98,276	0.464	20,122	5,737	0.115	0.229	1998
Skärholmen	0.111	1,837	127,207	0.124	16,495	15,124	0.048	0.319	1999
Farsta	0.115	2,338	131,694	0.048	20,279	21,758	0.047	0.302	2001
Kista	0.171	3,418	128,954	0.226	19,941	14,439	0.073	0.279	2001
Älvsjö	0.067	949	148,479	0.032	14,124	10,184	0.033	0.340	2002
Hägersten	0.072	1,479	137,375	0.032	20,453	14,437	0.032	0.349	2003
Liljeholmen	0.095	1,870	128,986	0.039	19,620	14,815	0.042	0.325	2003
Spånga-Tensta	0.149	2,739	134,051	0.214	18,364	15,795	0.058	0.289	2003
Bromma	0.058	1,070	157,602	0.025	18,456	28,318	0.026	0.352	2004
Enskede-Årsta	0.075	1,413	136,464	0.043	18,959	21,682	0.030	0.363	2004
Hasselby-Vällingby	0.071	1,222	144,869	0.048	17,197	30,094	0.032	0.342	2004
Vantör	0.122	2,378	127,248	0.067	19,459	16,943	0.048	0.298	2004
Total	0.102	1,928	137,062	0.085	18,859	209,326	0.039	0.333	2003
Panel B: Excluded City Districts									
Kungsholmen	0.072	1,441	139,860	0.028	19,882	19,616	0.036	0.340	
Norrmalm	0.072	1,357	146,137	0.031	18,941	31,823	0.032	0.369	
Östermalm	0.053	918	152,793	0.037	17,216	31,435	0.026	0.415	
Maria-Gamla stan	0.080	1,376	135,548	0.032	17,298	35,964	0.038	0.395	
Katarina-Sofia	0.081	1,369	134,195	0.024	16,877	20,464	0.041	0.418	
Skarpnäck	0.124	2,446	129,539	0.051	19,758	19,655	0.048	0.305	
Total	0.078	1,421	140,744	0.034	18,317	158,957	0.039	0.333	

Disposable income and SA are CPI adjusted to 2000 prices.
[a] Average welfare benefits in city district including entire population.
[b] For the year 1995, since only available for the years 1995–2005.
[c] Average welfare benefits among welfare recipients.

that, as expected, the central districts have low participation rates, higher disposable income, and lower shares of immigrants born in non-Western countries, but that the average benefits per recipients are about the same as that for the rest of Stockholm. Skarpnäck, in contrast, is more similar to the average of the sample included in our analysis, with 12.4 percent of its residents being welfare recipients in 1993.

According to the classification, the first city districts to implement activation requirements were Rinkeby (in 1998) and Skärholmen (in 1999). Eventually, other city districts followed, and by the end of the studied time period, all districts for which classification was possible had implemented mandatory activation. The last column of Table 1 gives the launching year for activation requirements in each city district. Note that when applying for SA, an individual must contact the SA office of the district in which he or she lives (or is registered). Individuals cannot choose which district to apply to and thereby avoid the programs or participate in activities in other districts.

Because we do not know why the different city districts implemented the programs at different times, a possibility exists that the adoption is somewhat endogenous. Because no overall municipal decision was made, each city district could decide whether they wanted to implement activation requirements. Thus, the politicians and social unit management in the city district decided whether and how to implement activation requirements (Thorén, 2008). Examining the observable characteristics, we find that the first districts to implement the reform had some of the highest shares of welfare recipients. However, this pattern is not consistent across the sample because both Spånga-Tensta and Vantör, both with very high participation rates, were among the last to implement activation programs. To formally examine whether endogenous factors may be driving the implementation of activation programs, we will also perform placebo estimations on data for the time period before the programs started.

The activation programs created the new so-called job centers that SA recipients were required to attend between 4 and 15 hours, depending on the city district (Edmark, 2009). Previously, welfare recipients were only in contact with the local social worker, and no mandatory programs were in place for all SA recipients. Unemployed recipients were directed to the unemployment office, but no sanctions were imposed if they did not participate in any activities. The activation program in Skärholmen is the most well-known program and is usually referred to as "the Skärholmen model". This program started as a measure to reduce welfare participation among students who were unemployed during the summer. In 1999, the program was extended to include all unemployed welfare recipients. The main feature of the program is that unemployed welfare applicants are sent to the job center. To retain eligibility for welfare, the applicant must visit the job center for 3 hours every day, following a rotating schedule to prevent black market work, until he or she finds a job. The required activity consists mostly of individual job searching. The job center provides computers with Internet access and assistance from staff when necessary.

As noted by Thorén (2008), resources are often limited at the job center; for example, clients can rarely use the computers for more than 15 minutes each day. Recipients' attendance is recorded daily, and because there is close cooperation between social workers and job center staff, absence is easily detected and can (and often does) lead to a reduction in benefits. This possibility of imposing sanctions is common to the programs in all the city districts. Activation starts when the individual applies for benefits; that is, when an unemployed individual applies for SA, he or she is sent to the job center immediately. The main goal of the activation programs is to improve individuals' chances of becoming self-supportive. However, Thorén (2008) concludes that many of the activities in the activation programs primarily aim to test the client's willingness to work.

DATA

The information about the starting years of the activation programs is combined with individual-level register data from the Louise database administered by Statistics Sweden. This database includes information on various individual characteristics, such as age, country of birth, number of children, level of education, place of residence, and information on income for all individuals aged 16−64 years living in Sweden.[10] Accordingly, we have data for the entire population, regardless of labor market attachment and welfare participation. Our sample consists of all individuals 18−64 years of age living in one of the 12 city districts of Stockholm between 1993 and 2005. People are excluded from the sample if they died or moved away from the municipality. The data also contain the share of the household's SA that the individual received during the past year and benefits collected from other parts of the social security system.[11] SA is directed at households rather than at individuals, and we define an individual as a welfare participant if he or she lived in a household that received SA sometime during a given year. This classification is commonly used, for example in

Jenkins and Cappellari (2014) and Hansen and Lofstrom (2006). What we refer to as SA is thus the individual's share of the household's total received benefit. All unemployed individuals living in a household receiving SA are directed to the job center to fulfill activation requirements. We also exclude all newly arrived immigrants for three years. The reason for excluding these individuals is that they are eligible for SA during their first 18 months in Sweden (*introduktionsbidrag*) under different eligibility criteria than other welfare recipients, and we do not want to capture their SA entry and SA exit due to this type of support.

Table 2 gives descriptive statistics for the population. The mean amount of welfare benefit received by an individual is slightly above 2,000 SEK (182 USD) per year. However, it should be noted that all zeroes are included here and that the mean amount of benefits among those who actually receive any benefits at all is approximately 23,500 SEK (2,100 USD) per year.

Fig. 2 presents the average SA entry and SA exit rates by year for the studied population together with the unemployment rate in the municipality of Stockholm. We can observe that SA entry and SA exit rates follow the unemployment rate, with high SA entry rates and low SA exit rates

Table 2. Summary Statistics.

	Mean	Std. Dev
SA	2,055	9,889
Share with SA	0.087	0.283
Income (100s SEK)[a]	1,626	2,644
Age	40.525	12.151
Age < 26	0.125	0.330
Female	0.499	0.500
Immigrant	0.241	0.428
Native	0.759	0.428
Born in Western country	0.102	0.303
Born in non-Western country	0.139	0.346
No. of children	0.657	0.995
Parent	0.372	0.483
Single parent	0.063	0.244
Compulsory schooling or less	0.195	0.396
Postsecondary schooling	0.350	0.477
N	2,986,175	

Disposable income and SA are CPI adjusted to 2000 prices.
[a]The income variable is only available for individuals from the year 1995.

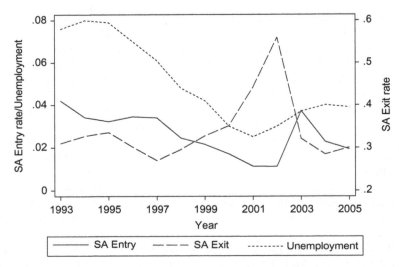

Fig. 2. Annual Unemployment Rate and Raw SA Entry and SA Exit Rates by
Year in Stockholm.

Table 3.   Raw SA Entry and SA Exit Rates by Different Populations.

	Entry	Exit
All	0.026	0.335
Women	0.025	0.337
Men	0.026	0.334
Age < 26	0.051	0.351
Immigrant	0.051	0.289
Born in non-Western country	0.072	0.277
Single parent	0.065	0.283
Unmarried individuals without children	0.028	0.352

during the first half of the time period. SA entry rates decreased and SA
exit rates increased with the economic recovery until 2003. This result is in
line with the development of the welfare receipt, as shown in Fig. 1.

We are also interested in how activation requirements affect more specific
subgroups in the population. Table 3 gives the SA entry and SA exit rates
for different subpopulations in our sample, averaged over the entire
time period. The table provides that young individuals have both higher SA
entry rates and higher SA exit rates, reflecting their mobility. Immigrants,

especially those born in a non-Western country, have high SA entry rates and low SA exit rates.[12] The high SA entry rates are consistent with the results of Hansen and Lofstrom (2006). The pattern observed for immigrants can also be observed among single parents.

EMPIRICAL STRATEGY

To determine the treatment effect on the treated (TT) when mandatory activation is introduced, we use a difference-in-differences (DD) approach over multiple events and time periods in a linear probability model (LPM). When we estimate the effects of mandatory activation on SA entry and SA exit rates, there will be different events of interest. In the case of SA entry, the population consists of those individuals who did not receive any SA at $t-1$, and the event of interest will be whether they then receive SA at t. Let $W_{it} = 1$ indicate that the individual received welfare at time t; then, the probability of SA entry is given by $Pr(W_{it} = 1 | W_{it-1} = 0)$. In the case of SA exit, the population consists of individuals receiving SA at $t-1$, and the event of interest is whether they do not receive SA at t, $Pr(W_{it} = 0 | W_{it-1} = 1)$. For completeness, we will also report the effect of mandatory activation on the probability to receive SA, that is, the probability of an individual receiving SA regardless of whether the individual was on welfare the previous year.

Because all the city districts have implemented mandatory activation, they will all be included in both the control group and the treated group. In a certain year, the districts that had changed their welfare policy are included in the treated group, whereas the rest of the districts are included in the control group. In the difference-in-differences approach in the LPM, we include city district and year dummies. By using this approach rather than only including dummies for treatment and control groups, we are able to control for time-constant unobserved city district-specific effects and systematic changes over time that are common for all city districts. The identifying assumption is therefore that the city districts would have developed similarly if no treatment had occurred. Thus, the implementation of activation requirements cannot be related to (unobserved) city district-specific conditions. This assumption cannot be tested explicitly, but in columns (4)–(6) of Tables 4 and 5, we estimate a model in which we include linear, city district-specific trends. If including these trends significantly changes the baseline estimates, it is an indication that the underlying assumptions are not fulfilled.

If an individual lives in city district j, where there are mandatory work requirements at time t, the treatment variable $D_{jt} = 1$; otherwise, $D_{jt} = 0$. If the probability for the event of interest (SA receipt, SA entry or SA exit) to occur is given by $Pr(W_{ij} = 1)$, $Pr(\text{entry})$ or $Pr(\text{exit}) = Y_{ijt}$, then

$$Y_{ijt} = \alpha_j + \tau_t + \beta D_{jt} + \gamma_t \mathbf{X}_{ijt} + \iota_i + \eta_{ijt} \tag{1}$$

where α_j and τ_t are city district and year dummies, respectively. β then gives us the effect, averaged across all the city districts and years, of mandatory activation on the probability of SA receipt, SA entry and SA exit. To control for individual heterogeneity that varies over time, $\mathbf{X}_{ijt}$ is included.[13] All individual covariates are time interacted (giving γ_t) to allow these individual characteristics to influence the probabilities differently over the business cycle. Note that both the SA entry and the SA exit populations may change over time because of the reform. Individuals closest to the labor market may never enter the population of SA recipients or may leave it faster due to the introduction of mandatory work requirements. To control for this possibility, we will include individual fixed effects, indicated by ι_i, in our estimation model. Our estimates will thus be based on individuals present both before and after the reform; therefore, the composition of the groups will not change. Finally, η_{ijt} is an error term.

A strength of our econometric analysis is that individuals in our data are part of the same labor market and therefore face the same economic conditions but live in areas where mandatory activation was implemented at different times. The time dummies will capture the common economic conditions within the municipality.

Because the effects of the reform may differ between the year in which mandatory activation was introduced and the following year, we will also examine whether the effects differ at t (when mandatory activation is introduced), $t + 1$, and $\geq t + 2$ (see the section "Results"). Thus the treatment variable is interacted with time since the start of the treatment and will be split into three parts: $\beta_1 D_{j,t=k+0}$, $\beta_2 D_{j,t=k+1}$, and $\beta_3 D_{j,t \geq k+2}$, where k indicates year of implementation.

Because treatment occurs only at the district level, the observations may not be independent, which could cause the standard errors to be downward biased (see, e.g., Donald & Lang, 2007). Due to the long time period of our analysis, namely, 13 years, the standard errors may also be serially correlated (Bertrand, Duflo, & Mullainathan, 2004). Because we only have 12 city districts, we are not able to use the common solution and cluster the standard errors at the level of treatment. In a first step, we will only cluster at the individual level, and if the result is significantly different from zero at that level, we will also use the Wild cluster bootstrap method proposed by Cameron, Gelbach, and Miller (2008). They show that a Wild cluster bootstrap works well with as few as five clusters. We base our inference on the sampling distribution obtained via a Wild cluster bootstrap with 99 replications. Since there is likely to be a positive correlation between observations in the same district, we expect the Wild bootstrap standard errors to always be larger than standard errors calculated using other methods.

RESULTS

In this section, we present the results of our estimations. Our main focus is the effects of mandatory activation on SA entry and SA exit, but we will also report how the implementation of activation requirements affected the overall SA receipt. We start by describing the average effects in the section "Average Effects", where we include the entire population. We also study whether the effects vary over time. In the section "Heterogeneous Effects", we determine whether the effects for different groups are heterogeneous. We also present results from placebo analyses, where we only use data from prereform years and move the launching year back in time five years. Throughout this section, we present the β parameter as defined in the section "Empirical Strategy".

Average Effects

In our estimations, the point estimates show a reduction in the SA receipt of 0.8 percentage points due to implementation of activation requirements, which is driven by a reduction in SA entry rates of 0.4 percentage points and an increase in SA exit rates of 1.6 percentage points. The results are presented in Panel A of Table 4. However, even though the receipt and entry estimations are significantly different from zero even when we use the Wild cluster bootstrap method and thus allow the standard errors to be correlated within the city districts, the results do not hold when linear trends are added to the model (columns 4–6). The point estimates are halved, and the p-values increase, yielding insignificant results. This result indicates that for this sample, the assumption of linear trends within the city districts is not fulfilled, and thus it is important that trends are included

Table 4. Estimation Results: Average Effects of Mandatory Activation.

	(1) SA receipt	(2) SA entry	(3) SA exit	(4) SA receipt	(5) Trends included SA entry	(6) SA exit
Panel A						
All	−0.008	−0.004	0.016	−0.003	−0.002	0.011
	(0.001)***	(0.000)***	(0.004)***	(0.001)***	(0.000)***	(0.004)**
	[0.020]	[0.060]	[0.240]	[0.140]	[0.140]	[0.300]
N	2,986,175	2,698,222	287,953	2,986,175	2,698,222	287,953
Panel B						
Year of implementation	−0.006	−0.004	0.016	−0.003	−0.002	0.013
	(0.001)***	(0.000)***	(0.005)***	(0.001)***	(0.000)***	(0.005)***
	[0.060]	[0.060]	[0.220]	[0.120]	[0.200]	[0.220]
One year after	−0.011	−0.006	0.014	−0.005	−0.003	0.010
	(0.001)***	(0.001)***	(0.005)***	(0.001)***	(0.001)***	(0.005)*
	[0.020]	[0.020]	[0.440]	[0.140]	[0.220]	[0.480]
Two years after	−0.024	−0.010	0.028	−0.008	−0.003	0.022
	(0.001)***	(0.001)***	(0.006)***	(0.001)***	(0.001)***	(0.007)***
	[0.020]	[0.020]	[0.560]	[0.180]	[0.600]	[0.640]
N	2,986,175	2,698,222	287,953	2,986,175	2,698,222	287,953

Individual fixed effects, year dummies, city district dummies, and time-varying controls are included in all estimations. Standard errors clustered on individuals in parentheses. *P*-values from Wild cluster bootstrap in brackets.
*$p < 0.1$, **$p < 0.05$, ***$p < 0.01$.

in the model to control for different time trends at the district level. Thus, our preferred estimates are the ones presented in columns 4–6. Our estimations of the effects of mandatory activation on the SA receipt with linear trends are very similar to those reported by Dahlberg et al. (2013), who reports a nonsignificant estimate of −0.2 percentage points even though a somewhat different sample is used and individual fixed effects are not included in the analysis. Although the effects are insignificant, the estimates translate into meaningful effects in economic terms. The estimate for welfare exit, 0.011, corresponds to a 3 percent increase in the probability to stop collecting SA (for SA entry the relative reduction corresponds to 7 percent). Of course, since we cannot reject the hypothesis that the true effect is different from zero, the economic significance should be interpreted with caution. However, the reform may still have had a significant effect at different times after implementation.

A shortcoming of our information on the implementation of activation requirements for SA recipients is that we do not know when during the year the activation programs were implemented. If the program was implemented at the end of the year, the treatment effects will be smaller during that year, and the estimates will suffer from attenuation bias. To illustrate this, we also present the results when we let the effect vary with time since implementation. Therefore, we have estimated a model in which we separate the treatment effects for the year of implementation, the first year after implementation, and two or more years after implementation. The results are given in Panel B of Table 4. For the SA receipt and SA entry, the effects are larger in magnitude, the greater the time since activation was introduced in the respondent's city district. However, when we include linear trends, we find a pattern similar to the pattern that emerged when we estimated the total effect for the entire population. The estimates become less negative, and the *p*-values resulting from the Wild cluster bootstrap method are all greater than conventional significance levels. Moreover, the estimates differ only slightly between the time periods, the estimates for entry are −0.002, −0.003, and −0.003, and thus it is very unlikely that there are any economically meaningful differences between the time periods.

In the SA exit estimations, all the point estimates are positive and increase with time since activation was introduced in the respondent's city district. However, when we use the Wild cluster bootstrap method, the estimates are not significantly different from zero, in the estimations both with and without linear trends. Here the differences between the estimates are larger, and two years after the reform the exit rate is estimated to be

2.2 percentage points lower in the treated districts. However, since the
p-value from the Wild cluster bootstrap is very large, 0.640, this estimate is
hard to interpret.

Our conclusion is therefore that we are not able to identify any effects
on the SA entry rates or the SA exit rates for the entire population when
mandatory activation is implemented, neither estimated as a total effect
nor when we let the effect vary over time. The point estimates are often
relatively large but are not estimated with enough precision. However, the
reform may still have had a statistically significant effect for different
subpopulations.

Heterogeneous Effects

The probability of becoming dependent on SA is clearly not uniformly
distributed over different demographic groups and across the income
distribution. Among the more welfare-prone groups are young individuals,
immigrants born in non-Western countries, single parents, and low-
educated individuals. Because these groups have a higher probability of
receiving benefits than others, we attempt to create a better-defined SA
entry sample by estimating the effects of mandatory activation on (SA
receipt and) SA entry rates with the use of a subpopulation consisting of
individuals with any of these characteristics. Thus, we reduce the problem
of estimating an effect for individuals who have close to zero probability of
ever participating in welfare (e.g., individuals with high education and
income are unlikely to change their behavior in response to a reform that
will most likely never affect them). We prefer to define the population
at risk of entering into welfare by using demographic characteristics rather
than income. Individuals with low income are likely more prone to receive
welfare benefits than others. However, Meyer (2000) argues that restricting
the sample to include only low-income individuals might create bias
because poverty is likely to be higher in an area with low benefit levels and
vice versa, and the higher level of poverty and lower levels of benefits might
affect welfare participation as well as SA entry and SA exit.

As shown by Dahlberg et al. (2013), the activation programs that we
study have a larger effect for single individuals, that is, unmarried individuals without children. Other groups that may have been affected differently are young individuals and immigrants born in non-Western countries.
Thus, we analyze the effect of mandatory activation for these groups
separately. Young individuals are likely to be more mobile than other

individuals, and we therefore expect activation requirements to have larger effects on these individuals. Young people may also have more opportunities to begin an educational program or to receive financial help from their families. Unmarried individuals without children, who are also very mobile (Fiva, 2009), compose a group with low probability of receiving SA, but because this group is large, a large portion of those receiving SA belong to this group.

To study whether activation requirements have heterogeneous effects, we perform separate estimations for the following subgroups: the population at risk of entering SA; unmarried without children; young individuals aged less than 26; and immigrants born in non-Western countries.[14]

The results for the population at risk of entering SA are given in Panel A of Table 5. The estimated effect of mandatory activation on the SA receipt and SA entry for this group is the same as that for the entire population, both when we estimate the effect as an average effect over all years and when we let the effect vary over time. As with the total population, the point estimates become less negative and insignificant when we use the Wild cluster bootstrap method and include linear trends. This result indicates that the assumptions for linear trends within the city districts are not fulfilled for this group either.

The point estimates for unmarried individuals without children, given in Panel B in Table 5, are rather similar to those for the entire sample; however, the estimated effect for the SA receipt and SA entry is more precise and our preferred estimates, where we include linear trends, are significantly different from zero when we use the Wild cluster bootstrap method. Thus, even if the point estimates are reduced when linear trends are included, they still show a reduction of 0.6 percentage points for the SA receipt and a reduction of 0.2 percentage points for the SA entry rate. These results should be compared to an entry rate of 2.8 percent on average for this group and thus a reduction in the entry rate of 7 percent. This implies both a statistically and economically meaningful effect. Although not statistically significant, the estimated effect for the SA exit is positive and large implying a 1.3 percentage point increase in the exit rate. Relative to the baseline exit rate in this group, this corresponds to an increase of 3.7 percent. It is also worth noting that in this group, the exit estimate does not drop as dramatically when we add linear trends as it does in most of our other samples.

When we estimate how the effects vary over time for unmarried individuals without children, the precision is diminished, and the point estimates are only marginally significant. However, the point estimates for the SA

Table 5. Estimation Results: Heterogeneous Results.

	(1)	(2)	(3)	(4)	(5) Trends included	(6) Trends included
	SA receipt	SA entry	SA exit	SA receipt	SA entry	SA exit
Panel A						
Population at risk of entering SA	−0.008	−0.005		−0.002	−0.003	0.013
	(0.001)***	(0.001)***		(0.001)*	(0.001)***	(0.007)**
	[0.100]	[0.100]		[0.460]	[0.300]	[0.220]
Year of implementation	−0.007	−0.004	0.017	−0.002	−0.002	0.015
	(0.001)***	(0.001)***	(0.006)***	(0.001)**	(0.001)**	(0.007)**
	[0.180]	[0.140]	[0.140]	[0.440]	[0.360]	[0.120]
One year after	−0.010	−0.007	0.017	−0.003	−0.004	0.014
	(0.002)***	(0.001)***	(0.007)**	(0.002)**	(0.001)***	(0.008)
	[0.080]	[0.080]	[0.120]	[0.460]	[0.280]	[0.520]
Two years after	−0.026	−0.012	0.016	−0.007	−0.003	
	(0.002)***	(0.002)***	(0.008)**	(0.002)***	(0.002)*	
	[0.080]	[0.080]	[0.400]	[0.500]	[0.600]	
N	2,986,175	1,022,523		2,986,175	1,022,523	
Panel B						
Unmarried w/o children	−0.010	−0.004	0.017	−0.006	−0.002	0.013
	(0.001)***	(0.001)***	(0.006)***	(0.001)***	(0.001)***	(0.007)**
	[0.040]	[0.040]	[0.140]	[0.040]	[0.060]	[0.220]
Year of implementation	−0.009	−0.003	0.017	−0.005	−0.002	0.015
	(0.001)***	(0.001)***	(0.007)**	(0.001)***	(0.001)***	(0.007)**
	[0.040]	[0.040]	[0.120]	[0.040]	[0.100]	[0.120]
One year after	−0.014	−0.006	0.016	−0.008	−0.003	0.014
	(0.001)***	(0.001)***	(0.008)**	(0.001)***	(0.001)***	(0.008)
	[0.040]	[0.040]	[0.400]	[0.080]	[0.100]	[0.520]

Two years after	-0.025 (0.002)*** [0.040]	-0.010 (0.001)*** [0.020]	0.028 (0.010)*** [0.440]	-0.009 (0.002)*** [0.240]	-0.003 (0.001)* [0.420]	0.024 (0.012)** [0.420]
N	1,395,995	1,249,097	146,898	1,395,995	1,249,097	146,898
Panel C						
Age <26	-0.013 (0.003)*** [0.100]	-0.010 (0.002)*** [0.040]	-0.000 (0.012) [0.860]	-0.009 (0.003)*** [0.120]	-0.009 (0.002)*** [0.040]	0.004 (0.012) [0.800]
Year of implementation	-0.013 (0.003)*** [0.060]	-0.010 (0.002)*** [0.040]	0.003 (0.012) [0.640]	-0.009 (0.003)*** [0.100]	-0.009 (0.002)*** [0.020]	0.008 (0.012) [0.300]
One year after	-0.018 (0.003)*** [0.080]	-0.014 (0.003)*** [0.040]	-0.007 (0.014) [0.560]	-0.011 (0.003)*** [0.140]	-0.011 (0.003)*** [0.040]	0.001 (0.015) [0.960]
Two years after	-0.032 (0.005)*** [0.080]	-0.021 (0.004)*** [0.040]	0.000 (0.018) [0.990]	-0.013 (0.005)** [0.360]	-0.012 (0.004)*** [0.140]	0.025 (0.021) [0.440]
N	372,325	312,850	59,475	372,325	312,850	59,475
Panel D						
Immigrants born in non-Western country	-0.004 (0.002)	-0.004 (0.002)**	0.010 (0.005)*	0.002 (0.002)	-0.002 (0.002)	0.005 (0.005)
Year of implementation	-0.003 (0.002)	-0.003 (0.002)*	0.010 (0.006)*	0.001 (0.002)	-0.001 (0.002)	0.006 (0.006)
One year after	-0.004 (0.003)	-0.006 (0.002)***	0.009 (0.006)	0.002 (0.003)	-0.002 (0.002)	0.004 (0.007)
Two years after	-0.021 (0.004)***	-0.010 (0.003)***	0.019 (0.008)**	0.001 (0.004)	0.001 (0.003)	0.008 (0.009)
N	414,978	290,331	124,647	414,978	290,331	124,647

Individual fixed effects, year dummies, city district dummies, and time-varying controls are included in all estimations. Standard errors clustered on individuals in parentheses. P-values from Wild cluster bootstrap in brackets.
*$p < 0.1$, **$p < 0.05$, ***$p < 0.01$.

receipt and SA entry indicate that the effectiveness of mandatory activation has increased somewhat since activation was introduced in the respondent's city district, as the point estimates become slightly more negative with time since activation started. For SA exit, the estimates remain positive and large, but none of them are significantly different from zero when the Wild cluster bootstrap method is used.

The results for individuals under the age of 26 years are presented in Panel C of Table 5. Young individuals have a somewhat higher reduction in the SA receipt compared to the entire population. This result seems to be driven only by lower SA entry rates for this group because the point estimates for SA exit are close to zero. Looking at our preferred estimates (column 5), the effect of mandatory activation on the probability of SA entry is reduced by 0.9 percentage points; the p-value from the Wild bootstrap method is 0.04. This effect is large, as the mean SA entry rate for this group during the studied period was approximately 5 percent (see Table 3) which corresponds to a reduction of 18 percent. Even for this group, the size of the effect seems to be increasing since activation was introduced in the respondent's city district. For the SA receipt, the effect becomes insignificant one year after implementation, and for SA entry the effect is only marginally significant.

Finally, Panel D of Table 5 gives the results for immigrants born in non-Western countries. Although all the estimates have the expected signs in the estimations without linear trends, they all become insignificant when linear trends are included, even when the standard errors are clustered only at the individual level (and some estimates even change signs).[15] Because the activities that immigrants participate in are likely to consist of mainly language training and thus likely differ from those offered to other SA recipients, the different results for this group compared with those for the other samples might not be surprising and may explain why we do not find any effect for the entire sample.

We have also conducted placebo analyses for the subpopulations.[16] These results are given in Table 6. Reassuringly, most of the estimations are close to zero, and many even have the opposite sign. This result indicates that we might have underestimated the effects for our subpopulations. The exception is immigrants born in non-Western countries, for which we find a larger reduction in the SA receipt in our placebo estimations than we do in the primary estimations for this group. This result indicates that mandatory activation for this group may increase rather than decrease the probability of receiving SA.[17]

Table 6. Placebo Results: Heterogenous Results.

	(1)	(2)	(3)
		Trends included	
	SA receipt	SA entry	SA exit
Panel A			
Population at risk of entering SA	0.000	0.001	
	(0.001)	(0.001)	
N	710,106	566,576	
Panel B			
Unmarried w/o children	0.002	0.001	−0.001
	(0.001)*	(0.001)	(0.007)
N	794,027	696,640	97,387
Panel C			
Age < 26	0.004	0.003	0.001
	(0.003)	(0.003)	(0.011)
N	218,712	177,790	40,922
Panel D			
Immigrants born in non-Western country	−0.010	−0.010	0.017
	(0.003)***	(0.003)***	(0.006)***
N	189,501	117,819	71,682

Year dummies, city district dummies, and time-varying controls are included in all estimations. Standard errors clustered on individuals in parentheses.
$*p < 0.1$, $**p < 0.05$, $***p < 0.01$.

CONCLUSIONS

In this article, we examine the effects of introducing mandatory activation in the city of Stockholm on the entry and exit rates of SA recipients. The variation we exploit is a sequential implementation of activation requirements in the different city districts of Stockholm. Earlier studies in the literature have found that mandatory activation reduces welfare participation. However, most of these studies have only captured SA exit effects by focusing on those individuals who are already welfare recipients. The results from studies analyzing the total population remain unclear since the effects of mandatory activation on the entry and exit rates are not considered separately.

Our results indicate that, for the overall population, there is no statistically significant effect of mandatory activation programs on either SA entry or exit. However, there are important differences between groups. In particular, for young and for unmarried individuals without children, activation reduces significantly the probability to start collecting SA benefits. For the group of unmarried individuals without children, we also find a large positive effect on the probability to exit SA, but this estimate is not statistically significant. Based on these findings, we conclude that individuals with fewer family responsibilities are more responsive to the incentives created by the programs. This can be explained by these groups being more mobile and accept job offers on short notice. For young individuals, in particular, the reduction in SA entry following the reform can also be explained by the fact that pursuing higher education, and thus qualify for study grants, becomes relatively more attractive when the requirements of SA take-up are more stringent.

Our results highlight the importance of having access to data on both SA participants and potential SA entrants in order to be able to capture the full effect of welfare reform on benefit take-up. We also show that it is important to consider that the effect of the programs varies across demographic groups, at least in settings where the SA population is heterogeneous. It is also important to keep in mind that the effect of the programs is likely to depend substantially on their design and the type of activities the participants are taking part in.

NOTES

1. We will use the words welfare and SA as equivalents.

2. See also, for example, Chambers (1989) and Brett (1998).

3. The hypothesis that regions with generous welfare systems attract welfare recipients (that is, that welfare-prone individuals relocate to places where SA is higher) is confirmed in several recent studies; Gelbach (2004), McKinnish (2007), and Fiva (2009).

4. We do not find any migration due to the reform in our sample. We have run the estimations both with and without movers, but the result does not change. If individuals fictitiously changed addresses to avoid activation, this information would also be captured in this study because we use information on where the individuals are registered to live and not self-reported information.

5. See Milton and Bergström (1998) and Giertz (2004) for Sweden, Graversen and Jensen (2010) for Denmark, and Dahl (2003) for Norway.

6. State waivers enabled states to give exceptions from the federal regulations to test new programs or combinations of programs.

7. Between 1983 and 2008, the exchange rate varied between 9 USD per 100 SEK and almost 19 USD per 100 SEK. For the years in our analysis (1993–2005), the exchange rate varied less, and in 2000, it was approximately 11 USD per 100 SEK, which we use for comparison in this article.

8. Some municipalities implemented activation programs prior to 1998.

9. The five most centrally located districts are Kungsholmen, Norrmalm, Östermalm, Maria-Gamla stan, and Katarina-Sofia.

10. Individuals who are 16 and 17 years old are excluded from our sample.

11. The individual's share of the household's benefits is calculated by using an equivalence scale determined by the National Board of Health and Welfare (Socialstyrelsen).

12. As non-Western countries, we include the former Soviet Union (due to data limitations, all these countries are coded in the same way in our data), Asia, Africa, and South and Central America.

13. The individual characteristics that we include in the model are age, age squared, and dummy variables for female, parent, single parent, born in a Western country except Sweden, born in a non-Western country, low education (compulsory schooling or less), and high education (at least some postsecondary schooling).

14. We also performed estimations for single mothers, who constitute another vulnerable group, but no effect of mandatory activation on either SA entry rates or SA exit rates could be found for this group.

15. Accordingly, we do not include p-values from the Wild cluster bootstrap method in this table sine they are larger than the conventional standard errors.

16. We perform the placebo analyses by using data from 1993 to 2000. For the years 1998, 1999, and 2000, we exclude Rinkeby, and for 1999 and 2000, we also exclude Skärholmen. Thus, we only use data for the period before the reform was implemented in any of the city districts. We move the launching year of the actual reform back in time five years.

17. Because the estimates in the placebo estimations are small and never significant for the groups for which we do find effects in our main analysis for SA entry and SA exit, we do not report any p-values from the Wild cluster bootstrap method.

ACKNOWLEDGMENTS

We thank Anders Björklund, Matz Dahlberg, Jon Fiva, Kajsa Hanspers, Eva Mörk, Oddbjørn Raaum, Michael Svarer, Johan Vikström, the seminar participants at the Department of Economics, Uppsala University, and the participants in the course Topics in Applied Microeconometrics in Aarhus and at the IZA/OECD/World Bank Conference on Safety Nets and Benefit Dependence in Paris for their valuable comments and suggestions. Finally, we have benefited significantly from the reports of two anonymous referees and comments by the editors of this journal.

REFERENCES

Acs, G., Phillips, K. R., & Nelson, S. (2005). The road not taken? Changes in welfare entry during the 1990s*. *Social Science Quarterly*, *86*(s1), 1060–1079.

Andrén, T., & Gustafsson, B. (2004). Patterns of social assistance receipt in Sweden. *International Journal of Social Welfare*, *13*(1), 55–68.

Bennmarker, H., Skans, O. N., & Vikman, U. (2013). Workfare for the old and long-term unemployed. *Labour Economics*, *25*, 25–34.

Bertrand, M., Duflo, E., & Mullainathan, S. (2004). How much should we trust differences-in-differences estimates? *Quarterly Journal of Economics*, *119*(1), 249–275.

Besley, T., & Coate, S. (1992). Workfare versus welfare: incentive arguments for work requirements in poverty-alleviation programs. *The American Economic Review*, *82*(1), 249–261.

Black, D. A., Smith, J. A., Berger, M. C., & Noel, B. J. (2003). Is the threat of reemployment services more effective than the services themselves? Evidence from random assignment in the UI system. *The American economic review*, *93*(4), 1313–1327.

Blank, R. M. (2002). Evaluating welfare reform in the United States. *Journal of Economic Literature*, *40*, 1105–1166.

Bonoli, G. (2010). *The political economy of active labour market policy*. Working paper 1/2010. The University of Edinburgh.

Brett, C. (1998). Who should be on workfare? The use of work requirements as part of an optimal tax mix. *Oxford Economic Papers*, *50*(4), 607–622.

Cameron, A. C., Gelbach, J. B., & Miller, D. L. (2008). Bootstrap-based improvements for inference with clustered errors. *The Review of Economics and Statistics*, *90*(3), 414–427.

Chambers, R. G. (1989). Workfare or welfare? *Journal of Public Economics*, *40*(1), 79–97.

Dahl, E. (2003). Does "Workfare" work? The Norwegian experience. *International Journal of Social Welfare*, *12*(4), 274–288.

Dahlberg, M., Hanspers, K., & Mörk, E. (2013). Mandatory activation of welfare recipients – Evidence from the city of Stockholm. In *Essays on welfare dependency and the privatization of welfare services*. Economic studies 137, Department of Economics, Uppsala University.

Donald, S. G., & Lang, K. (2007). Inference with difference–indifferences and other panel data. *Review of Economics and Statistics*, *89*(2), 221–233.

Edmark, K. (2009). Migration effects of welfare benefit reform. *Scandinavian Journal of Economics*, *111*(3), 511–526.

Fallesen, P., Geerdsen, L. P., Imai, S., & Tranaes, T. (2012). *The effect of workfare policy on crime*, Rockwoll Foundation Study Paper No. 41.

Fiva, J. H. (2009). Does welfare policy affect residential choices? An empirical investigation accounting for policy endogeneity. *Journal of Public Economics*, *93*(3–4), 529–540.

Forslund, A., & Skans, O. N. (2006). Swedish youth labour market policies revisited. *Vierteljahrshefte zur Wirtschaftsforschung*, *75*(3), 168–185.

Geerdsen, L. P., & Holm, A. (2007). Duration of UI periods and the perceived threat effect from labour market programmes. *Labour Economics*, *14*(3), 639–652.

Gelbach, J. B. (2004). Migration, the life cycle, and state benefits: How low is the bottom? *Journal of Political Economy*, *112*(5), 1091–1130.

Giertz, A. (2004). *Making the poor work. Social assistance and activation programs in Sweden*, Lund Dissertations in Social Work No. 19, Lund University.

Gittleman, M. (2001). Declining caseloads: What do the dynamics of welfare participation reveal? *Industrial Relations: A Journal of Economy and Society, 40*(4), 537—570.

Graversen, B. K., & Jensen, P. (2010). A reappraisal of the virtues of private sector employment programmes. *The Scandinavian Journal of Economics, 112*(3), 546—569.

Grogger, J. (2004). Welfare transitions in the 1990s: The economy, welfare policy, and the EITC. *Journal of Policy Analysis and Management, 23*(4), 671—695.

Grogger, J., Haider, S. J., & Klerman, J. (2003). Why did the welfare rolls fall during the 1990's? The importance of entry. *The American Economic Review, 93*(2), 288—292.

Grogger, J., & Karoly, L. A. (2005). *Welfare reform: Effects of a decade of change.* Cambridge, MA: Harvard University Press.

Hamilton, G. (2002). *Moving people from welfare to work: Lessons from the national evaluation of welfare-to-work strategies.* U.S. Department of Health and Human Services.

Hansen, J., & Lofstrom, M. (2006). *Immigrant—native differences in welfare participation: The role of entry and exit rates.* IZA Discussion Paper No. 2261.

Jenkins, S. P., & Cappellari, L. (2014). The dynamics of social assistance benefit receipt in Britain. In S. Carcillo, H. Immervoll, S. P. Jenkins, S. Königs, & K. Tatsiramos (Eds.), *Safety nets and benefit dependence* (Vol. 39). Research in Labor Economics. Bingley, UK: Emerald Group Publishing Limited.

Klawitter, M., Plotnick, R. D., & Edwards, M. E. (2000). Determinants of initial entry onto welfare by young women. *Journal of Policy Analysis and Management, 19*(4), 527—546.

Klerman, J. A., & Haider, S. J. (2004). A stock-flow analysis of the welfare caseload. *Journal of Human Resources, XXXIX*(4), 865—886.

Lødemel, I., & Trickey, H. (2001). *'An offer you can't refuse': Workfare in international perspective.* Bristol: The Policy Press.

McKinnish, T. (2007). Welfare-induced migration at state borders: New evidence from microdata. *Journal of Public Economics, 91*(3—4), 437—450.

Meyer, B. D. (2000). *Do the poor move to receive higher welfare benefits?* mimeo.

Milton, P., & Bergström, R. (1998). *Uppsalamodellen och social-bidragstagarna. En effektutvärdering,* CUS-rapport 1998:1, The National Board of Health and Welfare.

Moffitt, R. (2003). The role of nonfinancial factors in exit and entry in the TANF program. *Journal of Human Resources, 38,* 1221—1254.

Moffitt, R. A. (1996). The effect of employment and training programs on entry and exit from the welfare caseload. *Journal of Policy Analysis and Management, 15*(1), 32—50.

Olofsson, J. (1996). *Arbetslöshetsfrågan i historisk belysning: En diskussion om arbetslöshet och social politik i Sverige 1830—1920.* Dissertation, Lund University.

Riley, R., & Young, G. (2001). *Does welfare-to-work policy increase employment?: Evidence from the UK new deal for young people.* Discussion paper. National Institute of Economic and Social Research.

Salonen, T., & Ulmestig, R. (2004). *Nedersta trappsteget — en studieom kommunal aktivering.* Växjö: Institutionen för vårdvetenskap och social arbete vid Växjo Universitet.

Thoren, K. H. (2008). *Activation policy in action: A street-level study of social assistance in the Swedish welfare state.* Sweden: Växjö University Press, Växjö universitet.

USK. (2007). Ekonomiskt bistånd och introduktionsersattning 2007, Statistik om Stockholm, Stockholms stads utrednings och statistik kontor AB.

THE IMPACT OF TEMPORARY ASSISTANCE PROGRAMS ON DISABILITY ROLLS AND RE-EMPLOYMENT

Stephan Lindner and Austin Nichols

ABSTRACT

Workers in the United States who lose their job may benefit from temporary assistance programs and may apply for Disability Insurance (DI) and Supplemental Security Income (SSI). We measure whether participation in four temporary assistance programs (Temporary Assistance for Needy Families (TANF), Supplemental Nutrition Assistance Program (SNAP), Unemployment Insurance (UI), and Temporary Disability Insurance programs (TDI)) influence application for DI, SSI, and re-employment. We instrument temporary assistance participation using variation in policies across states and over time. Results from our instrumental variables models suggest that increased access to UI benefits reduces applications for DI. This result is robust to different sensitivity checks. We also find less robust evidence that UI participation increases the probability of return to work and reduces the probability

Safety Nets and Benefit Dependence
Research in Labor Economics, Volume 39, 219–258
Copyright © 2014 by Emerald Group Publishing Limited
ISSN: 0147-9121/doi:10.1108/S0147-912120140000039006

*of claiming SSI benefits. In contrast, some of our results suggest a posi-
tive effect of SNAP participation on claiming SSI.*

Keywords: Disability insurance; temporary assistance; duration
analysis

JEL classifications: H53; I38; J64

INTRODUCTION

Applications for disability insurance in the United States through Social
Security Disability Insurance (DI) and Supplemental Security Income (SSI)
are high during periods of high unemployment (Autor & Duggan, 2006;
Black, Daniel, & Sanders, 2002; Bound & Burkhauser, 1999; Rupp &
Stapleton, 1995). This correlation has been interpreted as evidence that
workers tend to move onto DI after having lost their job. Consistent with
this view are findings that applicants for DI (and to lesser extent, for SSI)
experience large income losses around the time of application, some
of which they can buffer by receiving temporary assistance (Bound,
Burkhauser, & Nichols, 2003). Whether these payments influence application decisions for DI and SSI, however, is largely unknown. This is an
important issue for policy makers because being on disability insurance is
expensive (especially for DI) and usually implies a withdrawal from the
labor market (Von Wachter, Song, & Manchester, 2011). Temporary assistance (TA) could be a less costly alternative for some workers at risk of
claiming disability benefits. If so, then policies that increase access to temporary assistance program could help these workers stay in the labor force
and reduce overall government expenditures. However, participation in
temporary assistance programs may also make it easier to get disability
insurance benefits, for instance, by providing income support during the
application process. Given these possible interactions and their implications,
there is considerable interest in understanding better how participation
in temporary assistance programs affects the decision to claim disability
benefits.

   The goal of this study is to shed light on this question by examining
four temporary assistance programs: Temporary Assistance for Needy
Families (TANF), Supplemental Nutrition Assistance Program (SNAP),
Unemployment Insurance (UI), and Temporary Disability Insurance (TDI)
programs. We analyze how participation in these programs affects claims

for DI and SSI both directly through applications and indirectly through re-employment, as employed workers are less likely to claim DI or SSI benefits. After discussing channels through which participation in one of the temporary assistance programs may affect re-employment and application for DI or SSI, we select a sample of workers who have lost their job and create spells of nonemployment ending in re-employment, application for DI, or application for SSI. Because OLS estimates are likely to be biased due to selection and simultaneity, we construct instruments based on state policies and rules for each of the temporary assistance programs.

Our OLS estimates show that participation in each of the four temporary assistance programs is associated with a lower re-employment probability. Furthermore, UI claimants tend not to apply for SSI, while TDI recipients tend to apply for DI. Workers who are more likely to receive SNAP benefits are also more likely to apply for SSI, but less likely to apply for DI. These results could signify causal effects of participating in temporary assistance programs on re-employment and applications for DI and SSI, but they are also consistent with selection by income and health status. Results from IV regressions are in most cases quite different. For re-employment, we do not find consistently negative effects of temporary assistance program participation on re-employment. We even find some evidence that UI participation increases the probability of becoming re-employed. Furthermore, participation in UI decreases applications for DI and SSI, which is consistent with the idea that UI is a substitute for claiming disability benefits. For SSI, we find a positive effect of taking up SNAP benefits on subsequent applications but this result is only significant for some specifications.

Our findings contribute to a growing literature on the interaction between temporary assistance and disability insurance programs. The finding of a negative effect of UI participation on applications for DI corroborates other research that has focused on this interaction in the United States (Lindner, 2011; Rutledge, 2011). Outside of the United States other studies have identified similar links between the two programs. For instance, Petrongolo (2013) examines an increase in job search requirements in the United Kingdom among UI claimants and finds that it increased disability insurance take-up. Lammers, Bloemen, and Hochguertel (2012) similarly examine the effects of a policy reform in The Netherlands that increase job search requirements and also find that these reforms increase disability insurance take-up. While all of these articles find that disability and UI programs function as substitutes, Inderbitzin, Staubli, and Zweimüller (2013) find both program substitution (for workers 55 years or older) and program complementarity (for workers 50—54 years old) when studying extensions to UI benefits and how they affect disability insurance take-up in Austria.[1] Our results show that program substitution is also relevant in the United States, where the disability insurance program is smaller compared to similar programs in European countries — albeit increasing at a faster pace (Burkhauser, Daly, McVicar, & Wilkins, 2013) — and therefore may target a more narrow group of workers with more severe health impairments.

Aside from the interaction between UI and DI, we also find evidence that SNAP program participation may be complementary to claiming SSI. This result is consistent with Coe, Lindner, Wong, and Wu (2014) who find that SNAP is used as income support during the months where claimants have little other income sources.

The following section provides an overview of the different programs. We then discuss the primary channels through which participation in temporary assistance programs may affect applications for DI and SSI. The sections "Empirical Approach," "Data and Sample Selection", and "Empirical Analysis" describe the econometric approach, data and sample selection, and main findings. In the section "Robustness Checks", we discuss additional robustness checks and in the last section, we offer some concluding remarks.

OVERVIEW OF TEMPORARY ASSISTANCE AND DISABILITY PROGRAMS

In this section, we describe institutional parameters of the temporary assistance programs and DI and SSI. Given the complexity of these programs, we focus on rules and regulations that are relevant for this study.[2]

Social Security DI and SSI for the Blind and Disabled

In 1956, Congress enacted DI to insure workers and their dependents against loss of earnings and higher health care expenses due to permanent disability by providing monetary benefits and access to Medicare. In 1974, SSI was added as a second program. Medical eligibility criteria and the application determination process are the same for both insurance programs, but their nonmedical eligibility criteria are different.[3] Individuals can apply for both programs if they meet all respective nonmedical requirements. Applicants either need to have a specific disabling condition or need to show that they cannot perform their previous work and any other type of work. Less than 40 percent of initial applications are accepted, and many of these are for categorically eligible conditions, such as blindness. One-third of all denied applicants file an appeal. The majority of such appeals are successful, but the appeal process often takes many months or even years.

DI benefits are calculated in the same way as retirement benefits and are substantial: in 2008, DI benefits for the average wage earner were $1,500 per month, or about 40 percent of earnings. In addition, beneficiaries are also eligible for Medicare two years after disability onset. Benefits for SSI are not tied to past earnings and tend to be lower. The maximum amount in 2008 was $637 per month for an individual. Because SSI is a means-tested program, other transfer income such as UI and DI benefits reduce SSI benefits dollar-for-dollar after a general deduction of $20. One dollar of earned income decreases SSI benefits by half a dollar after an earned-income deduction of $65. Besides cash transfers, beneficiaries also receive Medicaid in most states.[4]

UI

The UI system is a federal-state partnership aimed at providing short-term cash benefits to individuals who lose or quit their job through no fault of their own. Unemployed workers are eligible for UI benefits if they fulfill all monetary and nonmonetary requirements. We use variation in such requirements across states and over time in our empirical analysis. A number of states have changed eligibility requirements since 2009 because of the American Recovery and Reinvestment Act (ARRA) but changes in eligibility rules have also occurred before 2009.

Monetary entitlement requires sufficiently high wage earnings during the Base Period, which is the first four of the last five completed calendar quarters before the worker files a claim. In addition, a number of states require claimants to have earned wages during at least two of the four base period quarters, and we will make use of this variation across states. Over the past decades, more and more states have also considered the final completed quarter before job loss to determine monetary eligibility, known as the Alternative Base Period (ABP). The ABP allows applicants with insufficient earnings in the Base Period to be monetarily eligible, provided that they have sufficiently high earnings during the ABP. We will use variation in the prevalence of the ABP in our empirical analysis as well.

Nonmonetary eligibility criteria concern both the reason of job separation and ongoing claims. Workers must have lost their job through no fault of their own, that is, either involuntarily, or voluntarily but with a good cause (e.g., due to illness). UI claimants must also show that they continue to be able and available to work, but the standards are very low. Aside from these commonalities, states differ in a number of nonmonetary eligibility rules. We use variation in the following rules for our analysis: whether part-time workers can claim benefits and whether workers who stopped working because they care for their parents, move for their spouse, or experienced domestic violence are entitled to benefits.

UI claimants receive benefits for 26 weeks in most states during non-recession periods. During period of high unemployment, states or the federal government can extend the maximum duration of UI benefit payments. Formulas for weekly UI benefits specify a minimum and a maximum benefit amount as well as a percentage within these boundaries. UI benefits typically replace half of earnings in the highest or two highest quarters of the Base Period within the minimum and maximum amounts. These amounts vary considerably across states. For instance, Massachusetts had the highest maximum benefit amount with $639 per month in 2010, while Mississippi had the lowest one with $235 per month. We use this variation across states and over time in our empirical analysis. Moreover, states also differ in whether they have a waiting week during which new UI claimants do not receive benefits, whether claimants can receive dependency benefits, and whether UI claimants can receive benefits after 26 weeks while in approved training.

SNAP

The SNAP, also known as food stamps, is a means-tested program for poor households. Established with the Food Stamp Act in 1964, the program currently serves more than 40 million Americans, or more than 12 percent of the population. Households qualify for SNAP if their gross (or basic) household income does not exceed 130 percent of the federal poverty line and if their net monthly household income does not exceed 100 percent of the federal poverty line.[5] Liquid assets also cannot exceed eligibility limits, which are currently $2,000 for households with no elderly or disabled member and $3,000 for households with elderly or disabled members.[6] Benefits are calculated by subtracting 30 percent of net household income from the maximum benefit amount, which depends on the size of the household. Because SSI or DI benefits are included in household income, receiving these cash transfers reduces the amount of SNAP benefits a household receives.

While major eligibility rules and benefits are determined at the federal level, states have some control over program eligibility and participation. We use aspects of the program in which states differ for our empirical analysis. This includes outreach spending per person, use of biometric information, and eligibility for noncitizens.

TANF

TANF is the successor to Aid to Families with Dependent Children (AFDC), established in 1935 to provide income support for poor families. In 1996, AFDC was replaced by TANF. Both are means-tested programs but TANF has a stronger focus on promoting work and decreasing dependency among poor families. In most states, a family must have a child younger than 18 years and pass an income and asset test similar to those for SNAP in order to be eligible for TANF/AFDC.[7]

Benefits are calculated by subtracting families' net income from a so-called payment standard, which is set by the states and varies by family size. All but two states also disregard a portion of earnings before computing benefits. Benefits vary considerably by states. For instance, the maximum monthly benefit amount for a family of three was between $170 in Mississippi and $923 in Alaska. We use variation in benefits at zero earnings for our empirical analysis.

TDI

TDI is either provided by employers or by the state. Only five states currently administer a TDI program. The first state to introduce one was Rhode Island in 1942, followed by California (1946), New Jersey (1948), New York (1949), and Hawaii (1969).

In order to qualify for benefits, a worker needs to have sufficient past employment or earnings (depending on state laws) and must not be able to perform regular or customary work because of a physical or mental illness. In all states, a claimant cannot receive UI and TDI at the same time. Benefits are calculated similarly to UI benefits but tend to be more generous because of higher maximum levels. In California, the maximum weekly benefits amount in 2010 was $987 while the maximum weekly UI benefits amount was $450 per week. Benefits are paid for 26—52 weeks.

CONCEPTUAL AND EMPIRICAL BACKGROUND

Using Inderbitzin et al. (2013) conceptualization, receiving cash benefits through temporary assistance programs may generate both complementarity and substitution effects with respect to applications for DI and SSI and re-employment. Complementarity exists if receiving temporary assistance increases the likelihood that workers apply for DI or SSI or find new employment. Substitution exists if receiving temporary assistance reduces the likelihood that workers apply for DI or SSI or find new employment.

With regard to re-employment, a substitution effect exists because cash benefits from temporary assistance programs are reduced or terminated if a person starts working again. For instance, UI benefits are only paid while a person is not working. Similarly, increasing earnings by one dollar reduces SNAP benefits by 30 cents. The substitution effect leads to workers remaining unemployed for a longer time, which in turn can decrease the probability of finding a new job. For UI, studies have generally found that receiving UI benefits increases unemployment duration (Card, Chetty, & Weber, 2007; Meyer, 1990).[8]

Temporary assistance programs can also create a substitution effect for disability insurance applications. With regard to applications for SSI, such a substitution effect exists because other transfer income directly reduces SSI benefits dollar-for-dollar (after a general deduction of $20, see the section "Social Security DI and SSI and for the Blind and Disabled"). For DI, benefits are not reduced by other transfer income, but a substitution effect nevertheless exists because the value of applying for DI benefits is reduced if higher amounts of other income are available, and the application process itself is far from costless. Intuitively, receiving DI is less desirable if one already receives $10,000 per month as compared to $100 per month.[9] A substitution effect may also exist if receiving temporary assistance stabilizes health and thereby makes applying for DI or SSI less attractive.

Receiving temporary assistance can also create complementarity effects. With respect to re-employment, a higher income can enable individuals out of work to engage in job search activities, which increases their chance of finding a new job. For instance, Young (2011) finds that UI benefits increase search effort, especially among low-wage unemployed workers.

With respect to DI or SSI, other income might provide crucial support during applications and thereby make is easier to apply for benefits. For instance, Coe et al. (2014) find evidence that applicants for DI use SNAP as income support while awaiting the application decision. Finally, it is also possible that if workers remain unemployed for a longer time due to temporary assistance, such longer unemployment duration creates a "scarring effect," that is, loss of human capital and worsening of health, which in turn makes applying for DI or SSI more attractive. Overall, the net effect of program participation on applications for DI or SSI and on re-employment is ambiguous.

Temporary assistance programs do not only give out cash assistance, they also provide incentives and assistance for beneficiaries to find work. These program features, if effective, increase the chances of becoming re-employed. However, they may also have unintended consequences insofar as individuals faced with these requirements may look for other programs such as DI or SSI where they can avoid such requirements. Other features of the programs make them institutional complements or substitutes to DI and SSI. For instance, SNAP caseworkers might encourage clients to apply for SSI since it has similar income eligibility criteria.

The discussion so far assumes that workers are assigned randomly to a temporary assistance program. However, workers decide to apply for a program based on characteristics such as age, health, business conditions, or attitudes toward receiving cash transfers. Some of these characteristics are observed, but not all of them. This poses a problem if unobserved characteristics that influence temporary assistance take-up also influence job search and applications for DI and SSI. In this case, comparing program participants with nonparticipants based on observable characteristics alone is problematic because it confounds treatment effects with selection effects based on unobserved characteristics. Moreover, the decision to search hard for a job or to apply for DI or SSI may also influence whether or not to claim temporary assistance. Such simultaneous decisions make it hard to identify the causal effect of receiving temporary assistance benefits as well. The following section explains how we empirically address these issues of selection and reverse causality.

EMPIRICAL APPROACH

We estimate whether nonemployed workers' participation in a temporary assistance program affects their probability of becoming re-employed, applying for DI, or applying for SSI. The first econometric model that we estimate is a discrete-time duration model with person-month observations:

$$E[y_{isd}|d, \text{UI}, \text{TDI}, \text{TANF}, \text{SNAP}] = F[\beta_0 \log d + \beta_1 \text{UI}_{isd} + \beta_2 \text{TDI}_{isd}$$
$$+ \beta_3 \text{TANF}_{isd} + \beta_4 \text{SNAP}_{isd} + X_{isd}\gamma] \quad (1)$$

where y_{isd} is equal to one for individual i at month d of nonemployment spell s if one of the three ending events occur, and zero otherwise. Ending events include employment or application for permanent disability benefits (i.e., DI or SSI). We use only spells whose beginning we observe (i.e., fresh spells) and may observe more than one spell per person. Moreover, we only include months of a continuing spell and the first month of employment or application for disability following a spell of nonemployment (when either outcome is observed during the period covered by data). This makes Eq. (1) a hazard model, or a model of the probability of $y = 1$ conditional on not having transitioned to $y = 1$ by that date. The coefficient β_0 measures how the probability of outcome y_{isd} changes with the log of nonemployment duration, or the baseline hazard. $\text{UI}_{isd}, \text{TDI}_{isd}, \text{TANF}_{isd}$, and SNAP_{isd} are dummy variables for participation in one of the four programs during month d of spell s, and X_{isd} is a vector of demographic characteristics and the state unemployment rate.[10]

Using the identity function $F(x) = x$, Eq. (1) is a linear version of a discrete-time hazard model, whereas a logit link fits a close approximation to a proportional hazards model (Jenkins, 1995). Other researchers have proposed this person-month estimation of logit models for maximum likelihood estimation of proportional hazards discrete-time duration models, by first expanding the data to person-months, but our data comes in the form of person-months already.

We use the identity link for our analysis, that is, a linear version of Eq. (1). We prefer using such a linear specification over nonlinear specifications because it is much easier to introduce instrumental variables (IV) in linear models than in nonlinear models. Moreover, coefficients in a linear model directly measure marginal effects for the probability that an outcome occurs. However, using linear probability models assumes that program participation in temporary assistance is related to the probability outcomes in a linear fashion. Consequently, it does not restrict expectation of outcome values to be bounded between 0 and 1, although it still provides consistent estimation of the marginal effects of a comparable nonlinear model (though consistency does not imply lack of bias in a finite sample).

Therefore, our results are linear approximations to models where the link function is not the identity function. We explore how sensitive results are to alternative functional form specifications in the section "Robustness Checks".

Another assumption of our empirical approach is independence of outcomes conditional on observable characteristics, that is, we are not estimating competing risk models, where an increase in the probability of entering one state would necessarily reduce the probability of entering a competing state. We also assume in Eq. (1) that the baseline hazard is linear in the log of duration. In the section "Robustness Checks", we relax this assumption by estimating Eq. (1) using a flexible baseline hazard. Finally, Eq. (1) does not include an unobserved heterogeneity term, which is often included in duration models. However, we address possible correlation at the individual level by clustering standard errors, as we discuss in more detail at the end of this section.

Our primary interest is in measuring whether people participating in temporary assistance programs have different outcomes over the course of the spell than people who do not participate in these programs. We could also estimate how the timing of temporary assistance program participation relates to the timing of re-employment as well as disability insurance application by interacting the temporary assistance program participation terms with variable(s) measuring duration. We have explored this possibility but found it hard to discern patterns in our data. We therefore restrict our attention to investigating the relationship between the three outcomes and any temporary assistance program participation during nonemployment spells.[11]

This focus permits for an alternative specification using spells as unit of observation:

$$E[y_{is}|d, \text{UI}, \text{TDI}, \text{TANF}, \text{SNAP}] = \beta_0 + \beta_1 \text{UI}_{is} + \beta_2 \text{TDI}_{is} + \beta_3 \text{TANF}_{is}$$
$$+ \beta_4 \text{SNAP}_{is} + \gamma X_{is} + \varepsilon_{is} \qquad (1')$$

Eq. (1′) does not include a monthly subscript d because we use one observation per spell for this specification. For this specification, we collapse person-month observations used for Eq. (1) to person-spell observations. In this case, the outcome variable y_{is} is equal to one if the spell ends with the outcome of interest (i.e., re-employment, application for DI, or application for SSI) and zero if no such ending is observed.

In what follows, we report estimates for both equations since they both are legitimate ways to measure the effect of temporary assistance participation on re-employment and applications for DI and SSI. While similar, the two specifications have some important differences. Using months versus spells as unit of observation implies that longer spells receive more weight relative to shorter spells. Therefore, coefficients differ if people with shorter spells react differently to receiving temporary assistance program participation as compared to people with longer spells. A second important difference concerns right-censored spells. Right-censoring primarily occurs because our surveys observe people only for a few years but may also occur because of panel attrition. For such spells, we do not observe an outcome even though they may exit the nonemployment spell at some point. This is less of an issue for model (1) because it captures the longer duration of nonemployment of right-censored spells but more problematic for model (1') because we do not assign the correct outcome to such spells. We investigate the sensitivity of our results with respect to right-censoring in the section "Robustness Checks".

For both specifications, estimates are only consistent if the error term is uncorrelated with temporary assistance participation. However, this assumption is likely to be violated for two reasons, simultaneous equations bias and omitted variable bias.

An omitted variable bias exists if variables correlated with participation in a temporary assistance program and with the outcome variable are not included in the regression. For instance, individuals with unobserved health problems are more likely to receive TDI benefits and to apply for DI or SSI. Past labor force participation could also be such a confounding variable, if people with weak labor force attachment are more likely to qualify for TANF or SNAP as well as SSI. Furthermore, aggregate-level variables such as business conditions may contribute to correlated participation in temporary assistance programs, DI and SSI applications, and re-employment.

A simultaneous equation bias occurs if an outcome influences participation in a temporary assistance program. For instance, an individual who is very likely to become re-employed in the near future might not bother applying for UI or other cash assistance. Similarly, a person who plans to apply for DI might find it to be too much work to first claim other benefits. In such cases, OLS would be biased towards a negative value.

In order to address these issues, we instrument participation in temporary assistance programs. Regressions for participation in one of the temporary assistance programs may be written as follows:

$$TA_{isp} = \alpha_0 + \varphi Z_{is} + \delta X_{is} + \mu_{isp} \tag{2}$$

where TA_{isp} measures program participation in one of the four programs p, Z_{is} are instruments which are included in this equation, but not in Eqs. (1) or (1′), X_{is} are exogenous variables included in both equations, and μ_{isp} is an error term. There is one such equation for each of the four programs.

Proper instruments need to satisfy two requirements: being correlated with temporary assistance participation (instrument relevance) and affecting outcomes only through participation in the temporary assistance program (exclusion restriction). Regarding the first requirement, even if instruments are relevant, they might be weak. In that case, IV estimates may be inconsistent and imprecisely measured. As an indicator for weak instruments, we report F-statistics for the null hypothesis that coefficients for instruments in Eq. (2) are jointly zero. We also report the Kleibergen-Paap LM test for underidentification and associated p-values. This test determines whether the lowest correlation between an instrument and one of the endogenous variables is statistically significant from zero. As it turns out, the Kleibergen-Paap LM test statistic is relatively low for our main specification with the four temporary assistant models. In the section "Robustness Checks," we discuss how eliminating TDI, the smallest of the four temporary assistance programs, considerably improves identification.

If instruments also fulfill the monotonicity assumption[12] and there is one endogenous and one instrumental variable, then the IV estimator identifies the local average treatment effect (LATE), which is the average treatment effect for those who are induced to participate in a program because of variation in the instrument (Imbens & Angrist, 1994). As mentioned in the theoretical framework, this treatment effect could capture the effect of receiving cash transfers on outcomes, which could depend on the population involved, or it could identify the effect of other program characteristics. The LATE can be thought of as the effect on mean outcomes of manipulating the excluded instrument (program parameters) and thereby inducing greater participation, a kind of marginal treatment effect.

Instruments used here include state policies and rules for the four temporary assistance programs. We do not include state fixed-effects because our instruments are too weak if we do. Therefore, our identification assumption is that differences in policies across states are not correlated with other characteristics that vary on the state level and that influence outcomes. This is a plausible assumption because DI and SSI are administered at the federal level. Furthermore, policies do not change quickly and therefore are unlikely to reflect current economic conditions that may influence outcomes. However, even if exclusion restrictions do not hold, IV estimates are still of interest. In this case, they measure both the direct effect of policy variation on outcomes and the indirect effect of policy variation on outcomes through temporary assistance program participation.

We estimate Eqs. (1) and (1') for each of the three outcomes separately, both as OLS and as IV regressions. IV regressions are estimated in one step but we also present results of regressions as shown by Eq. (2) only to better assess the quality of our instruments.[13] Separate estimation of the different outcomes assumes that, conditional on observables, the occurrence of each outcome is independent from the others. We prefer this approach for computational simplicity.

We cluster all standard errors at the individual level to account for serial correlation in errors at the individual level because we repeatedly measure individual characteristics when observing multiple months (in Eq. 1) and spells per person. Clustered standard errors are not commonly used in discrete-time hazard models. Under the assumption of independently and identically distributed errors, logit regression models using months at risk of a transition are equivalent to maximum likelihood duration models (Jenkins, 1995). However, in simulations we have found that if there is a positive serial correlation of errors at the individual level, points estimate remain unaffected but standard errors are too small, implying high rejection rates of true null hypotheses.[14] Because errors are likely correlated in this way, we have clustered standard errors at the individual level.

DATA AND SAMPLE SELECTION

The primary data source is the Survey of Income and Program Participation (SIPP) for the years 1996–2010. The SIPP is a nationally representative sample of individuals 15 years of age and older of the civilian noninstitutionalized population. The SIPP interviews people once every four months, called a wave, for two to four years. Respondents provide information about the preceding four months, called reference months. Connecting reference months of different waves generates panels of two to four years. We restrict out attention to the years from 1996 on, since we have better instruments for this time period, especially for SNAP.

In order to identify applications for DI and SSI, SIPP panels are matched to administrative records (the 831 records) from the Social Security Administration (SSA). An 831 record is opened whenever a person applies for DI or SSI, and subsequently tracks administrative actions on open applications. We use 831 records to identify the date of the first application and the type of application, where we distinguish between applications for DI and SSI. The latter group also contains concurrent applications, that is, applications for both DI and SSI.[15]

The sample for this analysis includes workers who complete all interviews, are matched to Social Security data (either disclose their Social Security Number or have a match based on name, birth date, and address so that they can be matched to 831 files), and who experience a job loss (which could be voluntary or involuntary). A job loss occurs when a person works all weeks during the previous month (including being absent from work), but does not work for at least one week during the current month. An individual remains nonemployed after job loss until he or she finds a job or applies for DI or SSI. We disregard spells for which a worker is younger than 20 or older than 57 at the time of job loss. We chose age 57 as the highest age in order to ensure that all workers in the sample are younger than 62 throughout all spells and panels. In order to use prior earnings information, the sample is also restricted to individuals with an earnings history of more than three months prior to job loss. Finally, we also exclude temporary layoffs, spells with missing interview waves, and spells with missing state information.[16] The final sample contains 32,208 workers. Table 1 shows sample selection steps and corresponding sample sizes.

Respondents in the SIPP report the amount of income they receive from different types of programs. For UI and TDI, we simply consider an individual to be on one of these programs if he or she reports receiving cash income from it. For TANF, we use SIPP's relationship information within

Table 1.   Sample Selection and Sample Size.

Selection Steps	Sample Size
Universe	469,565
Complete interview	393,900
SSN disclosure	291,676
Nonemployment spell	201,323
Age 20–57 at first month of spell	68,926
Employment history >3 months	40,741
No temporary layoffs	34,867
Complete spell	32,829
State identified	32,613
No prior DI/SSI application	32,208

Notes: Sample sizes displayed are unweighted number of individuals. Each row shows the number of individuals who meet the respective requirements. See text for details of the selection steps.

households to identify whether a child or its parents receive such benefits. Finally, an individual participates in SNAP if anyone in the household receives benefits from the program.

We use several sources to construct instruments for participation in these programs.[17] Appendix A describes these instruments in detail. For UI, "Significant Provisions of State UI Laws" and the "Comparison of State Unemployment Insurance Laws" from the Department of Labor contain detailed information about states' policies.[18] Additional information comes from states' correspondence with the Department of Labor regarding compliance with the ARRA. We use the following rules as instruments: the maximum UI benefit amount, whether states stipulate an initial waiting week where benefits are not paid, whether UI claimants must have worked for at least two quarters during the Base Period, whether states have adopted the ABP, whether states have allowances for dependents, whether people stopped working because of domestic violence or filial obligations are eligible, whether people moved with their spouse and therefore stopped working are eligible, whether part-time workers are eligible, and whether qualified UI claimants can receive UI benefits after 26 weeks of payments.

Concerning TANF, benefits depend on states' payment standards. We use benefit formulas to create TANF benefits at zero dollar earnings. These benefits best reflect transfers that potential recipients currently out of work may claim.

SNAP benefit rules are set by the federal government and therefore do not change across states. However, states administer the program and in this capacity have control over some of its aspects, especially eligibility standards. We use information from the SNAP Program Rules Database (Finegold, Margrabe, & Ratcliffe, 2010) to construct three sets of instruments; these instruments are also used in a study examining the role of SNAP in reducing food insecurity (Ratcliffe & McKernan, 2010). The instruments are: outreach spending per person, use of biometric information, and eligibility for noncitizens. For the latter, we distinguish between full eligibility (all noncitizens) and partial eligibility (only noncitizens who either have a disability, are under 18 years old, or have been U.S. residents for more than 5 years). Based on this state-level information, we create household-level instruments indicating whether a household member is a noncitizen and lives in a state with full or partial eligibility for noncitizens.[19]

Workers can receive TDI benefits either through their employer or through the state if it has a TDI program and they have worked in covered employment. Domestic and family workers are generally not covered. California covers self-employed workers and Hawaii covers state and local government employees. Agricultural workers are covered in three states: California, Hawaii, and New Jersey. We interact state-level coverage with industry codes of last employment to create a variable measuring whether an individual is covered by a state-administered TDI program as an instrument for TDI participation.

EMPIRICAL ANALYSIS

We begin the empirical analysis with summary statistics for nonemployment spells as shown in Table 2. The average spell duration is 6.86 months and seven out of 10 spells end with re-employment (including self-employment). Another 0.74 percent and 0.84 of all spells end with an application for DI and SSI, respectively. The remaining spells are right-censored. Because right-censored spells tend to be longer than other spells, the average duration by spell outcome is smaller than the overall observed duration, namely 5.4 months for re-employment, 6.0 months for DI applications, and 6.1 months for SSI applications. The long nonemployment duration for DI and SSI applications is consistent with Lindner (2013) who shows that these people remain out of work for several months and engage in job search before applying for disability insurance.[20]

The two largest temporary assistance programs are UI (16.15 percent of all nonemployed workers receive UI benefits) and SNAP (16.56 percent). Participation in TDI and TANF is much lower, namely, 0.53 percent and 3.39 percent, respectively. Most TANF recipients (over 90 percent in the sample) also receive SNAP. In terms of benefits, UI and TDI are by far the most generous programs with an average monthly benefit amount of $738.54 and $1015.38, respectively. TANF and SNAP benefits are by contrast relatively modest, averaging $126.74 and $264.02, respectively.

Fig. 1 shows how participation in these programs evolves over the course of nonemployment spells. The four months preceding a job separation are shown as well. UI is the program most targeted at job loss events and designed to provide short-term benefits. UI participation jumps up at the first month of nonemployment, increases further to reach about 15 percent during the third and seventh month, and then declines steadily. The other programs show a more moderate increase at the beginning of nonemployment, followed by a constant or slightly increasing participation rate.

Table 2. Summary Statistics.

Variable	Mean/ Percentage	25th Percentile	Median	75th Percentile
Age	35.25	25	34	44
Male	42.11	0	0	100
White	80.9	100	100	100
Married	49.91	0	0	100
High-school degree	89.93	100	100	100
Some college	60.09	0	100	100
Noncitizen immigrant in household	11.77	0	0	0
Number of children <18	0.95	0	0	2
Medicaid coverage during month	10.16	0	0	0
Private health insurance during month	58.63	0	100	100
Monthly earnings last year	1,621.43	496.53	1,111.89	2,081.5
Work limitation	11.25	0	0	0
Work limitation during panel	23.47	0	0	0
Reason not working: health problem	6.38	0	0	0
Number of spells per person	1.31	1	1	1
Spell duration (in months)	6.86	3	5	8
Exit: Employment (spell)	70.67	0	100	100
Exit: DI (spell)	0.74	0	0	0
Exit: DI/SSI or SSI (spell)	0.87	0	0	0
Application for DI or SSI observed	1.74	0	0	0
Unemployment rate	5.67	4.4	5.2	6.3
UI recipient during spell	16.15	0	0	0
UI benefit amount	738.54	353.51	636.86	1,003.76
TDI recipient during spell	0.53	0	0	0
TDI benefit amount	1015.38	420	854	1,384
TANF/AFDC: Fam. recipiency (spell)	3.39	0	0	0
TANF/AFDC: Fam. amount	126.74	60.64	100.45	160.81
SNAP: Household recipiency (spell)	16.56	0	0	0
SNAP: Household amount	264.02	132.47	236.06	346.64
UI: Wages in two quarters	24.17	0	0	0
UI: Waiting week	81.32	100	100	100
UI: Alternative base period	29.81	0	0	100
UI: Dependency allowance	25.29	0	0	100
UI: Domestic violence	48.07	0	0	100
UI: Move with spouse	25.01	0	0	100
UI: Filial obligations	39.11	0	0	100
UI: Part-time work	37.34	0	0	100
UI: 26 weeks	15.13	0	0	0
UI: Maximum weekly benefit amount	301.6	253.91	291.39	345.03
Covered by state TDI insurance	11.77	0	0	0
Imputed TANF benefit at zero earnings	376.48	255.06	349.25	485.37
SNAP: Biometric technology used	20.29	0	0	0
SNAP: Outreach spending per person	0.02	0	0	0

Table 2. (*Continued*)

Variable	Mean/ Percentage	25th Percentile	Median	75th Percentile
SNAP: Noncitizen fully eligible × noncitizen in household	3.64	0	0	0
SNAP: Noncitizen partly eligible × noncitizen in household	7.51	0	0	0

Notes: Fractions are shown as percentages. Dollar amounts are in January 2000 values. Monthly observations are used if not otherwise stated. The first month of nonemployment spells is used for age, male, white, married, high-school degree and some college. Temporary assistance participation refers to whole spell. For a description of the instrumental variables, see Appendix A.

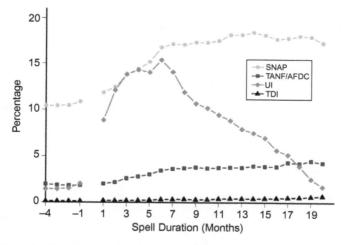

Fig. 1. Participation in Temporary Assistance Programs by Spell Duration. *Notes*: Negative spell duration refers to months prior to the beginning of nonemployment spells.

One should note, however, that these patterns are confounded by differential exit rates for individuals who are on a program versus individuals who are not. For instance, we could explain the increase in SNAP participation rates by longer nonemployment spell duration of participants.

Table 3 depicts results from estimating Eq. (2) using individual person-months as the unit of observation. As explained in the previous section, we estimate IV regressions in one step, but we present here results from

Table 3.   Regression Results for Temporary Assistance Participation (Full Sample, Individual-Month as Unit of Observation).

Instrument	UI Participation	TDI Participation	TANF Participation	SNAP Participation
UI: Maximum weekly benefit amount	0.2515***	−0.0110	0.0386	−0.1416**
	(0.0530)	(0.0168)	(0.0329)	(0.0486)
UI: Waiting week	0.0029	0.0015	0.0007	0.0172*
	(0.0073)	(0.0025)	(0.0044)	(0.0070)
UI: Wages in two quarters	−0.0082	−0.0007	0.0036	−0.0059
	(0.0071)	(0.0020)	(0.0050)	(0.0075)
UI: Alternative base period	−0.0187*	0.0033	−0.0043	−0.0080
	(0.0063)	(0.0023)	(0.0041)	(0.0061)
UI: Dependency allowance	0.0170	0.0024	0.0093*	−0.0059
	(0.0072)	(0.0024)	(0.0046)	(0.0067)
UI: Domestic violence	0.0041	0.0035	0.0071	0.0060
	(0.0072)	(0.0025)	(0.0045)	(0.0067)
UI: Move with spouse	−0.063	0.0029	0.0058	−0.0046
	(0.0078)	(0.0023)	(0.0048)	(0.0074)
UI: Filial obligations	−0.0034	−0.0014	−0.0120**	−0.0037
	(0.0062)	(0.0021)	(0.0041)	(0.0061)
UI: Part-time work	−0.0033	−0.0018	−0.0014	−0.0087
	(0.0063)	(0.0021)	(0.0038)	(0.0063)
UI: 26 weeks	0.0145	−0.0021	−0.0036	0.0267**
	(0.0091)	(0.0029)	(0.0057)	(0.0083)
TDI: Covered by state TDI insurance	−0.0246*	0.0090*	0.0164*	−0.0367***
	(0.0112)	(0.0041)	(0.0070)	(0.0091)
TANF: Imputed benefits at zero earnings	0.1328***	−0.0015	0.0438	−0.1549***
	(0.0313)	(0.0092)	(0.0236)	(0.0293)
SNAP: Biometric technology used	−0.0201*	0.0003	0.0000	−0.0144
	(0.0078)	(0.0025)	(0.0053)	(0.0076)
SNAP: Outreach spending per person	−0.0420	0.0040	0.0139	0.0442*
	(0.0219)	(0.0079)	(0.0124)	(0.0214)
SNAP: Immigrants fully eligible	0.0272*	0.0092	−0.0072	0.0086
	(0.0219)	(0.0052)	(0.0074)	(0.0106)
SNAP: Immigrants partially eligible	0.0001	0.0039	0.0017	−0.0022
	(0.0065)	(0.0022)	(0.0043)	(0.0062)
SNAP: Noncitizen fully eligible × noncitizen in household	0.0386	−0.0185	0.0045	0.0059
	(0.0271)	(0.0096)	(0.0187)	(0.0244)
SNAP: Noncitizen partly eligible × noncitizen in household	−0.0134	−0.0110	−0.0001	0.0435*
	(0.0217)	(0.0078)	(0.0153)	(0.0206)
F-statistic	11.70	4.77	3.45	13.21

Notes: Standard errors are in parentheses. Standard errors are clustered on the individual level. All specifications include demographic variables. Temporary assistance participation refers to spell. *F*-statistics test for the null hypothesis that all excluded instruments equal to zero. For a description of the instrumental variables, see Appendix A.

*Significantly different from zero at the 5 percent confidence level.
**Significantly different from zero at the 1 percent confidence level.
***Significantly different from zero at the 0.1 percent confidence level.

estimating Eq. (2) to better assess the quality of our instruments. All regressions use clustered standard errors at the individual level. The table also shows F-statistics for the test of the null hypothesis that coefficients for all instruments are jointly zero (i.e., the excluded instruments have no impact on participation).

For UI, we find that participation is higher in states and years with higher UI maximum benefit amounts. The other statistically significant instrument is the ABP, which is related to a lower participation rate. This is somewhat surprising because the ABP offers an alternative way for UI applicants to be monetarily eligible and therefore increases access to the program. Apparently, states with a lower UI participation rate are more prone to implement the ABP to boost participation rates. The significant coefficients for TDI coverage, TANF benefits at zero earnings, whether states use SNAP biometric information and whether immigrants are fully eligible for SNAP indicate that these instruments proxy characteristics of UI policies not fully captured by the other instruments. For instance, higher TANF benefits at zero earnings are correlated with higher UI maximum benefits ($\rho = 0.35$), suggesting that these TANF benefits proxy aspects of generosity or accessibility of the UI programs. Conversely, states with biometric systems also have more restrictive UI programs.

For TDI, workers residing in states with a state program are more likely to receive temporary disability benefits, as one would expect if the state program did not completely crowd out private coverage. For TANF, benefits at zero earnings predict participation rates but the coefficient is only significant at the 10 percent level. Other policies predicting TANF participation include: whether states have UI dependency benefits and whether people who stop working to care for their parents are eligible for UI benefits.

For SNAP, outreach spending per person and partial eligibility for noncitizens predict SNAP participation. In addition, UI benefits, TANF benefits, and TDI coverage are inversely related to participation. These negative coefficients likely indicate substitution effects: workers covered by TDI or receiving sufficient TANF benefits are less inclined to also claim SNAP benefits. Finally, whether states extend UI benefits beyond 26 weeks to workers in training also predicts SNAP participation. Overall, instruments for UI and SNAP have good power but F-tests for TDI and TANF are below 10, indicating that few policies can well predict participation of these programs but may also be influenced by the small number of people participating in these programs. We also find that policies from one temporary assistance program are correlated with participation in another program.

Such correlations do not necessarily imply that the exclusion restriction is violated because they can reflect similarities in policies across states.

Table 4 presents regression results from Eq. (1) with individual-month as unit of observation. Columns 1–3 show OLS results for re-employment, DI application, and SSI application, respectively, and columns 4–6 show corresponding IV results. All regressions use demographic variables from the SIPP and state unemployment rates from the Bureau of Labor Statistics as controls. Table B1 contains full regression tables for the IV regressions.

Starting with the OLS results in Table 4, the first column shows that participation in any of the temporary assistance programs is negatively associated with re-employment. This negative association could signify that the negative substitution effect outweighs the positive complementarity effect or that individuals receiving such benefits have other characteristics (such as worse health) that make it harder for them to find a job. While we include a dummy variable for work limitation in our regressions, it is conceivable that it does not fully capture all relevant dimensions of health. The next two columns show that the association between the different temporary assistance programs and applications for DI or SSI is less uniform. The negative coefficient for UI participation on SSI applications

Table 4. Regression Results, Individual-Month as Unit of Observation.

	OLS			IV		
	Employment	DI	SSI	Employment	DI	SSI
UI recipient	−0.0314***	0.0000	−0.0005**	0.2798***	−0.0061**	−0.0045
	(0.0017)	(0.0002)	(0.0002)	(0.0630)	(0.0023)	(0.0024)
TDI recipient	−0.0337***	0.0107***	0.0003	−1.4673**	−0.0252	0.0122
	(0.0044)	(0.0028)	(0.0016)	(0.5224)	(0.0214)	(0.0212)
TANF/AFDC recipient	−0.0131***	0.0002	0.0005	−0.5404*	−0.0021	0.0109
	(0.0026)	(0.0003)	(0.0006)	(0.2152)	(0.0088)	(0.0088)
SNAP recipient	−0.0170***	−0.0006**	0.0008**	0.0687	−0.0057	0.0056
	(0.0020)	(0.0002)	(0.0003)	(0.0831)	(0.0032)	(0.0032)
Kleibergen-Paap LM test				20.010		
				(0.172)		

Notes: Standard errors are in parentheses. Standard errors are clustered on the individual level. All specifications include demographic variables. The *F*-statistic is the Kleibergen-Paap *F*-statistic. See text for details.
*Significantly different from zero at the 5 percent confidence level.
**Significantly different from zero at the 1 percent confidence level.
***Significantly different from zero at the 0.1 percent confidence level.

could indicate that taking up UI deters people from applying for this program. Alternatively, it might indicate that people on UI tend to have stronger labor force attachment and higher past earnings, and for that reason are less likely to qualify for SSI based on their income and savings.

The estimate for TDI participation with respect to DI application is positive, but the corresponding estimate for SSI application is not significantly different from zero. The positive coefficient with respect to DI applications can result from a worse health status of TDI participants as compared to nonparticipants. However, the coefficient with respect to SSI application should then also be positive, which is not the case. One possible explanation is that workers who qualify for TDI tend to be high wage earners (similar to UI recipients) in better jobs that provide such benefits, and therefore likely to be ineligible for SSI.

TANF participation is not positively or negatively associated with either DI or SSI, but SNAP participation is negatively related to applications for DI and positively to applications for SSI. Presumably, SNAP recipients are more likely to be poor or lack a steady work history, which qualifies them for SSI but not for DI.

These results without correcting for endogeneity suggest that workers sort into different temporary assistance programs and DI or SSI based on their past labor force attachment and their health status. However, OLS coefficients could also represent program participation effects. The next three columns present second stage results for the IV regressions in order to identify possible causal effects of participation in temporary assistance programs on re-employment and application for DI and SSI.

Looking first at re-employment, we can see that UI participation significantly increases employment and TDI and TANF participation significantly reduces employment. The size of the coefficients and their standard errors tend to be large, which is typical in instrumental variables estimation. While it would be more desirable to have precisely estimated coefficients, these results still suggest that the negative association between program participation and re-employment in the OLS regressions is primarily due to selection for UI and SNAP. For TDI and TANF, we find negative and statistically significant effects but the corresponding first stages are not strong and these results could therefore reflect weak instrument problems. The Kleibergen-Paap LM test is also not statistically significant, indicating that at least some weakly related instruments do not contribute to identification. We address this issue in the section "Robustness Checks".

Turning to the next column for DI applications, one can see that the coefficient on UI participation is negative and strongly significant, consistent with other studies that have looked at the interaction between the UI program and applications for DI (Lindner, 2011; Rutledge, 2011). Moreover, coefficients for other temporary assistance programs, while not significant, are all now negative. Most notably, the OLS estimate for TDI participation was positive and significant, and the IV result is negative and insignificant. Overall, these results suggest that if participation in temporary assistance influences applications for DI, then they function as a substitute on average. In other words, though participation may act to both increase and decrease application rates, the net effect for those induced to participate by small increases in eligibility or generosity is to actually reduce applications, or at least to not increase them.

Results are more mixed for SSI, as shown in the last column. Only one coefficient (for UI participation) has a positive sign. Coefficients are not statistically significant at the 5 percent level but coefficients for UI and SNAP participation are statistically significant at the 10 percent level.

Table 5 presents results for Eq. (1') with spells as unit of observation. Most coefficients have the same sign as compared to Table 4, but the standard errors tend to be larger. The IV results show that the effect of UI participation on re-employment is still positive and significant (as in Table 4) but other coefficients for re-employment are not significant. Moreover, the coefficient for TANF changes its sign. In addition, UI

Table 5. Regression Results, Individual-Spell as Unit of Observation.

	OLS			IV		
	Employment	DI	SSI	Employment	DI	SSI
UI recipient	−0.0235***	0.0003	−0.0032**	0.2148**	−0.0384**	−0.0307*
	(0.0057)	(0.0011)	(0.0011)	(0.0775)	(0.0138)	(0.0147)
TDI recipient	−0.2459***	0.1408***	0.0247	−1.5441	0.0078	−0.1328
	(0.0321)	(0.0264)	(0.0176)	(1.1667)	(0.2236)	(0.2220)
TANF/AFDC	−0.0481***	0.0002	0.0095	0.1219	−0.0411	0.0212
recipient	(0.0138)	(0.0020)	(0.0052)	(0.3813)	(0.0715)	(0.0713)
SNAP recipient	−0.0407***	−0.0015	0.0139***	0.2003	−0.0333	0.0232
	(0.0071)	(0.0014)	(0.0023)	(0.1211)	(0.0241)	(0.0240)
Kleibergen-				20.571		
Paap LM test				(0.151)		

Notes: Standard errors are in parentheses. Standard errors are clustered on the individual level. All specifications include demographic variables.
*Significantly different from zero at the 5 percent confidence level.
**Significantly different from zero at the 1 percent confidence level.
***Significantly different from zero at the 0.1 percent confidence level.

participation is negatively related to DI and SSI application, with the latter coefficient being now statistically significant at the 5 percent level. The coefficient for instrumented SNAP participation on applications for SSI is not significant with spells as the unit of observation.

For spells as unit of observation, the results can be directly translated into a quantitative interpretation. Recall from Table 2 that 0.74 percent of all spells end in an application for DI and another 0.87 percent in an application for SSI. The mean spell values are therefore 0.0074 and 0.0087 for DI and SSI applications, respectively. The IV estimate for the effect of UI participation on DI application in Table 5 is −0.0384, or about 5 times as large as fraction of spells ending with an application for DI. The quantitative interpretation is similar for months as unit of observation. Here, 0.0074 DI applications per spell translate into about 0.001 applications per month (the average spell duration is 6.0 months for DI applicants and 6.1 months for SSI applicants), and the coefficient for UI participation is about 6 times larger. Similarly, the effect of SNAP participation on applications for SSI is about 5 times the average number of applications for SSI per month.

These results suggest that application decisions for DI and SSI are very sensitive to participation in temporary assistance programs, at least for those influenced by the instruments to participate. Treatment effects for people influenced by the instruments may be substantial if receiving cash benefits is very important for them in their current economic situation. This seems plausible because people who consider claiming temporary assistance benefits are likely very cash-strapped. Another reason why the treatment effect for these people could be large, at least for DI and SSI program participation, is their higher knowledge about various government programs as compared to people not affected by the instruments. However, large coefficient values together with nonsignificant Kleibergen-Paap LM test statistics could also indicate that our instrumental variable equations are not well identified. In the next section, we explore various checks to see whether our results presented thus far are robust to alternative specifications.

ROBUSTNESS CHECKS

In this section, we discuss several robustness checks.[21] The first of these checks concerns the use of linear probability models. In Table 6, we present logit and probit regressions results corresponding to OLS regressions as

Table 6. Logit and Probit Regressions Results.

	Months			Spells		
	Employment	DI	SSI	Employment	DI	SSI
Logit regressions						
UI: recipient	−0.0288***	−0.0000	−0.0003	−0.0265***	0.0004	−0.0015
	(0.0017)	(0.0002)	(0.0002)	(0.0055)	(0.0011)	(0.0014)
TDI: recipient	−0.0811***	0.0008***	0.0004	−0.2043***	0.0080***	0.0046
	(0.0131)	(0.0002)	(0.0003)	(0.0295)	(0.0014)	(0.0024)
TANF/AFDC:	−0.0192***	−0.0004	0.0003	−0.0467***	−0.0007	0.0036*
recipient	(0.0040)	(0.0005)	(0.0002)	(0.0119)	(0.0032)	(0.0017)
SNAP	−0.0193***	−0.0005*	0.0005**	−0.0387***	−0.0009	0.0081***
recipient	(0.0022)	(0.0002)	(0.0002)	(0.0066)	(0.0014)	(0.0012)
Probit regressions						
UI recipient	−0.0258***	0.0001	−0.0003	−0.0237***	0.0012	−0.0016
	(0.0017)	(0.0002)	(0.0002)	(0.0056)	(0.0010)	(0.0013)
TDI recipient	−0.0684***	0.0009***	0.0004	−0.2007***	0.0102***	0.0052
	(0.0106)	(0.0002)	(0.0003)	(0.0297)	(0.0017)	(0.0027)
TANF/AFDC	−0.0165***	−0.0004	0.0003	−0.0473***	−0.0014	0.0038*
recipient	(0.0037)	(0.0005)	(0.0002)	(0.0120)	(0.0031)	(0.0017)
SNAP	−0.0182***	−0.0004*	0.0005**	−0.0389***	−0.0004	0.0080***
recipient	(0.0022)	(0.0002)	(0.0002)	(0.0066)	(0.0014)	(0.0012)

Notes: The table shows average marginal effects for logit and probit regressions. Standard errors are in parentheses. Standard errors are clustered on the individual level. All specifications include demographic variables. Asterisks indicate significance levels as explained in Table 5.

shown in the left part of Tables 4 and 5. While this is no direct test whether the functional form assumption matter for our IV results, this comparison offers some indication whether our results might be sensitive to the choice of the link function.[22] We express all probit and logit coefficients as average marginal effects so that they are directly comparable to OLS coefficients. In general, we would expect the marginal effects of the three specifications to be similar because they are all consistent estimators, but finite sample properties could results in difference across the three specifications.

Marginal effects have in most cases the same sign across the three specifications. Moreover, magnitudes of coefficients are fairly similar in many cases, most notably for the coefficient of UI and DI participation. However, in some cases differences between the three specifications are large and are significantly different. These are cases where the IV results are not robust to further sensitivity checks discussed in this section, for example, effects of temporary assistance participation on re-employment.

To address the issue of underidentification in Tables 4 and 5, we explore whether excluding TDI recipiency as one of the temporary assistance programs could improve identification.[23] Table 7 displays results when TDI recipients and TDI participation as an endogenous variable and its instrument are excluded from the regressions. Three of the four effects of UI and TANF/AFDC participation on re-employment are not significant but the effect of UI participation on DI applications remains negative and significant. Remarkable is the much larger LM statistic and the much smaller associated *p*-values.

Next, we estimate OLS and IV regressions for two subsamples: a poverty sample that includes respondents with a family income less than twice the national poverty threshold and a work limitation sample that includes respondents who report having at least one functional limitation or problems with an Activity of Daily Living (ADL) during the time they are observed. The poverty sample has 12,328 people (about 40 percent of all spells) and the work limitation sample has 3,645 people (about 11 percent of all spells). For the poverty sample using months as unit of observation, we also find a significant positive effect of UI participation on re-employment and a negative significant effect of TDI or TANF/AFDC participation on re-employment. The effect of UI participation on DI applications is negative as in Table 4 but not significant. Coefficients have the same signs but are not statistically significant when we use spells as unit

Table 7. IV Regression Results Without TDI Participation.

	Months as Unit of Observation			Spells as Unit of Observation		
	Employment	DI	SSI	Employment	DI	SSI
UI recipient	−0.0162	−0.0057*	−0.0021	−0.1177	−0.0339*	−0.0129
	(0.0270)	(0.0024)	(0.0025)	(0.0879)	(0.0150)	(0.0162)
TANF/AFDC	−0.0383	−0.0054	0.0058	0.7759*	−0.0532	−0.0475
recipient	(0.0837)	(0.0078)	(0.0079)	(0.3546)	(0.0651)	(0.0660)
SNAP recipient	−0.0112	−0.0048	0.0055	0.0392	−0.0342	0.0316
	(0.0300)	(0.0027)	(0.0028)	(0.1138)	(0.0211)	(0.0217)
Kleibergen-Paap		24.365			39.926	
LM test		(0.059)			(0.000)	

Notes: Standard errors are in parentheses. Standard errors are clustered on the individual level. All specifications include demographic variables.
*Significantly different from zero at the 5 percent confidence level.
**Significantly different from zero at the 1 percent confidence level.
***Significantly different from zero at the 0.1 percent confidence level.

of observations. For the work limitation sample, two significant coefficients in the IV regressions of Tables 4 and 5 remain significant: the positive effect of UI participation on employment when months are the unit of observation and the negative effect of UI participation on DI participation when spells are the unit of observation. Moreover, the effect of SNAP participation on SSI application is positive and significant for spells as unit of observation. Overall, regressions using these subsamples find similar effects as in the main sample, but the smaller sample sizes often imply that we cannot estimate these coefficients precisely.

A fourth robustness check concerns the issue of right-censoring. To explore how right-censored spells influence our results, we estimate our OLS and IV regressions using only completely observed spells. For months as unit of observation, we find a positive and significant effect of UI participation on re-employment, a negative and significant effect of UI participation on applications for DI and SSI, and a negative and significant effect of TDI and TANF/AFDC participation on re-employment. For spells as unit of observation, only the effects of UI participation on re-employment and DI or SSI application are significant. Overall, these results suggest that the effect of UI participation on SSI applications is either concentrated among shorter spells (that tend not to be right-censored) or that some people with right-censored spells who do not receive UI benefits and who would be affected by changes in instruments apply for SSI after we can observe them. We also find that effects of TDI and TANF/AFDC participation on re-employment are not robust to excluding right-censored spells.

As a fifth robustness check, we estimate Eq. (1) with duration dummies instead of the log of duration. This alternative specification of the baseline hazard implies nearly identical results as compared to our IV results in Table 4.

Finally, we estimate our instrumental variable regressions excluding the SIPP 2008 panel. We do this for two reasons: there were many changes to the economy and some of the temporary assistance programs during the Great Recession and we do not have information on outreach spending for SNAP for the years starting with 2008. With respect to economic and programmatic changes, we suspect that the effect of UI on DI might be sensitive to excluding years covering the Great Recession because UI claimants remained on the program for a much longer time during that period. This longer program duration could imply that UI was more effective in keeping UI claimants from applying for DI during the recession. However, because of the slack labor market during the recession, unemployed could also have been more inclined to apply for DI whether or not they receive

UI. Therefore, the effect of receiving UI on the decision to apply for DI might be stronger or weaker during the Great Recession.

When estimating our models without the 2008 SIPP, we find that the effect of UI on DI participation remains relatively unchanged. Coefficients of SNAP participation on disability insurance application and re-employment change somewhat but these changes are not large enough to be statistically significant.

To summarize, the various checks have shown that the negative effect of UI participation on DI application is robust to alternative specifications. We also find a significant effect of UI participation on applications for SSI in some specifications but not in others. Coefficients for re-employment are also sensitive to various specifications, which is not surprising given their large standard errors. Results for TDI and TANF/AFDC participation do not appear to be well identified and are not robust. Finally, the effect of SNAP on SSI is always positive but only significant in some specifications.

CONCLUSION

This article addresses whether and how participation in temporary assistance programs influence re-employment and applications for DI and SSI. We focus on workers who have lost their job because temporary assistance payments are an important income support for them and because they are more likely to apply for DI and SSI than employed workers. After correcting for selection bias by instrumenting for temporary assistance participation using state policies and rules, we find evidence that temporary assistance programs may be substitutes or complements for DI and SSI application. The most robust evidence is that UI participation deters applying for DI. Moreover, in some specifications UI participation also reduces the probability of applying for SSI and increases the probability of re-employment. Together, these results suggest that UI participation reduces disability claims both directly and possibly also indirectly through a higher chance of finding new employment. We also find a positive effect of claiming SNAP benefits on applications for SSI, though evidence for this causal effects is mixed. Finally, coefficients for TDI participation and TANF participation do not appear to be well identified and we do not find robust causal effects for these two program.

The negative effect of UI participation on applications for DI and SSI suggests that the substitution effect dominates the complementarity effect, but the positive effect of SNAP participation on applications for SSI in some specifications suggests the opposite. One possible explanation is that the complementarity effect dominates for low levels of cash assistance (e.g., SNAP benefits), whereas the substitution effect dominates for high levels of cash assistance (e.g., UI benefits). Alternatively, the effect of receiving cash transfers could depend on the group receiving them. While UI beneficiaries with their strong labor force attachment may be more easily dissuaded from applying for DI or SSI, low-income job losers who receive SNAP might see their benefits as a step towards receiving SSI benefits or may learn by receiving benefits while not employed that they can survive on less income and no job. Finally, the different results could also indicate institutional complementarities or lack thereof. UI is a program for able and available workers, and recipients might therefore be reluctant to apply for DI or SSI even if they are eligible. For SNAP, parents with children on SNAP and SSI could find it easier to claim benefits for both programs, or SNAP caseworkers might direct people who qualify for SNAP to the SSI office since both programs have similar eligibility rules.

This article provides an overview of the interaction between temporary assistance programs and applications for DI and SSI. Our research indicates that such interaction exists for UI. For SNAP we find some evidence of a positive effect on SSI participation. This is not to say that participation in other temporary assistance programs such as TDI do not influence DI or SSI applications. Rather, these temporary assistance programs are smaller as compared to UI and SNAP and we cannot precisely identify possible interaction effects in our data. In future research, matched administrative temporary assistance disability claims records could provide better estimates of interactions between participation in smaller temporary assistance programs and applications for DI and SSI. Another area of future research concerns the link between applying for DI or SSI benefits and receiving them. It is quite plausible that workers influenced by policy changes to temporary assistance have different application success rates than other workers. Ultimately, estimating the effect of temporary assistance program participation on DI and SSI rolls is necessary to obtain estimates about the fiscal impact of such interactions.

Even though our analysis is only a preliminary step toward this goal, some policy implications follow. First, the negative effect of UI participation on disability insurance claims suggests that improving access to UI and increasing its benefits could help reduce the number of DI applications. Our results for SNAP participation on SSI are less robust but the positive relationship would imply that policy makers could reduce SSI claims by reducing access to SNAP. However, our discussion about these effects also shows that it is important to understand why these effects exist. For UI, is seems plausible that UI benefits support jobless workers and thereby make applying for DI less necessary. By contrast, SNAP claimants constitute a very different population and the complementarity with SSI could reflect a need of basic income support to be able to apply for SSI or a lack of knowledge about accessing the program. Therefore, policy makers might find it desirable to increase SSI applications through SNAP participation. Understanding these underlying reasons for program interaction in future research will be an important step toward formulating more effective policies that take program interactions into account.

NOTES

1. Two papers also study the effect of changes to the DI program on UI take-up. Karlström, Palme, and Svensson (2008) study the 1997 abolition of special eligibility rules for 60–64 year old workers in Sweden. They find that the reform increased take-up of sick pay and unemployment insurance. Borghans, Gielen, and Luttmer (2010) exploit a cohort discontinuity in the stringency of the 1993 Dutch disability reform to obtain causal estimates of the effect of decreased DI generosity on employment and other transfers.

2. Information in this section comes from: U.S. Committee on Ways and Means (1996, 2000, 2004), Comparison of State UI Laws and Significant Provisions of State UI Laws (see http://www.ows.doleta.gov/unemploy/comparison2011.asp), Rowe, Murphy, and Mon (2010), and Social Security Administration (1997).

3. Specifically, DI is an insurance for workers with a recent and relatively steady work history in covered work while SSI is a means-tested program for people with income and assets below certain limits (for assets, the limit is currently $2000 for individuals and $3000 for couples).

4. Most states grant Medicaid to SSI beneficiaries automatically. Some states, however, apply their Medicaid eligibility criteria to SSI beneficiaries who then do not necessarily qualify for these benefits.

5. Monthly gross household income is calculated by summing up income of all household members. SSI and DI benefits are part of gross household income. Net (or counted) household income is obtained from gross household income by adjusting for family size, child support payments, and shelter expenses.

6. Liquid assets include checking and savings accounts, stocks and bond, individual retirement accounts, and nonrecurring lump-sum payments such as insurance settlements. Non-liquid assets are personal and residential property or life insurance policies and pension plans.

7. In some states, pregnant women are eligible as well.

8. Longer unemployment duration due to higher UI benefits may also be attributed to a liquidity effect: higher UI benefits relax credit constraints, which in turns allow workers to search longer for jobs (Chetty, 2008).

9. More precisely, the net value of applying for DI or SSI decreases with other income if the utility function is strictly concave.

10. Demographic variables include: age, age squared, sex, race (white and not Hispanic, black, Native American, and Hispanic), marital status, high-school diploma, some college, number of children under 18 years, Medicaid coverage, health insurance coverage, last year's earnings, work limitation, state's unemployment rate, and dummy variables for calendar years and calendar months. Work limitation is a widely used, self-reported assessment whether the respondent has difficulties working because of a mental or physical impairment.

11. We also estimated eq. (1) using monthly dummies for temporary assistance participation. The results are qualitatively the same as the ones we find for eq. (1).

12. Monotonicity means that everyone who participates for one value of the instrument also participates for a different value of the instrument if on average more people participate under the latter value than under the former.

13. Technically, we use the General Method of Moments (GMM) approach to estimate coefficients of instrumental variable regressions. See for instance Wooldridge (2012) for a general discussion of the GMM approach to instrumental variables.

14. Specifically, a positive serial correlation implies rejection rates of true null hypotheses on the order of 50 percent with a nominal alpha of 5 percent.

15. Alternatively, we could have distinguished between three groups of applicants, DI only, SSI only, and concurrent applications. We treat the last two groups as one category since few applications for SSI are observed in the sample and the results for concurrent applications are similar to the results for SSI only applications if regressions are estimated for each outcome separately.

16. Temporary layoffs are job separations due to slack work, material shortage, or similar reasons where workers are expected to return to their employer and therefore not interesting for this study.

17. The instruments used in our analysis cover important aspects of the four temporary assistance programs and likely influence program participation. Given the complexity of these programs, it would be possible to construct further instruments. However, this would require substantially more time and thereby would have made the analysis infeasible.

18. See http://www.ows.doleta.gov/unemploy/statelaws.asp#sigprouilaws

19. The SNAP Rules Database currently covers the years 1996 to 2007. Since states have not changed their noncitizen eligibility rules and biometric technology since the early 2000s, we assume that rules remain the same between 2007 and 2010. We also assume zero outreach spending for 2008 to 2010 (because of lack of information), which effectively is an assumption that any outreach spending in 2008 to 2010 had no effect on participation.

20. We also explored whether people with right-censored spells are different in observed characteristics as compared to people with observed endings. Differences were minor in most cases, suggesting that selective attrition is not a serious concern in our data. However, right-censored spells have an average observed duration of 10.7 months, much longer than duration for people with observed outcomes.

21. Tables for robustness checks not included in this manuscript can be obtained from the authors upon request.

22. We did not estimate IV probit models as a comparison because they require endogenous variables to be continuous.

23. We also experiment with treating SNAP and TANF/AFDC participation as one temporary assistance program but such a change does not improve our models much.

ACKNOWLEDGMENTS

The research reported herein was pursuant to a grant from the U.S. Social Security Administration (SSA) funded as part of the Retirement Research Consortium (RRC). The findings and conclusions expressed are solely those of the authors and do not represent the views of SSA, any agency of the federal government, the RRC, or the Urban Institute, its board, or its funders. We received value feedback from a number of people, including: Gregory Acs, Pamela Loprest, two anonymous referees, editors of Research in Labor Economics and seminar participants at the Urban Institute, the Social Security Administration, and the IZA/OECD/World Bank Conference on Safety Nets and Benefit Dependence. We would also like to thank Tom Callan for excellent research assistance and Stephan Lindner would like to express his gratitude to Brian Rowe, Christine Cheu, and Louie for their support. We would not have been able to conduct this study without the support of Paul Davies, Thuy Ho, and Tom Solomon from SSA.

REFERENCES

Autor, D. H., & Duggan, M. G. (2006). The growth in the social security disability rolls: A fiscal crisis unfolding. *Journal of Economic Perspectives, 20*, 71–96.

Black, D., Daniel, K., & Sanders, S. (2002). The impact of economic conditions on participation in disability programs: Evidence from the coal boom and bust. *American Economic Review, 92*(1), 27–50.

Borghans, L., Gielen, A. C., & Luttmer, E. F. P. (2010). *Social support substitution and the earnings rebound: Evidence from a regression discontinuity in disability insurance reform.* IZA Discussion Paper No. 5412. Bonn, Germany.

Bound, J., Burkhauser, R. J., & Nichols, A. (2003). Tracking the household income of SSDI and SSI applicants. In S. W. Polachek (Ed.), *Worker well-being and public policy* (pp. 113–148). Amsterdam: JAI.

Bound, J., & Burkhauser, R. V. (1999). Economic analysis of transfer programs targeted on people with disabilities. In O. Ashenfelter & D. Card (Eds.), *Handbook of labor economics* (pp. 3417–3528). New York, NY: Elsevier.

Burkhauser, R. V., Daly, M. C., McVicar, D., & Wilkins, R. (2013). *Disability benefit growth and disability reform in the U.S.: Lessons from other OECD nations.* Federal Reserve Bank of San Francisco Working Paper No. 2013-40.

Card, D., Chetty, R., & Weber, A. (2007). Cash-on-hand and competing models of intertemporal behavior: New evidence from the labor market. *Quarterly Journal Economics, 122*(4), 1511–1560.

Chetty, R. (2008). Moral hazard versus liquidity and optimal unemployment insurance. *Journal of Political Economy, 116*, 173–234.

Coe, N. B., Lindner, S., Wong, K., & Wu, A. Y. (2014). How do the disabled cope while waiting for SSDI? *IZA Journal of Labor Policy, 3*(1), 1–27.

Finegold, K., Margrabe, W., & Ratcliffe, C. (2010). *SNAP program rules database documentation.* Washington, DC: The Urban Institute.

Imbens, G. W., & Angrist, J. D. (1994). Identification and estimation of local average treatment effect. *Econometrica, 62*, 467–475.

Inderbitzin, L., Staubli, S., & Zweimüller, J. (2013). *Extended unemployment benefits and early retirement: Program complementarity and program substitution.* IZA Discussion Paper No. 7330.

Jenkins, S. P. (1995). Easy estimation methods for discrete-time duration models. *Oxford Bulletin of Economics and Statistics, 57*(1), 129–136.

Karlström, A., Palme, M., & Svensson, I. (2008). The employment effect of stricter rules for eligibility for DI: Evidence from a natural experiment in Sweden. *Journal of Public Economics, 92*(10), 2071–2082.

Lammers, M., Bloemen, H., & Hochguertel, S. (2012). Job search requirements for older unemployed: Transitions to employment, early retirement and disability benefits. *European Economic Review, 58*(2), 31–57.

Lindner, S. (2011). *How does unemployment insurance affect the decision to apply for social security disability insurance?* Ann Arbor, MI: The University of Michigan.

Lindner, S. (2013). From working to applying: Employment transitions of applicants for disability insurance in the United States. *Journal of Social Policy, 42*(2), 329–348.

Meyer, B. D. (1990). Unemployment insurance and unemployment spells. *Econometrica, 58*(4), 757–782.

Petrongolo, B. (2013). The long-term effects of job search requirements: Evidence from the UK JSA reform. *Journal of Public Economics, 93*(11–12), 1234–1253.

Ratcliffe, C., & McKernan, S. M. (2010). *How much does SNAP reduce food insecurity?* Washington, DC: The Urban Institute.

Rowe, G., Murphy, M., & Mon, E. Y. (2010). *Welfare rules databook.* Washington, DC: The Urban Institute.

Rupp, K., & Stapleton, D. (1995). Determinants of the growth in the social security administration's disability programs – An overview. *Social Security Bulletin, 58*(4), 43–70.

Rutledge, M. (2011). *The impact of unemployment benefits extensions on disability insurance application and allowance rates.* CCR Working Paper No. 2011–17. Center for Retirement Research at Boston College, Chestnut Hill, MA.

Social Security Administration. (1997). *Social security programs in the United States.* Washington, DC: Author.

U.S. Committee on Ways and Means. (1996). *Green book.* Washington, DC: Author.

U.S. Committee on Ways and Means. (2000). *Green book.* Washington, DC: Author.

U.S. Committee on Ways and Means. (2004). *Green book.* Washington, DC: Author.

Von Wachter, T., Song, J., & Manchester, J. (2011). Trends in employment and earnings of allowed and rejected applicants to the social security disability insurance program. *American Economic Review, 101*(7), 3308–3329.

Wooldridge, J. M. (2012). *Econometric analysis of cross section and panel data* (2nd ed.). Cambridge, MA: MIT Press.

Young, C. (2011). *Unemployed workers and job search effort: Evidence from random audits.* Stanford, CA: Stanford University.

APPENDIX A: DESCRIPTION OF SELECTED INSTRUMENTS

UI Program Variables

Alternative base period: Historically, the base period has been used to assess monetary eligibility of UI claimants. The base period includes the first four of the last five completed calendar quarters. The base period therefore ignores up to six months of earnings prior to the date a claim is filed. For instance, if a worker claims benefits June 20, 2011, then the last completed quarter is January to March 2010, and the base period includes January to December 2010. The ABP reduces the gap between the quarters counted for monetary eligibility and the time a claim is filed by including the last four completed quarters to determine monetary eligibility. In some states, the ABP includes the last three completed quarters before filing a claim, plus the current quarter.

Wages in two quarters: UI claimants are only monetary eligible if they have earned wages in two of the four quarters under consideration (either base period or alternative base period).

Waiting week: UI claimants do not receive benefit during the first week of eligibility in such states.

Dependency allowance: UI claimants may receive additional benefits for dependent family members. In order to receive ARRA funds, states are required to pay at least $15 per dependent up to $50 per week.

Domestic violence/moving with spouse/filial obligations: These are good cause provisions for nonmonetary eligibility, that is, workers may quit employment for one of these reasons and still be eligible for UI. Filial obligations include taking care of ill or disabled immediate family member. These provisions are part of the ARRA.

Part-time work: Workers who only seek part-time work are still eligible for UI benefits. This provision is part of the ARRA.

26 weeks: UI benefits continue for at least 26 additional weeks after exhaustion of regular benefits while the UI claimant is in approved training. This provision is part of the ARRA.

TDI Program Variables

Covered by state TDI insurance: Five states currently offer TDI: California, Hawaii, New Jersey, New York, and Rhode Island. These states cover different groups of workers. California is the only state to include the self-employed, while Hawaii is the only state to cover local government workers. Agricultural workers are covered in California, Hawaii, and New Jersey. We use industry codes of the last job to identify whether a worker is covered in one of these states.

TANF Program Variables

Imputed TANF benefits at zero earnings: We use state benefit formulas to determine for each state and year TANF benefits of families with zero earnings.

SNAP Program Variables

Biometric technology used: Some states have introduced biometric technology (typically fingerprints) to verify an applicant's identity and thereby reduce multiple participation fraud. As of 2010, five states have such a policy in place: Arizona, California, Massachusetts, New York, and Texas.

Outreach spending per person: Amount of federal and nonfederal outlays as well as outreach grants per non-SNAP participants with a household income below 150 percent of the federal poverty threshold in as state.

Noncitizen fully eligible × noncitizen in household: Equals to one for a household if noncitizens are fully eligible for SNAP benefits in a state and at least one noncitizen lives in that household. Noncitizen were fully eligible for SNAP benefits prior to the 1996 welfare reform, but lost eligibility with the reform. After the welfare reform, some states introduced legislation to restore full eligibility for noncitizens. These changes occurred between 1997 and 2003, and since then, six states have restored full eligibility for noncitizens. These are California, Connecticut, Maine, Nebraska, Washington, and Wisconsin.

Noncitizen partly eligible × noncitizen in household: Equals to one for a household if noncitizens are eligible for SNAP benefits in a state under certain circumstances and at least one noncitizen lives in that household. Noncitizen were fully eligible for SNAP benefits prior to the 1996 welfare reform, but lost eligibility with the reform. Some states restore partial eligibility after the welfare reform, and the Farm Security and Rural Investment Act of 2002 restored eligibility for noncitizens if they have a disability, if they have been U.S. residents for at least 5 years, or if they are children under 18 years.

APPENDIX B

Table B1. IV Regression for UI/TDI/TANF/AFDC/SNAP Take-Up, All Months.

	Employment	DI	SSI
UI recipient	0.2798***	−0.0061**	−0.0045
	(0.0630)	(0.0023)	(0.0024)
TDI recipient	−1.4673**	−0.0252	0.0122
	(0.5224)	(0.0214)	(0.0212)
TANF/AFDC recipient	−0.5404*	−0.0021	0.0109
	(0.2152)	(0.0088)	(0.0088)
SNAP recipient	0.0687	−0.0057	0.0056
	(0.0831)	(0.0032)	(0.0032)
Age	−0.0063*	−0.0000	0.0003*
	(0.0029)	(0.0001)	(0.0001)
Age squared	0.0001	0.0000	−0.0000*
	(0.0000)	(0.0000)	(0.0000)
Male	0.0164	0.0004	0.0002
	(0.0087)	(0.0003)	(0.0004)
Black	0.0135	0.0015	−0.0011
	(0.0195)	(0.0008)	(0.0008)
American Indian	−0.0050	0.0001	−0.0007
	(0.0110)	(0.0004)	(0.0004)
Asian	0.0047	0.0005	−0.0012**
	(0.0120)	(0.0005)	(0.0005)
White, Hispanic	0.0237	0.0011*	−0.0012*
	(0.0128)	(0.0005)	(0.0005)
Married	−0.0290**	0.0001	0.0002
	(0.0103)	(0.0004)	(0.0004)
Noncitizen in household	−0.0062	−0.0008*	0.0004
	(0.0090)	(0.0003)	(0.0003)
High-school degree	−0.0065	−0.0007	0.0006
	(0.0124)	(0.0005)	(0.0005)
Some college	0.0100	−0.0003	−0.0000
	(0.0075)	(0.0003)	(0.0003)
Two children <18	0.0207	0.0006	−0.0013*
	(0.0145)	(0.0006)	(0.0005)
Three children < 18	0.0271	0.0008	−0.0015
	(0.0233)	(0.0009)	(0.0009)
Four children <18	0.0495	0.0011	−0.0026*
	(0.0324)	(0.0013)	(0.0013)
Five or more children <18	0.0274	0.0013	−0.0019
	(0.0355)	(0.0013)	(0.0014)
Medicaid coverage during month	0.0643	0.0015	−0.0038
	(0.0643)	(0.0026)	(0.0025)

Table B1. (*Continued*)

	Employment	DI	SSI
Private health insurance during month	0.0363*	−0.0004	−0.0003
	(0.0168)	(0.0006)	(0.0006)
WC: recipient during month	−0.0066	0.0084***	−0.0040**
	(0.0304)	(0.0026)	(0.0012)
Monthly earnings last year (in 1,000 USD)	0.0004	0.0002**	0.0001*
	(0.0017)	(0.0001)	(0.0001)
Work limitation	0.0385	0.0077***	0.0053***
	(0.0295)	(0.0013)	(0.0012)
Duration (log)	−0.0417***	−0.0002	−0.0007***
	(0.0048)	(0.0002)	(0.0002)
Number of spells of person	0.0088**	−0.0000	0.0001
	(0.0029)	(0.0001)	(0.0001)
Unemployment (percentage by state/month)	−0.0089***	0.0002**	0.0001
	(0.0022)	(0.0001)	(0.0001)
Year: 1997	−0.0093	0.0004	0.0003
	(0.0074)	(0.0004)	(0.0004)
Year: 1998	−0.0219*	0.0000	0.0006
	(0.0109)	(0.0005)	(0.0005)
Year: 1999	−0.0277	−0.0001	0.0007
	(0.0142)	(0.0006)	(0.0006)
Year: 2000	−0.0501**	−0.0014	−0.0000
	(0.0192)	(0.0008)	(0.0009)
Year: 2001	−0.0255*	0.0001	−0.0004
	(0.0108)	(0.0005)	(0.0005)
Year: 2002	−0.0549***	0.0006	0.0013*
	(0.0129)	(0.0006)	(0.0006)
Year: 2003	−0.0702***	0.0002	0.0008
	(0.0152)	(0.0007)	(0.0007)
Year: 2004	−0.0112	0.0001	−0.0004
	(0.0104)	(0.0005)	(0.0005)
Year: 2005	−0.0389***	0.0001	0.0000
	(0.0112)	(0.0005)	(0.0005)
Year: 2006	−0.0475***	−0.0000	0.0004
	(0.0131)	(0.0006)	(0.0006)
Year: 2007	−0.0636***	−0.0003	−0.0002
	(0.0163)	(0.0007)	(0.0007)
Year: 2008	−0.1218***	−0.0004	0.0001
	(0.0188)	(0.0006)	(0.0010)
Year: 2009	−0.1093***	0.0008	0.0004
	(0.0176)	(0.0007)	(0.0008)
Year: 2010	−0.1079***	−0.0002	0.0003
	(0.0193)	(0.0008)	(0.0009)
Month: 2	0.0128***	−0.0003	−0.0003
	(0.0033)	(0.0003)	(0.0004)

Table B1. (*Continued*)

	Employment	DI	SSI
Month: 3	0.0040	0.0001	−0.0001
	(0.0034)	(0.0003)	(0.0004)
Month: 4	0.0057	−0.0001	−0.0006
	(0.0037)	(0.0003)	(0.0004)
Month: 5	0.0007	−0.0001	−0.0002
	(0.0037)	(0.0003)	(0.0004)
Month: 6	0.0217***	−0.0001	−0.0003
	(0.0040)	(0.0003)	(0.0004)
Month: 7	0.0121**	−0.0004	−0.0006
	(0.0042)	(0.0003)	(0.0004)
Month: 8	0.0139**	0.0002	−0.0006
	(0.0043)	(0.0004)	(0.0004)
Month: 9	0.0342***	−0.0001	−0.0003
	(0.0044)	(0.0003)	(0.0004)
Month: 10	0.0202***	−0.0000	−0.0005
	(0.0044)	(0.0003)	(0.0004)
Month: 11	0.0057	−0.0002	−0.0002
	(0.0045)	(0.0003)	(0.0004)
Month: 12	−0.0177***	−0.0001	−0.0006
	(0.0046)	(0.0003)	(0.0004)
Constant	0.3611***	−0.0001	−0.0051
	(0.0668)	(0.0026)	(0.0026)

WHAT IMPACT DOES OLD-AGE PENSION RECEIPT HAVE ON THE USE OF PUBLIC ASSISTANCE PROGRAMS AMONG THE ELDERLY?

Norma B. Coe and April Yanyuan Wu

ABSTRACT

*This article estimates the causal effect of benefit levels on elderly enroll-
ment in two public assistance programs by using the variation in eligibility and benefit levels introduced by old-age pension benefits. The findings
are threefold. First, the low take-up among the elderly is not driven by
changes in the composition of the eligible pool. Second, old-age pensions
decrease the use of public assistance programs by decreasing the gain of
participation — the potential benefits. Third, we find program-specific
responses: a $100 increase in potential Supplemental Security Income
(SSI) benefits leads to a 4—6 percentage point increase in the take-up
probability, but we are unable to estimate consistent results for the
Supplemental Nutrition Assistance Program (SNAP). Together with
the fact that eligible individuals who begin receiving old-age pensions*

Safety Nets and Benefit Dependence
Research in Labor Economics, Volume 39, 259–295
Copyright © 2014 by Emerald Group Publishing Limited
All rights of reproduction in any form reserved
ISSN: 0147-9121/doi:10.1108/S0147-912120140000039007

continue to participate in SSI more often than they maintain SNAP enrollment, the different program response could be due to preference for cash over in-kind transfers.

Keywords: Old-age pension; Supplemental Nutrition Assistance Program; Supplemental Security Income; take-up decisions

JEL classifications: H53; H55; I3

INTRODUCTION

Low take-up by the elderly in most means-tested transfer programs is a persistent and puzzling phenomenon: estimated elderly take-up rates for Supplemental Security Income (SSI) range from 38 percent to 73 percent (e.g., Coe, 1983; McGarry, 1996; Shields, Barnow, Chaurette, & Constantine, 1990; Strand, Rupp, & Davies, 2009) and less than 35 percent for the Supplemental Nutrition Assistance Program (SNAP) (Haider, Jacknowitz, & Schoeni, 2003; Wolkwitz & Leftin, 2008; Wu, 2009). This low take-up is especially surprising since the elderly have fewer opportunities to work their way out of poverty, and might be expected to be more reliant on the safety net than their younger counterparts. To the extent that low take-up of the elderly in means-tested programs reflects serious unmet need, this is an issue of public concern.

Despite this well-documented counter-intuitive phenomenon, not much is known about the reasons behind the low take-up rate among the elderly in means-tested programs. While an extensive literature has explored program participation among the eligible population broadly, only a few have focused specifically on the elderly.[1] Further, most of these studies are limited to measuring correlations between potential benefit levels and program participation. SNAP and SSI are national programs with relatively uniform eligibility criteria and benefit levels;[2] though state SSI Supplement programs introduce state-level benefit variation, this variation is likely correlated with the cost of living within the state and is not ideal for identification. As a result, the inherent selection issue that must be dealt with before causal estimates can be measured – individuals who are in the program may be different from non-participating eligible individuals – is difficult to address. McGarry (1996) tries to identify the causal relationship between SSI benefit levels and take-up among the elderly. However, the validity of the exclusion restrictions of McGarry's instrumental variables has been questioned by other researchers (Elder & Powers, 2004). Thus, relatively little is known about what factors matter most in the take-up decision of the elderly, how these factors and their relative importance differ by age, or how enrollment in transfer programs might be increased. Since proposals for raising SNAP/SSI benefit levels have been put forward to increase elderly participation, it is crucial to estimate the effects of public assistance benefits to the elderly participation decision.

Using the *Health and Retirement Study* (HRS) linked to administrative earnings records and geographic identifiers, this study examines the take-up decision of the elderly in SNAP and SSI programs by exploiting the interaction between old-age pension benefits and public assistance programs.[3] Old-age pensions interact with means-tested transfer programs in two ways. First, by providing a considerable source of income, old-age pension benefits change who is eligible for means-tested transfer programs; in 2011, 14.5 million people were lifted out of poverty by old-age pension benefits (Van de Water & Sherman, 2012). If the likelihood of take-up varies among individuals, old-age pension benefits could have a large impact on the take-up rate by changing the composition of the eligible pool. Second, among those still eligible, receiving retirement income from old-age pensions changes the expected public assistance benefit amount individuals are eligible to receive from means-tested transfer programs. Since the take-up decision is likely impacted by the expected benefit of participating, this factor could be another explanation for the different take-up rates between the young and the elderly.

The program interactions with old-age pensions provide age-related variation in eligibility and benefit levels of means-tested public transfer programs that can be exploited to estimate the causal impact of the expected public assistance benefit level on the take-up of means-tested programs. We develop an instrumental variable using the exogenous variation in potential SNAP/SSI benefits caused by potential receipt of old-age pension benefits. This instrumental variable captures the fact that old-age pension benefits, the major source of income for the low-income elderly population, reduce SNAP/SSI payment on nearly a dollar-for-dollar basis.

This article contributes to the literature in several ways. First, we use instrumental variables techniques to exploit exogenous changes in the benefit level to estimate the causal relationship between take-up and benefit levels in two means-tested programs. Second, we improve on measurement error issues by using administrative earnings records available from the Social Security Administration matched to survey data. Finally, traditional economic theory suggests that cash transfers are superior to in-kind transfers in terms of the recipient's utility: in-kind transfers may constrain the behavior of the recipients, while cash transfers do not. This article examines whether the interactions with old-age pensions have different behavioral responses between these cash (SSI) and in-kind (SNAP) transfer programs.[4]

Our findings are summarized as follows. First, we do not find evidence that the low take-up among the elderly is driven by changes in the pool of eligible individuals that have differential take-up patterns. However, old-age pension receipt has a significant impact on the use of public assistance programs among the elderly because the increase in income decreases the potential benefits available from public programs. Our estimates are inconclusive about the behavioral response to a change in SNAP benefits,[5] but our estimates suggest that a $100 increase in SSI benefits leads to a 4–6 percentage point increase in the probability of participating in SSI, a smaller effect than traditionally found in the literature.[6] These findings are robust across different model specifications and different definitions of the eligible population. The average SSI benefit for eligible individuals aged 50–62 is about $472 per month, and the benefits for those above the earliest age at which one could claim an old-age pension (62) is approximately $229, a simple back-of-the-envelope calculation shows that old-age pensions decrease the take-up rate of SSI by 10–15 percentage points. Together with the fact that eligible individuals more often continue participating in SSI after receiving old-age pension benefits than they maintain SNAP enrollment, we posit that the different estimated behavioral response could be due to individual preference for cash over in-kind transfers.

The article proceeds as follows. The Background section briefly outlines the SNAP and SSI programs and reviews the existing literature. The "Data, Sample, and Determining Program Eligibility" section describes the data, sample construction, and measurement error, and presents the descriptive patterns of eligibility and participation. The "Do Old-Age Pensions Impact Take-Up by Changing the Composition of the Eligible Pool?" section discusses interactions between old-age pensions and means-tested transfer programs. The "Empirical Strategy" section discusses empirical methods and summarizes the main results. The "Sensitivity Tests" section summarizes sensitivity tests, followed by concluding remarks.

BACKGROUND

The SNAP

SNAP is the largest nutrition program for low-income Americans and a mainstay of the federal safety net. To receive SNAP, households must meet three financial criteria: a gross income test, a net income test, and an asset test.[7] A household is automatically, or "categorically," eligible for SNAP when they are receiving SSI, the Temporary Assistance for Needy Families, or General Assistance programs.

Eligibility rules for households with an elderly (age 60 and over) or disabled member are more liberal than for the rest of the population. First, these households are exempt from the gross income test. Second, the more generous net income test removes the cap on the shelter deduction and includes a deduction for out-of-pocket medical expenses.[8] Third, the asset limit increases from $2,000 to $3,250.

The amount of SNAP benefit that a household receives is equal to the maximum benefit level (which varies by household size) subtract 30 percent of the household's net income (reflecting that an average household will spend approximately 30 percent of its net income on food). In 2012, an eligible two-person household could receive SNAP benefits of between $16 and $367 each month.

SSI

Designed to provide financial support to low-income blind, disabled, and elderly individuals, the SSI program is currently the largest federal means-tested cash assistance program in the United States. The SSI program provides a guaranteed income to all eligible individuals. In 2012 the income guarantees were $698 ($1,011) per month for a single individual (couple) living in his own home. The SSI benefit individuals receive is the difference between the income guarantee and their countable income.[9] A resource test is also required for participation in SSI.[10]

Individuals between 18 and 64 must meet the income and resource tests and be determined to be unable to work for at least one year due to a medical impairment.[11] For the aged (65 and over), individuals need to meet only the income and resource tests to be eligible. In addition to the federal program, states have the option of offering supplemental SSI benefits. In 2012, 30 states offered supplements to elderly individuals, and a total of 45 states offered at least some form of supplemental benefit, which can be substantial. For example, the income guarantee for a couple living in California in 2012 is $1,407 ($396 above the federal level), while in New York the income guarantee is $1,115. If a state is willing to administer its own program, it is free to alter the eligibility requirements as it wishes, including imposing more or less stringent income and resource tests. While federal benefits are indexed for inflation, state benefits are not.

Literature Review

Numerous studies have examined why people eligible for government transfer programs do not participate in these programs. The cost/benefit framework has been the basis for investigations of nonparticipation in social
programs: individuals choose to enroll only if the benefits of participation
exceed the costs. The findings of Blank and Ruggles (1996) support this
claim. Using data from the *Survey of Income and Program Participation*
(SIPP), they show that low participation of women in the Aid to Families
with Dependent Children and the SNAP stems from would-be participants'
expectations of low benefits. In her study of SSI participation among the
elderly, McGarry (1996) reports that larger expected SSI benefits significantly increase the probability that an individual will participate in the program. Davies (2002) also suggests that the calculated benefits are positively
correlated to the participation decision. Wu (2009) finds that the elderly's
decision to participate in SNAP is strongly associated with economic incentives. The lower expected SNAP benefit level and relatively better financial
situation for the elderly account for about one-third of the difference in
SNAP take-up between the elderly and the non-elderly.[12]

While there is an extensive literature on nonparticipation, only a few
studies have focused specifically on older adults despite the fact that low
take-up by the elderly in means-tested programs has been perceived as a
serious problem for over a quarter of a century (Davies, 2002; Elder &
Powers, 2004; McGarry, 1996 on SSI; Cunnyngham, 2010; Gundersen &
Ziliak, 2008; Haider et al., 2003; Levy, 2008; Wu, 2009 on SNAP). While
the existing research attributes the low take-up among eligible elderly
largely to the fact that many elderly poor expect to receive only a very
modest cash payment, identification is difficult because SNAP and SSI are
national programs with virtually uniform eligibility criteria and benefit
levels. State SSI Supplement programs introduce state variation in benefits,
but this variation does not solve the identification problem if it is correlated
with the cost of living in the state.[13] Most of the existing studies are limited
to measuring correlations between potential public assistance benefit levels
and program participation.

McGarry (1996) proposes a two-stage procedure in which the computed
expected SSI benefit is first regressed on household characteristics and the
(federal + state) maximum benefit. This predicted value then enters into a
probit for the take-up decision. The two-stage procedure will yield consistent estimates only if (a) the variance of the measurement error in benefits
is correctly estimated, and (b) a researcher finds valid exclusion restrictions,

in this case variables which affect the expected benefit amount but have no influence on take-up decisions apart from their indirect effects through benefit levels. Elder and Powers (2004) argue that this assumption is invalid for four variables used by McGarry: average household income in the previous year; household head status; marital status; and SSI generosity in the state of residence. As a result, the inherent selection issue that must be dealt with before causal estimates can be measured — individuals who are in the program may be different from non-participating eligible individuals — is difficult to address. A recent study by Schmidt, Shore-Sheppard, and Watson (2013) uses simulated eligibility and benefits to instrument for imputed eligibility and potential benefits; however, their study focuses on families with children.

DATA, SAMPLE, AND DETERMINING PROGRAM ELIGIBILITY

Data and Sample

For the primary analysis, we use data from the 1992 through 2010 waves of the HRS linked to administrative earnings records and geographic identifiers. The HRS is a longitudinal data collection effort begun in 1992 with a cohort of about 10,000 individuals between the ages 51−61 who were born between 1931 and 1941. Additional cohorts have been enrolled over time so that the survey includes 30,500 individuals in 2010 and can be weighted to be nationally representative of the non-institutionalized population over the age of 50. Respondents are interviewed every two years.

Approximately 70 percent of respondents have given consent to have their earnings histories back to 1951 linked to the survey. For those who have not given permission, we estimate earnings histories based on survey data on previous jobs and wages (Gustman & Steinmeier, 2001), using the estimated returns to tenure from Anderson, Gustman, and Steinmeier (1999).[14]

As discussed in the background section, states have the option of offering supplemental SSI benefits, and ignoring such state-level differences will cause substantial error in estimated benefits and eligibility. We match the public use data with the restricted-access geographic identifier file. The match rate is 99.7 percent.

In each wave, respondents are asked whether they have received SNAP/ SSI at any time in previous two years, and if so, the amount of their last

SNAP/SSI benefit. In addition to the self-reported recipiency status and benefits information, the HRS includes detailed data allowing us to accurately determine eligibility and benefit levels for the SNAP and SSI programs: income, assets, living arrangements, state of residence, dependent, shelter, and medical expenditures, as well as other programs' participation status for the categorically eligible. These attributes of the HRS provide some important advantages over other nationally representative data sets that have been used to study take-up.[15] One drawback of the HRS, however, is that income from certain sources is available only on an annual basis. Therefore, our analyses of SNAP/SSI take-up among eligible households use annual measures of eligibility and take-up.[16]

Our primary sample consists of survey respondents aged 50–80, whose household provided a family and financial respondent interview, who were not institutionalized at the time of the survey, who answered the SNAP/SSI receipt questions, and for whom we have an administrative earnings record or imputed earnings record. These restrictions result in a sample of 24,039 individuals and 130,518 person-year observations for the SNAP analysis, and 24,445 individual and 134,919 person-year observations for the SSI analysis.

The HRS provides imputations for many of the income and wealth questions, and we use these imputations whenever they are available. Imputations are not provided for the earnings and income of non-respondent co-residents for every wave, which is necessary to determine eligibility for SNAP, so we impute these values using hot-deck methodology.[17] The unit of observation for all of our analysis is the individual. For household-level variables like income or wealth, the values represent the total income or wealth for the household in which an individual resides.

Determining SNAP and SSI Eligibility

We begin our analysis by calculating program eligibility and take-up rates among the eligible population. Since the determination of a unit's eligibility hinges on a number of assumptions and depends on the availability and accuracy of income and asset information, the classification is prone to error. As pointed out in previous studies, incorrectly classifying some individuals as eligible who are actually ineligible will result in a downwardly biased computed take-up rate (Blank & Ruggles, 1996; Daponte, Sanders, & Taylor, 1999; Haider et al., 2003; McGarry, 1996; Strand et al., 2009). The rich financial information in the HRS and in the administrative earnings records allows us to assess eligibility more accurately by account-ing for various deductions and the asset limit; we then compute the take-up rate among the eligible.[18]

We determine SNAP eligibility accounting for age/disability-specific gross and net income tests, the dependent, shelter, and medical expenditure deductions, categorical eligibility, and the age/disability-appropriate asset tests. Fig. 1(a) summarizes the patterns of eligibility and take-up by age. Overall, about 10 percent of our sample is estimated to be eligible for the SNAP, which is comparable to the literature (Haider et al., 2003; Wu, 2009). Eligibility increases with age: while about 8 percent of individuals under age 60 are eligible for SNAP, the rate for individuals over age 60 exceeds 10 percent. This is due to both differences in eligibility rules that are based on age and in the income/asset decline that occurs over the lifecycle. Not surprising, we also find that the take-up rate among the eligible elderly is low. Only 28 percent of the elderly who are eligible receive benefits. Consistent with the existing literature, we find a negative age gradient in take-up: while about 34 percent of eligible individuals age 60 and younger collects benefits, the proportion declines to 23 for those 70 and older.

We determine SSI eligibility by applying both the state-specific income and asset tests, and also by applying health tests to the population under age 65.[19] Fig. 1(b) summarizes patterns of eligibility and participation among the eligible. We find that 4.6 percent of our sample is eligible for benefits and only 47 percent of the eligible population takes up the benefit.

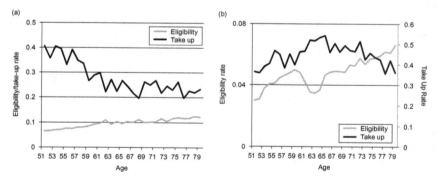

Fig. 1. (a) SNAP Eligibility and Take-Up Rates by Age. (b) SSI Eligibility and Take-Up Rates by Age. *Source*: Authors' calculation based on the HRS, 1992–2010.

Our analysis of SSI is also complicated by the fact that two distinct groups may enter the program: the aged and the disabled. At age 65, the disability standards are removed, and we observe an eligibility surge. In contrast to SNAP's negative age gradient for take-up, the take-up rate for SSI is relatively higher for the older group compared to those under age 60.

Even if program eligibility could be assessed entirely without error, the calculated take-up rate would still be biased if respondents' reports of participation contain errors. To assess the extent of this problem, we calculate the participation rates of those individuals we classify as ineligible. We find that about 1.5 percent of people classified as not eligible for SNAP/SSI report that they received SNAP/SSI, which is consistent with the literature.[20] The literature also documents that the HRS has relatively lower under-reporting compared to other surveys (Haider et al., 2003). Finally, when we compare the demographic characteristics of recipients, the average calculated SNAP/SSI benefits in the HRS, and estimates of other quantities based on the HRS versus administrative records, we find that the HRS tracks the administrative data fairly well.[21] Overall, these results suggest that the HRS can be used to analyze determinants of SNAP/SSI eligibility and take-up among the elderly.

DO OLD-AGE PENSIONS IMPACT TAKE-UP BY CHANGING THE COMPOSITION OF THE ELIGIBLE POOL?

Old-age pensions can impact the take-up of means-tested programs in two ways. First, by providing a considerable amount of income, pensions change who is eligible for means-tested transfer programs. In 2011, the U.S. old-age pension program lifted over 14.5 million elderly Americans above the poverty line, which directly made some individuals ineligible for the means-tested programs and compresses the bottom of the income distribution (Van de Water & Sherman, 2012). Since around 40 percent of Americans claim their old-age pension within one year of the Early Eligibility Age (62), the earliest one can claim their old-age pension (Bosworth & Burtless, 2010), and since our sample indicates that about 62 percent claimed between 62 and 63, it is not surprising to see the eligibility rate drop at this age for both SNAP (Fig. 1(a)) and SSI (Fig. 1(b)) programs.

Second, among those who are still eligible, old-age pension income can impact take-up by increasing their income relative to the poverty line, and thus decreasing the potential public assistance benefit level and the marginal utility of the additional income.[22] Fig. 2(a) and (b) illustrates that among eligible households, the income distribution shifts upward after age 62. Among the SNAP-eligible population, Fig. 2(a) shows that at the 25th percentile of the income distribution when SSI and SNAP benefits are excluded, total family income is around 58 percent of the poverty threshold at ages 61–62; it jumps to 70 percent for ages 63–64. Fig. 2(b) shows sharp drops in SNAP benefits level around age 62 (the EEA), particularly for those at the bottom of the benefit distribution. Similar patterns are observed for the SSI program (Fig. 3(a) and (b)). When following the same individual over time, we also find that the likelihood of being eligible declines around the EEA. Therefore, old-age pensions, by lifting elderly individuals above the poverty line, change the pool of eligible individuals.

If the likelihood of take-up varies among individuals, old-age pensions could impact the take-up rate simply by changing the composition of the eligible pool. These changes are largely overlooked in the take-up literature. Table 1A and B explores the take-up rates and benefit amounts, by age, based on eligibility before and after age 62. Surprisingly, we find little evidence of differential take-up, on average, among these groups: eligible individuals who become ineligible after they turn age 62 and ineligible individuals who become eligible after 62. For SNAP, the take-up rate is 8 percent for both groups; for SSI, the average SSI benefit is lower for

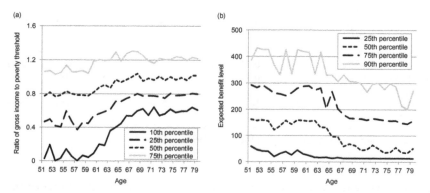

Fig. 2. (a) Ratio of Gross Income to Poverty Threshold by Age among SNAP Eligible Respondents. (b) Expected SNAP Benefit Level by Age among SNAP Eligible Respondents. *Source*: Authors' calculation based on the HRS, 1992–2010.

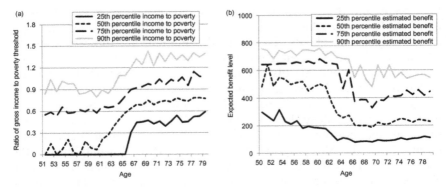

Fig. 3. (a) Ratio of Gross Income to Poverty Threshold by Age among SSI Eligible Respondents. (b) Expected SSI Benefit Level by Age among SSI Eligible Respondents. *Source*: Authors' calculation based on the HRS, 1992−2010.

Table 1. Take-Up Rate by Eligibility Status.

	Take-Up Rate		Number of Observations		Estimated Benefit (per Month)	
	Age 58−61	Age 62−64	Age 58−61	Age 62−64	Age 58−61	Age 62−64
A: SNAP Program						
Eligible both periods	0.38	0.32	547	504	$188	$161
Eligible first period, ineligible second period	0.08	N/A	376	N/A	$195	N/A
Ineligible first period, eligible second period	N/A	0.08	N/A	472	N/A	$189
B: SSI Program						
Eligible both periods	0.57	0.64	617	514	$421	$360
Eligible first period, ineligible second period	0.13	N/A	887	N/A	$165	N/A
Ineligible first period, eligible second period	N/A	0.09	N/A	482	N/A	$109

Source: Authors' calculation based on the HRS, 1992−2010.

those newly eligible after 62, which likely explains the slight difference that we do find (13 percent vs. 9 percent, a difference that is statistically insignificant). Not surprisingly, the take-up rate is higher among individuals who have longer eligibility spells; for instance, among those who are eligible for

SSI both before and after the EEA, about 58 percent took up the benefits before age 62, and 62 percent took up after age 62. Interestingly, we also find that SNAP/SSI recipients who remain eligible for SNAP/SSI after receiving an old-age pension are more likely to exit from in-kind transfer programs (SNAP) compared to the cash transfer program (SSI) (32 percent vs. 9 percent).

EMPIRICAL STRATEGY

Conceptual Framework

We start with McGarry's (1996) framework, which relates the net cost of enrolling in means-tested programs to the expected benefits and other variables thought to influence expected public assistance benefits and costs of enrolling. In particular, an eligible individual participates in SNAP/SSI if the utility gain from participating, P_{it}^*, is positive. One only observes the final participation decision, P_{it}, where $P_{it} = 1$ if $P_{it}^* > 0$, and $P_{it} = 0$ otherwise. In the estimation, P_{it}^* will be modeled as a linear function of the potential benefits of participating, as well as individual socioeconomic characteristics. That is,

$$P_{it}^* = \beta_1 B_{it} + X_{it}' \gamma + \varepsilon_{it} \tag{1}$$

where ε_{it} is distributed normally with mean 0 and variance σ_e^2, B_{it} is the monetary public assistance benefit associated with participating, and X_{it} are individual characteristics thought to affect preferences for participation, such as age, race, gender, marital status, education, household size, health status, and asset ownership.

Table 2 panel A and panel B presents descriptive information for our analytic sample − eligible elderly individuals − for the SNAP and SSI programs, respectively, by participation status and by age.[23] At any age, participants are more likely to be female or minorities and less likely to be married and they have somewhat less schooling. On average, the participants are poorer and less likely to own a home or a car; they also seem more likely to have a higher level of expected public assistance benefits − for instance, the mean calculated SSI benefit for participants is $366, compared to $279 for nonparticipants; and they are much more likely to receive benefits from other welfare programs.

Table 2. Summary Statistics.

	Pre-EEA				EEA and Older			
	Eligible, take-up		Eligible, no take-up		Eligible, take-up		Eligible, no take-up	
	Mean	Standard deviation	Mean	Standard deviation	Mean	Standard deviation	Mean	Standard deviation
A: SNAP Eligibles								
Age	56.26	3.10	56.74	3.09	71.10	5.00	70.84	5.14
Female	0.62	0.49	0.56	0.50	0.74	0.44	0.65	0.48
White	0.54	0.50	0.66	0.48	0.64	0.48	0.69	0.46
Married	0.31	0.46	0.44	0.50	0.22	0.41	0.37	0.48
Less than high school degree	0.42	0.49	0.56	0.50	0.33	0.47	0.44	0.50
Household size								
One person household (%)	0.36	0.48	0.34	0.48	0.56	0.50	0.48	0.50
Mean	2.45	1.71	2.35	1.54	1.72	1.17	1.81	1.10
Income to poverty	0.64	0.43	0.82	0.75	0.83	0.33	1.15	0.74
Own a home	0.34	0.47	0.54	0.50	0.36	0.48	0.58	0.49
Own a car	0.46	0.50	0.66	0.47	0.37	0.48	0.59	0.49
Receive SSI	0.28	0.45	0.08	0.27	0.49	0.50	0.16	0.37
Poor health	0.29	0.45	0.18	0.38	0.28	0.45	0.19	0.39
Mean estimated SNAP benefit	212.10	187.88	205.21	177.35	108.43	132.19	123.25	140.25
Ever previously eligible	0.54	0.50	0.36	0.48	0.84	2.38	1.24	3.21
Quarters of work	79.46	52.56	102.35	53.55	0.76	0.43	0.55	0.50
Mean % zip code below 130% of poverty	0.33	0.47	0.23	0.42	68.32	52.69	90.89	57.38
Number of observations	850		1,869		1,456		5,162	

B: SSI Eligibles

	Mean	SD	Mean	SD	Mean	SD	Mean	SD
Age	56.94	2.86	56.63	2.98	71.25	4.81	71.88	4.88
Female	0.71	0.45	0.58	0.49	0.75	0.43	0.77	0.42
White	0.59	0.49	0.61	0.49	0.61	0.49	0.66	0.47
Married	0.11	0.31	0.23	0.42	0.22	0.42	0.28	0.45
Less than high school degree	0.66	0.47	0.50	0.50	0.73	0.44	0.63	0.48
Household size								
One person household (%)	0.46	0.50	0.25	0.43	0.45	0.50	0.43	0.50
Mean	2.26	1.60	2.63	1.69	2.19	1.64	2.23	1.64
Income to poverty	0.04	0.21	0.44	0.68	0.48	0.43	0.91	0.56
Own a home	0.26	0.44	0.34	0.47	0.32	0.47	0.53	0.50
Own a car	0.29	0.45	0.49	0.50	0.29	0.45	0.47	0.50
Receive welfare	0.58	0.49	0.37	0.48	0.48	0.50	0.23	0.42
Poor health	0.49	0.50	0.42	0.49	0.28	0.45	0.21	0.41
Mean estimated SSI benefit	642.58	150.25	461.39	240.01	337.64	240.06	236.49	198.64
Ever previously eligible	0.66	0.47	0.39	0.49	0.76	0.43	0.58	0.49
Quarters of work	46.41	41.95	92.68	51.63	53.85	47.87	61.91	48.69
Mean % zip code below 130% of poverty	0.33	0.47	0.31	0.46	0.24	0.43	0.21	0.40
Number of observations	422		907		1,452		1,805	

Source: Authors' calculation based on the HRS, 1992–2010.
Note: Data on benefits are expressed in 2011 dollars using CPI-U.

Instrumental Variable Construction

To estimate how benefit levels from public assistance programs impact the likelihood of take-up among the eligible, we exploit the exogenous variation in potential public assistance benefits caused by old-age pension receipt. We develop an instrumental variable, the "Average Potential Benefit" (AvePotBen) to capture the variation in the programs' expected benefit levels upon potentially receiving old-age pension benefits at the EEA. This instrument will thus vary not just as someone ages (reaching the EEA). It will also vary between individuals based on their demographic characteristics, though not work history.

Before age 62, the AvePotBen is set at the maximum benefit level under the SNAP and SSI programs, by household size and state of residence. At age 62 and above, the AvePotBen equals the maximum SNAP or SSI benefits level, minus the old-age pension benefit an individual claiming at 62 would have, averaged over demographic cell. The demographic cell is constructed by five-year age groups, gender, race, education, and marital status; this approach is in the spirit of that used by Currie and Gruber (1996) in the context of Medicaid, and that used by Schmidt, Shore-Sheppard, and Watson (2013) to study five major safety net programs.

The validity of this instrument relies on two facts: that old-age pension benefits are the backbone of most people's retirement income; and it reduces SNAP/SSI payments on nearly a dollar-for-dollar basis. An examination of the income data of individuals further supports this approach. For instance, 27 percent of self-reported SNAP recipients and 37 percent of SSI recipients in out sample who are age 62 and older list their old-age pension as their sole income source. For over 40 percent of SNAP recipients and 50 percent of SSI recipients, old-age pension income accounts for 90 percent or more of their total income. This indicates there should be a high correlation between actual SNAP/SSI benefits one would receive and the Average Potential Benefits measure. Moreover, after claiming, the old-age pension benefits are largely fixed from the individual's perspective.[24] By construction, this variable reveals the decline in the SNAP/SSI benefits levels upon claiming old-age pension benefits.

Further, the average old-age pension benefit by demographic cell, has advantages over individual-specific benefit levels, which are based on earnings and marital status history and likely not validly excluded from the model. For example, "taste for work" is likely correlated with both earnings history (and thus old-age pension benefits) and one's likelihood of participating in a means-tested program, but likely unobserved. Using individual-level variation, especially the variation related to the preference for work, may raise concerns about the validity of the instrumental variable. On the other hand, the average old-age pension benefit at age 62, by demographic cell, is correlated with individual benefit levels but should not be correlated with individual-level unobserved characteristics, such as family shocks or a taste for work and welfare, conditional on the other variables. Further, we do not use earned income to define cells because labor market decisions are likely endogenous to safety net parameters.[25]

Administrative earnings records are necessary to calculate this instrumental variable, because we can include individuals over age 62 who have yet to claim their old-age pension benefits and individuals missing claiming ages or self-reported benefits level in the analysis, thus not introducing selection in the process of addressing endogeneity. Also, the self-reported benefit level and claiming age may contain measurement error, potentially biasing the calculated of the AvePotBen and, in turn, the estimates of the impact of potential benefit levels on the take-up decision. Further, measurement error in the calculated benefits may bias the estimation (Davies, 2002; Elder & Powers, 2004; McGarry, 1996), and the two-stage-least-square procedure help obtain a consistent estimate of the effect of the benefit on participation by minimizing the impact of measurement error in the calculated benefit (McGarry, 1996). After we estimate the old-age pension benefit level at individual level assuming he claims at age 62, we aggregate the estimation to the demographic cell level to construct the cell average.

Empirical Specifications

We start by estimating the linear probability model among eligible individuals as follows:

$$P_{it} = \beta_0 + \beta_1 B_{it} + X'_{it}\gamma + \tau_t + \varepsilon_{it} \tag{2}$$

where P_{it} is a binary variable equal to 1 if participating at time t and 0 if not. B_{it} is the expected benefit level in each of the means-tested programs examined for eligible individual i at time t.[26] Since the amount of expected public assistance benefits is observed only for those who actually participate, we calculate the expected SSI/SNAP benefit level for each eligible individual based on survey information and the rules of each program. Variables such as race, education, gender, marital status, family structure, disability indicators to proxy for permanent income, and total covered quarters worked are included in X.[27] τ_t are year of interview dummies, and ε_{it} denotes an idiosyncratic error term. The coefficient of interest is β_1, which measures the association between the expected public assistance benefit level and likelihood of take-up.

In one model, we exploit the longitudinal nature of the data set and include individual fixed effects in order to capture time-invariant unobservable characteristics that might be correlated with the participation decision. The specification takes the following form:

$$P_{it} = \beta_0 + \beta_1 B_{it} + X'_{it}\gamma + \tau_t + \alpha_i + \varepsilon_{it} \tag{3}$$

where α_i is the unobserved time-invariant individual effect.

To examine the causal relationship between expected benefits level and take-up behavior, we estimate a Two-Stage Least Squares (TSLS) model with the AvePotBen as the instrumental variable. While the individual fixed effect model takes into account time-invariant individual unobservable heterogeneity, the IV model has the advantages of accounting for time variant unobservables and for measurement error in the expected benefits level.

The first stage estimates the effect of the AvePotBen on the needs-based program benefit level:

$$B_{it} = \delta_0 + \delta_1 \text{AvePotBen}_{it} + X'_{it}\delta_2 + \tau_t + \varepsilon_{it} \tag{4}$$

where AvePotBen is the instrumental variable.

Instead of estimating the effect of actual public assistance benefit levels on participation, the predicted public assistance benefit level from the first equation will be used when estimating the participation equation:

$$P_{it} = \beta_0 + \beta_1 \hat{B}_{it} + X'_{it}\gamma + \tau_t + \varepsilon_{it} \tag{5}$$

where the coefficient of interest is β_1, which measures the causal impact of the expected public assistance benefit level on the take-up behavior.

While receiving old-age pension benefits leads to a decline in the benefit level, it may also impact ones knowledge about the SSI program, since SSI is also operated by the Social Security Administration.[28] The improved information about program eligibility may negate the effect of a benefit change on participation. Lack of information contributes to nonparticipation among the elderly (Blaylock & Smallwood, 1984; Coe, 1983; Daponte et al., 1999; Hill, 1990; Wu, 2009), and receiving information on program eligibility may lead to a higher taking up rate. Ideally, one would measure knowledge of SNAP/SSI directly using data individual perceptions of these programs. Lacking such data, we follow the example of recent literature that exploits geographical heterogeneity as a proxy for knowledge of the Earned Income Tax Credit or disability programs (Chetty, Friedman, & Saez, 2012; Furtado & Theodoropoulos, 2012). To proxy for knowledge, we include the poverty density by zip code as a control in our model, with the intention of capturing word-of-mouth communication.[29] Living in a zip code with a higher fraction of the population below poverty may lead to improved information about public assistance programs. Social interaction with members of one's community helps to convey information about program eligibility and the application process that may make it easier to apply for SNAP and SSI.

We present the participation estimates in Table 3 panel A and panel B. The results for a simple OLS model (Model 1, estimating Eq. (2)), an individual fixed-effects model (Model 2, estimating Eq. (3)), and an IV model (Model 3, estimating Eqs. (4) and (5)) are shown. The regression sample is smaller than the sample of all eligibles used for Table 2 due to the construction of AvePotBen; observations have negative values of AvePotBen are excluded from the analysis.[30] The bottom of Table 3 panel A and panel B reports the coefficients of the instrumental variables from the first stage.

For SNAP participation, the OLS yield different results from the FE and the IV models (Table 3 panel A). In the OLS model, the effects of most of the variables assumed to influence the participation decision operate in directions consistent with the literature that estimates the correlation between SNAP use and personal characteristics. These estimates clearly show that SNAP take-up is strongly associated with economic incentives. A higher expected monetary SNAP benefit increases the probability of participation, though the coefficient is only significant at the 10 percent level and the magnitude is fairly small. Even after controlling for the size of their expected SNAP benefits, elderly individuals who own a home or car are less likely to participate, as are the better-educated, those without children under 15 in the household, and those in good or fair health condition. Consistent with the literature, we find a negative age gradient in the participation decision. Individuals who have higher numbers of covered quarters also are less likely to participate. Further, we find that those receiving SSI are significantly more likely to participation in SNAP, suggesting the possible effects of better information, lower application costs, or/and a lower welfare stigma once one means-tested program is utilized. Interestingly, there is no remaining correlation between zip-code poverty density and SNAP participation.

Table 3.   Participation among the Eligible Elderly.

	Model (1) OLS	Model (2) FE	Model (3) IV
A: SNAP Participation			
Estimated SNAP benefit ($00s)	0.013*	0.008	0.052
	(0.007)	(0.006)	(0.033)
Age	−0.025*	0.051*	−0.026*
	(0.014)	(0.029)	(0.014)
Age square	0.000	0.000	0.000
	(0.000)	(0.000)	(0.000)
Female	0.008		0.007
	(0.017)		(0.017)
Married	−0.028	0.010	0.004
	(0.018)	(0.027)	(0.030)
White	−0.018		−0.015
	(0.017)		(0.017)
High school and above	−0.026*		−0.027*
	(0.016)		(0.016)
Household size	−0.001	0.004	−0.024
	(0.008)	(0.008)	(0.019)
Children under 15	0.079***	0.035	0.079***
	(0.027)	(0.026)	(0.027)
Poor health	0.041**	0.028*	0.039**
	(0.017)	(0.015)	(0.017)
Own a home	−0.086***	−0.020	−0.088***
	(0.017)	(0.021)	(0.017)
Own a car	−0.050***	0.041**	−0.047***
	(0.016)	(0.016)	(0.016)
Receive SSI	0.265***	0.095***	0.277***
	(0.020)	(0.018)	(0.022)
Quarters worked	−0.001***		−0.001***
	(0.000)		(0.000)
Poverty density by zip-code	0.012	−0.006	0.007
	(0.017)	(0.016)	(0.018)
Wave indicator	Yes	Yes	Yes
State indicator	Yes	Yes	Yes
IV (Average Potential Benefits)			0.345***
			(0.037)
F-test of excluded inst.			88
R square	0.196	0.031	0.189
Number of observations	8,797	8,797	8,797
B: SSI Participation			
Estimated SSI benefit ($00s)	0.043***	0.030***	0.060**
	(0.006)	(0.004)	(0.027)
Age	0.088***	0.174***	0.086***
	(0.020)	(0.043)	(0.020)

Table 3. *(Continued)*

	Model (1) OLS	Model (2) FE	Model (3) IV
Age square	−0.001***	−0.001***	−0.001***
	(0.000)	(0.000)	(0.000)
65 plus	0.069***	0.113***	0.092
	(0.022)	(0.032)	(0.042)
Female	−0.022		−0.013
	(0.027)		(0.036)
Married	−0.013	0.002	0.011
	(0.027)	(0.050)	(0.046)
White	0.019		0.020
	(0.020)		(0.020)
High school and above	−0.041*		−0.043**
	(0.023)		(0.022)
Household size	−0.021	−0.009	−0.002*
	(0.013)	(0.008)	(0.013)
Children under 15	−0.001	0.045*	0.002
	(0.044)	(0.030)	(0.044)
Poor health	0.001	−0.055**	−0.001
	(0.018)	(0.020)	(0.016)
Own a home	−0.069***	0.050	−0.066***
	(0.021)	(0.035)	(0.021)
Own a car	−0.054*	0.005	−0.050
	(0.029)	(0.026)	(0.031)
Receive SNAP	0.184***	0.026*	0.178***
	(0.022)	(0.020)	(0.025)
Quarters worked	−0.001***		−0.001*
	(0.000)		(0.000)
Poverty density by zip-code	−0.020	0.027	−0.025
	(0.020)	(0.023)	(0.023)
Wave indicator	Yes	Yes	Yes
State indicator	Yes	Yes	Yes
IV (Average Potential Benefits)			0.201***
			(0.024)
F-test of excluded inst.			62
R square	0.222	0.114	0.217
Number of observations	3,923	3,923	3,923

Source: Authors' calculation based on the HRS, 1992–2010.
* indicates significant at 10% confidence level; ** indicates significant at 5% level; *** indicates significant at 1% level.

The OLS model suggests that for every $100 in SNAP benefits, participation increases by about 1.3 percentage points. Turning to Model 2, we add individual fixed-effects to the OLS model to take into account time-invariant individual unobservable heterogeneity that affects the take-up decision. The expected SNAP benefits lose significance in the fixed-effects model, and the magnitude is roughly half of that estimated in the OLS model. Some of the coefficients that are significant in a cross-sectional setting are not significant in the fixed-effects model, such as home ownership and having kids under 15. The lack of significance could be due to fact that the fixed-effects are soaking up much of the variation at the individual-level, leading to imprecise estimates.[31]

Turning to Model 3 (IV), the first stage results show that the instrument tends to have the expected sign and is statistically significant ($F = 88$) — that is, the AvePotBen is positively correlated with the level of SNAP benefits. However, we find in the second stage that there is no significant relationship between the SNAP benefit amount and take-up, indicating that individuals whose benefit levels are impacted by old-age pension income are insensitive to expected public assistance benefits. Interestingly, the estimated coefficient, while imprecisely estimated, is larger than the OLS coefficient. This suggests that classical measurement error is confounding the OLS relationship more than the traditional selection issues.[32,33]

Turning to the SSI take-up decision (Table 3 panel B), we add an additional control variable — age 65 and over — to capture the removal of the disability test for eligibility. The results for the SSI program are broadly consistent across the model specifications. A higher expected SSI monetary benefit increases the probability of participation. Elderly individuals who own a home or car are less likely to participate, as are the better-educated, and those with longer work histories. Individuals receiving other welfare benefits are also more likely to participate. Unlike the SNAP model where we find a negative correlation between age and SNAP take-up, age is positively associated with the probability of take-up, especially for those 65 and older, suggesting the role of differential eligibility. Similar to the SNAP analysis, there is no remaining correlation between zip-code poverty density and SSI participation.

The OLS model suggests that for every $100 increase in SSI benefits, participation increases by 4.3 percentage points. Once we add individual fixed-effects to the OLS model (Model 2), the estimate decreases slightly, to 3.0 percentage points. Either model suggests that individuals are more sensitive to benefit amounts for SSI's cash benefits than for SNAP's in-kind benefits.

Turning to Model 3 (IV), the first stage results show that the instrument — the AvePotBen — is highly positively correlated to the level of calculated SSI benefits ($F = 62$). In the second stage, there is a significant relationship between SSI benefits amount and take-up. When comparing the OLS and IV results, the magnitude of the estimated effect of SSI benefits on participation is slightly increased, 4.3 versus 6.0 percentage points, again suggesting that classical measurement error is confounding the OLS estimate even more than selection concerns. The IV results suggest that for individuals whose SSI benefit increases by $100, participation increases by 6 percentage points. The average SSI benefit drops from $472 to $229 around the EEA, suggesting that old-age pension benefits decrease SSI participation by about 15 percentage points due to the decrease in benefit level.

In a set of model specification tests, we also include eligibility status in previous wave as a control variable, in order to test the hypothesis that individuals who have longer eligibility spells are more likely to participate, possibly due to the information about the program or/and persistent poverty status. The lagged variable is statistically significant and an important predictor of take-up (for SNAP, in the OLS, the coefficient is equal to 0.122; the t statistic is equal to 8.83; for SSI, the coefficient is 0.265; the t statistic $= 17.90$). However, the estimated effect of the relationship between benefit level and take-up remains largely unchanged with those presented in Table 3 panel A and panel B. To test for a nonlinear relationship between benefit levels and participation we add a square-term of benefit level in regressions. In all specifications we find that the square-term is insignificant and small in magnitude, and the main results are largely similar across various specifications compared to those without square-term.

Taken together, our estimates are inconclusive about the behavioral response to changes in SNAP benefits, but a $100 increase in SSI benefits leads to a 4−6 percentage point increase in the probability of participating in the SSI.

SENSITIVITY TESTS

In this section, we test the robustness of our findings in three ways: (1) relaxing the asset eligibility requirement in our eligibility definition; (2) estimating the take-up equations among those with income less than 130 percent of the poverty line for SNAP program; (3) estimating the take-up equation among eligible individuals age 65 and older for whom the disability test is removed for SSI program.

Relaxing the Asset Eligibility Requirement

The literature suggests that households tend to under-report asset holdings (Czajka, Jacobson, & Cody, 2003, for example), but the under-reporting is less a concern for the study of the low-income and elderly populations in general (Strand et al., 2009). Nevertheless, we examine how robust our results are when relaxing the asset eligibility requirement.

Not surprisingly, the eligibility rate for SNAP increases to 16 percent when relaxing the asset tests, and the take-up rate declines to 19 percent. A similar pattern is observed for SSI, with eligibility rate rising to 8.6 percent and take-up declining to 31 percent.

The results of estimating the take-up equation among these new eligible samples are summarized in Table 4. For SNAP, again, while there is a statistically significant relationship in the OLS model, we find that individuals are insensitive to changes in the expected benefits level in the instrumental variable estimations and the fixed-effects estimations. For SSI, the broad conclusions are the same, but the magnitude of the effect increases (7.5 percentage points).

Using 130 Percent of the Poverty Line to Determine Eligibility for SNAP

To address concern about measurement error in other income components or expenditures that we used to calculate various deductions, we also estimate the take-up equation for SNAP among individuals whose household income is under 130 percent of the poverty line (using only the gross income test).

In this analysis, our eligibility rate increases to 13 percent with a take-up of 24 percent. Again, while the OLS estimate on expected SNAP benefits is significant, the instrumental variable estimate, and the fixed-effects estimate lose their significance (Table 4).

Estimate the Take-Up Equations among Those over Age 65 for SSI

As discussed before, the SSI analysis is complicated by the fact that two distinct groups may enter the program — the aged and the disabled. Since the disability standards are removed at age 65, we observe an eligibility

Table 4. Sensitivity Tests.

	Model (1) OLS	Model (2) FE	Model (3) IV
Relaxing the asset eligibility requirement			
Estimated SNAP benefit ($00s)	0.027***	0.009*	0.032
	(0.006)	(0.005)	(0.034)
IV (Average Potential Benefits)			0.253***
			(0.035)
F-test of excluded inst.			52
Estimated SSI benefit ($00s)	0.025***	0.019***	0.075***
	(0.003)	(0.003)	(0.038)
IV (Average Potential Benefits)			0.099***
			(0.020)
F-test of excluded inst.			22
Using 130 percent of the poverty line to determine eligibility for the SNAP			
Estimated SNAP benefit ($00s)	0.015**	0.009	0.025
	(0.007)	(0.007)	(0.034)
IV (Average Potential Benefits)			0.284***
			(0.033)
F-test of excluded inst.			75
Estimate the take-up equations among those over age 65 for the SSI			
Estimated SSI benefit ($00s)	0.044***	0.042***	0.128***
	(0.008)	(0.006)	(0.044)
IV (Average Potential Benefits)			0.209***
			(0.032)
F-test of excluded inst.			25

Source: Authors' calculation based on the HRS, 1992–2010.
* indicates significant at 10% confidence level; ** indicates significant at 5% level; *** indicates significant at 1% level.

surge. Additionally, while the work-limitation measure is not a perfect representation of the Social Security Administration's disability criteria, our disability eligibility for individuals under 65 may be noisy. For these reasons, we estimate a separate take-up equation among eligibles age 65 and older for whom the disability test is removed for the SSI program.

The broad conclusions are the same regardless of the estimation model (Table 4). When comparing the OLS and instrumental variable results, however, the change in the estimated effect of SSI benefits on participation is relative substantial, increasing from 4.4 to 12.8 percentage points.

The instrumental variable results suggest that for older individuals whose SSI benefit increases by $100, participation increases by 13 percentage points.

CONCLUSION

By providing income to elderly households, old-age pensions potentially influences take-up of means-tested programs among the elderly in two distinct ways. First, by lifting households out of poverty, the composition of the pool of eligible individuals changes. To the extent that there is heterogeneity in individual take-up decisions, changing the eligible pool could help explain the difference in take-up rates. However, we find very little support for this theory. While individuals who are serially eligible have higher take-up rates, there is no differential average take-up among those who become eligible versus those who become ineligible as they become old enough to claim old-age pension benefits.

Second, old-age pensions could influence take-up decisions by providing income and thus decreasing the expected public assistance benefit level for which one may claim, decreasing the benefit of participation. While our estimates are inconclusive about the behavior response to the benefit change of the SNAP, we estimate that a $100 increase in SSI benefits leads to a 4−6 percentage point increase in the probability of participating in the SSI. These results are robust to numerous model specifications.

Further, our data and methodology have advantages over many existing studies: using administrative earnings rather than self-reported ones improves the measurement of one component of income used in computing SNAP/SSI eligibility. The instrumental variable approach and sensitivity tests using different definitions of the eligible population help to address the measurement error in the potential means-tested benefit level, further confirming that our findings are robust.

Finally, by examining two programs − SSI and SNAP − in consistent ways, we can compare the estimated relationship between the expected public assistance benefits level on the take-up decision with little worry that the model assumptions are driving differences in the results. By comparing these two programs, we find two pieces of suggestive evidence that indicate individuals prefer cash to in-kind transfers. First, take-up in SSI is more sensitive than SNAP to the expected public assistance benefit level, and second, after receiving old-age pension benefits, eligible individuals remain on SSI more often than they maintain their SNAP benefits.

The policy implications of these results are straightforward. Our estimates suggest that a 10–15 percentage point decrease in SSI take-up among the elderly can be explained by the lower benefit level. The different behavioral response to SSI and SNAP also suggest that effective policy interventions should take into account the type of benefits – cash or in-kind – when targeting poverty relief for the elderly.

Further, our findings highlight important interactions between old-age pensions and public assistance programs, which are needed to understand the full fiscal implications of potential changes to old-age pension programs. Countries around the world are struggling to respond to the increasing cost of their public old-age pension programs due to the pressures of population aging. Many countries, including the United States, Germany, Canada, Italy, Austria, and the United Kingdom, are responding by increasing the age of eligibility for old-age pension benefits. The findings of our study implies that the increase in old-age pension eligibility age may increase outlays for public assistance programs and therefore the overall fiscal savings may be overestimated due to the spillover effects of old-age pension programs on other government spending programs.

ACKNOWLEDGMENTS

The research reported herein was pursuant to a grant from the U.S. Social Security Administration (SSA), funded as part of the Retirement Research Consortium (RRC). The findings and conclusions expressed are solely those of the authors and do not represent the views of SSA, any agency of the federal government, the RRC, Boston College, or the University of Washington. The authors would like to thank Matthew Rutledge, Alexander Strand, Konstantinos Tatsiramos, two anonymous reviewers and participants at the APPAM fall research conference, SSA workshop, and IZA workshop for thoughtful comments and suggestions, and Lauren Dahlin, Miguel Matamoros and Kara Bradley for research assistance. All errors are authors'.

NOTES

1. Examples include Choi (1998), Davies (2002), Haider et al. (2003), Levy (2008), McGarry (1996), and Wu (2009).

2. There are some very recent variations in SNAP eligibility rules across states. In 2009, 13 states had exempted all or almost all households from the asset test, and all states exclude some or all vehicles from countable assets. Many states supplement federal SSI benefit levels.

3. Specifically, we are talking about the Social Security program within the United States.

4. SNAP benefits are now received as a debit card balance, so could be considered as a cash equivalent; however, the benefits can still be used only in a subset of stores to buy a subset of goods.

5. Haider et al. (2003) find that SNAP benefits are negatively correlated to participation decision among the elderly, while Wu (2009) finds a positive correlation but the magnitude is fairly small.

6. The literature fails to reach a consensus on the impact of SSI benefits on program participation. Estimates range from zero (Elders & Powers, 2004) to a 15 percentage point increase (Davies, 2002) in participation due to a $100 increase in benefits.

7. Under SNAP rules, a household is defined as individuals who share a residential unit and purchase and prepare food together. *Gross income* is defined as the total income for all household members, including that gained from working, investment, and transfers, but excludes most noncash income and in-kind benefits. The gross income limit is set at 130 percent of the poverty line ($1,640 per month for fiscal year 2012 for a two-person household). *Net income* is then computed by allowing for various deductions, including standard, earned income, excess shelter, medical expense, child support payments, and dependent care deductions from the household's gross income, with the net income limit set at 100 percent of the poverty line ($1,261). The asset limit in 2012 was $2,000.

8. Household out-of-pocket medical expenses in excess of $35 per month can be deducted.

9. Countable income disregards the first $20 of income from all sources, the first $65 of earned income, and one-half of additional earnings per month. Other disregards are home energy assistance payments, tuition benefits, disaster relief, and the value of SNAP benefits.

10. A resource test is also required for participation in SSI. Generally, countable assets cannot exceed $2,000 for an individual and $3,000 for a couple, but owner-occupied housing, regardless of value, and one car that used for transportation of the beneficiary or member of the beneficiary's household are excluded. There is a complex set of rules regarding how assets other than cash are considered.

11. The disability definition and determination process is identical to that of the Social Security Disability Insurance (DI) program. See Wixon and Strand (2013) for details on the disability determination process.

12. Wu (2009) estimates the correlation between the benefits level and the take-up decision, rather than the causal impact; those estimates fall within the broad range of the estimates in this paper using OLS models.

13. Some work uses within-state over-time variation (e.g., Neumark & Powers, 2005), but states that have changed their state SSI supplemental program over time, may not be representative of all states.

14. To project earnings beyond the year at which the individual last gave permission to match to the administrative data, we follow Gustman and Steinmeier (2001).

For individuals with self-reported earnings, the assumption is that the average of their real earnings observed in the last three reported periods persist until their expected claiming date. The actual claiming age is used if respondents have already claimed old-age pension benefits. For those yet to claim, we assume that respondents claim old-age pension benefits at their self-reported expected retirement ages. If the expected retirement age was greater than 70, or if the individual indicated that he never expected to retire, a retirement age of 70 is used unless the individual had already worked beyond that age. If the respondent did not provide an expected retirement age, we assign them a claiming age so that the age distribution of claiming matches the Social Security Administration reported claiming ages (U.S. Social Security Administration, 2010, Table 6.B5.1). Combining the actual earnings with the simulated earnings yields a complete earnings profile for each individual in the HRS sample from 1951 to retirement age.

15. The March *Current Population Survey* (CPS) does not ask questions about wealth, housing expenditures, or medical expenditures. The quality of the wealth data in the SIPP is questionable (Gustman & Juster, 1996) and the administrative earnings record linked to the SIPP is not readily accessible. Further, the longer panel structure of the HRS allows us to observe the transition into and out of the program around the early eligibility age.

16. This inevitably introduces measurement problems; part-year eligibles may be classified as "ineligible" based on annual income.

17. A detailed description of imputation method and the summary statistics are available from authors upon requests.

18. Tables A1 and A2 provide a detailed discussion of the information that is available in the HRS for assessing eligibility, as well as the assumptions made given its limitations.

19. We determine if someone is disabled if they answer that they have a work-limiting condition. While there is concern about the reliability of self-reported health and disability in survey data sets (e.g., Institute of Medicine, 2002), Benítez-Silva, Buchinsky, Chan, Rust, and Sheidvasser (1999) find that disability self-reports are unbiased in predicting the Social Security disability awards among disability applicants. Since we are trying to identify disability as determined by SSA, we also use disability self-reports as a proxy.

20. For instance, Haider et al. (2003) find that less than 1.5 percent of people classified as ineligible for SNAP report that they receive benefits.

21. We compare characteristics of SNAP recipients in our sample with those reported in the SNAP Quality Control data and characteristics of SSI recipients in our sample with the SIPP matched to SSI administrative files (Table A-2 of Elder & Powers, 2004), and find that our sample matches fairly well with the administrative record in terms of age, race, gender, marital status, and health status.

22. While it is well known that U.S. Social Security's replacement rate is less than one (80–90 percent for low-wage earners on average), the replacement rate is computed based on annualized lifetime income, not as a fraction of income in the years just prior to claiming benefits. As such, many low-income households – especially individuals who are widowed or not working – experience an increase in income due to claiming retirement benefits.

23. For the regression analysis, we exclude individuals who receive Social Security Disability Insurance income, because they are automatically converted to

old-age pension benefits at their full retirement age (age 65–67, depending on birth year), and thus will not be impacted by the EEA.

24. The Social Security Administration will recalculate the Primary Insurance Amount – the amount one's benefits are calculated from – as long as the individual keeps working, but under most circumstances, this recalculation leads to modest increases in benefits. Delaying claiming is the primary way to influence retirement benefits after age 60.

25. The average cell size is 36 for the SSI analytical sample, with a standard deviation of 22; the average cell size is 69 for the SNAP sample, with a standard deviation of 34.

26. Benefits use average monthly measure based on the annual information.

27. Using demographic variables to capture permanent income makes this work comparable to the program participation literature.

28. When individuals claim early old-age pension benefits, they may learn that they are also eligible for SSI benefits (U.S. Social Security Administration, 2010). Thus, at the same time as being eligible for fewer benefits, they also learn of their eligibility status.

29. Previous research has found neighborhood effects in outcomes such as educational achievement, dropout rates, transition from welfare to work, social and occupational mobility, health, subjective well-being, and stock ownership (Brown, Ivkovic, Smith, & Weisbenner, 2008; Dietz, 2002; Durlauf, 2004; Ellen and Turner, 1997; Galster, 2002).

30. To test if sample selection drives any results, we have also estimated the OLS model using the full sample (available from authors upon request). The estimates are largely consistent.

31. The fixed effects in an IV model also soak up much of the variation and lead to insignificant results, which are not reported here.

32. On the one hand, correcting for the positive bias of the OLS due to endogeneity concerns leads to smaller IV estimates. On the other hand, the IV estimates may be larger than the OLS estimates due to the presence of classical measurement error (e.g., Hyslop & Imbens, 2001).

33. Partially due to relatively large estimated standard errors in the three SNAP take-up models, we cannot reject the null that all three models estimate the same relationship between SNAP benefits and the take-up decision.

REFERENCES

Anderson, P. M., Gustman, A. L., & Steinmeier, T. L. (1999). Trends in male labor force participation and retirement: Some evidence on the role of pensions and social security in the 1970's and 1980's. *Journal of Labor Economics, 17*(4), 757–783.

Benítez-Silva, H., Buchinsky, M., Chan, H. M., Rust, J., & Sheidvasser, S. (1999). An empirical analysis of the social security disability application, appeal, and award process. *Labour Economics, 6*, 147–178.

Blank, R. M., & Ruggles, P. (1996). When do women use aid to families with dependent children and food stamps? The dynamics of eligibility versus participation. *Journal of Human Resources, 31*(1), 57–89.

Blaylock, J. R., & Smallwood, D. M. (1984). Reasons for non-participation in the food stamp program. *Western Journal of Agricultural Economics, 9*, 117–126.

Bosworth, B. P., & Burtless, G. (2010). *Recessions, wealth destruction, and the timing of retirement*. Working Paper No. 2010-22. Center for Retirement Research at Boston College, Chestnut Hill, MA.

Brown, J. R., Ivkovic, Z., Smith, P. A., & Weisbenner, S. (2008). Neighbors matter: Causal community effects and stock market participation. Journal of Finance, *American Finance Association, 63*(3), 1509–1531.

Chetty, R., Friedman, J. N., & Saez, E. (2012). *Using differences in knowledge across neighborhoods to uncover the impacts of the EITC on earnings*. NBER Working Paper No. 18232.

Choi, N. (1998). A comparative study of elderly ssi recipients, denied applicants, and eligible nonapplicants. *Journal of Aging and Social Policy, 10*(2), 7–28.

Coe, R. D. (1983). Participation in the food stamp program, 1979. In G. J. Duncan & J. N. Morgan, (Eds.), *Five thousand American families – Patterns of economic progress* (Vol. 10, pp. 121–177). Ann Arbor, MI: University of Michigan.

Cunnyngham, K. (2010). *State trends in supplemental nutrition assistance program eligibility and participation among elderly individuals*. Final Report. Mathematica Policy Research.

Currie, J., & Gruber, J. (1996). Health insurance eligibility, utilization of medical care, and child health. *The Quarterly Journal of Economics, 111*(2), 431–466.

Czajka, J. L., Jacobson, J. E., & Cody, S. (2003). *Survey estimates of wealth: A comparative analysis and review of the survey of income and program participation*. Washington, DC: Mathematica Policy Research, Inc., under contract to the Social Security Administration, contract number 0600-01-60121/0440-02-51976.

Daponte, B. O., Sanders, S., & Taylor, L. (1999). Why do low-income households not use food stamps? Evidence from an experiment. *Journal of Human Resources, 34*(3), 612–628.

Davies, P. S. (2002). SSI eligibility and participation among the oldest old: Evidence from the AHEAD. *Social Security Bulletin, 64*(3), 38–63.

Dietz, R. D. (2002). The estimation of neighborhood effects in the social sciences: An interdisciplinary approach. *Social Science Research, 31*(4), 539–575.

Durlauf, S. N. (2004). Neighborhood effects. In J. V. Henderson & J. F. Thisse (Eds.), *Handbook of regional and urban economics* (1st ed., Vol. 4, pp. 2173–2242).

Elder, T., & Powers, E. (2004). *SSI for the aged and the problem of "Take-Up"*. Working Paper No. 2004-076. Michigan Retirement Research Center.

Ellen, I. G., & Turner, M. A. (1997). Does neighborhood matter? Assessing recent evidence. *Housing Policy Debate, 8*(4), 833–866.

Furtado, D., & Theodoropoulos, N. (2012). *Immigrant networks and the take-up of disability programs: Evidence from U.S. census data*. Working Paper No. 2012-23. Center for Retirement Research.

Galster, G. C. (2002). An economic efficiency analysis of deconcentrating poverty populations. *Journal of Housing Economics, 11*(4), 303–329.

Gundersen, C., & Ziliak, J. P. (2008). The age gradient in food stamp program participation: Does income volatility matter? In D. Jolliffe & J. P. Ziliak (Eds.), *Income volatility and food assistance in the United States*. Kalamazoo, MI: W.E. Upjohn Institute.

Gustman, A. L., & Juster, T. F. (1996). Income and wealth of older American households: Modeling issues for public policy analysis. In E. A. Hanushek & L. Nancy (Eds.), *Assessing knowledge of retirement behavior* (Vol. 1, pp. 1–60). Washington, DC: National Academy Press.

Gustman, A. L., & Steinmeier, T. L. (2001). How effective is redistribution under the social security benefit formula? *Journal of Public Economics, 82*(1), 1–28.

Haider, S. J., Jacknowitz, A., & Schoeni, R. F. (2003). Food stamps and the elderly: Why is participation so low? *Journal of Human Resources, 38*, 1080–1111.

Hill, D. H. (1990). An endogenously-switching ordered-response model of information, perceived eligibility and participation in SSI. *The Review of Economics and Statistics, 72*(2), 368–371.

Hyslop, D. R., & Imbens, G. W. (2001). Bias from classical and other forms of measurement error. *Journal of Business and Economic Statistics, 19*(4), 475–481.

Institute of Medicine. (2002). The dynamics of disability: Measuring and monitoring disability for social security programs. In G. S. Wunderlich, D. P. Rice, & N. L. Amado (Eds.), *Committee to review the social security administration's disability decision process research*. Washington, DC: National Academy Press/National Research Council.

Levy, H. (2008). *Food stamp use among the elderly: Evidence from panel data*. Unpublished manuscript.

McGarry, K. (1996). Factors determining participation of the elderly in supplemental security income. *Journal of Human Resources, 31*(2), 331–358.

Neumark, D., & Powers, E. T. (2005). The effects of changes in state SSI supplements on pre-retirement labor supply. *Public Finance Review, 33*(1), 3–35.

Schmidt, L., Shore-Sheppard, L., & Watson, T. (2013). *The effect of safety net programs on food insecurity*. NBER Working Paper No. 19558. National Bureau of Economic Research, Inc.

Shields, J. F., Barnow, B. S., Chaurette, K. A., & Constantine, J. M. (1990). *Elderly persons eligible for and participating in the supplementary security income program*. Washington, DC: U.S. Government Printing Office. Final report prepared for the U.S. Department of Health and Human Services.

Strand, A., Rupp, K., & Davies, P. S. (2009). *Measurement error in estimates of the participation rate in means-tested programs: The case of the US supplemental security income program for the elderly*. Washington, DC: U.S. Social Security Administration, Office of Retirement and Disability Policy, Office of Research, Evaluation, and Statistics.

U.S. Social Security Administration. (2010). Online social security handbook. Retrieved from http://www.ssa.gov/OP_Home/handbook/handbook.html

Van de Water, P. N., & Sherman, A. (2012). *Social security keeps 21 million americans out of poverty: A state-by-state analysis*. Center on Budget and Policy Priorities, October.

Wixon, B., & Strand, A. (2013, June 1). Identifying SSA's sequential disability determination steps using administrative data. Research and Statistics Note No. 2013-01.

Wolkwitz, K., & Leftin, J. (2008). *Characteristics of the food stamp household, fiscal year 2007*. Nutrition Assistance Program Report Series, Report No. FSP-08-CHAR. U.S. Department of Agriculture, Food and Nutrition Service, Alexandria, VA.

Wu, A. Y. (2009). *Why do so few elderly use food stamps?* Working Paper No. 10.01. The Harris School of Public Policy Studies, The University of Chicago, Chicago, IL.

APPENDIX

Table A1. HRS Information and Adjustments for Determining SNAP Program Eligibility.

	Eligibility Rules	Differences in Rules for Elderly and Disabled Households	Source of Information in the HRS	Data Limitations and Adjustments Made
Gross income test	Total income ≤ 130 percent of HHS poverty line	Not subject to gross income test	Income of respondent and spouse, plus income of additional household members (for the 1992 through 2000 data collections) Ratio of household income to the U.S. Census poverty threshold times the poverty threshold (for the 2002 through 2010 data collections)	Income data for additional household members often bracketed or missing. Use hot-deck procedure to impute Reported household size is occasionally inconsistent with the number of observed residents. For 1992 through 2000 data collections, use the number of observed residents. For the 2002 through 2010 data collections use the reported household size
Net income test	Total income less deductions ≤100 percent of HHS poverty line	No difference	See above	See above
Deductions				
Standard	Standard deduction	No difference	No information necessary	N/A
Earned income	20 percent of earned income	No difference	Sum of earnings, self-employment earnings, business income, and rental income	Income of additional household members not broken down by source. Do not include their income as earned income

Table A1. (Continued)

	Eligibility Rules	Differences in Rules for Elderly and Disabled Households	Source of Information in the HRS	Data Limitations and Adjustments Made
Dependent care	Uncapped deduction for dependent care needed for work, training, or education	No difference	Data unavailable	Ignored
Excess shelter deduction	Excess shelter costs > 1/2 of the household's income. Capped	No cap	Sum of mortgage payments, rental payments, park and association fees, and real estate taxes	Some costs reported in brackets. For closed brackets, use the midpoint. For open brackets, use the lower bound. Utility expenditure data are unavailable. Ignored
Child support payment	Legally owed child support to a non-household member	No difference	Data unavailable	Ignored
Medical expense	None	Elderly medical expenses ≥ $35 per month	Respondent's and spouse or partner's out-of-pocket medical expenses	None
Asset test				
Limit	Assets ≤ $2,000	Assets ≤ $3,000	Net value of real estate and secondary residences (excluding primary residence), businesses, IRA/Keogh accounts, stocks, checking accounts, CDs, bonds, and other savings and debts	Data does not distinguish between Keogh Plans (included) IRAs (excluded). Include both
Excluded assets	Primary home and vehicle under $4,650	Value of vehicle used to transport a disabled household member, no maximum	Value of primary residence and transportation assets	No data available on vehicle use. Exclude all transportation assets

Other *AFDC/TANF and SSI*	If all household members receive program then eligibility presumed	No difference	Respondent and spouse's SSI income	Data on TANF receipt unavailable. Assume no TANF receipt Data on SSI receipt by additional household members is unavailable. Assume additional household members do not receive SSI
Work requirements	Able-bodied household head may be required to work	Not subject to work requirements	Data unavailable	Ignored
Citizenship	Some permanent residents are eligible	Eligible if > 65 years older and in the United States on August 22, 1996	Place of birth	Ignored
Institutionalized	Not eligible if institutionalized	In nursing home is not eligible	Institutionalized individuals are assigned zero weight	Limit the sample to observations with nonzero weight

Table A2. HRS Information and Adjustments for Determining SSI Program Eligibility.

	Eligibility Rules	Source of Information in the HRS	Data Limitations and Adjustments made
Health eligibility	Respondent is considered aged, blind or disabled		
Aged	Respondent's age ≥ 65	Age is derived from the year for which income is reported less the respondent's birth year	
Blind	Respondent is considered blind	Self-report of vision	No objective report of vision is available
Disabled	Respondent is considered disabled	Whether disability limits work or if labor force status is listed as disabled	No objective report of disability is available
Income eligibility	Countable earned and unearned income is less than the federal benefit rate		
Earned income	One-half earned income less the first $65 or $85 if the respondent has no unearned income	Earnings from employment + self-employment, in the previous year	Income information is annual rather than monthly. Annual income is divided by 12. Self-employment income is available at the household level for wave 2
Unearned income	Unearned income less the first $20	Rental income + social security retirement income (old-age pension in the United States) + social security disability income + pension income + unemployment and worker's comp + veteran's benefit + welfare + lump sum and other income, in the previous year	Income information is annual rather than monthly. Annual income is divided by 12
Living in the household of another		Federal benefit rate is reduced by one-third if living in the household of another and not paying rent	Not owning house and not paying rent
	Deemed income from an ineligible spouse is reduced	Children in HRS family data	Data for other family members (not respondent or spouse) is unreliable and

Deduction for the children of an ineligible spouse	based on the number of ineligible children	may not match the self-report of household size
Resource eligibility	Countable resources under $2,000 for an individual and $3,000 for a couple	
Countable resources	IRA + trusts not reported elsewhere + Stocks, mutual funds, and investment trusts + Checking, savings, money market accounts + CD, government savings bonds, T-bills + Bonds and bond funds + Other savings, assets + Net value of 2nd home + Net value of other real estate + Net value of businesses	Assets are reported at the household level. Assets are divided equally between respondent and spouse. No data is available for burial plots. The total value of all vehicles is given without the number of vehicles, so a potential second vehicle is not included. Face value of life insurance is not included

HARVARD UNIVERSITY

http://lib.harvard.edu

**If the item is recalled, the borrower will
be notified of the need for an earlier return.**

Thank you for helping us to preserve our collection!